Standard 1

A school administrator is an educational leader who promotes the success of all students by **facilitating the development, articulation, implementation, and stewardship of a vision of learning that is shared and supported by the school community.**

Standard 2

A school administrator is an educational leader who promotes the success of all students by **advocating, nurturing, and sustaining a school culture and instructional program conducive to student learning and staff professional growth.**

Standard 3

A school administrator is an educational leader who promotes the success of all students by **ensuring management of the organization, operations, and resources for a safe, efficient, and effective learning environment.**

Standard 4

A school administrator is an educational leader who promotes the success of all students by **collaborating with families and community members, responding to diverse community interests and needs, and mobilizing community resources.**

Standard 5

A school administrator is an educational leader who promotes the success of all students by **acting with integrity, fairness, and in an ethical manner.**

Standard 6

A school administrator is an educational leader who promotes the success of all students by **understanding, responding to, and influencing the larger political, social, economic, legal, and cultural context.**

Source: Council of Chief State School Officers.

The Human Resource Function in Educational Administration

NINTH EDITION

I. Phillip Young
University of California–Davis

PEARSON

Merrill
Prentice Hall

Upper Saddle River, New Jersey
Columbus, Ohio

Library of Congress Cataloging-in-Publication Data

Young, Ila Phillip–

    The human resource function in educational administration / by I. Phillip Young.—9th ed.
      p. cm.

    Includes bibliographical references and index.

    ISBN 0-13-243541-1 (alk. paper)

  1.   School personnel management—United States. I.   Title.

    LB2831.58.C37 2008

    371.2'01093—dc22

                              2006037417

Vice President and Executive Publisher: Jeffery W. Johnston
Executive Editor: Debra A. Stollenwerk
Assistant Editor: Elisa Rogers
Production Editor: Kris Roach
Production Coordination: Carlisle Publishing Services
Design Coordinator: Diane C. Lorenzo
Cover Designer: Ali Mohrman
Cover Image: SuperStock
Production Manager: Susan Hannahs
Director of Marketing: Ann Castel Davis
Senior Marketing Manager: Darcy Betts Prybella
Marketing Coordinator: Brian Mounts

This book was set in Photina MT by Carlisle Publishing Services. It was printed and bound by Courier/Westford. The cover was printed by Phoenix Color Corp.

Pearson Education Ltd.
Pearson Education Singapore Pte. Ltd.
Pearson Education Canada, Ltd.
Pearson Education—Japan

Pearson Education Australia Pty. Limited
Pearson Education North Asia Ltd.
Pearson Educación de Mexico, S.A. de C.V.
Pearson Education Malaysia Pte. Ltd.

10 9 8 7 6 5 4 3 2 1
ISBN-13: 978-0-13-243541-3
ISBN-10:   0-13-243541-1

To my wife, Karen
My daughter, Rebecca
My son Phillip, and his wife Maggie

I.P.Y.

PREFACE

The future of the United States within the global world market depends more today than ever before on its public education system. Core to the success of public education systems within the United States is the effectiveness and the efficiency of the human resource function. The human resource function is a viable part of the strategic planning process for moving school systems from their current state of operation to a desired state of operation.

Fundamental to the strategic planning process is proactive decision making on the part of all stakeholders. Some of the decisions involve old issues ever new, whereas other decisions involve new issues yet to be broached by many educational organizations. Within this edition, both types of issues are addressed. Issues that have been and continue to be a mainstay of the human resource function are examined from both traditional and novel perspectives. Emerging human resource issues are introduced, and best practices relating to these issues are examined.

Organization of This Text

This edition, like the eighth edition, is organized into three parts. However, many major revisions have been made in this edition. All chapters have been revised extensively as well as expanded in scope, and new chapters have been added in Parts II and III. Without exception, all chapters contain important Web links and cite recent research to guide informed decision making at the local school district level.

Nested within many of these chapters are informational needs as identified by the Interstate School Leaders Licensure Consortium (ISLLC) for administrators in the public school setting (Council of Chief State School Officers, 1996). Specific attention is given to certain types of knowledge and specific indicators for evidence of this knowledge. Although these standards are under current review, most of them are likely to survive the test of time.[1] The standards are listed on page i for reference.

The three parts of this edition reflect preemployment considerations from a strategic planning perspective, core human resource functions common to every organization, and continuity of employment considerations for enhancing the employment life of individuals. The examples in this text benefit students as well as practicing professionals.

Part I introduces the human resource function and places it within the strategic planning context, with special attention to the external and internal environmental factors as addressed across ISLLC standards. Informational needs for linking human resource functions and strategic planning processes are examined from a policy perspective and are linked to actual practice. Enrollment projection techniques are illustrated, and staffing plans are provided as a foundation for executing the human resource function in the field setting.

In Part II, core human resource functions associated with recruitment, selection, orientation, performance appraisal, and compensation are addressed from several perspectives. Emphasis is placed on policy decisions and administrative decisions relative to these different human resource functions, and current research is brought to bear on these topics. Practical examples from the field setting are provided to inform decision making and to illustrate models or processes that can be used at the local school district level. These examples complement knowledge requirements and performance indicators as identified in many ISLLC standards.

The focus of Part III is on the employment continuity process and benefits associated with continued employment. Staff development processes and procedures to maintain a level of proficiency in the current position and/or to prepare for future positions are discussed. Finally, collective bargaining within the school setting is described, as well as the role of the human resource function in collective bargaining.

What's New in This Edition

This edition follows the general systems approach to the human resource function from a strategic management perspective as set forth in previous editions. It expands current knowledge in this area from several viewpoints by drawing from emerging research, by expanding current knowledge about human resource practice, by addressing new systemic reform efforts confronting public school districts, by linking recent Web-based information about current practice of the human resource function, and, most importantly, by providing actual examples of human resource practices from the field setting. Again, as with past editions, attention is devoted to the concerns of those administrators who administer the human resource function in the educational setting and to employees who must fulfill job assignments. Both perspectives are addressed in this new edition by:

- Taking strategic planning from an academic exercise to an operational perspective at the local school district level
- Describing the components comprising an integrated information system that focuses on operational needs of a public school district
- Using a linear enrollment projection system based on succession for projecting student enrollments necessary for informed staffing of a public school district
- Illustrating a nonlinear enrollment projection technique capable of combining objective and subjective factors affecting the informed staffing of a public school district
- Analyzing staffing trends for a public school district both across time and among work units
- Identifying policy decisions relative to staffing allocations required by strategic planning at the local school district level
- Integrating enrollment projections and staffing needs within the strategic planning process

- Developing staffing charts for administering and auditing the staffing process at the local school district level
- Differentiating between proactive (affirmative action) and facially natural (equal employment opportunity) policy statements for recruitment and selection
- Focusing on recruitment and selection both from an individual and an organizational perspective
- Offering actual examples of validation techniques for selection processes that meet federal standards and enhance the efficiency of the selection process at the local school district level
- Outlining the steps involved with designing, developing, and implementing an effective orientation process for newly assigned and newly employed personnel
- Presenting a decision matrix to be used in constructing and applying the performance appraisal process
- Detailing auditing criteria for assessing compensation structures and incorporating these criteria into new compensation structures that are internally consistent and externally competitive
- Deconstructing entitlements and privileges within the employment continuity process
- Approaching development as a process and focusing on design and on evaluation issues as an integral part of development
- Expanding the scope of the collective bargaining process to include procedural and substantive process concerns for recognition, negotiation, dispute resolution, and grievance processing

Finally, by addressing past practices, examining present practices, and suggesting future practices, the ninth edition offers those responsible for, and those subjected to, the human resource function in the school setting with viable options. The underlying philosophy of this textbook is that a singular approach to human resource management in the school setting does not exist and that knowledgeable choices must be made by all stakeholders. If easy answers and fixed solutions existed for most human resource issues, then many of the current educational problems would have been resolved decades ago.

Note

1. For a complete listing of the ISLLC standards without cost see (**http://www.ccsso.org/content/pdfs/isllcstd.pdf**).

Supplements

This edition has two additional support features that are available for download at **http://www.prenhall.com**. One is PowerPoint slides that have been developed for each chapter to guide classroom discussion. The other one is a test bank.

Acknowledgments

Foremost I wish to acknowledge the help of my wife Karen. She provided insight, motivation, and editing skills. In addition, I would like to acknowledge the following practicing professionals from the public school setting for their efforts and insights relative to the ninth edition of this text. They took time from their busy schedules and administrative responsibilities to provide a much needed service without the benefit of any compensation: Xavier De La Torre, Assistant Superintendent for Human Resources–Elk Grove School District, Elk Grove, CA; Dane Delli, Assistant Superintendent for Assessment and Research, Aptakisic-Tripp School District–Buffalo Grove, IL; Fernie Marroquin, Assistant Superintendent for Human Resources, Tulare Joint Union High School District–Tulare, CA; Todd Oto, High School Principal, Visalia Unified School District–Visalia, CA; and David Waggener, Director of Finance, Union County School District–Morganfield, KY.

I also want to thank the reviewers for their thoughtful insight and comments. They are: Bruce T. Caine, Vanderbilt University; W. Keith Christy, University of Arkansas at Little Rock; Marla Susman Israel, Loyola University Chicago; and Donnie Snider, Abilene Christian University.

BRIEF CONTENTS

CONTENTS

NOTE: Every effort has been made to provide accurate and current Internet informaiton in this book. However, the Internet and information posted on it are constantly changing. It is inevitable that some of the Internet addresses listed in this textbook will change.

PART I

Foundations of the Human Resource Function

1 The Human Resource Function

2 Information Systems and Enrollment Projections

3 Strategic Planning and Staffing

Part I introduces the reader to the content and to the context of the human resource function as applied to educational organizations within the public school setting. The intent of Part I is to

- Provide an overview of the human resource function, link the human resource function to other organizational functions, and illustrate how the human resource function is a vital part of the overall operation of an educational organization.
- Describe strategic planning from a human resource perspective and discuss ways in which it can be employed to enhance attainment of the strategic goals and objectives of an educational organization.
- Emphasize the vital importance of information within the strategic planning process and its power to affect the efficacy and efficiency of human resource outcomes.
- Illustrate different enrollment projection techniques based on actual field data that can be utilized by public school districts within the strategic planning process and that can provide a foundation for the human resource function.
- Incorporate enrollment projections into a comprehensive staffing model following a strategic planning process, provide a staffing analysis, and compile staffing charts to guide operational objectives for meeting organizational needs.

The Human Resource Function

1

Goals of This Text

This book addresses the **human resource function** in educational institutions as practiced in the public school setting. The aim of this book is to provide important insights about human resource issues and to illustrate sound managerial practices relative to these activities. Because the human resource function in the public school setting impacts either directly or indirectly every aspect of the schooling process, information provided in this book is useful to a variety of stakeholders when fulfilling their role assignments.

Included among these stakeholders within the public school setting and addressed in this book are policy makers, district-level employees, school administrators, and aspiring educational leaders. Although each of these stakeholder groups has a vested interest in the human resource function within the public school setting, these interests are often unique to a particular group and warrant specific attention. Following is a description about how each group is served by this book both from an individual and from an organizational perspective within the human resource context.

The role of policy makers, as related to the human resource function, is to select a particular human resource option from a variety of viable alternatives, and various alternatives for different human resource functions will be noted throughout this text. For most human resource issues, more than a single option exists, and these options vary in process as well as in outcome. As such, the task of policy makers is to weigh these different human resource options and to choose the one best suited for their particular school district in light of specific external and internal environmental constraints impacting the organization and the operation of their particular public school district.

Functionally, the choice among human resource options by policy makers serves two distinct purposes concerning the organization and the operation of their particular school district. One purpose served by a specific choice is the formal authorization for following a definitive course relative to the direction of a public school district with respect to approved human resource functions. Another purpose served by a specific choice of policy makers is the legitimization to commit fiscal resources of the school district by following a designated course of action involving the implementation of specific human resource directives.

To guide policy makers in their deliberation process about alternative human resource activities from an organizational and an operational perspective, district-level employees must provide legislative groups with valid information to direct informed decision making on the part of either elected or appointed officials. In all instances, policy makers are either elected or appointed officials, with most being elected rather than appointed (Cunningham & Cordeiro, 2006) and with most not being professional educators. As such, most policy makers bring judgment rather than content expertise when making decisions about the organization and operation of a public school district relative to the human resource function within the public school setting.

Once policy decisions are made by a legislative group, executive-level personnel within the school district must develop administrative processes and operational procedures for executing the intent of approved human resource policies. In so providing this service, goals must be established, objectives must be defined, operational procedures must be instituted, and audit mechanisms must be put in place. Within the following chapters, executive-level personnel will be provided with the information they need to accomplish these tasks from a strategic planning perspective.

In keeping within this general flow for the human resource function as a process involving strategic planning, site-based administrators complete, in most instances, the operational cycle. These line administrators are charged with taking rhetoric to reality or policy to practice. That is, site-based managers must develop, administer, and evaluate human resource policies in the field setting and guide the pivotal employees in the implementation and evaluation process. Specific information is provided in the ensuing chapters about both policy and practice relative to policy selection, implementation, and evaluation within the field setting, and actual illustrations are provided from the field setting.

With respect to aspiring educational leaders seeking to enter the managerial ranks as practicing administrators, this book seeks to serve this last group from at least two perspectives. First, this book provides insights about one of the most important functions performed by an educational organization, which is the management of the human resource function in the public school setting. Second, the ensuing chapters describe different aspects or subsystems of the human resource function that aspiring administrators are likely either to encounter or to be subjected to in their educational careers within the public school setting that can be either adopted or modified to meet the needs of a particular public school district.

Collectively for all readers of this book, important information can be gleaned about the human resource function as executed in a public school system. Most importantly, the human resource function in a public school system will be nested within the overall vision of a school district aligning values and goals with system objectives relative to specific human resource functions from a strategic planning perspective. For each of these activities comprising the human resource function within the public school setting, procedures and processes will be discussed and related research will be provided to inform decision making as well as practice for various stakeholders.

As noted in the previous paragraphs, the human resource function in a public school district is not a stand-alone activity but is interrelated with all aspects of the organization and operation of a public school district. As a managerial activity involving either directly or indirectly all operations of a public school system, the human resource function must be sensitive to many forces impacting policy choices and implementation strategies. Fundamental to guiding decision making and to choosing among alternative plans of action is the awareness both of past impediments and of potential opportunities hampering as well as serving the human resource function within the public school setting.

Impediments and Opportunities for the Human Resource Function

For many public school districts, several aspects of the human resource function have yet to be realized fully and have yet to be capitalized on effectively within the education setting. Several impediments exist for this shortcoming. Underlying these impediments is a failure to realize the potency of systematic planning relative to the human resource function.

Without the aid of systematic planning, many human resource polices will be poorly conceptualized. Poorly conceptualized human resource policies are difficult to interpret and are difficult to implement. Furthermore, subsequent evaluations of human resource practices according to poorly conceptualized polices, when conducted, will likely be unsatisfactory.

Within the public school setting there has been a reluctance or inability of stakeholders to apply emerging knowledge about human resource practices. In some instances this can be attributed to the rigidity of individuals responsible for administering the human resource function in a school district. Change is always difficult, and human resource management is no exception to this difficulty.

Compounding these impediments are, in many instances, internal and external political constraints on the school system over which little discretion can be afforded and goes unrecognized. Often overlooked, goals and objectives defining the human resource function are interrelated rather than stand-alone events. Relationships exist both within the human resource function and between other organizational functions necessary for operating a public school system. Figure 1.1 depicts the centrality of the human resource function in a public school system relative to other required functions performed by most school districts.

As Figure 1.1 shows, the human resource function is central to the different operations, tasks, and/or processes necessary in all public school districts. When fulfilling the human resource function relative to external relations, educational planning, educational programming, and logistical support, designated personnel within the public school setting should perform each of these collaborated activities. Failure to perform or at least tend to any one of these processes will limit substantially the effectiveness and the efficiency of a school system at present as well as in the future.

In all public school districts, school boards function as a policy-making body. Beyond this commonality as performed by school boards, different divisions of labor exist. Within small school districts, operational responsibilities for the human resource function may be delegated among several different position holders. The superintendent may perform some responsibilities associated with the human resource function, whereas building-level administrators within the school district may perform other responsibilities. In large school systems, specific personnel or entire departments may be assigned to perform most all human resource functions.

The purpose of depicting the relationships, as found in Figure 1.1, is to identify, classify, and relate major functions and subfunctions of human resource management that must be performed within a school system if the mission of the school system is to be fulfilled. The human resource function, it should be noted, is divided into ten areas: forecasting, planning, recruitment, selection, induction, appraisal, compensation, employment continuity, development, and unionism. These processes form the foundation of subsequent chapters addressed in this book.

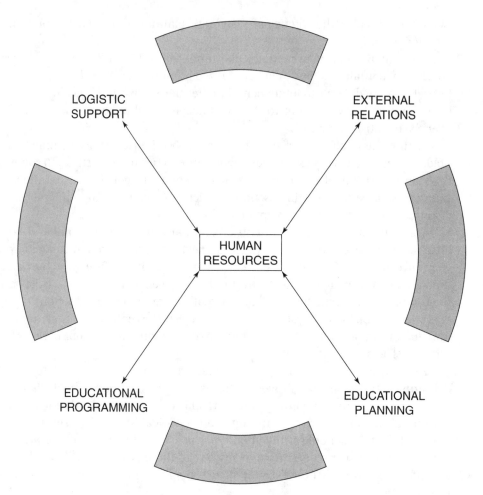

FIGURE 1.1 *Centrality of the human resource function to other organizational endeavors.*

From the preceding introduction of the human resource function, one can examine the significance of this important subsystem of a school organization. For example,

■ In contrast to some other major functions, human resource is concerned with activities related primarily to individuals as employees. The scope of the human resource function, as can be judged from the activities listed in Figure 1.1, is extensive. These functional activities exercise a pervasive influence on system personnel throughout their employment careers.

■ Design and operation of the human resource function can have either positive or negative effects on the individual, the work unit, and/or the system at large. Individuals' behavior influences organizational effectiveness. A proactive role of the human resource function is to develop a structure within which individuals and work units are able to work cooperatively and to perform productively when fulfilling assigned job requirements.

■ With the maelstrom of contemporary challenges posed by external and internal governmental, political, educational, economical, and social change, the human resource function must be shaped so that it occupies a pivotal position to link system purposes to human resource practices. System purposes and human resource procedures depend largely on personnel.

Personnel needed by a school system are those who will have the ability, motivation, and creativity to: (a) enable the system to surmount its infirmities; (b) adjust the educational program continually to the needs of individuals living and competing in a dynamic society; (c) provide leadership that shapes the human organization in such a way that there will be congruence between the individual and the system; (d) create a climate conducive to maximizing voluntary growth and individual effectiveness; and (e) influence ordinary personnel to perform in an extraordinary fashion. This kind of human resource strategy calls for a leadership focus that is intent on achieving the goals of the organization; that provides opportunities for its members to bring initiative and creativity to their tasks, which will result in both individual satisfaction and effective position performance; and that will mesh administrative processes so that greater congruence between organizational goals and individual efforts becomes a reality.

Educational organizations, like all organizations, are created and maintained to achieve specific purposes (Hoy & Miskel, 2005). It is important that the reader understands the significance of the relationship between organizational purposes and the human resource function. Figure 1.2 will enable the reader to visualize the interaction among three types of goals and the human resource function within a productive school setting.

As can be observed in Figure 1.2, these goals have unique as well as shared properties. The focus of the human resource function is to capitalize on the shared properties among goals as well as the unique properties of specific goals. Far too often the emphasis in the field setting has been to ignore unique aspects of goals.

Contemporary thought about organizations in general and about educational organizations in particular emphasizes the human resource function as a vital part of system operation. Human resources are the basis for addressing problems encountered within the work setting. This viewpoint includes, among other values, careful attention

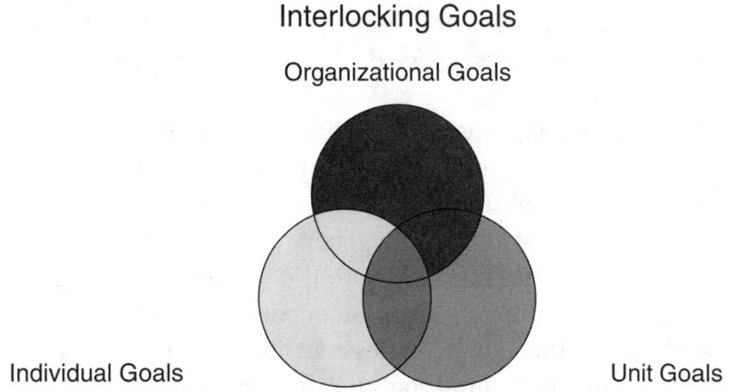

FIGURE 1.2   *Interconnecting goals of the human resource function.*

to formulation, clarification, adherence, and internalization, as well as development of plans within the human resource function for improving interpersonal relationships, to seeking better methods of resolving conflict, and to increasing mutual understanding among system personnel.

Goal setting and goal achieving were established long ago as significant organizational activities within the human resource context (House, 1971). An acceptance of these activities is the result of a number of factors which include the need for greater unity of direction in all organizations, the pressure to clarify system and individual roles, and the importance of feedback to reduce gaps between both individual and organizational needs and actual performance expectations for on-the-job behaviors.

Considerably less attention has been devoted by the human resource function within the public school setting, however, to the behavioral aspects of the goal-setting process as they apply to members of a school system. Although it is clear that numerous benefits can be derived from goals established at the top level of the system, it is equally true that unless members of the system are committed to general organizational goals and specific position objectives as established, the intended outcomes will fail to be realized. As will be stressed in subsequent chapters, setting organizational goals involves consideration of the impact of this process and of the outcomes on the people it will affect when it leads to internalizing organizational goals as part of an individual's value system as a member of the school community.

One of the major tasks of human resource administration is to understand employees' reactions to system processes designed to achieve organizational goals. By understanding employees' reactions to system processes and to expected outcomes, it is possible to modify those processes and expected outcomes when it is apparent that there is incompatibility between goals/outcomes and human reactions to mechanisms for attainment. Goal acceptance, commitment, and internalization are behavioral aspects involved in and essential to the outcomes of the goal-setting process when utilized as part of the human resource function (Marshall & Gerstl-Pepin, 2005).

There is a kernel of truth to the often-stated criticism that educational establishments suffer from "purpose ambiguity" within the human resource function. Not only does clarification of organizational expectations for the individual contribute to security and to position satisfaction, but achievement of both organizational and individual goals also gives the individual a significant sense of accomplishment. The more clearly individuals understand what they are expected to do, the more likely they are to achieve expectations and goal obtainment.

In fact, other objectives of the human resource function (see Figure 1.2) indicate that the clearer the organizational expectations on behalf of individuals as position holders, the easier it is to evaluate their progress in attaining the goals established by the organization. Individuals cannot know where they are going or what they are doing until the school system defines clearly where the district is going. If the goals of the system are known and if the individual has an opportunity to participate meaningfully in meeting these objectives through activities contributing to self-actualization, then attainment of both system and individual goals will be enhanced through an effective human resource strategy. Collectively, the purposes, goals, and objectives of the human resource function must be tempered in light of certain impinging realities faced by all public school systems.

Impinging Realities Influencing the Human Resource Function

As an organization, the school district in totality, as well as the human resource function within a school district, is impacted by many forces. Collectively, these forces should help shape decision making about human resource policies and should dictate specific modes of action to be followed by a public school district. Contained in Figure 1.3 is a depiction of specific forces impacting both the school district at large and the human resource function in particular.

Included among these forces, as found in Figure 1.3, are environmental factors, organizational constraints, ethical considerations, and cultural realities. Each of these entities has a unique as well as an interactional implication for shaping the human resource function in the public school setting. As such, attention is warranted to understand the human resource function from a broad perspective through an examination of these impinging realities relative to their effects on polices, procedures, and implementation processes.

Environmental Factors Impacting the Human Resource Function

Within the United States of America, school systems are created to serve our society through the education of the populace (Valente & Valente, 2005). This societal goal for educating the populace is extremely noteworthy relative to the organization and

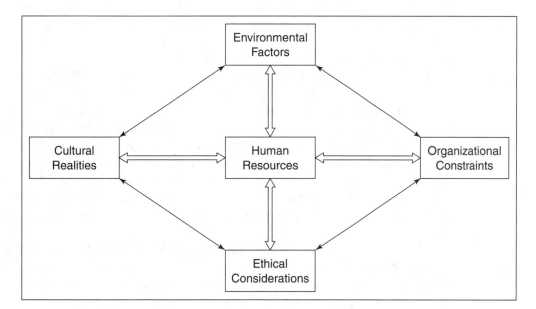

FIGURE 1.3   *Forces impacting the human resource function.*

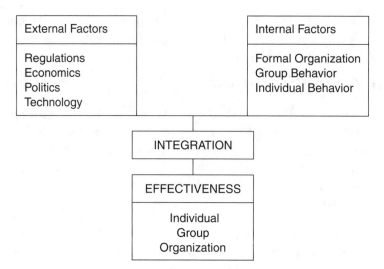

FIGURE 1.4 *External and internal environmental factors affecting individuals, groups, and the organization.*

operation of the human resource function in the public school setting. Unlike many nations of the world, public education in the United States is for all and not just for the academic/economic elite (Owings & Kaplan, 2006).

Given this humanitarian goal for public education in the United States, the human resource function in the public school setting takes on special responsibilities. Stakeholders within the United States need a working knowledge about the relationship between environmental factors and the operation of the human resource function in the public school setting. Consequently, a model for understanding the interaction of the school system environment and the influence of this environment on individual, group, and organizational behavior is presented in Figure 1.4.

This schematic portrayal of the environmental factors as found in Figure 1.4 depicts two types of environments: (1) external and (2) internal. With respect to the human resource function in the public school setting, most changes, in the evolution of human resource management, have been brought about by the **external environment** over which public school districts have little control. Major external forces that affect the human resource function have been grouped arbitrarily into clusters (as outlined in Figure 1.4) in order to establish a framework for analyzing the complex interaction between environmental factors and the human resource activities of a public school system.

Environmental-organizational interaction suggests that there are constraints, forces, and options to which a system must respond to achieve stability and viability in an ever-changing environment. The human resource function plays a vital role in helping the system operate within economic structures, meet legal mandates, honor contractual obligations, address pressures of special-interest groups, adapt to emerging technologies, and uphold ethical standards while maintaining centrality of purpose. Striking this balance between the external environment and the ongoing operations of a school system

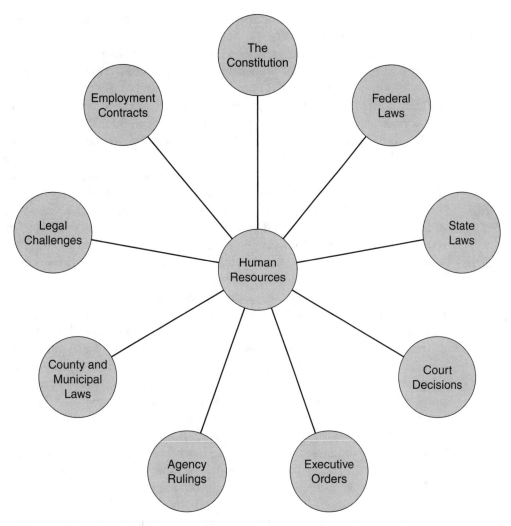

FIGURE 1.5   *Regulatory factors influencing the human resource function.*

requires considerable organizational effort on the part of the human resource function as well as those responsible for its operation.

Contextually, education in the United States operates within a framework of regulatory controls of varying degrees. As indicated in Figure 1.5, these elements include the Constitution; federal laws; state, county, and municipal laws; court decisions; executive orders; administrative agency rulings; legal challenges; and employment contracts. It is agreed generally that provisions governing employment in both the public and private sectors have a far-reaching influence on the operation of the human resource function. Each state system controls the school curriculum and supporting services, determines who shall teach, decides how schools are financed, and oversees school board policy-making authority. In addition, there are regulatory controls governing taxation limitations, salaries, benefits, collective bargaining, performance appraisal, tenure, grievance procedures, and budgetary requirements.

Because school systems operate within an external environment over which school districts exercise little control, knowledge of the present external environment, especially its direction and organizational impact, is an essential aspect of human resource management. In addition to the regulatory factor, there are other factors noted in Figure 1.4 (economical, political, and technological) that affect conditions in the workplace. Following are some indicators illustrating the external environmental impact on people, positions, and direction of human resource activities within the public school setting.

Economic factors are variables that influence the human resource function within the public school setting because most of the costs associated with operating a public school district are related to human resource expenditures. Public school districts, as nonprofit organizations, depend on the ebb and flow of available funds to operate. Although there are recent efforts to reduce the dependency on public funds through school–business relationships, only a minute portion of the funds necessary to operate a public school district come from private sources.

Most of the funds needed to operate a school district are derived from public coffers. Federal funds are awarded usually through entitlements for ongoing programs or through grants for new initiatives. State monies, the largest contributor to public school districts, are generated through some type of formula funding process designed to provide a minimum level of acceptable education for the students (Thompson & Wood, 2001). Most recently, many states have instituted public lotteries as a means for supplementing public school coffers, but outcomes from lotteries, like outcomes from school–business relationships, provide only a very limited level of support for the operation of most public school districts (Owings & Kaplan, 2006).

Also, many public school districts use local revenues to supplement outside sources of income and to provide services beyond those funded by external sources. All sources of revenue for public school districts are subject to political agendas shaped largely by sociocultural phenomena. As the political climate changes, funding sources and funding amounts can and do change. Among many recent factors influencing the political climate fueled by sociocultural phenomena are testing, teacher certification, sex education, and drug/alcohol testing, to mention only a few.

The last, but by no means least, of the external influences on the operation of a school district is technology. Technology within the present context refers to the sum of ways in which the school system attains the information needed to carry out the processes, mechanisms, and techniques it employs to deliver educational services. Among the emerging challenges for the human resource function created by the advent of modern technology and the quickening pace of its development are these pressing agenda items:

- *Technology assimilation:* Ensuring that technology is available and is used to its best advantage by the system and its members.
- *Comprehensive information system:* Using a modern, systematic plan designed to acquire, store, maintain, protect, retrieve, and communicate data in a valid and accurate form.

■ *Staff development:* With the widespread adoption of electronic technology, a critical shortage of computer-literate support staff has developed. Programs for assisting personnel, especially those in a temporary position, are necessary to acquire the skills needed to satisfy burgeoning demands for information.

■ *Office operations:* An information-driven school system requires application of new technology to increase the efficiency and effectiveness of office operations.

■ *Computer applications:* Examples of computer applications vital to the human resource function include recruitment and selection tracking, attendance monitoring, training and developing management, position control, compensation (including benefits), regulatory adherence, payroll, forms management, and computer-assisted instruction.

The second environmental dimension portrayed in Figure 1.4 is the **internal environment** of a school district. A school district's internal environment interacts with the external environment to change almost every aspect of schooling. Interaction among these influences creates administrative challenges, especially concerning their impact on individual and group behavior, as well as the need for strategies to cope with the inexorable tendency toward environmental change.

An internal factor that has changed the way school districts operate in recent years is the formal organization of a school district. To meet emerging needs and to respond to political pressures, some of which have been imposed by the external environment, school districts have decentralized decision making and have created new positions. Vogue within the human resource area today is **site-based decision-making councils** assuming increasing levels of responsibility (Young & Miller-Smith, 2006).

Today, unlike in the past, "two forms of governance exist in the United States" (Winter, et al., 2005, p. 435) relative to decision making within the public school context. One form is the traditional model following line staff from a top-down perspective. The other form involves decentralizing the decision-making process through the use of site-based councils involving parents, teachers, and administrators.

Accompanying changes in decision making are the creation of new positions within the organizational structure, and these new positions alter the formal structure of the organization. One of the new positions created by many school systems is for testing and/or accountability. This position is designed to address accountability issues related to proficiency test scores linking to federal legislation (No Child Left Behind) and state mandates. Not long ago, responsibilities associated with student achievement would have been subsumed under curriculum, but have more recently assumed an independent status with direct reporting relationships to the superintendent.

Another new position that has altered the formal structure of school systems pertains to technology. Technology, as initially conceived within public school districts, was viewed as an operational position responsible for the business functions of the school district. In recent times, technology has expanded to cover educational as well as operational concerns and commands a prominent place within the educational hierarchy.

Within a short period of time, technology positions have been reconceptualized. Initially, individuals with a math background were recruited for these positions, and subsequently, individuals possessing undergraduate- and graduate-level degrees in technology were sought. More recently, associate degree graduates are recruited to provide technical expertise, and technology demands have been redelegated to general educators.

Group behavior within public school districts has changed due largely to collective bargaining. Since the first public law was passed by Wisconsin in 1959, many states (n = 34) have followed in the adoption of public sector laws and have afforded employees greater decision-making ability relative to most human resource functions. What was once entirely a management decision regarding the educational process has become a bilateral decision that requires the concurrence of union leadership.

Individual behavior, like group behavior, has changed within public school districts during recent times. Different populations are seeking and acquiring positions in the educational setting. Changes in employment populations for individuals are due to several external and internal causes.

Certificated personnel, at one time, entered the ranks of educators fresh out of college. Because of certification requirements and entrance requirements being altered, many individuals now enter the certificated ranks in nontraditional ways. Alternate certification routes have allowed individuals to become teachers and administrators without following traditional career progressions, and these individuals have different human resource needs than traditional educators.

Many changes may be observed concerning noncertificated employees in school systems. For example, not so long ago, most bus drivers were males seeking merely to supplement their incomes. Today, most bus drivers are females who rely on the position as a major, if not the sole, source of income.

Collectively, these changes in the internal environment of a school district alter substantially the way school districts operate. In response to these changes, the human resource function must make certain adaptations to ensure the effective and efficient operation of a school district. Functionally, many of these necessary changes may be limited by certain organizational constraints.

Organizational Constraints Hampering the Human Resource Function

When viewed from an organizational lens, all public school districts have an **organizational structure.** That is, every school district has a structure for linking positions and people to purposes. The structure may be one that has been adopted formally by the board of education and described by organizational charts, position guides, and organizational manuals. On the other hand, the structure may be informal, without documentation or evidence of any kind to describe specific characteristics of alignment.

In both cases, all public school districts are composed of people who occupy positions, employees that interact with each other, and individuals concerned about being compensated, both for responsibilities inherent to the work they perform and for their individual contributions to organizational effectiveness. To align individuals with an

Purposes	Every organization has a structure or a plan for linking positions and people to purposes. The purpose of an organization forms the starting point of planning because all activities flow from purpose.
Activities	Activities are divided into positions; positions are grouped into major functions; functions are grouped into units.
Reporting Relationships	Every structure has a hierarchy to coordinate organizational activity. Some positions report to other positions. The number of positions reporting to another position is referred to as the span of control.
Line and Staff Relationships	Line positions have the authority to initiate and to carry out basic activities of the organization. Staff positions complement the activities of line positions.

FIGURE 1.6 *Elements of an organizational structure.*

organizational structure from a human resource perspective, an analysis is needed by those responsible for the human resource function (see Figure 1.6).

As illustrated in Figure 1.6, elements of organizational structure should include purposes, activities, reporting relationships, and line–staff relationships designating a **span of control.** One inference that can be drawn from an analysis of an organization's structure is that its design as well as its implementation involve individual and group participation through which system purpose is transformed into policies, functions, processes, activities, operations, and audit mechanisms aimed at achieving specific organizational outcomes. Another inference is that there are compelling questions to be answered about the design of the organization's structure from a human resource perspective such as these:

- What are the key activities that need to be performed to serve the interests of students, position assignments, regulatory agencies, community groups, parents, and the school system?
- What is the most appropriate way to group these key activities into positions?
- How should positions be grouped into attendance units, departments, administrative and supervisory groups, support services, and temporary personnel requirements?
- How many positions should be in the structure? What major tasks, reporting relationships, and performance criteria should be established for each position?
- To what extent should the system be decentralized or centralized for decision-making purposes?
- What integration devices such as communication and coordination are most suitable for bringing together positions, position holders, and work units into a cohesive whole for system betterment?

- What chain of command should be established? How many levels of management are needed in the system?

Structural questions such as these force designers of human resource systems to focus on how to utilize best the structure, and how to choose from among the feasible options the ones most likely to improve individual, group, and system performance from a district-wide perspective. An inescapable circumstance of school management is that the complexity, as well as the politically and intellectually demanding tasks associated with school restructuring, requires an appreciation of a host of factors. These factors must be taken into consideration when designing an organizational structure for a school system. Failure to consider these tasks defeats many of the concerns associated with an effective and efficient human resource system from a strategic planning perspective.

Despite all the criticisms about school system structures that have surfaced in the long-running debate about restructuring schools, especially regarding hierarchies, levels of management, types of supervision, and top-down decision making on the part of administration; some mode of procedure, of fusing human and nonhuman resources into a cohesive effort toward purpose attainment, is inescapable. A system approach is essential to implement improvements in a public school district through direction and coordination. Without concerted effort from a system perspective, school districts are reactive rather than proactive to emerging situations and fail to capitalize on opportunities.

To monitor organizational constraints in a school system, audit mechanisms are essential to all human resource functions. At least two kinds of audit mechanisms exist: (a) **system controls** and (b) **functional controls.** System controls are focused on the total organization and include policies, position descriptions, strategic plans, and mission statements. Functional controls pertain to those measures that guide the human resource function relative to the actions of employees.

Several compelling reasons exist as to why audit mechanisms are essential to all human resource functions in a public school district. One compelling reason is that every plan that the school system initiates and allocates resources to should have a built-in means for judging its effectiveness. There are numerous other justifications for audit mechanisms, such as preventing and correcting deviations from standards as in curbing turnover, absenteeism, sick leave, and other benefit abuses and minimizing behaviors that are antiorganizational, self-serving, defiant, rebellious, or in violation of the system's culture. With respect to this last reason for audits involving the actions of employees, ethical considerations come into play for a variety of reasons because they reflect **values.**

Ethical Considerations

It is an inescapable fact that decisions give life to a school system and that most decisions are permeated by **ethics.** Following this stream of thought, exercise of authority through the decision-making process includes consideration of ethical implications for the operation of a school district, especially in the human resource domain. Ethics, according to most definitions (see the National Education Association (n.d.), refers to the rightness or wrongness of certain actions, to the goodness or badness of the motives, and to the outcomes of such actions from a value perspective.

What is or is not ethical, in many instances, is a matter of personal interpretation (Kowalski, 2004). Because ethics are a matter of interpretation, ethical standards to which a school system is committed in the human resource area need to be clearly and extensively communicated. Mechanisms for clarifying and for communicating ethics pertaining to human resources include personnel handbooks, policy manuals, and a code of ethics adopted by the school system.

A broader understanding of ethical behavior in the workplace, especially as it applies to the human resource function, is an important step in dealing with personnel problems and enhancing system betterment. The relationship between ethical sensitivity and the human resource function is intertwined, as the following concepts demonstrate:

- Leadership is involved with decisions about such matters as organizational purpose, goals, objectives, strategies, and their implications.
- Ethical considerations, when factored into the decision-making process, uphold human dignity as a contributor to positive personal and organizational behavior.
- Decisions made by leaders have a direct impact on both internal and external environments.
- The orientation of individuals and groups to the educational system is influenced by ethical sensitivity to their expectations, aspirations, well-being, conditions of work, compensation equity, and the reward system.
- Decisions and power are inseparable within the public school setting. Those who have authority to make decisions are able to exert control over others, either directly through position power or indirectly through various forms of expertise.

Issues of ethical concern for the school system include obligations as well as various kinds of responsibilities. For example, system and member obligations, such as those following, have the inherent potential for unethical conduct when behavioral obligations and responsibilities are unfulfilled:

- Member ethical obligations to the school system
- Personnel ethical obligations to the profession
- Teacher ethical obligations to students
- System and member commitment to professional employment practices
- System and member obligations and responsibilities to stakeholders in the external environment such as taxpayers, creditors, suppliers, governments, unions, accrediting agencies, and recruitment sources (colleges and universities, other school systems, and placement agencies).

From the foregoing points, it may be assumed that power to decide can influence member behavior and that the power to decide has important ethical considerations. However, as noted in this section, ethical considerations are context specific and what is ethical in one situation may not be ethical in another situation. Ethical considerations associated with the human resource function must be tempered in light of cultural realities associated with particular school systems.

Cultural Realities

Every organization has a culture, and school districts are no exception to this generality (Sergiovanni, 2006). The culture of a school district is defined by several constructs including norms, values, expectations, and ideas. As such, the culture of a school system is rooted within local traditions and community expectations.

Well stated by Smithers (1988) some time ago, an organization's culture can serve a variety of useful functions for new as well as continuing employees. For employees new to a school system, the system's culture provides a range of behaviors that the employees must exhibit before becoming fully assimilated within the work environment. Existing employees rely on their knowledge of a school system's culture to help them select behaviors in uncertain situations lacking a clear directive.

The culture of a school system is difficult to observe directly but is recognizable by astute employees. Culture is something that is felt and that renders a particular school district unique (Cunningham & Cordeiro, 2006). It is "the ways things are done" in that school district.

What might be appropriate behavior for employees in one school district might be entirely inappropriate behavior for employees in another school district. Appropriateness of behavior for employees, in many instances, may depend more on the culture in which the behavior occurs rather than on the behavior itself. This explains, at least in part, why different school districts can adopt similar mission statements but utilize quite different procedures and processes to implement the intent of a similarly defined mission statement.

A school district's culture has important implications for most of the human resource functions listed in Figure 1.1. Although a school district's culture is always present, it is not beyond change (Giancola & Hutchison, 2005). Indeed, many of the planning techniques used within the human resource function are designed to alter a school system's culture to move the district from the current state to a desired mode of operation.

Cultural factors in the human resource function that can be changed by those in leadership positions include envisioning, bringing to life, reinforcing, rewarding, and embedding constructive behaviors. Beyond helping members to understand their culture, leaders create the means to enhance its positive features, and these means aid in neutralizing tendencies toward system instability. Leaders can use their knowledge of a school district's culture to enhance the performance of several other human resource functions.

For example, research addressing the recruitment of educators has revealed the importance of culture for the recruitment process (Winter, Newton, & Kirkpatrick, 1998). Several studies have shown that many applicants are more interested in the cultural aspects of a school system than in the economic rewards provided by school systems (see Young, Place, Rinehart, Jury, & Baits, 1999). Empirical research has shown that applicants for teacher positions are more likely to pursue job offerings when recruitment interviews with the school district's representative focused on the work and the work environment rather than on salaries and fringe benefits.

Much recent research addressing the selection of employees has been expanded to incorporate issues related to an organization's culture within the human resource process.

Traditional selection paradigms focused almost exclusively on person-position fit. More recently, organizations have begun to examine selection from a person-organization fit perspective (see Heneman & Judge, 2006; Parsons, Cable, & Liden, 1999).

For many school districts, the format for orientation and development activities and programs can be quite similar, but the content of these activities and programs should vary considerably due to a district's unique culture. Culture of a school district comes into play even in those economic activities performed by the human resource function. Often, the pay rate for employees of a public school district is influenced by a district's culture as well as by a district's ability to pay (Young, 2006; Young, Delli, Miller-Smith, & Alhadeff, 2004).

One of the continuing questions about school system culture is what is its relationship to the human resource function? One response is that to a considerable extent, culture is tied to the impact of change in the workplace. There are shifting human values and changes in the demographics of the workforce (in ethnic background, in cultural diversity, and in graying of the instructional cadre), and these changes alter the existing culture for a school system.

There is another set of culture-driven forces with the potential to affect individual and group behavior: the environmental dimension. The environmental dimension includes regulatory agencies, community groups, boards of education, school management, unions, standing committees, work units (such as elementary schools), and support groups (maintenance, operation, clerical, food service, security, and transportation). In one way or another, each of these system entities and their constituents is affected by changes that have personal, organizational, legal, state, national, and international causes.

Collectively, all the impinging realities described in the preceding sections of this chapter interact to shape the educational process in every public school district and the human resource function supporting this process. To bring a broad perspective to the human resource function and to provide insight into the purposes, policies, plans, procedures, and projects, as well as the impact of these human resource aspects on work, working arrangements, and work motivation of school administrative, teaching, and support personnel is the intent of this book. To accomplish this intent, one type of strategic planning process is used as a basic framework.

Strategic Planning

The particular **strategic planning process** used in this book involves several different but related planning concepts and linking these concepts into a managerial mosaic for directing the human resource function in the public school setting. Although many planning processes and procedures exist within the published literature, the one chosen as a guide for this book is both simple and effective. It involves the following:

- Utilizing a school system's mission statement to guide a strategic planning process for the human resource function.
- Placing in perspective different goals of the human resource function as linked to a school district's mission.

- Identifying general objectives of the human resource function pertinent to most human resource goals.
- Specifying operational functions necessary for accomplishing both specific goals and general objectives.

As will be illustrated throughout this book, the human resource function is related directly or indirectly to all organizational functions found within any public school district. Because the human resource function fails to be a stand-alone activity, it must be an extension of and reflection of the basic values for a public school system through a concerted planning effort. Key to identifying these values, the realization of these values, and the necessary linkages within the strategic planning process is an understanding of the relationships among planning concepts as found in the following diagram (see Figure 1.7).

Mission Statement

The **mission statement** of a school system identifies the purposes for which it has been created, its boundaries, its activities, as well as its governmental and collateral purposes. A mission statement should encapsulate these conditions and should represent the foundation for providing all educational programs and supporting services that will enhance the mental, moral, social, and emotional development of children, adolescents, and adults served by the school district. Purposes addressed in a mission statement establish parameters for human resource planning in the public school setting and following are examples of mission statements from three different school districts:

(1). The Mission of the Upper Arlington City School District is to provide each student with an innovative and superior education that instills integrity and promotes personal achievement in an ever-changing society (Upper Arlington School District, 2006).

(2). To educate and empower our students to reach their potential as productive citizens through a unified commitment to excellence (Clarksville County School System, n.d.).

FIGURE 1.7   *Components of the strategic planning process.*

(3). Farmersville Unified School District is committed to improving education through the use of technology. It is the intent of Farmersville Unified School District to make technologies an integral part of the District's curriculum and operations. The District will ensure that tools of technology become an expected and routine part of the education of our students, staff, parents and the community (Farmersville Unified School District, n.d.).

To some policy makers and to some educators, developing a mission statement to guide a school system in strategic planning and in selecting from among the multitude of underlying choices that must be made to coordinate diverse system activities represents a meaningless exercise in academic nonsense. However, the mission statement, when properly constructed, is arguably the most basic property of a school system, and one possessing considerable practical utility for shaping the human resource perspective. The mission statement reflects the system's overarching plan from which a set of subplans is derived relative to the overall system and subsystems of the human resource function.

Subplans include definitions of the types of work to be done, the division of labor, the specification of the number and kinds of jobs needed, how the jobs are structured, how resources are allocated, and articulation of system directives and their content through such processes as personnel involvement, goal acceptance and commitment, as well as member induction and socialization. Examination of the mission statements provided above leads to the realization that they embody the potential for the following:

- Clarifying the ultimate purpose of a school system's existence
- Identifying services that the public expects the system to deliver in exchange for financial support
- Providing a framework for judging the extent to which the mission is being realized
- Creating a focus for defining the scope and limitations of the system's endeavors
- Establishing a point of reference for deciding which key activities need to be performed
- Deciding how financial, technical, human, and organizational resources will be allocated
- Focusing on the end state rather than on the means of getting there
- Developing a frame of reference by which controls are generated to implement the mission (strategies, policies, programs, projects, rules, and regulations).

Another important value of a clearly defined mission statement is that it serves as a boundary guide. As a boundary guide, the mission statement determines what the school system should not do as well as stating what the school system should do. However, any boundary guide established by a mission statement must be tempered by regulatory mandates.

There is, for example, a hierarchy of laws, rules, and decisions that have operational mandates for school systems. These include such factors as federal mandates; the state constitution; statutes; state Board of Education rules; Department of Education regulations; court decisions; and system policies, labor contracts, and rules (see Figure 1.5). Collectively, these governing influences eliminate discretionary consideration of certain decisions within the strategic planning process while also leaving important permissive decisions to the school system.

A reality-based mission statement serves as an important anchor for defining the scope of acceptable choices regarding such current education issues as integrating sex education, preschool day care, pressures for extensive extracurricular programs, the extent of special education and pupil disability arrangements, various types of age-group plans, continuing education classes for pregnant teenagers, desegregation, bilingual education, and issues relating to cultural diversity, quality of work life, and restructuring the system. Viewed in the context of this discussion, the mission statement is important because it provides a focal point for debating, discussing, and arriving at a consensus among system members concerning their expectations and beliefs, as well as to their expressed wishes about what the organization's common purpose should be.

In practice, the mission statement for a school district reflects the philosophy of a school district by capturing the ultimate goals of the system in a succinct manner (see Figure 1.2). A mission statement provides a background for assessing current programs and activities within the district and offers a measuring stick for choosing among potential programs and activities for a district. However, the creation and the application of a unified purpose through a mission statement is frequently hindered by short-term perspectives and obscured by the business at hand.

For all of these considerations, the system's mission, if clearly understood, can be conducive to internalizing commitment and dedication to an explicit set of goals, identified objectives, and operational procedures. The school system is ill served when stakeholders fail to appreciate the interactive potential of a system mission and to use it consistently as a standard in making decisions regarding transformation from the present to a desired state. To move from the present state of operation to a desired state of operation in an effective and efficient manner requires the specification of goals, objectives, and operational procedures for the human resource function (see Figure 1.7).

Organizational Goals

By design, the mission statement for a public school system sets broad parameters for directing decision making within the strategic planning process. Based on these broad parameters, additional planning efforts are needed to identify means and methods for implementation of the mission statement within the public school setting. In keeping with the flow of the strategic planning process as applied to the human resource function, the next stage involves the identification of specific goals to capture the thrust of the mission statement.

Goals, as defined within the strategic planning process, define the purpose and lend direction to the human resource function. From a system's perspective, goals indicate which programs/activities should be implemented and the rationale for implementation of these programs/activities. Implied by goals are insights about such matters as what work is needed, what work activities are to be undertaken, and what competencies are needed to accomplish the goals. In addition, goals lead to consideration of performance requirements for the work and for determining a structure appropriate to facilitate achievement of objectives and operational procedures.

As a planning tool for guiding the human resource function in the public school setting, goals can be prioritized. Prioritization of goals provides a basis for capturing the intents of policy makers and for coordinating the work efforts of system personnel. Well illustrated in the professional literature is that the attainment of strategic outcomes is enhanced when human resource practices are focused, prioritized, and translated into plans of action according to preestablished goals.

For example, it would be senseless to make decisions about recruitment, selection, induction, compensation, appraisal, and tenure of system members without connecting these administrative tasks to the mission statement, goals, objectives, and operational functions of the system. Following is both a recap of and additional reasons to support the contention that strategic planning is an empowerment tool for meeting some novel as well as traditional human resource challenges through the development of goals:

- Goals define the purpose and direction for activities.
- Goals of a school system can be arranged hierarchically.
- Goals create system, unit, and individual expectations.
- Goals affect virtually all types of plans relating to system membership, from the quantity and quality of personnel to their recruitment, selection, and related processes.
- Goals provide the basis for coordinated effort.
- Goals provide standards against which to evaluate not only system parts but the total system as well.
- Goals are conducive to self-regulated behavior.
- Goals set the tone for members' behavior.
- Goals are antecedents to human resource policies, procedures, rules, methods, and strategies.
- Organizational effectiveness is enhanced when individual, unit, and system goals are compatible (see Figure 1.2).

Within the public school setting, the identification and the adoption of goals for the human resource function serves to facilitate the effective and the efficient operation of a public school district through further refining the thrusts of the mission statement and bringing the mission statement one step closer to actual practice in the field setting. Although goals give preference for activities on the part of educational administrators, goal statements lack identifiable objectives for guiding this preference. To provide identifiable objectives for the implementation of goal statements is the purpose of the following section.

District Objectives

Although goals derived from the mission statement are specific to a particular school district, the objectives for accomplishing these goals relative to the human resource function are somewhat universal across all public school districts. Succinctly stated, these **objectives** are identifying human resource needs, procuring individuals to fill these needs, and retaining a competent workforce. Following is an overview of each objective as part of the total human resource planning process.

Identifying Human Resource Needs

Fundamental to all human resource goals derived from the mission statement within a strategic planning process is information about staffing needs of the organization. Staffing information is needed about the number of and the types of employees required/desired for accomplishing specified goals stemming from the mission statement. To provide this information and to fulfill this objective within the planning process from a human resource perspective, a staffing plan must be devised.

When shaping the staffing plan according to human resource needs, educational administrators must consider that staffing levels within all school districts are driven to varying degrees largely by three factors. These factors include preferences of policy makers for specific goals/programs, constraints of the labor market relative to available resources, and enrollment levels of students within defined programs. Although certain exceptions exist relative to the number of staff needed to satisfy a particular goal of the mission statement, especially concerning special education, the number of staff is always an important issue to be resolved for most human resource activities.

Another important part of identifying human resource needs is determining the type of individuals required to execute each goal. Attention must be afforded within the staffing plan to educational and experiential qualifications of individuals expected to fulfill goal directives. When identifying human resource needs as an objective within the strategic planning process, consideration should be provided both to minimum and to desired qualifications of individuals as well as the means for procuring quality employees to meet identifiable human resource needs of a public school district.

Procuring Individuals to Fill Human Resource Needs

Once the human resource needs of a public school district have been identified through a well-determined staffing plan, another objective of the strategic planning process focuses on the procurement of quality employees required to execute specific goals emanating from the mission statement. Procurement of quality individuals to assume defined staffing needs for a public school requires strategic planning. Strategic planning is needed to identity applicant sources, to generate applicant pools, and to select among the most qualified job candidates.

Few school systems today enjoy the luxury of an adequate unsolicited applicant pool from which to choose among job candidates (Young, Jury, & Reis, 1999). This is especially true for those districts seeking to diversify their current workforce within the public school setting. As such, the strategic planning process for the human resource function must seek to identify sources of applicants differing from the racial/ethnic composition of current workforces as found in most public school districts, and must seek applicants aligning with the populations served by a public school district.

Identification of applicant sources is no assurance of increasing the diversity and quality of individuals seeking employment with a public school district. Indeed, individuals as applicants must make proactive decisions for seeking employment in a public school district. To capture the interests of job candidates and to motivate their application requires strategic planning on the part of a public school district.

It goes almost without stating, the aim of selection is to match individuals and jobs within the public school setting. A sound strategic human resource plan should provide information that facilitates this process both for applicants and for organizational representatives. Inappropriate pairings between applicants and jobs fail to serve all involved parties and lead to dysfunctional organizational behaviors such as turnover, discontent, and less-than-effective performance. Appropriate pairings between applicants and jobs must be reinforced through retaining a competent workforce once selection decisions are consummated.

Retaining a Competent Workforce

The attraction to and the attainment of individuals for a public school district is only part of the organizational process addressed within strategic planning from a human resource perspective. Marketable employees having employment options must enjoy at least a moderate level of job satisfaction with their current job assignment (Young, Chounet, Buster, & Sailor, 2005), and strategic planning addresses this need. Strategic planning within the human resource context should provide a means for reducing differences between actual and desired job situations as encountered by employees in an educational system.

From a system-level perspective, all employees benefit in knowing how their assignment fits within the total organizational design of the school district. Being apprised of the school system's mission statement, goals, and objectives is an often-overlooked aspect of the planning process, but an important one for maintaining the commitment of employees for accomplishing the mission of a public school district. An objective of the strategic planning process relative to the human resource function is to provide all employees with this information from a system's perspective.

At the basic level, most public school employees desire information about job expectations and organizational commitments/obligations for meeting job expectations. Far too often in most public school districts, employees lack this basic information about expectations, commitments, and obligations. As a managerial tool for human resource activities, the strategic planning process fills these voids.

When conceptualized appropriately and when implemented properly, a strategic planning process stemming from a mission statement and driven by specific goals can fulfill the objectives associated with identifying human resource needs, procuring individuals to fulfill these needs, and maintaining the services of these employees. To meet all these demands, certain operational functions must be performed by a public school system relative to the organization and to the operation of the human resource function. These operational functions required for a public school district are addressed in the following section of this chapter, and this information serves as a preview of the remaining content covered in this book.

Operational Functions of the Human Resource Process

As noted in Figure 1.1, components of this figure depict operational functions as part of the strategic planning process for effective public school systems. Operational functions reflect the means by which human resource activities are executed within the public school setting. To guide policy makers, executive-level personnel, site-based administrators, and aspiring educational leaders in fulfilling their obligations relative to the human resource function is the purpose of the ensuing chapters, and an overview of these chapters in content as well as perspective follows.

Organizationally, these chapters are allocated among three different sections of this book. The first section contains three chapters, provides an overview of the human resource process, identifies certain informational needs, and illustrates specific human resource planning techniques.

Within the first section, Chapter 1 emphasizes the centrality of the human resource process for the organization and operation of a public school district and provides a framework for the strategic planning process. Chapter 2 introduces readers to the informational needs associated with the human resource process and suggests guidelines for fulfilling these needs in terms of system design. One particular type of informational need identified in Chapter 2 is student enrollment data.

To determine the number and types of staff required for implementing goals derived from the strategic planning process through operational functions, attention is afforded in Chapter 2 to analyzing and to projecting student enrollments. For analyzing and for projecting student enrollments, specific techniques are addressed. Actual data from the field setting are used to illustrate different projection techniques with attention afforded to suitability for any particular school district. More specifically, attention is devoted both to linear and to nonlinear enrollment projection techniques as tools for strategic planning.

After fulfilling these basic informational requirements as set forth in Chapter 2 involving analyzing past enrollments and projecting future enrollments, Chapter 3 advances the strategic planning process through developing a staffing plan for a school district. To develop a functional staffing plan for a public school district, attention is afforded to analyzing enrollment trends, assessing current staffing levels, and determining desired staffing goals. For all these different components comprising a staffing plan, actual examples of staffing plans from the field setting are provided, and audit mechanisms for compliance to the strategic planning process are illustrated through the construction of staffing charts.

Having projected future enrollment needs and developed a functional staffing plan in Part I, the second part of this book addresses those human resource operatives pertaining to recruitment, selection, orientation, compensation, and performance appraisal. To attract a willing and capable pool of diverse candidates for filling identifiable needs as set forth in a functional staffing plan is the focus of Chapter 4. The thrust of Chapter 4 is recruitment and the various phases of the recruitment process. Recruitment as an operational function within the strategic planning process for the human resource function is examined both from legal and functional perspectives.

From a legal perspective, issues related to equal employment opportunities and to affirmative action are discussed from a policy-making perspective. Functionally, different sources for applicants are explored both externally and internally to a school district. Most importantly, information is presented about how applicants as individuals choose to seek employment with particular school districts and strategies that school districts can utilize to attract applicants.

Once viable applicant pools have been obtained through the recruitment procedures presented in Chapter 4, the emphasis of Chapter 5 is on selection or the means for delimiting the applicant pool seeking gainful employment with a public school district. In Chapter 5, selection is viewed as a process rather than as an event, and different phases of the selection process are detailed in this chapter. Bearing on all phases of the selection process are external regulatory requirements and internal functional demands governing selection practices, and Chapter 5 provides information about necessary requirements for this phase of the strategic planning process for implementation in the field setting.

Requirements of federal and state guidelines are discussed concerning statutory requirements related to validity paradigms. Different validity paradigms and their structural requirements are explored within the public school setting. Specific do's and don'ts of the selection process are noted both from a policy and from an operational perspective.

Selection of individuals either new to the school district or new to the job assignment within a school district requires an orientation process as a means for inducting them to their work assignment. Orientation as part of the strategic planning process is the topic of Chapter 6. When viewed from a strategic human resource planning perspective, orientation involves aligning values of the school system with goals of the organization and the means by which a position complements the purpose. At a more practical level, orientation involves placing an employee's position within the greater educational enterprise and specifying definable job expectations to be performed. An effective orientation program fulfills all these requirements and is the focus of Chapter 6.

Moving from orientation to other operational concerns, Chapter 7 addresses the human resource function relating to appraisal as part of the strategic planning process bearing on the human resource function within the public school setting. Appraisal addresses the assessment of current performance and for directing of future performance.

The focus of Chapter 7 is on performance appraisal systems for those employees that have been recruited, selected, and oriented. Depending on the focus of the strategic planning process, various employee appraisal systems are presented and critiqued. Emphasis is given to norm-referenced systems, criterion-referenced systems, and self-referenced systems as a means for complementing the strategic planning process adopted by a public school system.

Specific performance appraisal methods are presented in Chapter 7. Included among these methods are graphic rating scales, goal-setting processes, and self-constructed portfolios. Each evaluation system and each performance assessment method are discussed from a strategic planning process perspective.

Attention is given to designing and assessing compensation structures for all employee groups through application of auditing criteria in Chapter 8. Actual examples from the field setting are provided for rationality, compression, earning potentials, and elasticity associated with compensation structures in public school districts. Specific auditing criteria are examined to pinpoint operational concerns with current compensation systems and to design new compensation systems.

Issues concerning traditional and nontraditional pay systems are discussed in light of organizational goals as specified in the strategic planning process. Advantages as well as disadvantages of pay for performance systems are discussed. Policy concerns for identifying a relevant labor market and for using these data to update a compensation system are illustrated.

To maintain the continuity of individuals as viable employees of a public school system is the focus of the last part of this book and is covered in the remaining chapters (Part III). Within the last part of this book, attention is directed toward separate but related aspects of the human resource function within the strategic planning context. Chapter 9 concerns the entitlements and privileges of individuals relative to certain fringe benefits of public employment. A differentiation is made between entitlements and fringe benefits as part of the strategic planning process related to the human resource function. For each of these designated categories (entitlements and privileges), various options are provided for policy makers, executive-level employees, site-based administrators, and aspiring educational leaders that have implications for the planning process in the human resource domain.

Chapter 10 continues issues of the continuity process by examining career development opportunities for ongoing personnel. Different types of career development programs are presented and methods of evaluating these programs are discussed. Specific types of evaluation designs are presented and different threats to the internal validity of these designs are discussed.

The focus of the final chapter (Chapter 11) is on collective bargaining within the public school setting. An overview of the entire collective bargaining process is addressed from a public school perspective. From a procedural point of view, attention is given to unit recognition, unit identification, and the bargaining process.

Within the bargaining process, ground rules are discussed and criteria for analyzing a labor contract are illustrated. Different types of impasses are described for failing to negotiate an item or agree to an item. A differentiation is made between interest and rights arbitration when administering a labor contract.

Review and Preview

One of the main purposes of studying the human resource function of a school system is to develop a broader understanding of the forces, factors, conditions, and circumstances that shape its role as a contributor to organizational effectiveness. The intent of Chapter 1 is to convey the viewpoints that follow.

Evolving models of the human resource function extend well beyond traditional tasks of record keeping, social work, and collective bargaining. Today's designs consider the human resource function to be a vital unit in any organization. The organized and unified arrays of system parts interact through human performance to establish a productive public institution. The personnel processes within the human resource function (Figure 1.1) are linked to the organization infrastructure

(Figure 1.4). Dimensions of the infrastructure include system mission, human resources, regulatory requirements, environmental factors, and ethical considerations.

Chapter 2 examines the planning process as a component of the human resource function and its linkage to the elements in the organizational infrastructure. Social change and educational reform movements brought about by a combination of sociological, political, economic, regulatory, technological, and human resource forces require changes in models for enhancing the potential of the function to clarify problems and develop plans for their solution. Informational needs of a public school district are addressed and enrollment projection techniques are provided.

Discussion Questions

1. Identify one change-related issue facing your school district that has important implications for the human resource function. Please consider: (1) What factors from the external environment influence how the organization responds to that issue? (2) What factors from the internal environment influence how the organization responds to that issue? (3) How can the organization assess these factors comprehensively in developing a solution to the issue?

2. Consider a change or school district improvement issue receiving attention in the public press. How can this issue be addressed through the mission dimension of the human resource function pertaining to the different human resource directives?

3. Identify three system ethical obligations of your school district to the public. Identify three system ethical obligations of your school district to its employees.

4. Educational organizations often suffer from "purpose ambiguity" as a result of poor clarification of organizational expectations and goals. Identify one example of this ambiguity within your school district. What could be done to eliminate or minimize this ambiguity?

5. Organizational efficiency can be measured by the amount of effort it takes the organization to accomplish its work. (1) What is the impact of organizational structure on organizational efficiency? (2) How can human resource activities influence organizational efficiencies?

Case Study

Assume that you are responsible for developing a human resource plan in your school district and that your school district lacks a clearly defined mission statement. From a strategic planning perspective how would you go about refining the mission statement? What organizational goals would be important and how would you prioritize these goals? What human resources would need to be refined and would be needed to meet district needs?

References

Clarksville County School System. (n.d.). Mission Statement. Retrieved January 29, 2006, from the Clarksville County School System Web site: http://www.cmcss.net/

Cunningham, W. G., & Cordeiro, P. A. (2006). *Educational leadership: A problem-based approach* (3rd ed.). Upper Saddle River, NJ: Merrill/Prentice Hall.

Farmersville Unified School District. (n.d.). Mission Statement. Retrieved January 29, 2006, from the Farmersville Unified School District Web site: http://www.farmersville.k12.ca.us/

Giancola, J. M., & Hutchison, J. K. (2005). *Transforming the culture of school leadership.* Thousand Oaks, CA: Corwin Press.

Heneman, H. G., & Judge, T. A. (2006). *Staffing organizations* (6th ed.). Middleton, WI: Mendota House.

House, R. J. (1971). A path-goal theory of leader effectiveness. *Administrative Science Leadership Review, 16,* 321–339. Retrieved December 29, 2005, from the College of St. Scholastica Web site: http://www.css.edu/users/dswenson/web/LEAD/path-goal.html

Hoy, W., & Miskel, C. (2005). *Educational administration: Theory, practice and research.* New York: McGraw-Hill.

Kowalski, T. J. (2004). *Public relations in schools.* Upper Saddle River, NJ: Pearson.

Marshall, C., & Gerstl-Pepin, C. (2005). *Re-framing educational politics for social justice.* New York: Pearson.

National Education Association. (n.d.). Meeting the Challenges of Recruitment and Retention. Retrieved December 29, 2005, from http://www.nea.org/aboutnea/code.html

National Education Association. (n.d.). Retrieved June 10, 2006, from http://www.nea.org/index.html

No Child Left Behind Act 2001, Pub. L. No.107–110, 115 Stat. 1425 (2002).

Owings, W. A., & Kaplan, L. S. (2006). *American public school finance.* Belmont, CA: Thomson Wadsworth Corporation.

Parsons, C. K., Cable, D. M., & Liden, R. C. (1999). Establishing person-organization fit. In R. W. Eder & M. M. Harris (Eds.), *The employment interview handbook.* Thousand Oaks, CA: Sage.

Sergiovanni, T. J. (2006). *The principalship: A reflective practice perspective.* Boston: Pearson.

Sharp, H. M., & Sharp, W. L. (1995). Preparing for the future in the next stage. *National Forum of Educational Administration and Supervision Journal, 13*(1), 25–33.

Smithers, R. D. (1988). *The psychology of work.* Harper and Role: New York.

Thompson, D., & Wood, C. (2001). *Money and schools.* Larchmont, New York: Eye on Education.

Upper Arlington School District. (2006). *Strategic plan.* Retrieved January 29, 2006, from the Upper Arlington School District Web site: http://www.uaschools.org/strateg.htm

Valente, W. D., & Valente, C. M. (2005). *Law in the schools* (6th ed.). Upper Saddle River, NJ: Merrill/Prentice Hall.

Winter, P. A., Millay, J. D., Bojork, L. G., & Keedy, J. L. (2005). Superintendent recruitment: Effects of school councils, job status, signing bonus, and district wealth. *Journal of School Leadership,* 154, pp. 433–455.

Winter, P. A., Newton, R. M., & Kirkpatrick, R. L. (1998). The influence of work values on teacher selection decisions: The effects of principal values, and principal–teacher value interactions. *Teaching and Teacher Education, 14*(4), 385–400.

Young, I. P. (2006). Establishing the economic worth of teachers: A superintendent's guide for advising school boards. *Journal of Scholarship and Practice, 2*(2), 39–45.

Young, I. P., Chounet, P. F., Buster, A. B. & Sailor, S. (2005). Effects of student achievement on satisfaction of newly appointed teachers: A cognitive dissonance perspective. *Journal of School Leadership, 15*(1), 35–51.

Young, I. P., Delli, D. A., Miller-Smith, K. A., & Alhadeff, A. B. (2004). An evaluation of the relative efficiency for various relevant labor markets: An empirical approach for establishing teacher salaries. *Educational Administration Quarterly, 40*(3), 366–387.

Young, I. P., Jury, J. R., & Reis, S. B. (1997). Holmes versus traditional candidates: Labor market receptivity. *Journal of School Leadership, 7*(4), 330–344.

Young, I. P., & Miller-Smith, K. (2006). Effects of site-based councils on teacher screening decisions in high and low performing school districts: A policy capturing study. *Public Policy Analysis in Education, 14*(6).

Young, I. P., Place, A. W., Rinehart, J. S., Jury, J. C., & Baits, D. F. (1999). Teacher recruitment: A test of the similarity–attraction hypothesis for race and sex. *Educational Administration Quarterly, 33*(1), 86–106.

Information Systems and Enrollment Projections

2

CHAPTER OVERVIEW

OBJECTIVES

- Emphasize the importance of information for the human resource function.
- Relate human resource information to the strategic planning process.
- Identify components of an information system process model for the human resource function.
- Illustrate different enrollment projection techniques for providing basic information needs for human resource planning.

Demands for Human Resource Information

A distinguishing characteristic of school districts today is the demand for information by various stakeholders (Kowalski, 2004). Information demands exist for large and small school districts located in urban, suburban, and rural settings. These demands will continue to exist with little foreseeable abatement given the passage of federal legislation (e.g., No Child Left Behind, n.d.), the demands of state requirements (e.g., mandated proficiency testing), and the thirst of the public.

Within the total information demands experienced by public school districts, informational needs of the human resource function occupy a large portion. The nature and variety of information needed to conduct the human resource function can be inferred from the outline of information demands shown in Figure 2.1. More specifically, there is an insatiable demand from outside and within the system for an extensive array of human resource information to: (a) conduct day-to-day operations, (b) resolve short- and long-term personnel problems, (c) comply with external demands, (d) satisfy system needs for research and planning data, and (e) negotiate and implement collective bargaining agreements.

Because school administrative units are becoming more complex as a result of impinging external and internal factors influencing operation, the demand for more and

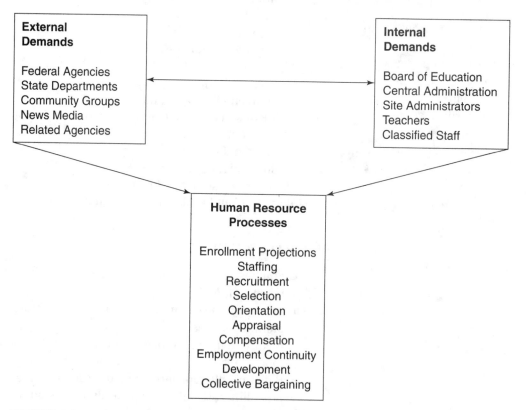

External Demands

Federal Agencies
State Departments
Community Groups
News Media
Related Agencies

Internal Demands

Board of Education
Central Administration
Site Administrators
Teachers
Classified Staff

Human Resource Processes

Enrollment Projections
Staffing
Recruitment
Selection
Orientation
Appraisal
Compensation
Employment Continuity
Development
Collective Bargaining

FIGURE 2.1   *Information demands for human resource functions.*

varied types of information has and continues to increase at a rapid unforeseen pace. Today, the necessity for creating, collecting, processing, storing, retrieving, integrating, and disseminating information to aid in the administration of an organization is hardly a matter for debate. It is becoming increasingly clear that sole dependence on the time-honored manual system of data management is no longer appropriate to keep a modern educational institution in step with the informational requirements necessary for an efficient and effective operation serving an ever-diversifying population of constituents with divergent needs and expectations.

As more school administrative units become large enough to offer comprehensive educational programs, it is inevitable that improved data-processing methods must be employed to integrate information for major areas of the school system involving instruction, funds, facilities, and personnel. The operation of a modern school system, with all the organizational, legal, political, governmental, and social ramifications, has caused the need for information acquisition and utilization to soar over past requirements in an exponential manner. To cope with this demand and to make effective use of information that is collected and utilized, a new approach to information acquisition and management is needed by public school districts to keep abreast in an ever-changing environment.

Information needs of a public school district can be met, in part, by making technological improvements in the information system as used by most school districts. Innovation can and should be geared not only to improvement of the human resource function in general, but also to improvements in the welfare of each individual employed in the system. Considerable advances have been made recently in the use of electronic data-processing procedures to facilitate the collection of data and the dissemination of information for planning and for decision making that will aid the system as well as improve the work life of employees.

These advancements in information processing and utilization make possible the storage and the retrieval of highly detailed and organized data that are useful as well as necessary in administering the human resource function within the school setting. Although it is true that many personnel decisions cannot be programmed, it is reasonable to assume that personnel decision making can be improved by data that are better organized, more accurate, more complete, and more available. Without reliable and valid data for human resource planning and decision making, much is left to chance in the organization and operation of a public school district.

Surprisingly, it is rare to find a school district that has an information system capable of providing, on request, information about various personnel and related aspects such as enrollment projection, position requirements, employee data, contractual agreements, regulatory requirements, litigation, disclosure, decision fairness, discrimination, and personnel file access and records. Few present-day school systems can readily and fully meet information demands such as those noted, as well as those listed in Figure 2.1 concerning the human resource processes. The gap between information supply and information demand in many institutions can be due to a variety of problems. Many of these problems can be linked to the absence of reliable records, outdated records, fragmentation of record creation and record keeping, needless files, record duplication, and inattention to transforming quantitative data into qualitative information as well as transforming qualitative data into quantitative information.

Moreover, and most important, the absence of a centrally directed and appropriately staffed information process often leads to the inability to resolve satisfactorily questions or disputes about student achievement, student enrollments, discrimination, personnel performance, salary, wage, fringe benefit issues, disciplinary actions, and unauthorized disclosure of personnel data. Failure to refine an information system is an open invitation to a host of human resource problems and charges because of a lack of appropriate information to resolve challenges such as those mentioned. In view of these potential problems, considerable attention is needed for this important area by most public school districts in meeting the information needs of stakeholders.

Information Needs and the Human Resource Function

As viable organizations having a defined mission, public school systems can be viewed from several perspectives relative to needs for information (Cunningham & Cordeiro, 2006). For the purpose of illustration and application relative to information demands, school systems can be deconstructed according to separate but related subdivisions having complementary as well as unique information needs relative to the human resource function. These divisions are academic and operation.

Broadly defined, the academic division encompasses most instruction provided to a specified clientele served by a public school district. Although the majority of clientele served by a public school district is school-age children, most school districts expand their client base to include adults and often fulfill educational needs of other organizations within the community through selective programming. Included among the programs provided by many public school districts are academic, vocational, cocurricular, and recreational programs (Sergiovanni, 2006).

To accomplish any of the instructional activities, logistic support is required and is provided by the operation division of a public school system (Owings & Kaplan, 2006). Personnel needs must be identified, staffing assignments must be filled, and employees/programs must be supervised. With few exceptions, facilities must be provided and maintained, and employees must be acquired as well as managed for the purpose of organizational continuity.

Connecting these two broadly defined functional divisions (academic and operation) within the public school environment is the overarching goal of the human resource function (see Figure 1.1, Chapter 1). This connection can be accomplished most successfully when following a strategic planning process for connecting these two basic divisions. As noted in the previous chapter (see Figure 1.7, Chapter 1), one strategic planning process as used in this book involves linking specific planning elements: (a) mission statement, (b) organizational goals, (c) district objectives, and (d) operational procedures. Collectively, these elements interact to provide both direction and motion to a public school district from a strategic planning perspective.

The building blocks for these elements and the mortar for their linkages within the strategic planning process is information. Pivotal to the operation of a public school district today as well as in the future is the collection, analysis, synthesis, and utilization of appropriate information to guide planning efforts and decision making of policy makers, district-level personnel, site-based administrators, and aspiring educational leaders. Indeed, acquisition and utilization of valid information differentiates largely between effective and ineffective school systems in our ever-changing environment.

In effective school systems, policy makers need information to develop, sustain, and/or modify the mission statement and to establish organizational goals reflecting the intent of the mission statement for the organization and operation of a public school system. For effective school districts, the mission statement is viewed best as a work in progress rather than a static product not amenable to change. Over time, external and internal environmental events have the potential for altering a mission statement, and policy makers must consider this emerging information in meeting their statutory assignments when overseeing the organization and operation of a public school system.

Continuing this line of progression from a strategic planning perspective for policy makers, district-level personnel must keep policy makers apprised of emerging information that can impact the organization and the operation of a public school district. Even if the mission statement remains intact, then the organizational goals could/should change in light of some new information. As such, district-level personnel are both information providers and information users within the strategic planning process.

Likewise, site-based administrators seek information for implementing objectives derived from organizational goals emanating from the mission statement. As line administrators, these managers rely on information to guide their practices in the field setting. Information for these personnel stems often from audit outcomes revealed through the strategic planning process.

Similar to site-based administrators, aspiring educational leaders need and benefit from information in several ways. As novices considering a managerial career, information equates with knowledge for this group. Most importantly, information promotes understanding and acceptance of the human resource function as practiced within the public school setting for this particular group of stakeholders.

Indeed, both the school system at large and each stakeholder group within a school system require and benefit from timely information. No doubt, information is intimately and indelibly linked to planning, organizing, directing, and monitoring the overall system and separate subsystems of which it is comprised. As such, the focus of this chapter is on the acquisition and compilation of information as related to the human resource function within the strategic planning process.

Information and the Strategic Planning Process

Today, within the public school setting, it is a given that information plays a critical role not only in maintaining the daily life of the organization but also in providing for the organization's survival and enhancement through strategic planning rather than through

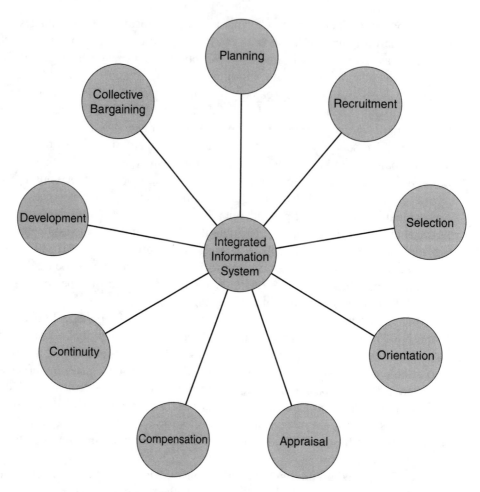

FIGURE 2.2   *Centrality of an integrated information process for linking human resource functions.*

a fixed mode of operation following past practices. Figure 2.2 illustrates relationships among subsystems within an organization through linking information needs to various operation functions as described in Chapter 1. To illustrate, many major functions of a school system, shown in Figure 2.2, must be linked to the system as a whole by means of an integrated information system.

The concept of information integration is illustrated by reference to the human resource functions and such operational activities as human resource planning, recruitment, selection, orientation, appraisal, compensation, continuity, development, and collective bargaining. Construction of an integrated information system for the human resource function involves establishing goals and objectives that stem from the basic mission statement of a school district. Goals and objectives depend, at least in part, on

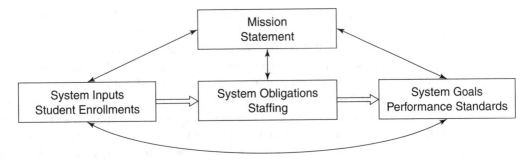

FIGURE 2.3   *Information flow model.*

information about current activities and capabilities of the school system through linking system inputs (student enrollments) with system obligations (staffing) and aligning this information with system goals (performance standards) (see Figure 2.3)

To begin the human resource process from an operational perspective relative to information needs for planning, an overall staffing plan must be constructed. Fundamental to this plan is anticipatory information. Anticipatory information is needed to project future enrollments of students (inputs), staffing needs of the district (obligations), and performance expectations of work units as well as individuals (goal alignment).

By reflecting the goals and objectives derived from the mission statement in the overall staffing plan, parameters are established for recruitment that impact other human resource operatives. To guide recruitment efforts, information is needed about current staffing capabilities, staffing needs, and staffing assignments in an ongoing operation. Failure to consider these different information sources would result in a nondirected recruitment program that serves neither potential applicants nor the system at large, and a directed recruitment program requires specific information about human resource needs, particular positions, and personnel requirements for filling these positions.

Once recruited by a public school system through the formulation of an applicant pool, potential job candidates must be selected to fill identified vacancies. To select from among those candidates seeking employment with a particular school system or with a specific work site within the school district, a variety of information is needed. Information is needed about applicants as well as about vacant positions to match job candidates with vacant positions and organizational goals.

After selection of desired job candidates is completed through appropriate matching of applicants with job requirements, individuals must be oriented relative to their assigned position. Information is needed about how their position fits into the whole of the organization. Likewise, information is needed about expectations of them as employees in fulfilling specific job assignments, meeting system demands, and assimilating within the community.

Following orientation, information is needed for establishing levels of compensation for newly hired employees as well as continuing employees accepting new positions. Compensation information is required about the external market and about internal rules and regulations governing compensation processes and practices within a particular school district. As ultimately determined for all employees, compensation information must be obtained that reflects both an ability to pay and a willingness to pay on the part of a public school district.

To assess the fit of individuals to the organization and to their jobs, all employees should be appraised. Appraisal of employees is not an isolated activity but relies on contextual information. Contextual information is needed about the job and about the candidate for appraisal to be a meaningful activity within the total employment process.

All continuing as well as new employees are concerned about the employment continuity process. They are aware on a superficial level of certain statutory provisions associated with their jobs and many privileges that come with a new job assignment. Information about these benefits is needed in a timely manner because some employment continuity processes have windows of opportunity that can close.

Most employees, including those employees new to their position or new to their assignment, are concerned about development opportunities. Information about development opportunities improves the retention of all employees. For this reason, an adequate information system should provide all employees with development opportunities on an ongoing basis.

Collective bargaining is an important process for many employees as well as for management. Information is needed about current labor contracts by all involved parties. Only through a well-designed information system can consistent information be provided to all stakeholders.

As can be surmised from the foregoing elaboration enrollment projections, staffing needs, recruitment, selection, orientation, appraisal activities, compensation, continuity processes, and development opportunities and collective bargaining functions cannot be performed effectively without information pertaining to personnel planning. Hence, there is an interdependence of personnel activities within the human resource function. The need for integration among the major functions shown in Figure 2.2 becomes readily apparent when, for example, newly appointed personnel are to be fully integrated within the ongoing operation of a school system and continuing employees are to be appropriately assigned.

It must not be overlooked from a strategic planning perspective that a school system, like other organizations, is composed of purposes, people, plans, tasks, technology, and a structure for fitting these parts together. The ability of the system to function effectively and efficiently depends on the bonding of these elements because each element has an impact on other elements and, thus, on the whole from a strategic planning perspective. Interaction of the various parts to achieve broad system purposes is affected through a human resource information process.

The Human Resource Information System Process

A general process model for developing a human resource information system is found in Figure 2.4. This process model can be viewed as an organizational mechanism through which efforts are made to achieve a desired state of operation relative to personnel information in the school setting. Within this model, the human resource information system process is characterized as being composed of separate but interrelated

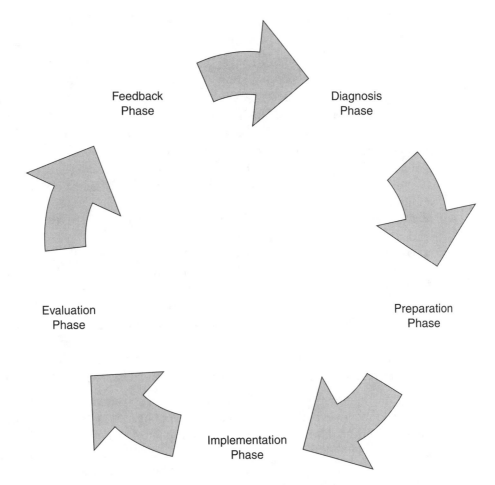

FIGURE 2.4   *Phases of a structural model for the information process.*

phases. These phases are as follows: (a) diagnosis, (b) preparation, (c) implementation, (d) evaluation, and (e) feedback.

The first phase of the information system process model outlined in Figure 2.4 is diagnostic. This diagnostic phase of the model is designed to assess the extent to which the present information system is providing essential data for achieving the goals and the objectives of the human resource function within the school setting. Diagnostic efforts within this phase of the model should focus on questions relating to what information is now collected, the ability of the system to retrieve this information, the accuracy of this information, and the relationship of this information to the system's goals and objectives as related to the mission statement of a public school district.

Information obtained in the diagnosis phase is used in the preparation phase of the human resource information system process. The second phase as reflected in Figure 2.4

is concerned with translating phase one (diagnosis) into decisions that lead to a series of action plans to improve the personnel information system. Central to the preparation phase is a set of goals for the human resource information system from a strategic planning perspective. The following are examples:

- Improvement and enhancement of the information system for collecting routine data
- Reduction of information duplication
- Elimination of useless information
- Standardization of methods for gathering information
- Justification of information from the standpoints of efficiency and effectiveness
- Improvement in availability, accuracy, flexibility, consistency, accessibility, and utility of information
- Involvement in the design of the information system of key people who will actually use both routine and nonroutine types of data
- Development of criteria that will govern identification, acquisition, refinement, storage, protection, and retrieval of information
- Organization and administration of the human resource information system in an effective and efficient manner (The information system should be part of a master plan to use funds, facilities, people, technology, and machines to achieve system objectives. This means appointment of knowledgeable personnel with authority to manage the information system; update the plan annually; and focus on specific objectives for hardware, software, personnel, budgets, space, and applications.)

Within the present context, information may be viewed as either programmed or nonprogrammed depending on the use of this information by other human resource functions. Certain data can be automated but other information of a conceptual, hypothetical, or judgmental nature is not readily amenable to computer programming by today's standards. However, both types of information are necessary for planning and for decision making within the human resource context.

After the school system has defined the objectives of the human resource information system, determined what kind of information is needed, reviewed information sources and acceptance criteria as outlined in Figure 2.3, and allocated responsibilities for administering various activities related to the system, the next phase (implementation) of the personnel information process can be initiated. This third phase, as outlined in Figure 2.4, consists of six key activities: identification, acquisition, refinement, storage, retrieval, and protection (see Figure 2.5). Each of the foregoing activities is important for the design and implementation of a human resource information system and is examined within the context of the human resource information system process in the following sections of this chapter.

Identification of Information

The initial activity in the implementation phase of the human resource information process, as depicted in Figure 2.5, is identification of information needed by a human resource information system. A primary focus of this activity in phase three of the

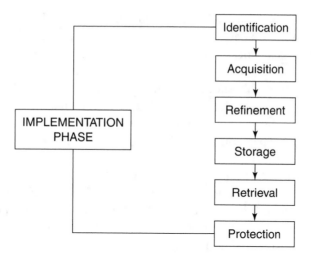

FIGURE 2.5 *Key activities of the implementation phase.*

implementation of the human resource information process is on identifying decisions required by the central administration governing what information is needed to achieve the goals of the system; purposes for which the information is needed; who will use the information; and what means shall be employed to gather, store, retrieve, and communicate information most effectively and efficiently for human resource planning and for decision making. Consequently, the initial act in the information process during this phase is to identify the central administration's conceptualization of the type of personnel information system the school system plans to operate to influence personnel behavior in ways conducive to goal attainment as specified by the mission statement.

This perspective, which governs the purpose of all information, needs to be mission oriented. School administrators should link information to actions necessary for accomplishing various goals identified previously by the system within the strategic planning process. Some of the information will indicate what has happened in the past, some other information will focus on what is happening at present, and still some other information needed should focus on the future. All three types of information, regardless of temporal orientation, should be directed toward influencing the behavior of people for satisfying both individual and system needs.

Acquisition of Information

Information acquisition, as noted in the personnel information process shown in Figure 2.5, follows plans for identification of needed information that is linked to the objectives of the system, as well as to the objectives of users' needs (including the needs of administrators, staff, school board members, clients, and the public). Acquisition includes identification, selection, and development of information. In many instances, purchase of source material from commercial databases is required within the information acquisition process.

When choosing among source information for inclusion in a human resource information system, acquisition of information should be governed by criteria such as purpose, value, relevance, completeness, cost, validity, reliability, and timeliness. Of these various criteria that can be used to determine what information is acquired for incorporation into the human resource information system for a school district, timeliness is the criterion most often overlooked. Timeliness, or the currency of data, is an important criterion in determining whether information should be acquired.

For example, a personnel roster is of little use to the payroll department if it is not kept current. Information files on recruitable talent, promotable personnel, and position holders who have reached performance plateaus are useless if this information has not been updated. Validity of information on collateral benefits for bargaining unit personnel in negotiations will be determined, for example, by its timeliness and by the aforementioned criteria.

Without doubt, timely information is expensive to acquire and to maintain. Although always desirable, timely information must be judged in terms of the cost-benefit concept. Certain kinds of information cost more money to obtain than other kinds of information, and the worth of all information must be judged in terms of benefits to the system within the human resource planning and decision-making context.

Refinement of Information

Most data acquired by the system need to be refined (see Figure 2.5), some to a greater and some to a lesser degree, before data are stored for retrieval and usage. Refinement includes checking data for accuracy. Information on student enrollments, staffing assignments, paychecks, retirement contributions, and certification of personnel, for example, must be precise and must be audited continuously within an integrated information system.

Complete and accurate information concerning the skill of every staff member is essential to conduct the human resource planning process efficiently and effectively from an organizational perspective. On the other hand, any data collected should include only those items the system really needs, inasmuch as the collecting and storing of information is a relatively expensive undertaking within the public school setting. Far too often, data are collected by school districts that have little utility for informing, planning, and decision making within the human resource context.

Other types of data-refinement processes include editing all forms of information entering the human resource information system, eliminating redundant information or overlapping information-gathering efforts, and incorporating error checks into the information system in order to call attention to missing or erroneous data as well as incongruence among data collected. In effect, the purpose of refining information is to ensure that data meet the acceptance criteria mentioned earlier in this chapter. Refinement is conceived as a kind of screen to separate useful from useless information, to code and prepare acceptable information for entrance into the information system, to ensure that the information is valid and reliable, and to bring together one form of data with another form of data, when combined, will create new information and perhaps new perspectives that were not possible before the information was available through an integrated human resource information system.

The concept of information refinement includes many and varied activities aimed at acquiring and storing data in forms that enhance the work of the system. Refinement of data may include editing information inputs (such as payroll verification), combining quarterly performance appraisal reports for a performance profile, employing statistical techniques for meaningful summary descriptions of raw data, and drawing inferences from personnel data under conditions characterized by uncertainty. Information refinement helps to make complex system phenomena more understandable and, in some cases, enables the system to achieve a new level of understanding about managing human resource problems as well as capitalizing on human resource opportunities.

Storage of Information

After information has been identified, acquired, and refined, arrangements must be made to store this information for future use by the human resource information system and in a manner that informs human resource planning and decision making. Information can be stored in manual systems, microfilm systems, or electronic systems. Manual storage systems, although less used today, include direct files, inverted files, optical coincidence cards, edge-notched cards, and punched cards. Microfilm storage systems include rolls of film, microfilm jackets, aperture cards, microfiche, and opaque micro-cards.

An electronic storage system is one that processes data by computers quickly, accurately, and automatically. Data processed by a computer are stored on memory devices, such as magnetic tapes, compact discs, zip discs, memory sticks, hard drives, and floppy discs. These storage mechanisms are not unfaultable and should be backed up in several ways in the event of a system crash or computer virus.

The decision as to which system or combination of systems will be used to store personnel information within an integrated information system will depend on a variety of factors, including size of staff, uses to be made of the information, availability of fiscal resources, and whether or not there are competent staff personnel to design and operate the system. Because the primary function of any personnel information system is to provide information when it is needed, where it is needed, and in the form in which it is needed, the storage system should be designed to enhance these objectives. Generally speaking, manual and microfilm storage systems are used to record historical information, and an electronic storage system is used to address current information needed by the human resource function.

Usage of multiple information storage mechanisms for an integrated information system is common practice in school districts because a variety of information is needed to inform human resource decisions. Some of the information needed for human resource decision making is amenable to a mechanized system of storage, while some of the other types of information needed for human resource decision making may not be amenable to a mechanized system of storage. A point to consider is that mechanized storage of certain kinds of information, such as the historical performance profile of an individual staff member or applications submitted by potential job candidates, may be prohibitive from a cost-benefit standpoint when attempting to codify specific information.

Retrieval of Information

Information retrieval, one of the activities in the implementation of the human resource information system process as outlined in Figure 2.5, refers to methods and procedures for recovering specific information from stored data. It goes without saying that information users should be able to retrieve stored information readily and in the form needed for planning and for decision making. Sadly, for many school districts, retrieval of information is a difficult process, and, in many instances, information retrieved may be in a form that fails to inform human resource planning and decision making.

Information stored manually, for example, is sometimes irretrievable because the procedures employed in storing this information lack appropriate organization for recovery. Information not properly classified, indexed, and/or coded will create problems when retrieval queries are posed for planning and decision making. Consequently, one of the requirements for operating an effective information storage-retrieval system is training staff personnel in procedures for classifying, indexing, and coding all incoming material.

Retrieval begins with a search strategy or a probe designed to locate information to solve problems posed by the user of a human resource information system. This search strategy includes evaluation of stored information to determine its relevance to such problems. The search is conducted also with consideration for the breadth and depth of information needed.

The foregoing observation indicates that there are various constraints affecting the search for and retrieval of human resource information, including time, funds, and personnel. Because information is the substance that holds an organization together and keeps the organization viable within external and internal markets, designing the storage-retrieval system and training personnel to operate the information system efficiently and effectively are matters of prime importance to the administrative team relative to the human resource function. Having problems associated with retrieval of information, concerns about access to this information by "need-to-know" parties surfaces often within the public school setting.

Protection of Information

Any public school district and all private school systems receiving federal funds must be concerned about privacy issues relating to a human resource information system. Information contained within a human resource information system is subject to certain federal and state laws concerning information access. Federal laws applicable to information contained within a human resource information system are the Freedom of Information Act of 1966 (United States Department of Justice, 1966), amended in 1974, and the Privacy Act of 1974 (United States Department of Justice, 1974).

The Freedom of Information Act requires government agencies to make available certain records that are requested by the public, and the Privacy Act is designed to resolve problems relating to disclosure, recording, inspection, and challenges to information maintained by government agencies or political subdivisions such as public school systems. Accompanying these federal acts are state laws addressing accessibility to public information.

Because the Freedom of Information Act applies only to federal agencies, states have developed their individualized set of laws pertaining to public information. These laws have been labeled as "sunshine laws" and address both access to public records and open meeting requirements. Most of the state legislation is modeled after the Freedom of Information Act.

In view of the existing legislation concerning access, school districts should develop policies for protecting the integrity of data contained in a human resource information system. These policies should indicate what records may be disclosed, by whom, and for what purposes; how disclosures are to be recorded; what controls an individual inspection of records; and resolving disagreements about stored information. General guidelines for the policy formation process include the following:

- Establish policies and guidelines to protect information in the organization: types of data to be sought, methods of obtaining the data, retention and dissemination of information, employee or third-party access to information, release of information about former employees, and mishandling of information.
- Inform employees of these information-handling policies.
- Become thoroughly familiar with state and federal laws regarding privacy.
- Formulate a policy that states specifically that employees and prospective employees cannot waive their right to privacy.
- Establish the policy that any manager or nonmanager who violates these privacy principles will be subject to discipline or termination.
- Avoid fraudulent, secretive, or unfair means of collecting data. When possible, collect data directly from the individual concerned.
- Do not maintain secret files on individuals. Inform them what information is stored on them, the purpose for which it was collected, how it will be used, and how long it will be kept.
- Collect only job-related information that is relevant for specific decisions.
- Maintain records of individuals or organizations that have regular access to or request information on a need-to-know basis.
- Allow employees to inspect, update, and/or append information to their personnel files.
- Gain assurance that any information released to outside parties will be used only for the purposes set forth prior to its release (Cascio, 1998; Cook, 1987).

Evaluation and Feedback Phases

The human resource information process outlined in Figure 2.4 includes evaluation and feedback as activities essential to its operation and improvement. Every organization should assess how well the system as a whole and each of its subparts are achieving assigned objectives. This is accomplished through assessment procedures by which the outcomes achieved are compared to the outcomes desired.

When meaningful differences are detected between achieved and desired outcomes, remedial action is warranted. Specific information to be gleaned from evaluation and feedback processes should provide answers to the questions that follow:

- Is the present system operating effectively?
- Do portions of the present system need to be preserved or modified?
- Is the system providing information that enhances the operation of the human resource function?
- How well does the system respond to changes in the environment relative to data collection?
- Do information security tests meet the criteria emphasized by legislative guidelines?
- Does the human resource information system interface properly with the total organization information system?

Securing answers to these questions involves various types of diagnoses, including determining what the major problems in the information system are, forces causing the problems, timing of the changes needed to resolve the problems, goals to be achieved by the change, and how goal attainment will be measured. Through evaluation and feedback, needed improvements in the information system can be brought about through a planned program of assessment. These improvements will facilitate organizational decisions regarding personnel processes, policies, and the organization's structure and have implications for the architecture of an integrated human resource information system.

Enrollment and the Human Resource Information System

Implicit in the administration of any organization is the realization that it is an entity in which people perform tasks to achieve established outcomes, and outcomes contribute to the system's goals (Cunningham & Cordeiro, 2006). As noted previously, school systems fail to be an exception to this generality as found in the general organizational literature (Hoy & Miskel, 2005). Indeed, the work to be done in school systems is structured into divisions (e.g., academic or operation), into groups (e.g., elementary schools), into jobs (e.g., instruction), and into specialized tasks (e.g., accounting, clerical, maintenance, etc.).

To ensure that decision makers have both the type of and the quality of information necessary for operating the human resource function in an effective and efficient manner, an integrated information system is required. Although information systems vary greatly in complexity, all effective systems rely on certain basic information sources as a foundation. At minimum, one source of information required early on within the strategic planning process by all public school districts is data depicting actual and expected student enrollments because student enrollments influence most operational processes from a strategic planning perspective (Tanner & Lackney, 2006).

These sources of information involving actual and expected student enrollments, when interconnected, provide the basic framework or structure of an integrated information system for the human resource function in a public school district. Information imparted by these different sources of system inputs lends direction to goals and objectives, enlists the support of decision makers through informed data, and suggests ways and means for directing a school system's organization and operation. As such, specific attention is devoted to actual and expected student enrollments as basic information requirements for all school districts within the strategic planning process from an information acquisition perspective.

Student Enrollment Information

Actual as well as expected student enrollments have important implications for the organization and operation of any public school system (Tanner & Lackney, 2006). The school system acquires, creates, and disseminates enrollment information to bring individuals, groups, and the organization into congruence with its strategic direction and to enlist the support of members to reach higher levels of performance in their assigned job duties. This type of information is used to create an institutional vision of expectations, as well as to establish purposes, structures, plans, policies, programs, and projects for their realization. As such, enrollment information is directed toward shaping outcome goals for most human resource functions within the strategic planning process.

Enrollment information at the basic level lends direction to the mission statement of a public school system. The mission statement establishes broad parameters for the organization and operations of a school district. Contents of a mission statement must be tempered by external and internal environmental considerations that bear on the operation of a public school district at the present as well as in the future given actual and expected student enrollments.

As noted in the introductory chapter and as echoed in this chapter, human resource planning is influenced greatly by the external and the internal environment. Because the number and types of environmental variables influencing a school district are virtually limitless, one must determine which variables appear to be critical in charting a specific school district's human resource planning process. Listed below are some of the most salient external considerations impacting most school districts in the past, today, and in the foreseeable future, relative to organization and operation of the human resource function.

Provisions of the No Child Left Behind Act
Performance on standardized competency tests
Special education students
Funding for federal entitlements
Block grants from the state
State-mandated education programs
Resources from state formula funding
Development of charter schools
Emergence/decline of parochial schools
Housing developments
Zoning changes within a district
Economic developments/declines in the local community

Actual choices among external environmental variables depend on specifics associated with a particular school district. External influences selected and guiding the development of a mission statement should be chosen on the basis of assumed relevance for achieving both system and human resource goals relative to student enrollments and in the design of the human resource processes. The preceding list as well as emerging issues pertinent to the construction of a mission statement merit continuous monitoring in order to enhance more systematically approaches to strategic decision making as related to human resource planning in the public school setting.

In addition to external environmental factors, human resource planning in any public school district is influenced by certain internal factors. Among these are student enrollments and staffing obligations to meet enrollment demands/declines. To provide information about student enrollments, an **enrollment projection** must be made and must be encapsulated within an integrated information system from a strategic planning perspective.

It is the acquisition of this basic information as required of all public school systems following a strategic planning process for the human resource function that is the focus of the remaining portion of this chapter. Indeed, within the following sections of this chapter, theory is linked to practice relative to basic enrollment information needs as part of the strategic planning process focusing on the human resource function in the public school setting.

Enrollment Projection Techniques

With the exception of special education having statutory requirements beyond local control, student enrollments are a viable source of data from a human resource planning and decision-making perspective. Information about student enrollments is needed both from a historical and from an anticipatory viewpoint within the strategic planning process. To provide means and methods for providing stakeholders within the strategic planning process information concerning student enrollments, two techniques for projecting enrollments are presented in this chapter: (1) **survival ratio technique** and (2) **Bayesian estimation process.**

These enrollment projection systems differ in some important ways, and each system has certain advantages depending on external/internal environments characterizing a particular school district. More specifically, the survival ratio technique is a linear projection process and relies strictly on known/objective data. In contrast to the survival ratio technique, the Bayesian estimation process is a nonlinear system and utilizes both objective and subjective information for projecting student enrollments.

However, common to both approaches is the simplicity of mathematical procedures utilized in projecting student enrollments. From a mathematical perspective, both approaches involve only addition, multiplication, and division. As such, these enrollment projection techniques are within the grasp of educational planners, all practicing public school administrators, and aspiring educational leaders as a technology to be used within the strategic planning process for the human resource function in the public school setting.

In fact, it is not unusual in many public school districts for principals to provide enrollment projections for their specific buildings within the strategic planning process.

These projections, as provided by principals, are compiled across buildings to formulate district-wide staffing plans as an integral part of the human resource function within the strategic planning process. Procedurally, this mode of data compilation involves a "bottom-up" rather than a "top-down" approach within the planning process.

Following are illustrations of both techniques as applied to an actual school district in the compilation of required information for strategic planning as a means for providing necessary information to decision makers relative to the organization and operation of a public school district. The first example utilizes the survival ratio technique, relying only on objective data and the principle of succession. For the second example, the same database is used but is enhanced by the inclusion of subjective information accommodated by the Bayesian estimation procedure.

Survival Ratio Technique

The survival ratio technique (SRT) is by far the most common method used by school districts, by state departments of education, and by external consultants for projecting student enrollments. As a method for projecting student enrollments, the SRT relies exclusively on the construct of succession as the only factor influencing student enrollments. **Succession** is defined within the SRT as movement of individuals/students from one point in time to another point in time relative to their enrollment status with a school district/school building.

Within the SRT, succession is operationalized from two perspectives: (1) entrance of individuals as students into the system at the entry level and (2) matriculation of students within the system once enrolled. The first perspective involves the succession rate for individuals born (live birth rates) within a particular time period that enrolled subsequently in the public school district at the initial entry level (either kindergarten or first grade at the elementary school level). For the SRT, this involves calculating the percentage of students entering a school district/school building based on live birth rates (enrollees/live birth rates).

The other perspective involves the succession rate for students enrolled in a school district/school building to matriculate to the next grade level in an expected linear progression. For example, the SRT is based on the linear succession rate for kindergarten students to advance to the first grade within a particular enrollment period. In continuing this line of reasoning, succession is defined further by calculating the percentage of students in the first grade that matriculate to the second grade, and this process is followed across all grade levels for which enrollment projections are provided (K–12 grade levels).

For projecting student enrollments according to the SRT, the compilation of three different data matrices is required. One matrix contains historical information, another matrix reflects succession ratios, and the third matrix provides projected enrollments for each level of instruction. To illustrate the SRT technique as a planning tool for providing information necessary for the strategic planning process, a specific example from the field setting is used. This example involves projecting enrollments for an actual elementary school building but the principles, as illustrated, can be generalized to projecting enrollments on a systemwide basis across all grade levels for different organizational configurations.

As a means for presenting the SRT that is temporally neutral relative to specific time periods (so the examples will not become dated by these illustrations), the concept of base

TABLE 2.1
Enrollment Data

Historical Enrollment Information							
Birth Year	Base Yr.-11	Base Yr.-10	Base Yr.-9	Base Yr.-8	Base Yr.-7	Base Yr.-6	Base Yr.-5
Birth Rate	13555	13428	12759	12420	12192	11998	12281
Enroll. Year	Base Yr.-6	Base Yr.-5	Base Yr.-4	Base Yr.-3	Base Yr.-2	Base Yr.-1	Base Yr.
K. Enroll.	56	64	54	54	55	47	59
Gr. 1 Enroll.	77	53	68	70	66	66	50
Gr. 2 Enroll.	74	77	51	57	63	61	64
Gr. 3 Enroll.	73	74	71	62	58	64	62
Gr. 4 Enroll.	69	70	75	74	65	72	62
Gr. 5 Enroll.	70	73	75	74	77	72	66
Gr. 6 Enroll.	74	73	69	74	70	74	64

year is used. **Base year** is defined in these examples as the current year of operation within a particular system/building. Depending on when enrollment projections are made, actual dates should be used for the base year and should be prorated accordingly across the different time periods as noted in the following tables (Base Year [plus/minus] actual date).

Contained in Table 2.1 is the basic data matrix used by the SRT. The first column of this matrix contains identifying labels for required historical information as used by the SRT: (1) birth year, (2) birth rate, (3) enrollment year, and (4) grade-level enrollments (K–6 grades). Within the first row of Table 2.1, birth year is a lagged variable reflecting the time period when individuals are born that could potentially enroll in a school district after meeting minimum age requirements (lagged five years for kindergarten enrollment).

Data acquisition for actual measures of live birth rates (row two of column 1 in Table 2.1) can be obtained from several sources. Included among these sources of information for live birth rates are state databases that can be assessed online, through annual reports issued by chambers of commerce, and/or by personal contacts with local hospitals. The unit of analysis used by most public school districts for assessing live birth rates is the county of location for a school district and can be obtained from any of the aforementioned sources.

The remaining labels found in column 1 of Table 2.1 depict either year of student enrollments (Enroll. Year) or grade levels of enrollments (K–6 grade enrollments). These data within respective rows of corresponding columns reflect historical information and are readily available in all school districts through established data files. Encompassed by these data as contained in Table 2.1 are the current enrollments of this particular elementary school building broken down by historical data enrollment information for the previous years (Base-6 through Base Year) and by grade levels (K–6).

Given this information as provided in Table 2.1, survival ratios are calculated to reflect successions across both time periods (entry and matriculation) and grade levels in this elementary school building. These ratios are found in Table 2.2. For those students born in Base Year-11 (n=13,555) and entering kindergarten in Base Year-5 (when they

TABLE 2.2
Enrollment Calculations for the SRT Technique

	Calculated Survival Ratios						
Base Yr.-11 13555	Base Yr.-10 13428 Base Yr.-5	Base Yr.-9 12759 Base Yr.-4	Base Yr.-8 12420 Base Yr.-3	Base Yr.-7 12192 Base Yr.-2	Base Yr.-6 11998 Base Yr.-1	Base Yr.-5 12281 Base Yr.	Mean SR
K. Enroll.	0.005	0.004	0.004	0.005	0.004	0.005	0.00443
Gr. 1 Enroll.	0.946	1.063	1.296	1.222	1.200	1.064	1.13188
Gr. 2 Enroll.	1.000	0.962	0.838	0.900	0.924	0.970	0.93241
Gr. 3 Enroll.	1.000	0.922	1.216	1.018	1.016	1.016	1.03126
Gr. 4 Enroll.	0.959	1.014	1.042	1.048	1.241	0.969	1.04553
Gr. 5 Enroll.	1.058	1.071	0.987	1.041	1.108	0.917	1.03016
Gr. 6 Enroll.	1.043	0.945	0.987	0.946	0.961	0.889	0.96177

become of age), the survival ratio for entering kindergarten is 0.005 (64/13,555), and this pattern is followed across the rows of Table 2.2 for every cohort group (exception in Table 2.2 being the last column, Mean SR, to be discussed below).

Focusing on the last column found in Table 2.2 is the heading for Mean SR (SR= survival ratio). Contained in this column is a calculated arithmetic average for survival ratios across time found in the respective rows (e.g., 0.00443 for kindergarten enrollments). This statistic is assumed by the SRT to reflect the best estimate of succession between birth rate and subsequent enrollments because it is based on historical data and assumes past enrollments are indicative of future enrollments given only observed data (live birth rates for kindergarten and matriculations rates for first–sixth grade levels) as used by the SRT.

Based on the succession assumption of the SRT, the **mean survival ratio** statistics (see last column of Table 2.2) are used to project future enrollments by the SRT. Projected enrollments for this particular example assessed for an actual elementary school building are found in Table 2.3. To illustrate the SRT as well as the simplicity of the SRT technique, specific computational examples are provided.

More specifically, the Mean SR statistics are assumed as a constant for projecting enrollments within any time period by the SRT. To project student enrollments at the kindergarten level, the Mean SR (0.00443) is multiplied by the appropriate live birth rates for an entering cohort groups. That is, 54 kindergarten students are projected for the Base Year+1 by multiplying the mean survival rate (0.00443) times the live birth rate (12,092) for this cohort group.

This same constant (0.00443) is used to project all kindergarten enrollments within this particular school building. For each cohort birth year entering kindergarten five years hence, this number (0.00443) is used as a multiplier to obtain a projected kindergarten enrollment.

As can be observed in Table 2.3, 61 students are projected to matriculate from the kindergarten class of Base Year+1 (n=54) to Base Year+2 first graders (n=61). This number was obtained by multiplying the Base Year+1 kindergarten students (n=54)

TABLE 2.3
Enrollment Project for the SRT Technique

		Projected Enrollments for Base Year+1 through Base Year+5				
		Birth Year	Base Yr.-4	Base Yr.-3	Base Yr.-2	Base Yr.-1	Base Yr.
		Birth Rate	12092	12211	11788	12000	11894
		Enroll. Year	Base Yr.+1	Base Yr.+2	Base Yr.+3	Base Yr.+4	Base Yr.+5
	Mean SR						
K. Enroll.	0.00443		54	54	52	53	53
Gr. 1 Enroll.	1.13188		67	61	61	59	60
Gr. 2 Enroll.	0.93241		47	62	57	57	55
Gr. 3 Enroll.	1.03126		66	48	64	58	59
Gr. 4 Enroll.	1.04553		65	69	50	67	61
Gr. 5 Enroll.	1.03016		64	67	71	52	69
Gr. 6 Enroll.	0.96177		63	61	64	68	50

times the mean SR for matriculation to the first grade (1.13188) from kindergarten. This succession pattern for computations is followed throughout to complete the matrix reflecting projected student enrollments using the SRT.

On reflection of the SRT as a method for projecting student enrollments, it is obvious that only succession drives student enrollment projections. Given the methodological constraint for the SRT, this particular linear technique is appropriate for school systems/buildings that can be characterized by stable enrollments and/or changing enrollments following only a linear progression across time (consistently either increasing or decreasing). However, many school districts have enrollments that fluctuate unsystematically (nonlinear) due to external and internal environmental influences over which little control is exercised, and other methods of projecting student enrollments are needed for informing the human resource planning process in these later types of school districts.

Bayesian Estimation Process

For many public school districts, student enrollments fail to follow a linear pattern of progression based on succession/matriculation due to emerging external and/or internal environmental events. That is, some school districts may experience declining enrollments due to reasons other than normal succession/matriculation. For example, major local employers may outsource their workforce, and many families are likely to follow job opportunities involving relocation beyond school district boundaries. Also, new charter or parochial schools within the locale may open and attract students away from their assigned location within a public school district.

In contrast, other school districts may incur increased student enrollments not reflected by succession or matriculation. New businesses may be acquired within the enrollment boundaries, thus attracting families with schoolage children, and/or new housing developments may emerge due to the availability of undeveloped land. To capture these changes in enrollments caused by recent external and internal environment influences other than live birth rates and/or normal succession patterns, methods other than the SRT are needed to project student enrollments for some public school districts within the strategic planning process.

One such method that can be used to capture nonlinear enrollment patterns is the Bayesian estimation process (BEP) as suggested initially by Tanner (1971) and used by more progressive school systems, only recently, to project student enrollments. Unlike the SRT, the BEP is a nonlinear technique. Rather than relying solely on historical information like the SRT (succession), the Bayesian method utilizes objective information (historical) as well as subjective information (external and internal factors) that influences student enrollments. To illustrate the BEP from a strategic planning perspective relative to the human resource function in the public school setting, another example is provided.

This example focuses on the same elementary school building used for the SRT (described above in Tables 2.1–2.3) but incorporates external and internal variables involving actual data collected in the field setting supplementing succession information for this particular school building. Indeed, it is not unusual for public school districts developing their first strategic plan for the human resource function to project student enrollments by both systems (SRT and BEP). By using both techniques, the value of each system can be determined through auditing processes as to which system is more accurate within the strategic planning process for any public school setting.

Like the SRT, the BEP relies on three basic data matrices. However, the data utilized in these matrices are configured in separate ways and impart different information than the SRT. The first data matrix used by the BEP is based solely on historical information using aggregated enrollments for grade levels and a **Bayesian normalization process** unique to the BEP. Again, within the BEP method—like the SRT method—mathematical procedures involve only addition, multiplication, and division.

Contained in Table 2.4 is the initial data matrix for the BEP. This matrix contains three columns. The first column reflects grade levels as contained within this particular elementary school building (K–6 grades). Within the second column of Table 2.4 is cumulative data aggregated for each of the grade levels during the past five years (Base Year-4 through

TABLE 2.4
Historical Data Required by the BEP

Grade	Sum of Enrollments for Last 5 Years	Step 1 Normalization
K	269	0.118764
1	320	0.141280
2	296	0.130684
3	317	0.139956
4	348	0.153642
5	364	0.160706
6	351	0.154967
Total	2,265	1.0000

Base Year, see Table 2.1 for verification). The last column contained in Table 2.4 reflects Step 1 statistics utilized by the BEP in projecting nonlinear student enrollment patterns.

To calculate the Step 1 statistics unique to BEP as found in Table 2.4, each grade-level enrollment is divided by the total enrollment (n=2,265) for this particular elementary school building. More specifically, the total kindergarten enrollments over the last five years (n=269) are divided by the total building enrollments (n=2,265) during this same time period, and similar calculations are performed for every grade level throughout this matrix. Within the BEP, these calculations are labeled as the Step 1 normalization process and represent a distributional summary of historical information relative to past enrollments for a specified unit of analysis (school building in this example). As an audit check, the normalized statistics should sum to unity (1.00) and failure to do so represents a computational error.

Subjective information influencing the enrollments of a public school district/building (external and internal factors) enters the BEP within the second stage of this procedure, and these influences are found in the second data matrix (see Table 2.5). This matrix contains seven columns, with the first column denoting grade levels within the building (K–6).

The second column within this matrix (Table 2.5) contains expected enrollment values for the Base Year+1 school year reflecting only historical information (with the exception of kindergarten). For the kindergarten enrollments set apart (n=54), the value used in this example was obtained from the SRT because Base Year+1 data are unknown for students entering kindergarten (see Table 2.3 for verification). This estimate (n=54) was used to link the SRT with the BEP for purposes of continuity in these examples but other values could have been substituted for the initial unknown kindergarten enrollments (i.e., average rate of kindergarten across time or the previous year enrollment for kindergarten).

With respect to other initial enrollment estimates found in column 2 for the different grade levels (i.e., 1–6), Base Year data are used. That is, within the Base Year, all students are promoted to the next grade level as per the BEP. To illustrate, all Base Year kindergarten students (n=59 see Table 2.1) are promoted to the first grade. Likewise, all students in the first grade during the Base Year (n=50) are promoted to the second grade

TABLE 2.5
External and Internal Environmental Factors Impacting Enrollments

Grade Levels	Initial Enroll. Estimates	Charter Schools	School Redistricting	Policy Changes	Net Expected Enrollments	Step 2 Normalization
K	54	−6	5	3	56	0.1217
1	59	−7	7	5	64	0.1391
2	50	−3	6	4	57	0.1239
3	64	−1	4	2	69	0.1500
4	62	0	7	2	71	0.1543
5	62	0	5	1	68	0.1478
6	66	0	6	3	75	0.1630
Total	417				460	1.00

(see Table 2.1), and this process is followed across the grade levels when compiling initial enrollment estimates as found in column 2.

Having established initial enrollment estimates for grade levels as found in column 2, columns 3–5 in Table 2.5 reflect external and internal environmental factors likely impacting this particular school building. Within this example, only three factors were used (charter schools, school redistricting, and policy changes) but this number could have been expanded both for other external factors and for other internal factors appropriate for a particular school district/building. No doubt for other school districts/buildings, the number of and the type of variables would be different from those found in this example applicable to this particular school building (one external and two internal factors).

The single external factor is the opening of a charter school that will attract potential enrollees from this particular school building. This impact is noted in column 3 for each grade level and was obtained from estimates provided by the building-level principal possessing in-depth knowledge about the school's community and potential enrollees.

In addition to the external environmental factor (charter schools), internal environmental events bearing on this particular school building are redistricting of enrollment boundaries for the upcoming year and policy changes by the Board of Education. For this specific school district, the Board of Education authorized free transportation to all students regardless of their location to school buildings. This convenience, as provided by the Board of Education, was perceived to have a positive impact by the principal on student enrollments as noted in column 5 for the different grade levels.

Contained in column 6 (Table 2.5) is an estimate for net expected enrollments. These numbers for net enrollments are obtained by considering both positive and negative effects (columns 3–5) due to external and internal events on initial enrollment estimates (as can be noted, there is a net change of 43 students). For data contained in column 6, a normalization process is performed similar to that found in Table 2.4 involving only objective information (historic enrollment data), and these results for normalizing subjective information are depicted in column 7 and labeled as Step 2 Normalization statistics (see Table 2.5).

The final stage of the BEP process involves combining normalized objective information based on historical data (see Step 1, Figure 2.4) with normalized subjective information based on perceptions of the principal (see Step 2, Figure 2.5) and making enrollment projections incorporating these sources of potential variance. Contained in Table 2.6 are the computations involved when combining both objective (see Step 1, Figure 2.4) and subjective information (see Step 2, Figure 2.5) as normalized by the BEP. Again, the first column of this table reflects grade levels contained in this particular school building.

Columns 2 and 3 of Table 2.6 reflect the normalization statistics as computed for objective information (Step 1, see Table 2.4) and for subjective information (Step 2, see Table 2.5). Values in these two columns are multiplied to obtain a joint probability distribution (see column 4 in Table 2.6) incorporating objective and subjective information within the enrollment projection system. The joint probability distribution is subjected to a normalization process similar to that used for calculating Step 1 and Step 2 statistics (as found in Tables 2.4 and 2.5).

Results of this last normalization process for Step 3 statistics are depicted in column 5 of Table 2.6. To obtain enrollment projections for the Base Year + 1 school year using the

TABLE 2.6
Projected Enrollments Based on Objective and Subjective Information

Grade Levels	Step 1 Normalization	Step 2 Normalization	Joint Probabilities	Step 3 Normalization	Base+1 Projected
K	0.1188	0.1217	0.0145	0.1004	46
1	0.1413	0.1391	0.0197	0.1365	63
2	0.1307	0.1239	0.0162	0.1124	52
3	0.1400	0.1500	0.0210	0.1457	67
4	0.1536	0.1543	0.0237	0.1646	76
5	0.1607	0.1478	0.0238	0.1649	76
6	0.1550	0.1630	0.0253	0.1754	81
Total			0.1440		460

BEP, Step 3 normalized statistics for each grade level are multiplied by the total net expected enrollment (n=460, as found in Table 2.5). For the kindergarten level Base Year+1 projected enrollment (n=46), the calculations involve multiplying the Step 3 normalization statistic (0.1004) times the total net expected enrollment (n=460). Other projected enrollments for the different grade levels using the BEP are computed following similar computational procedures. Because external and internal environmental factors are not constant across time within any particular school district/building, the BEP requires that the second and third data matrices as used in the examples be reconstituted for each subsequent base year for projecting student enrollments.

On reflection about the SRT and the BEP methods for projecting student enrollments with this same school building, both techniques provide information about actual and anticipated system inputs (students). Worth noting is that the projections are different, and this difference has some staffing implications (at least an additional FTE teacher as per the BEP for this particular example). Because the enrollment systems utilize different information, the particulars of a public school system relative to external and to internal factors must be considered when selecting an enrollment projection technique for providing planning information relative to the human resource function.

Linking Student Enrollments to Staffing Needs

From a strategic planning perspective involving an **integrated information system**, data about past, present, and expected student enrollments provide a foundation for guiding further human resource activities within the public school setting. Initially, this information must be incorporated into a total staffing plan as part of the strategic planning process to guide the planning and the decision making of policy makers and site-based administrators relative to other human resource processes. As such, the purpose of the following chapter is both to provide methods for incorporating this information depicting enrollment projections within a human resource staffing plan through an actual field example involving public school districts and to provide a foundational base for other human resource operatives necessary for conducting the human resource function in the public school setting.

Review and Preview

This chapter on the information system and the human resource function indicates that human resource practices are influenced by external and internal environmental factors that impact most human resource processes within the public school setting. A structural model for an integrated information system is presented and related to all human resource processes from a strategic planning perspective. Within this model, procedural steps are discussed relative to acquiring and to using information for planning and for decision making within the human resource function.

To link the strategic planning process as a management tool for planning and decision making with the information needs of public school districts, attention is devoted to different enrollment projection techniques. As a result, the astute reader is armed with both theoretical knowledge and technical skills necessary for constructing the basic elements of a human resource information system. Information is imparted within this chapter about both linear (SRT) and nonlinear (BEP) enrollment projection techniques, and the skills necessary for using either technique for projecting student enrollments within the public school setting.

In the following chapter, the general notion of strategic planning will be expanded relative to the human resource function. Skills obtained relative to enrollment projection techniques will be utilized in the configuration of staffing plans for a public school district. As such, both theory and practice continue to be commingled relative to the human resource function from a strategic planning perspective.

Discussion Questions

1. How can an organization close the gap between information demand and supply? What structures should be initiated to close the gap? How can technology be utilized to close the gap? What is the impact of organizational culture on this gap?

2. What are the particular external and internal environmental factors impacting your school district? How can these factors be addressed by an integrated information system?

3. Given both the linear (SRT) and nonlinear (BEP) student enrollment projection techniques, which is most applicable to your school district and why?

4. If you were going to use the BEP, what are the external and internal environmental factors impacting enrollments in your school district? How would you measure these factors?

5. Has computer technology increased access to the organizational information system, or has it decreased access? Has computer technology increased the efficiency of the organizational information system? Why or why not?

Case Study

In the past little attention has been given to long-range planning. However, because your school district hired a new superintendent, things have begun to change. As part of the job as a human resource director, you have been assigned the responsibility for projecting student enrollments. After reviewing the literature, you find two different systems: (1) survival ratio technique and (2) Bayesian estimation method. Which of the techniques would you recommend for your district? What is the rationale for your recommendation? How would school board members and principals in your district react to your recommendation? What steps would you take and what data would be required?

References

Cascio, W. F. (1998). *Managing human resources* (5th ed., pp. 548–549). New York: McGraw-Hill.

Cook, S. H. (1987). Privacy rights: Whose life is it anyway? *Personnel Administrator, 32*(4), 58–65.

Cunningham, W. G., & Cordeiro, P. A. (2006). *Educational leadership: A problem-based approach* (3rd ed.) Upper Saddle River, NJ: Merrill/Prentice Hall.

Hoy, W. K., & Miskel, C. J. (2005). *Educational administration: Theory, research, and practice* (7th ed.) New York: McGraw-Hill.

Kowalski, T. J. (2004). *Public relation in schools.* Upper Saddle River, NJ: Pearson.

Owings, W. A., & Kaplan, L. S. (2006). *American public school finance.* Belmont, CA: Thomson Wadsworth Corporation.

Sergiovanni, T. J. (2006). *The principalship: A reflective practice perspective.* Boston: Pearson.

Tanner, C. K. (1971). Designs for educational planning. Lexington, KY: Health Lexington.

Tanner, C. K., & Lackney, J. A. (2006). *Educational facilities planning: Leadership, architecture, and management.* Boston: Pearson.

United States Department of Justice. (1966). *The Freedom of Information Act.* Retrieved August 30, 2005, from the U.S. Department of Justice Web site: http:// www.usdoj.gov/04foia/foiastat.htm.

United States Department of Justice. (1974). *The Privacy Act of 1974.* Retrieved August 30, 2005, from the U.S. Department of Justice Web site: http:// www.usdoj.gov/04foia/04_7_1.html.

Strategic Planning and Staffing

3

CHAPTER OVERVIEW

OBJECTIVES

- Introduce the concept of strategic planning and discuss its relationship to the human resource function as applied in the public school setting.
- Emphasize the importance of developing a strategic plan for staffing the human resource function.

- Highlight key stages of the strategic planning and the staffing function as well as emphasize their major components and their linkages.
- Differentiate between policy decisions and administrative decisions within the planning and staffing process.
- Stress that strategic plans for staffing are temporary and are subject to change as internal and external challenges emerge within the public school setting.
- Illustrate the different phases of the strategic planning process related to staffing the human resource function.
- Provide working examples of the strategic planning process drawn from the field setting.
- Develop a staffing model based on actual field data obtained from a public school district.
- Construct a staffing chart for monitoring the staffing process within a public school district.

The Need for Strategic Planning and Systemic Changes

It is well established in the professional literature that public school districts are dynamic organizations constantly changing due to external and to internal influences altering the status quo operation (Hoy & Miskel, 2005). External influences include political and environmental changes that impact the organization and operation of a public school district. From the political perspective, new legislation has been and will continue to be passed that alters the schooling process and impacts the management of human resources in the public school setting (Kowalski, 2004).

Legislations and informed reports have been adopted at the national, interstate, and intrastate level, all of which have important implications for the human resource function in public school systems at the present time as well as in the future. At the national level, the No Child Left Behind Act (NCLB, 2001) has had and continues to have extremely important implications for the organization and operation of public school districts (Sunderman, Kim, & Orfield, 2005). Many parts of this act address specifically the human resource management issues for public school districts.

Several interstate commissions have been formed in recent times and have produced recommendations adopted in part or in whole by many states. Most notable are standards as set forth by the Interstate School Leaders Licensure Consortium (ISLLC), addressing the certification of public school employees for administrator positions. Based on these concerted efforts, many states have adopted standards that directly impact the human resource staffing function in the public school setting (Owings, Kaplan, & Nunnery, 2005).

Within most states of the union (intrastate), a new era of accountability has been entered and has been sustained. Pivotal to the accountability movement within many states is mandated competency-based testing for students and the advent of report cards for school districts, and research is emerging about how to use these outcomes within the human resource environment to shape decision making in guiding the organization and operation of a public school district (Creighton, 2001). Each of these outcome measures has profound implications for the human resource functions and the strategic planning process at the local school district level. These implications range from recruiting and selecting applicants, compensating and appraising all employees, as well as developing and motivating continuing employees (Cunningham & Cordeiro, 2006).

Likewise, internal influences impacting the human resource functions of a school district continue to emerge in every school district. Memberships on school boards change, employees turn over, and student populations are diversifying. As policy makers directing the overall operation of a school district, school board members serve limited terms through either an elected or an appointed process (Howell, 2005) and bring different philosophies about how a school district should operate when assuming their newly appointed positions.

Each year, some public school employees leave the school district for a variety of reasons. Some employees retire and a lesser number of employees are nonrenewed, while other employees either seek job opportunities in a different school district or leave the profession at their own choice (Ingersoll, 2002). Based on estimates of professional associations, extensive vacancies are expected at all organizational levels in the very near future and have dire implications for managing the human resource function.

Student populations served by public school districts are changing consistently in demographic composition and educational needs (Lindsey, Roberts, & Campbell-Jones, 2004). As compared to the not-so-distant past, fewer mono-cultural student bodies exist in public schools, more special education students are being accommodated (Gibson & Blandford, 2005), at least in part, and all students need basic technological groundings beyond yesterday's standards (Mayo & Kajs, 2005). As a result of these changing student bodies, traditional staffing patterns and assumptions are becoming obsolete for staffing America's public schools today, tomorrow, as well as in the foreseeable future (Lehr, Clapper, & Thurlow, 2005).

To accommodate all these external and internal events bearing on the human resource needs of a public school district, a strategic plan addressing the staffing needs of a public school district is needed now more than ever if a school district is to thrive as well as prosper in a changing and challenging environment that creates obstacles as well as opportunities. Although in the past, strategic planning from a human resource perspective may have been considered a luxury rather than a necessity, the outcomes of this omission are well noted in the public school setting. Instances of the lack of strategic planning in educational institutions relative to the human resource function are abundant within the professional literature. Examples from the literature include:

- Failure to incorporate the human resource function of staffing as a viable part of the total organizational structure
- Failure to link organizational expectations to the human resource staffing needs of public school districts
- Failure to obtain reliable and valid student enrollment projections for staffing consideration
- Failure to staff the human resource function adequately within a public school district
- Failure to develop accurate and realistic staffing specifications

- Failure to maintain aggressive, imaginative, and well-designed recruiting programs to attract new personnel to a public school district
- Failure to validate predictors used to delimit applicant pools and to select employees
- Failure to develop effective orientation programs for assimilating staff to positions, the system, and the community
- Failure to use collective bargaining positively to resolve human resource staffing problems in the operation of a public school district
- Failure to anticipate personnel shortages and surpluses in specific target areas

In light of these failures as noted for many public school districts, this chapter examines the relationship between the strategic planning process for staffing and the behavior of system members. When setting forth these premises associated with the strategic planning process, several goals will be addressed:

- To examine human resource planning and staffing in the context of educational system planning as it relates to overall objectives and goals of a school system
- To designate appropriate decision-making groups within the human resource function pertaining to staffing a public school district
- To identify basic components of a human resource plan addressing the staffing function in a public school setting
- To illustrate actual examples of each component comprising a strategic plan for human resource staffing in the public school setting
- To reinforce the necessity of approaching strategic planning and staffing as a process rather than an event

Human Resource Planning and Educational System Planning

Planning is a methodological mechanism for projecting intentions and actions rather than reacting to causes and events impacting education and the schooling process. Because planning addresses the future, planning is a challenging endeavor to be undertaken by any public school district having both immediate and long-range implications for the organization and the operation of a public school district. In most instances, planning is the antithesis of expediency and of laissez-faire modes of operation for a public school system. As such, planning is an effort to set a course of action and to guide a school system toward a set of expectations that align the school district with predetermined objectives and goals derived from sound decision making based on a systematic plan of action.

A pivotal human resource issue in any school district that requires systematic planning is the staffing of the organization relative to employees because employees determine ultimately the success of any public school district. Employees are needed to administer the organization, to instruct the students, and to provide necessary support services for students. The numbers of and the allocations of employees assigned to each of these functions fall within the realm of strategic planning as related to the human resource function.

Strategic plans for staffing should be devised to consider the immediate human resource needs as well as the future human resource needs of the school district. These plans must be tailored to the uniqueness of the district, the instructional units, and the classroom settings relative to student needs. Furthermore, these plans need to direct the school district in a systematic manner toward identified objectives and goals complementing student needs and impacting organizational efficiency.

Planning must consider both existing and emerging needs of a public school district. Different configurations of staffing are required for special education students, English as a second language students, vocational education students, college preparatory students, and regular education students. To meet the needs of all students, strategic human resource planning must consider these different configurations in the formulation of a strategic plan for staffing.

Human resource plans concerning the allocation of employees relative to student needs are governed by many constraints external or internal to the school system as noted in the previous chapters. At the national level federal mandates (NCLB) and learned groups (ISLLC) point out important staffing needs for all public school districts. To fill these needs within most public school districts, a strategic staffing plan of action is required.

Like mandates and recommendations emanating at the national level, state departments of education have certain minimum requirements concerning the staffing of school districts for particular employee classification groups. In many states, collective bargaining agreements have been negotiated that establish additional requirements concerning staffing levels that exceed state-mandated requirements.

Beyond legislative requirements of state departments and collective bargaining agreements, most accreditation associations impose restraints on the staffing of a school district that still differ and exceed minimum requirements. Also, certain local prerogatives come into play relative to staffing preferences and organizational design to capture individual school district needs as perceived by the public, policy makers, and local educators. To accommodate all these concerns in an efficient and effective manner, extensive planning is needed.

An effective strategic plan for human resource staffing must be tempered, however, by each of the concerns mentioned relative to the staffing of a school district. Failure to do so on the part of school administrators and policy makers will render unsuccessful any planning attempts on the part of well-intentioned stakeholders and will also be unproductive in guiding a school district toward maximizing educational opportunities for students. Although any strategic plan should be tailored to a specific school district, there exist certain common elements to any plan, and these elements are addressed in this chapter by illustrations that link staff planning to processes through relying on actual applications in the field setting.

For every school district, strategic plans should set broad directives and specific actions for guiding the school district in achieving system objectives and goals. One kind of planning tool in the family of strategic plans is referred to as a process model in this chapter. This process model can be employed to address the complexities of strategic planning as the system is guided from the present mode of operation into the future mode of

Steps	Activities
One	Define and articulate expectations for the system's human resources.
Two	Assess the overall operation of the human resource system.
Three	Develop a human resource strategic plan.
Four	Provide an implementation strategy for the human resource plan.
Five	Construct auditing mechanisms for monitoring the human resource plan.
Six	Realign the human resource plan to meet current as well as emerging conditions.

FIGURE 3.1   *Sequential model for the planning process.*

operation. To move from a present state to a desired state requires, in most instances, incremental actions on the part of decision makers within a school district.

Process, as the term is used here within, refers to a series of progressive and interdependent steps designed to: (a) enhance actions to bring about positive change in the human resource function, (b) establish a systemic approach for coping with routine and nonroutine human resource problems, and (c) improve human resource problem solving at the local school district level. This process includes six different stages or activities on the part of human resource planners, school administrators, and school board members (see Figure 3.1).

An examination of the processes illustrated in Figure 3.1 highlights certain aspects/functions to be performed when constructing a human resource staffing plan. It should be noted that the processes consist of a series of steps or activities that serve to systematize the manner in which managerial judgments are made relative to people plans and planning activities. The ultimate ends toward which the overall policy process is directed include: (a) heightening the impact of the human resource function on organizational purpose, (b) developing ways to bring about desired changes in system performance, (c) orienting the planning process beyond short-term needs, and (d) assessing the internal and external environments likely to influence planning choices.

To implement a strategic planning process within a public school district requires the continued and active involvement of several stakeholders. Without this level of commitment on the part of all stakeholders, the strategic planning process will, no doubt, fail. Consequently, it is important within the early stages of the strategic planning process to identify personnel and to delegate responsibilities for designing, implementing, and monitoring a strategic staffing plan addressing the human resource function within the public school setting.

Responsibilities of Personnel for Strategic Planning and Systemic Changes

An initial, as well as an important, issue that surfaces early in the strategic planning process for staffing concerns the delegation of responsibilities among personnel for constructing a human resource staffing plan. To execute strategic planning and systemic changes in a public school district today as well as in the future, responsibilities must be assumed by some designated personnel within every public school system. Ideally included among these personnel are public school administrators and school board members (sometimes outside consultants are used as facilitators). Both school administrators and school board members are needed because strategic planning for staffing relative to the human resource function requires two types of decisions: (1) administrative decisions and (2) policy decisions.

Administrative decisions within the staffing planning process should govern the design of the strategic plan, collection of data for the strategic plan, and the grist on which policy decisions are made. On the other hand, policy decisions should address desired future human resource outcomes and should commit resources for accomplishing the desired human resource goals. Collectively, these different decision-making bodies are interdependent and necessary partners within the strategic planning for staffing process.

Indeed, every school system, regardless of size or organizational structure, must perform certain basic human resource functions to maintain the ongoing operation. At a minimum within every school system, personnel must be recruited, selected, orientated, compensated, appraised, developed, and maintained. These human resource tasks are ongoing and reoccurring due to the fluidity of school systems as dynamic organizations (Cunningham & Cordeiro, 2006).

Particular personnel responsible for administering the human resource functions, as required of all educational organizations, vary depending on the size of the school district. For small school districts, human resource tasks may be decentralized and may be shared among position holders as a supplement to their regular job assignments. This point cannot be overemphasized. In fact, this is the mode of operation for most school districts having a student enrollment of less than 5,000 **full-time equivalent** (FTE) students, and the majority of school districts fall within this category in almost all states.

Because most school districts in the United States have student enrollments of less than 5,000 (FTE) students, responsibilities for human resource activities are frequently delegated among personnel within a particular school district. Most generally, this delegation involves other central office administrators (if available), and almost always, building-level principals. Consequently, the need to understand the strategic planning process from a human resource perspective is extremely important both for actual as well as aspiring building administrators as implied by recent ISLLC standards adopted by several states of the Union and required within certification programs for administrators in many states.

In contrast to the operation of small school districts relative to the human resource staffing functions and the strategic planning process, is the management of human resource functions in large districts (generally greater than 5,000 FTE students). For large school districts, the human resource functions are assigned to a specific administrative position. This position carries usually the title of human resource director (often not certificated) or an assistant superintendent for human resources (a certificated position).

In large school districts, like in small school districts, strategic planning relative to the human resource staffing function should progress from the bottom up and not from the top down. Building-level administrators should be charged with providing base line data about staffing levels, with performing student enrollment projections, and with complying to human resource plans as well as processes. By including all administrative levels in the strategic planning process, acceptance of and commitment to a strategic plan for staffing is increased greatly among stakeholders.

Importantly within the present context, regardless of the public school district's enrollment (small and delegating responsibilities or large with an appointed position), the same human resource requirements for strategic planning and systemic change must be met if a school district is either to move forth or to sustain academic efficiency relative to current as well as to future academic standards. Consequently, the goal of this chapter is to provide factual information about the human resource responsibilities of staffing to position holders regardless of their assigned role (either as an assigned administrator or as a specific human resource administrator) within the public school setting.

Phases of a Strategic Human Resource Plan for Systemic Change

Without a doubt, this is an age of budget limitations; mandated assessments; a diversifying society; changing social mores; and confusion regarding ends, means, and methods of improving public education in the United States. In light of these changes and challenges endured by most public school districts, the task of developing strategic staffing plans for an education system appears, initially, to be a rather daunting undertaking on the part of those responsible for developing human resource plans from a strategic perspective. Many of the concerns associated with strategic planning can be overcome, however, by considering staff planning as a process rather than as an event and by moving through this process in a systematic manner.

As a process, strategic staff planning in the human resource area can be broken down initially into phases, and phases can be broken down into stages/tasks to be performed in a sequential manner. The phases of a strategic planning process for staffing consist of seven separate but related endeavors: (1) analyzing **enrollment trends,** (2) assessing current staffing deployments, (3) calculating existing staffing ratios, (4) determining desired staffing levels, (5) providing staffing projections, (6) designing compliance mechanisms, and (7) monitoring and providing feedback. Following is an overview of each phase of the strategic planning process as related to the human resource staffing function as a prelude to specific examples taken from the public school setting. It should be noted that this process is circular rather than linear, and once completed the process begins again prior to each academic year (see Figure 3.2).

As noted in Figure 3.2, initial steps within the strategic planning process for staffing the human resource function in a public school district concerns analyzing enrollment trends (see Phase 1, Figure 3.2). Data must be compiled for student enrollments from a historical perspective to capture potential trends within any particular public school district. This information is used to provide school administrators and policy makers with baseline data necessary for guiding future decision making relative to the staffing function in a public school district.

Collectively, this phase of the strategic planning process follows the old adage "any journey starts with a first step." Implied by this adage is that there is a focal point of origin,

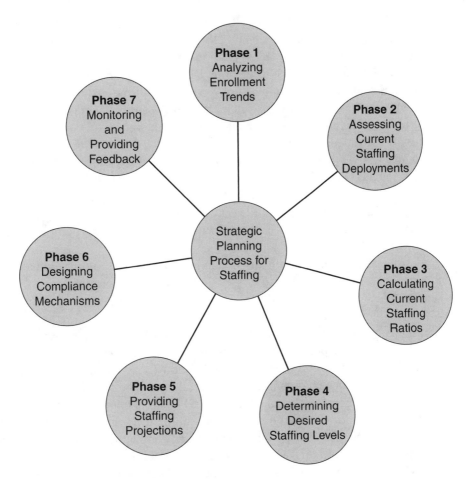

FIGURE 3.2 *Phases of a human resource staffing model.*

and strategic planning in the human resource area for staffing public school districts follows this colloquialism in a fundamental way. That is, the origin or starting point is based on historical enrollment information.

Only by possessing historical information about enrollment trends can sound strategic staffing plans be made by those charged with strategic planning for a public school district. Once enrollment trends have been analyzed, Phase 2 of the strategic planning process is invoked. The purpose of the second phase of the strategic planning process is to examine current staffing deployments within a particular school district. More specifically, information is needed about different classifications of employee groups, and their assignments within the public school district.

Given that baseline data are obtained about student enrollments (see Phase 1, Figure 3.2) and staffing deployments (see Phase 2, Figure 3.2), Phase 3 of the planning process is addressed. Phase 3 of the strategic staff planning process relative to human resource function involving personnel staffing commingles data from Phases 1 and 2. It does so by calculating staffing ratios reflecting the school district's current mode of operation relative to particular employee classification groups.

In contrast to the first three phases of the strategic planning process relative to the human resource function involving personnel staffing is the fourth phase. Importantly, the focus of Phase 4 of the strategic planning process is on goals and not on processes (a means to an end). These goals address a desired state of operation relative to the staffing function needed to operate a public school district in an effective and efficient environment given a particular school district's fiscal and physical constraints as moderated by external and internal environmental factors over which little control is afforded.

To transition from current human resource standings (see Phases 1, 2, and 3, Figure 3.2) to desired human resource conditions (Phase 4), the fourth phase of the strategic planning process is entered. Phase 4 of the strategic planning process relative to the human resource function involving staffing is future oriented. Attention is devoted to desired levels of the staffing function in light of previous information addressing current levels of staffing and leads to Phase 5 of the strategic planning process.

A major outcome from Phase 5 of the strategic planning process is the construction of a staffing plan to guide future actions on the part of the school system to obtain preestablished objectives identified in Phase 4 of the strategic planning process. This plan of action (Phase 5) should provide incremental steps that guide the school district from the current staffing situation to the desired staffing situation in a systematic manner. Within this plan of action both fiscal and organizational constrains must be considered as well as anticipated.

Having developed a plan of action (see Phase 5, Figure 3.2) for guiding a public school district from current staffing to desired staffing levels in the strategic planning process, techniques are required to ensure continued compliance to the strategic plan of action (Phase 6). To maintain desired staffing functions within a public school district across time, staffing charts must be constructed to protect the integrity of the strategic human resource plan. Staffing charts depict personnel requirements used by building-level administrators in the operation of local school buildings (examples are provided later in this chapter).

Phase 7 of the strategic planning process completes the cycle. At the final stage of the strategic planning process for staffing, an assessment, including feedback, relative to the effectiveness and to the efficiency of the strategic staffing plan is needed. Information derived from this stage of the planning process is used as an input for future planning.

Given the importance of each phase of the strategic planning process for the human resource staffing function relative to personnel staffing within the public school setting, specific examples from one practicing school district are provided as a means of illustration. It is important to note that these examples, although from a practicing school district, should serve as a guide and not be interpreted as a definitive model to be adopted by any school district without due consideration for external and internal environmental factors. What is appropriate for one school district may well be inappropriate for another school district, but the general format/process, as illustrated in the forthcoming sections of this chapter, is appropriate for all school districts desiring to develop and to implement a strategic planning process staffing.

Conduct of a staffing analysis for any particular school district should be made from a contextual perspective that considers external, internal, and local concerns as well as tempered by the mission statement that varies no doubt across school districts (see Chapters 1 and 2). That is, no specific organization configuration is controlling, and several schemes exist when formulating and executing the strategic planning process for staffing. Included among these schemes are several configurations for presenting a staffing analysis to guide the decision makers in formulating strategic human resource plans designed to induce systemic changes.

For purposes of illustration, only two schemes/configurations will be presented in this chapter. One of these schemes will depict data from a systemwide perspective, while the other scheme will decompose these same data according to organization units of instruction. In actual practice, these data could be further deconstructed to reflect either specific building-level assignments or particular classroom organizations within a school building (e.g., science, social studies).

To provide examples utilizing actual data from the field setting, a strategic planning process involving the human resource function related to staffing in a particular school district is used. In order to provide this public school district with a level of confidentiality, it is referred to in this chapter as the Sturgis Public School District. However, these are real data assessed in the public school setting, and within the following sections of this chapter, the reader will be taken through the formal steps necessary to construct a strategic plan to guide a public school district relative to the staffing function from a strategic planning perspective.

Phase 1 of the Strategic Planning Process: Analyzing Enrollment Trends

The purpose of Phase 1 of the strategic planning process as it relates to the human resource staffing function is to provide baseline information to school administrators and policy makers to guide their decisions based in part on enrollment trends. Student enrollment should be examined initially from a historical perspective because any given year of enrollment will reflect only a single point of observation, ignoring any trend or cyclical pattern occurring within a public school district. To illustrate the advantage for assessing historical data for a particular school district, actual enrollment data are collected for a specific public school district having a masked identity (Sturgis Public School District, see Table 3.1).

Initially, historical enrollment information is presented at a systemwide level (see Table 3.1, Section A), and subsequently enrollment trends are decomposed into functional units in this particular example (see Table 3.1, Section B). By moving from a systemwide perspective to a building-level perspective, additional insights are garnered about the strategic planning process for staffing in incremental stages. Based on past experiences of this author, this direction of information flow from a macro to a micro level is advantageous in the public school setting as a means of orienting both school administrators and policy makers to the strategic planning process addressing the human resource function involving personnel staffing in the public school setting.

TABLE 3.1

Phase 1 Historical Enrollment Trends

Historical Systemwide Enrollment Levels (A)							
	Base Year-6	Base Year-5	Base Year-4	Base Year-3	Base Year-2	Base Year-1	Base Year
Total	4014	3923	3762	3717	3722	3720	3600

Historical Instructional Enrollment Levels (B)							
Level	Base Year-6	Base Year-5	Base Year-4	Base Year-3	Base Year-2	Base Year-1	Base Year
Elementary Schools	2282	2229	2073	2015	1988	2003	1916
Middle Schools	620	635	634	636	622	603	635
High School	1112	1059	1055	1066	1112	1114	1049
Total	4014	3923	3762	3717	3722	3720	3600

These types of data for the Sturgis School District, as found in Table 3.1, are readily assessable for those seeking to conduct a strategic human resource plan focusing on staffing in their particular school district. As noted in Table 3.1, the top row of the enrollment matrix is defined by **"Base Years."** Base years are used in this example involving real data rather than actual dates to maintain the temporal stability of the illustration beyond the publication of this book. In actual practice, when conducting a specific strategic human resource plan for staffing in a particular school district, the Base Year is the current year in which data are collected, and subsequent years (i.e., Base Year-1, etc.) reflect historical data departing from the Base Year by a specific annual increment. For example, the Base Year in this example indicates that the Sturgis Public School District has a current total enrollment of 3,600 students, and this enrollment is down from a high of 4,014 enjoyed six years earlier (Base Year-6, see Table 3.1).

When compiling enrollment data, attention must be afforded to the unit of analysis used to describe students. At least two different units of analysis exist within this body of literature: (1) **head count** (HC) and (2) full-time equivalent (FTE). Head counts reflect the total number of actual students, while FTE reflects the total number of students prorated according to time in attendance within a particular school district. This differentiation between these units of analysis is important particularly for school districts having half-day kindergarten classes, school districts transporting students to vocational centers, or school districts providing only partial support to special education students. For purposes of presentation, these data as reflected throughout this chapter are always presented as FTEs.

However, it should be noted, FTEs are not always the preferred mode as a unit of analysis within the planning phase of the human resource process for staffing. For some human resource planning perspectives, head counts should be used. More specifically, head counts may well be more appropriate than FTEs concerning transportation needs, building accommodations, and food-service appropriations. Within these later contexts, all students must be served and not prorated students based on a FTE count.

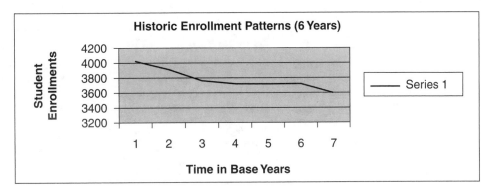

FIGURE 3.3 *Depiction of phase 1 enrollments for a system perspective.*

From a strategic human resource planning perspective involving a staffing analysis, information contained in Table 3.1 is extremely valuable. That is, this particular school district is experiencing a declining enrollment across several years. To capture this phenomenon from a systemwide basis relative to a declining enrollment more pointedly for administrators and policy makers in the conduct of strategic planning focusing on a staffing analysis, a graph is provided (see Figure 3.3) that yields important insight about this particular school district for decision makers when formulating strategic staffing patterns for guiding this district relative to future staffing needs (desired condition; Phase 4 to be discussed later in this chapter).

This graph depicts on the ordinate axis actual student enrollments, and on the abscissa axis, time as specified for each year spanning the data-collection sampling frame (the number 7 as contained in Figure 3.3 represents the Base Year). As readily ascertained by observation of these data, and graphed in Figure 3.3, this particular school district is likely to continue in a declining mode of enrollment, at least in the near future. Given the information imparted by these data, better decisions can be made about future human resource needs than if only the current year (Base Year) is considered as a starting point within the strategic planning process and reinforces the need for collecting historical data to guide decision makers relative to the construction of a strategic plan for addressing the staffing needs of a public school district.

Although these data, as contained in Table 3.1 (see Section A) and in Figure 3.3, provide a systemwide overview from a historical perspective, these data mask potentially important information needed to guide the development of a strategic plan. To provide more detailed information for administrators and policy makers in the formation of a strategic plan addressing the human resource staffing needs of a public school district, these data are recast (see Table 3.1) to be more revealing relative to instructional units. The specific instructional units of analyses are for the high school (grades 9–12), combined middle schools (grades 7–8), and combined elementary schools (grades K–6) (see Table 3.1).

By examining these systemwide data broken down by instructional levels, additional insights are provided for those involved in the strategic planning process concerning the

Section A

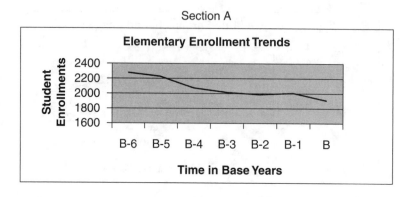

Section B

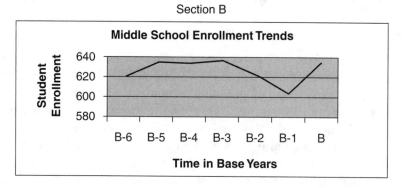

Section C

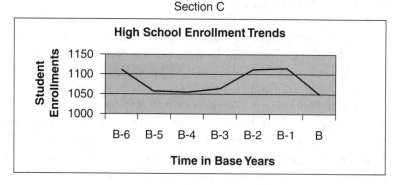

FIGURE 3.4   *Phase 1 historical enrollment trends decomposed by instructional levels.*

human resource staffing function in a public school district. Most notable is that all instructional units (elementary schools, middle schools, or high school) comprising this particular school district fail to follow the same linear enrollment trend as suggested by the systemwide analysis of enrollment data. This observation is obvious by examining the following graphs for each instructional level (see Figure 3.4).

Data, as displayed in the graphs contained in Figure 3.4, indicate enrollments at the elementary level are failing to recover from historical highs as enjoyed in the past (see Section A, Figure 3.4). However, for middle schools, these data suggest strong growth within recent time periods (see Section B, Figure 3.4), and that this growth may well carry over, at least in the near future, to the high school (see Section C, Figure 3.4). These seemingly abnormalities in enrollments moderated by instructional level have logical explanations when interpreted within a contextual context factoring in external and internal environmental factors impacting this particular public school district across time periods covered by these analyses.

When conducting this particular strategic planning process for this specific school district, parents, school board members, and building-level principals were interviewed according to an environmental scanning protocol. That is, enrollment data were presented to stakeholders, and stakeholders were requested to provide their own interpretation of enrollment trends. Results of these interviews indicate that parochial schools continue to open within the district boundaries, and many families desire to ground the early education experience of their children according to certain secular perspectives as espoused by parochial schools. For fiscal reasons, many of these parochial schools have had to increase tuition levels in most recent times, and parents indicate that these increases have altered their perspectives about the economic value of parochial education, at least beyond the elementary school level.

According to parent interviews, after their children are grounded at the elementary level in parochial schools, they are less willing to encumber tuition increases and more willing to enroll their children in the public school setting. This information explains, at least in part, the spike in enrollment at the middle school level for the Base school year (see Figure 3.4). Furthermore, this trend involving leaving parochial schools for public schools has important implications for enrollments at the high school level in the immediate as well as the not-so-distant future.

These data, as collected for the first stage of the strategic planning process focusing on the human resource staffing function, illustrate the necessity of analyzing historical information addressing enrollment trends. Without such a background framework to project future human resource needs, strategic errors are likely to be committed both by school administrators and policy makers in the formulation of, and execution of, a strategic plan addressing the human resource function involving the staffing of public schools. Given that the enrollment information has been collected and synthesized, attention is devoted to the second phase (Phase 2) of the strategic planning process, addressing staffing deployments within a public school district.

Phase 2 of the Strategic Planning Process: Assessing Current Staffing Deployments

Having collected enrollment data for students attending a public school district and having presented this information from a systemwide perspective as well as from instructional organizational levels, the second phase of the strategic planning process focuses on the deployment of staff within a public school district. Phase 2 of the strategic planning process differs in a very important way from Phase 1. Rather than focusing on historical information as was the case with enrollment data (see Phase 1, Figure 3.2), staffing statistics are compiled generally only for the current year of operation (Base Year) in Phase 2 of the strategic planning process for the human resource function involving staffing.

Information about the current year's staffing deployment within a public school district (see Phase 2, Figure 3.2) serves as a baseline condition to guide decision making about desired levels of staffing relative to current levels of staffing as required by the strategic planning process. A pivotal issue to be resolved by those responsible for constructing a strategic human resource plan addressing the staffing function in a public school district at Phase 2 is to determine particular staffing configurations to be included in the strategic planning process. Indeed, many possible configurations for classifying employees exist in the public school setting when performing a staffing analysis, and strategic planning for the human resource function suggests that individualized plans should be tailored to the specifics of a particular school district rather than follow a set mode of operation failing to exist for all public school districts.

In some instances, the classification for teachers within the strategic staffing planning process has been decomposed to include regular teachers, special education teachers, vocational education teachers, Title teachers (Title I and Title IV), and specialty teachers (art, music, and/or physical education teachers), to mention some options. Likewise, other classification schemes exist for noncertificated personnel that could include differentiation by job assignments (e.g., food service involving cashiers, servers, and cooks) or by budget category (soft vs. hard money). The more precise a strategic plan is for staffing the human resource function in a particular school district, the more clearly delineated the employee classifications must be within the planning process.

Within the examples provided, four different employee classification levels (teachers, aides, clericals, and custodians) are used for a very important reason. These particular levels were selected by the target school district under consideration as a policy decision made by a specific Board of Education but are by no means exhaustive, and other classification levels could have been so designated within the strategic planning process from a policy perspective. However, these levels, as chosen by this particular policy-making group in the Sturgis Public School District, reflect a variety of employee classification groupings and expand the strategic planning process for staffing the human resource function beyond instructional units to a systemwide perspective involving several predetermined employee classification levels, as noted in Table 3.2.

Levels of staffing for these particular employee classifications, as used in the strategic planning example for the Sturgis Public School District, are found in Table 3.2. In keeping with the model used for presenting enrollment information in Phase 1 for the strategic planning process (see Table 3.1), these staffing numbers are displayed both at the system level (see Table 3.2, Section A) and at the organizational instructional level (see Table 3.2, Section B).

As can be observed as well as could be anticipated from Table 3.2, current staffing patterns within this particular school district vary considerably by employee classification levels. More informative is the variation among classification levels of employees when broken down by instructional groupings (high school, middle school, or elementary schools). Collectively, these data provide important information for guiding decision

TABLE 3.2
Phase 2 Staffing Deployments for Base Year

Systemwide Staffing Levels (A)			
	Teachers	Aides	Clerical	Custodial
Total	305	44	22	22

Instructional Unit Staffing Levels (B)			
Levels	Teachers	Aides	Clerical	Custodial
High School	93	8	8	5
Middle Schools	58	6	4	5
Elementary Schools	154	30	10	12

making in Phase 3 of the strategic planning process involving the calculation of current staffing within a public school district.

Phase 3 of the Strategic Planning Process: Calculation of Current Staffing Ratios

The planning processes as previously shown (see Phases 1 and 2, Figure 3.2) lead to Phase 3, and Phase 3 is designed to assess the system and the system's linkage to the human resource function relative to the system's inputs concerning the allocation of staffing according to the current organizational configuration. This phase (Phase 3) within the human resource planning process is pivotal for creating desired outcomes for the system, its members, and those for whom the system renders service. When executed appropriately, this phase of the strategic planning process increases the likelihood that the system will perform effectively and efficiently under conditions of continuous change exerted by external and internal environments.

Meeting these requirements calls for addressing several questions such as the following:

- How can human resource staff planning be linked closely to the school system's mission statement?
- What is the system's current situation regarding attainment of educational expectations?
- What will the future external environment likely require in terms of demand for school system services?
- Which priorities should be established for the allocation of anticipated resources?
- Which internal or external factors might inhibit attainment of the system's educational aims?

Answers to these questions require information that must be acquired for guiding decision making of policy makers. In recent years, many school systems have come to realize that information is one of the key assets possessed by the district along with buildings and equipment, fiscal resources, and human resources. For example, managing all subprocesses of the human resource function effectively and efficiently requires information from both the internal and external environmental forces that influence human resource decisions within the public school setting.

Some information needed for human resource planning for staffing is depicted by established databases reflecting historical enrollment trends (Phase 1) and current staffing deployments (Phase 2). Other information needed for human resource planning must be compiled from these initial data sources (Phases 1 and 2) by those responsible for human resource planning (Phase 3, staffing ratios). To provide information that includes both sorts of data as contained in Tables 3.1 and 3.2 in a meaningful fashion to guide decision making, attention is directed to the third phase of the strategic planning process involving the calculations of ratios reflecting staffing patterns.

Because student enrollments drive staffing needs in the public school setting under most circumstances (special education being an exception), strategic planning within the human resource setting must consider simultaneously both sources of information (student enrollments and staffing allocations). To consider both sources of information simultaneously, the generally accepted index for presenting this collective information to administrators and to policy makers is a **staffing ratio**. Technically, a staffing ratio is calculated by dividing student enrollment data by particular employee classification levels included in the human resource plan (student enrollments/particular classification levels). Functionally, a staffing ratio depicts organizational demands (student enrollments) relative to organization commitments (staff allocations) on the part of administrators and policy makers directing a public school system, and reflects, to some extent, a philosophy of education exhibited through function if not through form.

Specific staffing ratios are provided for the Sturgis Public School District in Table 3.3. In keeping with the past classification systems as used in this chapter, these data are broken down on a systemwide perspective (see Section A in Table 3.3) and on a functional instructional level (see Section B in Table 3.3). These data, as depicted in Table 3.3,

TABLE 3.3
Phase 3 Staffing Ratios for Base Year

Systemwide Staffing Ratios (A)			
	Teachers	Aides	Clerical	Custodial
Total	11.8	81.8	163.6	163.6

Instructional Level Staffing Ratios (B)			
Levels	Teachers	Aides	Clerical	Custodial
High School	11.3	131.1	131.1	209.8
Middle Schools	10.9	105.8	158.8	127.0
Elementary Schools	12.4	63.9	191.6	159.7

indicate varying staffing ratios among employee groups within the district as well as within different organizational instructional levels.

Based on these data as contained in Table 3.3, policy decisions are needed about desired staffing levels relative to these employee classifications to guide this public school district in an anticipated future educational environment. Either to maintain existing staffing performance levels or to move from current staffing performance levels (see Phase 3, Figure 3.2), policy decisions must be made relative to desired staffing levels. Phase 4 of the strategic planning process addresses the formation of these policy decisions.

Phase 4 of the Strategic Planning Process: Determining Desired Staffing Levels

The goal of Phase 4 of the strategic planning process for staffing the human resource function in a public school system involves determining a desired level of staffing for a public school district. Phases 1–3 of the human resource planning process include (a) analyzing historical enrollment trends, (b) assessing current staffing deployments, and (c) computing operating staffing ratios, respectively. Moving from Phases 1–3 within the planning process, Phase 4 involves drawing inferences, considering planning options, and making planning decisions based on information derived from earlier phases of the strategic planning process. Many factors are involved with decision making for human resource planning at Phase 4 of the strategic planning process involving the human resource staffing function. Some examples follow:

- What are the planning implications derived from the current staffing analysis?
- What are the planning implications derived from the calculations of current staffing ratios?
- Will there be a shortage or surplus of system personnel to meet future needs as required by the human resource plans?
- To what extent do current job incumbents have the skills, abilities, and attitudes to fill projected positions?
- What assumptions should be made about professional staff size and about support staff size?
- Should staffing ratios be the same in all buildings across the district?
- Should staffing ratios be differentiated by organizational levels?
- Should staffing ratios be the same in all grade levels within a building?
- To what extent should existing jobs be redesigned and new jobs be developed?
- What decisions should be made about various kinds of staff balance (system; work unit; staff category; staff utilization; staff load; staff competency; and racial, ethnic, gender, age, and instructional balance)?

Based on the information obtained from the different phases of the strategic planning process (historical enrollment patterns [Phase 1 of the planning process], staffing deployments [Phase 2 of the planning process], and employee ratios [Phase 3 of the planning process]) as depicted for this particular school district (Sturgis Public School District) as well as answers to the above probes, policy makers (school board members) in conjunction with advice from public school administrators made specific decisions about desired staffing ratios as used in the following examples. This particular decision-making body, as used in this example for the purpose of illustration in the strategic planning process, decided from a policy capturing perspective to maintain the status quo relative to staffing ratios, as indicated in Table 3.3, except for teachers at the elementary school level.

With respect to teachers, this policy-making group for the Sturgis Public School District chose to maintain staffing ratios for the high school (11.3) and the middle schools (10.9). However, this policy-making group chose to reduce the staffing ratios for the elementary schools. As a policy decision, this informed group elected to reduce staffing ratios for elementary schools from the current level of operation (12.4) to a desired level of operation (10.5). Data contained in Table 3.4 reflect these policy decisions.

It is important to note for Phase 4 of the strategic planning process that the establishment of desired staffing levels is a policy decision and not an administrative decision. From a functional point of view, policy decisions are needed at this phase of the strategic planning process to guide staffing levels beyond those mandated by state departments of education. Also, policy decisions relative to staffing ratios exceeding state mandates are needed for encumbering fiscal resources necessary either to meet staffing ratios required by external accreditation agencies or to satisfy the staffing desires reflected by local preferences.

Given the anticipated declining enrollments for this particular school district as used in the example (Sturgis Public School District), a strategic plan concerning staffing desired levels is needed to ensure that future staffing levels align with desired staffing levels. As such, the strategic planning process moves from Phase 4 to Phase 5, based on policy decisions concerning desired staffing ratios for a particular public school district.

TABLE 3.4
Phase 4 Data Reflecting Actual/Desired Staffing Ratios

Systemwide Staffing Ratios For Actual/Desired (A)			
	Teachers	**Aides**	**Clerical**	**Custodial**
Total	11.8/11.2	81.8/81.8	163.6/163.6	163.6/163.6

Instructional-Level Staffing Ratios For Actual/Desired (B)			
Levels	**Teachers**	**Aides**	**Clerical**	**Custodial**
High School	11.3/11.3	131.1/131.1	131.1/131.1	209.8/209.8
Middle Schools	10.9/10.9	105.8/105.8	158.8/158.8	127.0/127.0
Elementary Schools	12.4/10.5	63.9/63.9	191.6/191.6	159.7/159.7

Phase 5 of the Strategic Planning Process: Providing Staffing Projections

To transition from a Base Year of operation (Phase 3) to a target year of operation (Phase 4) for a strategic plan involving the human resource function of staffing, incremental steps are required in the strategic planning process (Phase 5). Incremental steps in a strategic planning process are required for public school districts seeking either to maintain current staffing ratios or to alter existing staffing ratios to reflect some predetermined standard relative to new staffing ratios as established from a policy perspective. Making the transition from an existing organizational state reflecting current staffing ratios to a future state reflecting desired staffing ratios requires planning and the development of a strategic plan of action (Phase 5). The planning process described in this chapter for Phase 5 should help to chart managerial direction, reduce uncertainty, and minimize random behavior in efforts to achieve the aims of both the school organization and its members relative to desired staffing ratios.

After initial human resource plans have been developed, Phase 5 of the human resource planning process involves constructing a strategy for implementation of the human resource plan of action. The goal of the implementation strategy (Phase 5) is to provide an executable plan of action that directs the school district's relative staffing across time to a future state of operation for a public school district. As such, Phase 5 of the strategic planning process is future oriented and must be tempered by both the fiscal and the physical restraints of a particular public school district involving funds and building capacities.

Far too often these constraints delimiting the strategic planning process relative to the human resource function of staffing fail to be tempered by temporal considerations. That is, movement from the current state of operation to the desired state of operation is viewed from an immediate as opposed to a long-range perspective, and as a result, the strategic staffing plan is perceived to be impractical when viewed from a short-range perspective. In actual practice, the strategic staffing plan of action should span at least five years to accommodate the acclimation of a public school district from a current state of operation to a desired state of operation.

An example of a strategic plan of action for the Sturgis Public School District covering a five-year implementation period is found in Table 3.5. Examination of this table reveals some new information as compared to previous information presented in the earlier sections of this chapter addressing the strategic planning processes relating to the staffing function. On the first row of this table, the concept of base year is expanded from a historical perspective (see Table 3.1, "Base Year-6"–"Base Year") to a future scenario involving unknown data (see Table 3.4, "Base Year"–"Base Year+5").

Again, Base Year (see first row) is designated as the target year of data collection and reflects known information about the particular school district under consideration. The reader should note for the purpose of continuity that the Base Year data as contained in Table 3.5 is the same as the Base Year data contained in Table 3.3. However, what differs in Table 3.5 is that the Base Year concept is projected to a future period of time, again by using annual increments (Base Year + 1, Base Year + 2, etc.) departing from the Base Year.

TABLE 3.5
Phase 5 Long-Range Staffing Projections

Systemwide Staffing Ratios (A)						
Enrollments	Base Year 3600	Base+1 3629	Base+2 3610	Base+3 3561	Base+4 3528	Base+5 3494
Classifications						
Teachers	305	308	311	315	319	323
Aides	44	44	44	44	43	43
Clerical	22	22	22	22	22	21
Custodians	22	22	22	22	22	21

Instructional-Level Staffing Ratios For High School (B)						
Enrollments	Base Year 1049	Base Year+1 1043	Base Year+2 1072	Base Year+3 1053	Base Year+4 1040	Base Year+5 1038
Classifications						
Teachers	93	92	95	93	92	92
Aides	8	8	8	8	8	8
Clerical	8	8	8	8	8	8
Custodians	5	5	5	5	5	5

Instructional-Level Staffing Ratios For Middle Schools (C)						
Enrollments	Base Year 635	Base Year+1 623	Base Year+2 586	Base Year+3 590	Base Year+4 601	Base Year+5 592
Classifications	58	57	54	54	55	54
Teachers	58	57	54	54	55	54
Aides	6	6	6	6	6	6
Clerical	4	4	4	4	4	4
Custodians	5	5	5	5	5	5

Instructional-Level Staffing Ratios For Elementary Schools (D)						
Enrollments	Base Year 1916	Base Year+1 1964	Base Year+2 1952	Base Year+3 1918	Base Year+4 1886	Base Year+5 1863
Classifications						
Teachers	154	158	162	167	172	177
Aides	30	31	31	30	30	29
Clerical	10	10	10	10	10	10
Custodians	12	12	12	12	12	12

Within the second column of Table 3.5, student enrollment data are listed. For the Base Year, the enrollments are actual FTE students attending this school district (Sturgis Public School District) within the target year (see Table 3.1, Base Year enrollments). FTE enrollments, associated with the "Base Year+", are projected enrollments reflecting anticipated students entering and continuing with this particular school district in the future.

To obtain the enrollment data necessary for the "Base +" years, an **enrollment projection** is required. For some school districts, enrollment projections are provided by state departments of education at no cost to the public school districts, and in other school districts, enrollment projections are calculated by district personnel or through the use of external consultants. However, in all instances, enrollment projections are a necessary part of the strategic planning process involving the human resource function addressing personnel staffing.

Because of the importance that enrollment projections play within the strategic planning process for staffing, a major portion of the previous chapter in this text was devoted to this topic (see Chapter 2). Within Chapter 2, attention was provided both to linear as well as to nonlinear enrollment projection techniques to accommodate the needs of particular school districts relative to external and internal environmental impacts. In keeping with the previous chapter, those enrollment projections are used in this chapter as a point of illustration for the strategic planning process.

Based on these enrollment projections as found in Chapter 2, staffing allocations are depicted for the different employee classification groupings across a five-year time period. To obtain the desired staffing ratios (as determined in Phase 4) in an environment of declining enrollments (as projected in Phase 5), specific staffing actions are required by educational administrators at the school building level. To guide staffing decisions at the school building level, Phase 6 of the strategic planning process provides certain mechanisms from a strategic planning perspective either to maintain or to alter the current staffing configuration.

Phase 6 of the Strategic Planning Process: Designing Compliance Mechanisms

Introducing changes in the human resource function of staffing involves a variety of activities to improve existing arrangements, as well as to develop new approaches and capabilities based on a review of external and internal environmental conditions, threats, and opportunities for improving the effective and efficient operation of a public school district. Stage 6 of the human resource planning process presumes that there is organizational commitment to implement the design of the strategic staffing plan as construed from the previous phases of the planning process. Without commitment on the part of policy makers, administrators, and staff, even the best human resource plans are doomed to fail.

To provide direction governing administrative actions and to facilitate formal commitment to a strategic plan addressing the human resource staffing functions, formal mechanisms are required. The mechanisms used by many public school districts within the strategic planning process are **staffing charts** to guide decision making after desired

TABLE 3.6
Phase 6 Desired Staffing Ratios (Excluding Special Education) at the Elementary School Level

Enrollments	Teacher Positions	Aide Positions	Clerical Positions	Custodial Positions
210	20	3.3	1.1	1.3
221	21	3.5	1.2	1.4
231	22	3.6	1.2	1.4
242	23	3.8	1.3	1.5
252	24	3.9	1.3	1.6
263	25	4.1	1.4	1.6
275	26	4.3	1.4	1.7
286	27	4.5	1.5	1.8
297	28	4.6	1.6	1.9
308	29	4.8	1.6	1.9
319	30	5.0	1.7	2.0
330	31	5.2	1.7	2.1
341	32	5.3	1.8	2.1
351	33	5.5	1.8	2.2
362	34	5.7	1.9	2.3
374	36	5.9	2.0	2.3

enrollment levels have been obtained. Staffing charts provide a functional guide to building-level administrators in staffing their school buildings each spring relative to anticipated fall enrollments.

For the purpose of illustration for staffing charts within the strategic planning process, an example is provided only for elementary school buildings (see Table 3.6), even though staffing charts are needed for all instructional levels in a staffing plan (elementary schools, middle schools, and high schools). This staffing chart, as found in Table 3.6, assumes that the school district has met desired staffing levels as defined in Table 3.5 and has provided a means of complying with the staffing plan relative to predetermined desired staffing levels (see Table 3.4) in subsequent years. Contained in Table 3.6 are position entitlements for elementary schools within the Sturgis Public School District needed to maintain desired staffing ratios indicated by the strategic planning process. When interpreting these data it should be noted that statistics are based exclusively on only policy decisions at this particular local school district level.

For the Sturgis Public School District, enrollments in elementary schools (excluding special education students) range from a low of 230 FTE students to a high of 350 FTE students. Included in Table 3.6 are staffing ratios exceeding both minimum and maximum enrollments along with desired staffing ratios for each enrollment level. An example of how this staffing chart is used by elementary school principals is provided.

To illustrate, the reader is asked to assume that a particular elementary school building within the Sturgis Public School District has a projected fall enrollment (Base + 1 year) of 319 FTE students. According to this staffing chart, this elementary school building would earn 30 FTE teachers, 5.0 FTE aides, 1.7 clerical positions, and 2.0 custodial positions. Following this staffing chart, the elementary school principal would base fall staffing patterns according to these entitlements.

Phase 7 of the Strategic Planning Process: Monitoring and Providing Feedback

Within Phase 7 of the human resource planning process (see Figure 3.2), attention must be given to monitoring, assessing, and adjusting the implementation of the strategic planning process for staffing. Inherent in this phase of the planning process are three closely related steps that must be addressed: (a) reviewing plans (including goals, objectives, programs, and standards), (b) checking results against expectations, and (c) adjusting to correct deviations from staffing plans relative to the mission statement.

Ideally, every human resource plan that a school system places in operation should have a built-in means for judging the effectiveness of the plan relative to specified objectives and goals. Viewed in this manner, monitoring and evaluating the effectiveness of plans is an omnipresent function of school administration, an aspect of the administrative process designed to keep means and ends in balance relative to the human resource plan. To expect even the best designed human resource plans to flow flawlessly from initiation through fruition is unrealistic.

Through continuous monitoring on the part of system administration, adjustments can be made within the ongoing implementation process. To help with monitoring, assessing, and adjusting the strategic staffing plan for human resources, specific questions are posed for consideration. School members as well as public school administrators need to know the following:

- How feasible are the planning assumptions on which the function of staffing is based?
- Is the current organizational structure conducive to system effectiveness?
- Are positions being filled according to position guides?
- Which steps have been taken to implement systemwide development and career paths for personnel?
- Are the numbers and quality of personnel satisfactory?
- Are personnel deployed, balanced, and utilized effectively?
- Which initiatives are needed to adjust differences between actual and expected planning outcomes?

Answers to these questions serve as a basis for refining the strategic planning process relative to the human resource staffing needs of a public school district. As such, the strategic planning process for staffing is cyclical rather than linear. Following is a description of the cyclical aspects associated with the strategic planning process for staffing from a human resource perspective.

Cyclical Aspects of the Strategic Planning Process

Strategic planning relative to the human resource function involving the staffing of a public school district, as described in this chapter, should be an ongoing process in all educational organizations. To begin this process, six different planning activities are noted in Figure 3.1. These activities provide the basic directions for developing and for implementing the strategic planning process of staffing at the local school district level.

Functionally, seven different phases were used to depict data necessary for informing decision making and for guiding the staffing of a public school district from a strategic planning perspective. The different phases (1–7) of the human resource process should be performed on an annual basis by every public school district. By compiling data as required in each phase, errors either in omission or commission can be reduced from an organizational and an operational perspective. Errors encountered with the Base+1 year of operation can be avoided in subsequent years, if the strategic human resource plan is revisited annually and is updated according to known as well as anticipated external and internal environmental changes.

Obviously, effectiveness is the ultimate test of any strategic initiative implemented by a school district. Within the human resource context, effectiveness is defined broadly as the realization of objectives and goals associated with the planning process when aligning with the mission statement of a public school district. Consequently, district leadership has a strong obligation to define what effectiveness means and how effectiveness should be measured within the school setting in keeping with the intents of a school district's mission statement.

Exercising this obligation on behalf of district leadership is extremely important for many reasons. Interest groups and constituencies, both internal and external to the school system, have a stake in whether schools are effective or ineffective. Taxpayers, politicians, government bodies, home buyers, students, other employers, and employees have more than a passing concern about school system quality. All will use this interest to assess effectiveness if district leadership is remiss in their obligation to assess the effectiveness of school district operations relative to human resource staffing plans. Indeed, a well-designed and a well-executed human resource staffing plan serves as a mainstay for most all public school districts.

Review and Preview

Within this chapter, a model is presented for constructing a human resource staffing plan that can be used to guide a public school district from its current mode of operation to a desired level of operation. In so doing, information needed for seven different aspects of the strategic planning process for staffing are presented:

(1) analyzing enrollment trends, (2) assessing current staffing deployments, (3) calculating existing staffing ratios, (4) determining desired staffing ratios, (5) providing staffing projections, (6) designing compliance mechanisms, and (7) monitoring and providing feedback. For each of these components of the strategic

planning process, actual data obtained from the field setting are used as a point of illustration that others can follow.

As the culminating chapter of the first part of this book, this chapter builds on the previous chapters and provides a foundation for the future chapters. By building the notion of strategic planning as detailed in Chapter 1 and capitalizing on informational needs as described in Chapter 2, this chapter takes theory to practice in the real-world setting by using actual data. By constructing a human resource staffing plan as described in this chapter for taking a school system from current to desired levels of performance, a foundation has been provided for guiding operational procedures as described throughout the remainder of this book concerning specific human resource tasks and issues influencing recruitment, selection, orientation, compensation, appraisal, continuity, development, and collective bargaining, all of which are human resource topics to be addressed in the ensuing chapters of this book.

Discussion Questions

1. Within this chapter, enrollment and staffing data were broken down from a system and from a building-level perspective. What other meaningful configurations could have been used to conduct a similar analysis within the building level?

2. What would be some of the important hindrances in conducting a strategic staffing plan as illustrated in this chapter for your school district?

3. Within your school district, how would you go about determining desired staffing ratios? Who would be the influential stakeholders?

4. What types of resistance would you likely encounter if you developed formalized staffing charts derived from a strategic planning process? How would you address these concerns?

5. If your school district fails to have a strategic staffing plan, what are some of the consequences?

Case Study

Using your school building as the unit of analysis, develop a current staffing analysis for the positions comprising the workforce within your building. What levels of certificated personnel and what level of classified personnel would you include? What would be of concern for differentiating between a full-time equivalent and a head count for employees and for students? What issues are the Board of Education and the school administrators likely to have about this type of plan?

References

Creighton, T. (2001). *Schools and data: The educators guide for using data to improve decision making.* Thousand Oaks, CA: Corwin Press.

Cunningham, W. G., & Cordeiro, P. A. (2006). *Educational leadership: A problem-based approach* (3rd ed.). Upper Saddle River, NJ: Merrill/Prentice Hall.

Gibson, S., & Blandford, S. (2005). *Managing special education needs: A practical guide for primary and secondary schools.* Thousand Oaks, CA: Sage Publications.

Howell, W. (2005). *Besieged: School boards and the future of education politics.* Washington, DC: Brookings Institution Press.

Hoy, W. K., & Miskel, C. J. (2005). *Educational administration: Theory, research, and practice* (7th ed.). New York: McGraw-Hill.

Ingersoll, R. M. (June 2002). The teacher shortage: A case of wrong diagnosis and wrong prescription. *NASSP Bulletin, 86,* 18–27.

Kowalski, T. J. (2004). *Public relation in schools.* Upper Saddle River, NJ: Pearson.

Lehr, C. A., Clapper, A. T., & Thurlow, M. L. (2005). *Graduation for all: A practical guide to decreasing school dropouts.* Thousand Oaks, CA: Sage Publications.

Lindsey, R. B., Roberts, L., & Campbell-Jones, F. (2004). *The culturally proficient school: An implementation guide for school leaders.* Thousand Oaks, CA: Sage Publications.

Mayo, N. B, & Kajs, L. T. (2005). Longitudinal study of technology to prepare future teachers. *Educational Research Quarterly, 29*(1), 3–15.

National Education Association. (n.d.). "Meeting the Challenges of Recruitment and Rentention." Retrieved December 29, 2005, http://www.nea. org/aboutnea/code.html.

No Child Left Behind Act, 2001, Pub. L. No. 107–110, 115 Stat. 1425 (2002).

Owings, W. A., Kaplan, L. S., & Nunnery, J. (2005). Principal quality, ISLLC standards, and student achievement: A Virginia study. *Journal of School Leadership, 15*(1), 99–119.

Sunderman, G. L., Kim, J. S., & Orfield, G. (2005). *NCLB meets school realities: Lessons from the field.* Thousand Oaks, CA: Sage Publications.

PART II

Human Resource Processes: Recruitment, Selection, Orientation, Performance Appraisal, and Compensation

4   Recruitment

5   Selection

6   Orientation

7   Performance Appraisal

8   Compensation

Part II of this book examines five major human resource processes from a strategic planning perspective as applied to the public school setting: recruitment, selection, orientation, performance appraisal, and compensation. The intent of Part II is to expand an understanding of the key activities that make up organizational staffing within the public school setting. These activities include the following basic operational directives:

- Generating applicant pools through proactive recruitment, focusing on external and internal applicant pools.
- Matching individual talents with present and future position demands by selection with attention being provided to legal and practical aspects associated with procuring employees.
- Orienting recently assigned employees relative to job, system, and community expectations through considering the needs of newly selected and newly assigned employees.

- Examining different performance assessment techniques for evaluating the performance of employees and developing a decision model to direct policy and administrative deliberations with implications and applications for a performance assessment process tailored to the specific needs of a school district.
- Auditing current compensation practices, establishing new compensation structures, and maintaining an equitable compensation system for all employees that has internal consistency and external equity.

Recruitment

4

OBJECTIVES

- Develop and describe a model for recruitment of human resources from a strategic planning perspective.
- Differentiate the relationship between Equal Employment Opportunity and Affirmative Action Perspective.
- Discuss permissive policy issues affecting the recruitment process in the public school setting.
- Provide formal methods for informing the recruitment process.
- Identify and discuss different recruitment incentives used by public school districts.

- Differentiate among different labor markets for attracting potential job candidates.
- Examine different modes and mediums for communication within the recruitment process.
- Develop an overview of the recruitment process from a process perspective.

Part I of this book provides an overview of the human resource process from a strategic planning perspective as can be practiced in the public school setting. A specific structural model containing a mission statement, organizational goals, district objectives, and operational functions was used to link elements of the strategic planning process to the human resource function within the public school setting. Practical applications from a human resource perspective were provided in these chapters for basic planning processes (Chapter 1), for performing enrollment projections using alternative techniques (Chapter 2), and for constructing a workable staffing plan based on actual data from the field setting (Chapter 3).

Within the following section of the book (Part II), attention is directed toward moving from the initial stage of the strategic planning process to the operational stage of the strategic planning process. This involves linking the mission statement of the district with predetermined goals and objectives tailored to a local school district. Indeed, when fulfilling the intents of the mission statement through defined organizational goals and objectives, all school districts must identify, attract, select, orientate, compensate, and retain competent personnel to be effective as an organization in providing education to America's youth. To accomplish these operational functions in an effective and efficient manner requires deliberate planning and informed decision making on the part of both school board members and educational employees.

Beyond a doubt, acquiring and retaining competent personnel necessary for accomplishing the mission of a school district has become more difficult in recent years (Winter, Millay, Bjork, & Keedy, 2005). This seems to be true for all types of school districts (suburban, urban, or rural), and special types of employees. "Perhaps the single most important factor in attracting qualified candidates is the reputation and image of the school district and community" (Cunningham & Cordeiro, 2006, p. 283).

To depict an image for any public school district aligned with community expectations, several topics are explored in Part II of this book. Chapter 3 in Part II addresses recruitment as an organizational objective with attention afforded to the attraction and to the motivation of potential job candidates for vacant positions within a school district. Issues related to equal employment opportunity as well as to affirmative action perspectives are discussed, and informational needs for an effective and efficient recruitment process are described.

To delimit an initial applicant pool containing a willing, capable, and diversified pool of potential job candidates generated through a well-formulated program of recruitment as described in Chapter 4, Chapter 5 examines procedures and processes involving selection. Specific attention is afforded in Chapter 5 both to a conceptual and operational model for selecting employees. Methods and means are discussed for assessing commonly used predictors within the educational setting. Alternate mechanisms are presented to assess discrimination for particular groups of individuals receiving a protected class status by federal and state guidelines.

Within Chapter 6, emphasis is diverted to the orientation of employees. Employees new to the system and employees new to their assignment have special needs. Processes and procedures for these special needs are addressed from a strategic planning perspective.

All employees of a public school system must be evaluated relative to their "on job" performance. Different systems for assessing the job performance of employees are addressed in Chapter 7. Special attention is afforded to purposes of the performance appraisal process and to aligning purposes to processes.

Core to the employment relationship between public school districts and employees is compensation. Fundamental to any compensation process are concerns about internal consistency and external competitiveness. Both of these concerns are the focus of Chapter 8.

Recruitment

Given the dynamic as well as the contentious environment characterizing most school districts today relative to federal acts (e.g., No Child Left Behind, n.d.), national commissions (e.g., Interstate School Licensure Consortium, n.d.), and high-stakes testing implemented by most states, as well as the changing demographics of actual workforces comprising school systems, vacancies occur each year in every school district. In keeping with this changing environment and with the emerging vacancies, the workforce of a school district must be, at minimum, continuously replenished to meet these demands. The administrative process for replenishing the workforce is selection, and selection requires an effective and efficient recruitment program attracting willing as well as able potential job candidates.

An effective and efficient recruitment program is proactive rather than reactive relative to the human resource needs of a public school district and addresses both short- and long-range staffing needs. From a strategic planning perspective, as noted in the previous chapters, one of the major operational functions to be performed within the human resource context in a school setting is **recruitment.** As an operational function, recruitment has two distinct but related goals.

One of these goals involves the identification of viable applicants sought by an educational organization to fill vacant positions. Another goal entails motivating these individuals, once identified, to seek employment with the organization. Both of these goals are necessary components of a functional recruitment process from a strategic planning perspective.

As an operational task within the human resource process, recruitment is not an easy administrative endeavor for school districts. Effective recruitment requires extensive planning on the part of school boards as well as on the part of educational administrators and requires commitments of both to be executed in a meaningful manner. Although being far from a costless operational directive, recruitment efforts and funds can yield dividends in many ways within the public school setting when designed appropriately and executed effectively.

Frequently, recruitment has been overlooked as an unnecessary administrative directive by some school systems, and often it has been underutilized by many public school districts as a means for filling vacant positions. Indeed, far too many school districts have and continue to rely on "walk-ins" to staff vacant positions and have devoted little or no effort toward developing a formalized recruitment program to attract potential job candidates aligning their interests and their expertise with position requirements. However, such a practice involving the reliance on "walk-ins" is no longer feasible today for many reasons.

Unlike the past labor markets for potential candidates having limited opportunities, many viable applicants for educational positions have had and continue to have several options (Young, Jury, & Reis, 1997). These options include private sector jobs offering different types of incentives involving higher pay and greater career advancements than found in the public education setting. Consequently, no longer can school districts rely exclusively on "walk-ins" as a means of filling vacancies needed to operate an educational organization and must direct specific efforts toward the development and the implementation of a recruitment process to attract applicants that were once taken as a given in the recent past.

The most typical source for vacancies fueling the recruitment process in most school districts is retirements. Retirements within the public school setting come about in two separate but related ways. Most common among these ways is when individuals maximize their earning potential within state retirement systems based on their years of creditable service, and additional service on their part within the profession produces diminishing returns for continuous employment from an economic perspective. To capitalize on these earned benefits accrued through continuous services, many individuals retire and create vacant positions within a public school district (Winter, Rinehart, & Munoz, 2002).

Another way that retirements occur and create vacancy opportunities for filling positions is through retirement incentives (also known as early "buy-out" programs) promoted by a public school district and permitted by some state retirement systems. Functionally, "buy-out" programs involve paying forward service to the retirement system for time yet to be served by an employee as a means of inducing an employee to retire. Underlying "buy-out" programs are two basic assumptions as a means of justification from an organizational perspective.

One basic assumption is that more experienced and more expensive personnel can be replaced by less experienced and less expensive personnel equally capable of performing the same job assignment. The other basic assumption for "buy-out" programs is that new personnel possessing desired characteristics (as defined by NCLB/ISLLC/special competencies) can replace existing personnel devoid of desirable knowledge, skills, and abilities. For both of these reasons, "buy-out" programs create vacancy opportunities for a public school district that can potentially improve the current workforce if competent individuals are recruited and are selected to fill voids created by departing personnel.

In addition to retirements, turnovers among existing employees provide recruitment opportunities for most public school districts. Like retirements stemming either from "maxing out" or from "buy outs," turnovers result from two primary, yet different, sources for creating vacancies to be filled by recruitment efforts: (1) voluntary or (2) nonvoluntary. These sources for creating vacancies are resignations (voluntary) and/or nonrenewals (nonvoluntary), which are sometimes blurred within the public school setting.

Voluntary resignations of system employees stem either from personal or from professional reasons. From the personal perspective, individuals may choose to opt out of the profession early on in their careers because of unfulfilled expectations or to follow the career opportunities of a spouse being relocated. Also, professionally, voluntary resignations result in individuals capitalizing on career opportunities afforded by other school districts and in advancing their career progression by leaving one school district for employment in another school district.

Involuntary resignations on the part of employees affording recruitment opportunities for a public school district result largely from nonrenewals. For most educational positions within a public school district, a probationary period of employment is required as specified by a particular time frame. This time frame is legislated in almost all states for teachers and can be regulated in every school district for any position through enactment of policies specifying a specific period of time for exhibiting proficiency in a newly assigned position. Within this time frame, as defined by the probationary period either through statutory requirements or policy enactments, unsatisfactory employees can be nonrenewed at the prerogative of management without infringing on any property rights of employees.

Nonrenewals involve failing to reemploy rather than failing to discharge unsatisfactory employees. By using nonrenewals rather than discharges as a method for addressing less than satisfactory performance, many legal entanglements can be avoided because statutory conditions associated both with due process and property rights of employees fail to come into play (Valente & Valente, 2005). As such, the nonrenewal of existing employees creates recruitment opportunities to replace departing personnel once part of the current workforce.

Beyond maintenance needs replacing departing personnel within the recruitment context due to either voluntary or nonvoluntary departures, some vacancies occur in a public school district because new positions are created to fill organizational needs. New positions are created to accommodate expanding enrollments, to bring in special talents, or to accommodate newly configured organizational structures. For school districts experiencing enrollment growth, additional personnel must be recruited to meet emerging organizational needs attributed to growth.

To meet mandates of federal legislation (NCLB) and to acquire employees as suggested by ISLLC standards, most all public school districts need to recruit special talents. Likewise, to address concerns of the public relative to competency-based testing; new organizational configurations are being considered by some public school districts. As such, recruitment involves both short- and long-range planning activities in the staffing of a public school district.

Short-range staffing efforts are needed to meet current demands for personnel that exist in every organization as a result of retirements, turnovers, nonrenewals, expanding enrollments, and new organizational configurations. On the other hand, long-term staffing activities are designed to ensure a future supply of qualified personnel through a well-established program involving proactive recruitment. Both short-term and long-term activities are important because an extensive and aggressive program of recruitment are critical to the effectiveness of the organization by having a well-qualified

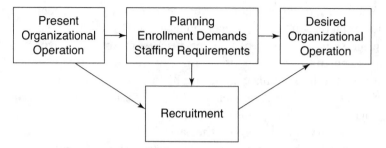

FIGURE 4.1   *Linking functions of the strategic planning process with recruitment.*

workforce as required by the No Child Left Behind Act (n.d.) and as suggested by ISLLC (n.d.) standards for administrators in guiding a public school district.

The links with the human resource planning process (Chapter 1), student enrollment demands (Chapter 2), and staffing requirements (Chapter 3) dictate the need for an effective recruitment program to advance a public school district from the current state of operation to a desired state of operation as determined from a strategic planning perspective. Functionally, this organizational metamorphosis is illustrated in Figure 4.1 through interconnecting specific elements as found within the strategic planning process to the operational directive involving recruitment.

As an operational function within the strategic planning process, recruitment should be driven by the organizational goals and by the district objectives emanating from the mission statement of a public school district. Lending purpose and direction to organizational goals and to district objectives within the recruitment process are formal policies adopted by a school district. Formal policies are needed at the local school district level because several viable yet competing avenues exist for directing recruitment strategies relative to the accomplishment of these strategic planning objectives.

When viewed from an organizational perspective, there is a set of internal and external environmental circumstances (facts and events—the recruitment contexture) that must be considered in developing the recruitment strategies, the programs, and the processes by which these strategies are implemented in the field setting. Many of these factors must be determined long before the recruitment process is implemented and long before the recruitment process reaches individuals as potential applicants. Some of these factors involve policy directives by boards of education, and many of these factors impact administrative actions on the part of educators implementing the recruitment process from a strategic planning perspective.

Administrative actions are warranted in situations where decision makers require data on specific recruitment alternatives and in situations where procedures are needed to implement certain policies. More specifically, data are needed concerning immediate as well as long-range staffing needs, as illustrated in Chapters 2 and 3, and for guiding the diversification of the present workforce relative to a relevant labor market (to be discussed). Based on the information provided by administrators, school boards should formulate specific recruitment policies that guide recruitment practices complementing the mission statement, district goals, and organizational objectives derived from the strategic planning process.

Most importantly and as noted previously, recruitment policies are needed in situations where more than one acceptable alternative exists, and where each alternative produces either a unique outcome or a specific recruitment directive-informing practice. The task of the school board is to evaluate the impact of various recruitment alternatives for the district and to develop recruitment policies and practices for guiding the district among choices. By approving certain recruitment policies and practices, boards of education set both the tone and the direction for recruitment activities from a strategic planning perspective.

Indeed, effective recruitment must be sensitive to changes and must be guided by the intent of policies. It is through the activities of the recruitment process that the system attracts specific types of willing and able candidates to fill existing as well as anticipated position vacancies meeting the human resource needs of any particular school district. Each of these activities is examined as an interdependent element, along with other components of the planning system relative to recruitment.

It is important to emphasize that effective recruitment can minimize problems that may follow the selection, the **placement,** and the maintenance of personnel in the pursuit of goals and objectives as set forth by a mission statement adopted by a public school district. Without an adequate as well as a willing pool of applicants from which to choose among potential job candidates, the execution of many of the operational directives comprising the human resource function will be rendered ineffective. For example, when recruitment yields the same number of candidates as the number of position vacancies to be filled in a public school district, selection is replaced by assignment, and an important operational directive (selection) within the strategic planning process is underutilized.

Within the recruitment phase of the strategic planning process, attention must be given early on to specific policies for guiding the recruitment activities. Although all these policies involve discretion, some of these policies are mandatory (with nested discretionary intents), while other polices are permissive (requiring a preferred stance on the part of a public school district). Within the following sections of this chapter, a differentiation is made between mandatory and permissive policy stances either to be adopted or to be considered by a public school district in the operation and implementation of the recruitment function from a strategic planning perspective.

Mandatory Recruitment Policies

By law, all public school districts must follow mandated public employment legislation in the recruitment and selection of employees and should develop well-formularized policies reflecting their intentions. Failure to do so by boards of education may bring about judicial sanctions for the district as well as for those responsible for decision making within the district if formal challenges are made by parties with a vested interest (Valente & Valente, 2005). Given the potential for legal challenges, it behooves those responsible for the recruitment and selection of employees to be knowledgeable about federal and state legislation pertaining to the recruitment and the selection processes both from a legal and from a practical perspective relative to fulfilling system needs and obligations for staffing the organization.

Federal and state legislation pertaining to recruitment and to selection is designed to prohibit illegal discrimination, and, in some instances, to correct for past discrimination associated with specific protection protected class groups. This legislation does so by identifying certain individuals or groups on the basis of definable characteristics such as gender, race, age, national origin, and so on. Individuals or groups possessing at least one of these definable characteristics are afforded protection from discrimination within the employment context if discrimination within the employment context is related, at least **in part,** to a defined group characteristic as defined by existing legislation (i.e., sex, age, national origin).

The term in part is bolded in the previous sentence for a reason. Within the employment context, it is a legal term and it has an important interpretation for describing outcomes. In part is interpreted literally to mean only tangentially related and not to mean controlling/influencing outcomes in totality.

Individuals covered by these legislative acts are said to have a protected class status within the employment process. The general term **protected class status** replaces the earlier term **minority** within the general human resource literature due to the categorical inclusion of females as a protected class group of individuals. Because females represent the majority sex and have a protected class status as defined by Title VII of the Civil Rights Act **(http://www.eeoc.gov/laws/vii.html),** the term minority, within the human resource context, is no longer applicable in this general body of literature and has been replaced by the term *protected class status.*

Examples of some of the major legislation defining protected class status pertaining to the employment process are found in Figure 4.2. This list is by no means exhaustive, but it is meant to be illustrative and contains only examples of some federal laws particularly applicable to the recruitment and selection processes in the public school setting. These laws, many of which have been in existence for decades, establish minimum requirements for recruitment and selection within the public sector but have been overlooked by many public school districts in actual practice when planning and executing many operational procedures comprising the human resource functions in the public school setting (recruitment, selection, compensation, assignment, and retention).

Premier among these federal acts as noted in Figure 4.2 is Title VII of the Civil Rights Act. Title VII of the Civil Rights Act is one of the oldest acts and has set both the tone and the direction for most other federal/state legislation concerning equal employment

Title VII Civil Rights Act	Section 504 of Rehabilitation Act
Age Discrimination in Employment Act	Americans with Disabilities Act

FIGURE 4.2   *Important federal legislative acts impacting human resources in the public school setting.*

opportunities. This act covers all private employers with fifteen or more employees, and all federal, state, and local governments including all public school systems as well as most private school systems.

Encompassed by Title VII of the Civil Rights Act are several protected class groups. Protected class groups are defined by this act on the basis of race, color, religion, national origin, and sex. With only a few exceptions (to be discussed later), it is illegal to discriminate within the employment context on the basis of these particular protected class statuses.

Another legislative act with important employment implications is the Age Discrimination in Employment Act (n.d.). Protective class status is afforded within the Age Discrimination in Employment Act (ADEA) to all individuals 40 years of age and older. Interestingly, initially the ADEA exempted from coverage educators but was amended later to include specifically educators as a protected class group worthy of protection on the basis of chronological age.

At present, only one specific group of employees within the educational setting have been exempted from ADEA by state laws. This group is bus drivers, and several states set an upper limit for age requirements of bus drivers beyond once exceeded can no longer be employed by a public school district in this specific capacity. Functionally, for this particular group of employees, age is a **bona fide occupational qualification** (BFOQ).

Section 504 of the Rehabilitation Act (n.d.) was the first piece of federal legislation to address handicapping conditions of individuals within the employment context and affording a protected class status to these individuals. In general, this act was interpreted initially to cover individuals having only physical handicaps (mobility, sight, hearing, etc.) that failed to affect their performance of required job functions with reasonable accommodations on the part of the employer. However, due to narrow interpretations of disabilities, the basic intents of this act were expanded to include other groups through more specific legislation.

Specifically, for individuals "otherwise" qualified to perform essential job duties with the aid of reasonable accommodations on the part of employers, the Americans with Disabilities Act (n.d.) was passed. More clearly defined within the Americans with Disabilities Act (ADA) than within Section 504 of the Rehabilitation Act are physical as well as mental impairments. The ADA addresses physiological conditions (such as AIDS, cancer, etc.) as well as psychological conditions (mental illness, substance abuse, etc.).

In addition to the requirements as set forth by existing federal legislation, states and school boards can define additional protected classes as long as these newly defined protected classes do not conflict with those characteristics addressed by existing federal legislation and represent a group disproportionably represented in the labor force due to a group characteristic. For example, several states have awarded protected class status on the basis of sexual preference of potential applicants as well as existing employees (see Table 4.1). Because federal legislation is silent with respect to sexual preference, these states have expanded beyond existing federal legislation the legal obligations for public school districts within the recruitment, selection, and employment process in particular states.

To guide the recruitment and the selection processes of a system, school boards should adopt district policies prior to executing any recruitment or selection activities. One important policy concerns whether the school district will be proactive or reactive

TABLE 4.1
States Passing Sexual Preference Legislation

California	Massachusetts	New Jersey
Connecticut	Minnesota	Rhode Island
Hawaii	Nevada	Vermont
Maryland	New Hampshire	Wisconsin

relative to protected class groups within the recruitment and selection processes. That is, a school district can adopt either an **equal employment opportunity** perspective (proactive) or an **affirmative action** perspective (reactive). Differences between these policy perspectives have a profound influence on the actual recruitment and selection practices exercised by a school district from a strategic planning perspective.

The equal employment opportunity perspective should be proactive both in intent and in application. "As applied to staffing, EEO refers to practices that are designated and used in a **'facially neutral'** manner, meaning that all applicants and employees are treated similarly without regard to protected class characteristics such as race and sex" (Heneman, Judge, & Heneman, 2000, p. 62). This perspective implies that recruitment and selection practices, procedures, and policies will be based solely on the principle of merit and that recruitment and selection practices will be followed without regard to the protected class status of individuals within the decision-making context.

In contrast to the equal opportunity perspective that is facially neutral relative to the protected class status of individuals, the affirmative action perspective is proactive and favors certain protected class groups within the recruitment/selection context. Justification for this favoritism is rooted in correcting past injustices incurred by protected class groups. To correct past injustices, a school board can adopt recruitment and selection policies that give preferential treatment to certain protected class groups using an affirmative action policy as opposed to an equal employment opportunity policy.

To illustrate the difference between the equal employment opportunity and affirmative action perspectives via formalized policy adopted by a particular school district, consider the following examples. An equal employment opportunity policy would state that "all recruitment and selection decisions will be made without regard to any protected class status." On the other hand, an affirmative action policy would state that "if a protected class individual and a nonprotected class individual are deemed to be equally qualified for employment, preference will be given to the protected class individual."

Given some confusion about equally qualified employees, more permissive language has surfaced in this area. Equally qualified has been substituted in some instances with qualified. Qualified has been interpreted to be possessing only the minimum qualifications for performing the job under consideration.

Depending on the school board's choice between the equal employment opportunity perspective and the affirmative action perspective, a distinct message is communicated, specific recruitment directives are set forth, and certain legal obligations are established relative to recruitment/selection. Problems, including legal difficulties, may occur when the actions and intentions of school boards and system employees are counter to the school board's formal employment policy. For example, if a school board adopts the equal employment opportunity perspective and later gives preferential treatment to individuals on the basis of their protected class status, then a violation has been committed.

That is, if a protected class person and a nonprotected class person are deemed to be equally qualified, then the final employment decisions must be made on the basis of facially neutral criteria from an equal employment opportunity perspective. Interestingly, one facially neutral criterion is the flip of a nonbiased coin. This decisional criterion favors neither individual on the basis of a protected characteristic and is a facially neutral method for selecting employees otherwise equally qualified.

Along the same line of reasoning, if a school board adopts an affirmative action policy, then preferential treatment should be provided for an identified protected class person over a nonprotected class person possessing equal qualifications. Controlling outcomes when qualifications are equal is protected class status. Failure to afford this deference on the part of a school district to a protected class person is a violation of an affirmative action policy.

However, the actual choice on the part of policy makers between the equal opportunity and the affirmative action perspective is not entirely arbitrary. This choice should be tempered by system specifics relative to certain external and internal information relative to the composition of the current workforce. External and internal information needed for informing the policy-making process relative to these two different perspectives (equal opportunity vs. affirmative action) can be obtained through well-established procedures that impart poignant information about the workforce of a public school district.

Information Needs and Mandatory Recruitment Policies

As noted previously in this chapter, policies related to recruitment and selection should not be formulated in a vacuum but should be guided by the recruitment contexture of a public school system. Factors external and internal to the school district must be considered when constructing policy about recruitment and selection in light of mandatory policies. One external factor that must be considered is the **relevant labor market** because the relative labor market determines what the composition of a school district should be for different protected class groups within any particular public school district from a legislative perspective.

The relevant labor market is a legal term. As a legal term, it is defined as the distance that an applicant could reasonably be expected to travel for employment consideration when seeking a position with a particular school system. Most important within this definition, distance, as used in defining a relevant labor market, is related only "to the consideration" of an applicant for employment, not to "the daily commute of an employee" once an individual is selected. More succinctly, a differentiation is made between consideration and selection in the above definition.

Because different kinds of applicants (classified employees, faculty members, or administrative groups) could be expected to travel varying distances for employment consideration at the preemployment stage of the selection process, the relevant labor market varies by the type of position within a school district. For some positions, the distance may be only a few miles (clerical), for still others it may be several hundred miles (teacher), and yet for other positions it may be national in scope (administrators). Consequently, for any particular protected class group, their representation in the composition of a district's workforce varies by occupational grouping (type of position—classified, certificated, or administrative) rather than being a fixed number for the school district at large and applicable to all school districts in general.

In addition, a relevant labor market can vary not only by employee groupings but by geographical regions depending on the availability of the potential labor market. For some school districts located in highly populated states (e.g., New York), the relevant labor market is smaller than in other states with sparse populations. In contrast, for less populated states (e.g., Montana), individuals, as applicants, might be expected to travel greater distances to be considered for employment opportunities.

It is important to note, however, that the composition of the educational workforce comprising a specific school district is not directly related to the composition of the student body within any said school district, at least from a legal perspective. From a practical perspective in some school districts, it may be highly desirable to have the composition of a workforce within a school district mirror student bodies. This would be true especially when role models are needed or desired for student bodies.

At first glance, the legal requirement based on a relevant labor market may appear to be detrimental for diversifying school systems. However, to link diversity of staffing strictly to diversity of students would be more detrimental than the use of a relevant labor market because many districts across the nation have few, if any, diverse students. However, the relevant labor market for these districts will reflect almost always a need for a diverse workforce beyond the composition of student bodies as well as the diversity of the current workforce.

In addition to the external assessment of relevant labor markets for protected class persons, an internal assessment should be made relative to the distribution of protected class persons employed by a school district. This latter assessment or **diversity analysis** should reflect the number of protected class persons employed by the district and the types of positions held by protected class persons within the district. By obtaining data on the number of persons employed and the types of positions they hold, the school board can assess the organizational distribution of protected class persons within a district and can tailor their recruitment and selection policies accordingly.

Data concerning the relevant labor markets for different positions and for the distribution of protected class persons within a school district are captured by two different statistics: (a) a stock statistic and (b) a concentration statistic. **Stock statistics** provide information about the employment of protected class persons in relation to the relevant labor market for these persons. **Concentration statistics** provide information about the assignment of protected class persons at various organizational levels within the district's hierarchy.

Both stock statistics and concentration statistics should be calculated for each group of protected class persons within the relevant labor market for various occupational groupings comprising the workforce of a school system. Without this information it is unlikely that a school district can formulate adequate recruitment and selection policies necessary for attracting and retaining a diverse group of employees. To illustrate stock and concentration statistics, several examples are provided.

Within these examples, for simplicity of presentation, the general term *protected class* is used rather than *specific protected classes* as found in Table 4.1. In actual practice, these statistics would be computed for each protected class group when performing analyses for diversity of a workforce in the public school setting. Also, these statistics should be calculated for all employee groupings but only selective groupings (classified, instructional, and administrator) are used in these examples for purpose of illustration. Again, as just stated, an aggregated group classification label is used for all protected classes rather than addressing each specific group of protected class persons separately (i.e., race, sex, national origin) as should be done in the field setting when performing a diversity analysis (see Table 4.2).

The stock statistics in Table 4.2 indicate a distinct difference in the distribution of protected class persons employed by the school district and protected class persons available in the relevant labor market. The percentage of protected class persons employed by the school district is only 6 percent and their workforce potential is 15 percent. On the other hand, the percentage of nonprotected class persons employed by the school district is 94 percent and their workforce potential is 85 percent. This difference between those available and those employed indicates an underutilization of protected class persons relative to their availability in the relevant labor market and an overrepresentation for nonprotected class individuals.

To illustrate concentration statistics for informing mandatory recruitment policies, two examples are provided. In the first example, protected and nonprotected groups are broken down by classification levels (support, certificated, and administrative). These data are found in Table 4.3.

TABLE 4.2
Stock Statistics for a Hypothetical School District

Available Applicants	Current Employees	Differences
Protected = 15%	Protected = 6%	9%
Nonprotected = 85%	Nonprotected = 94%	−9%

TABLE 4.3
Concentration Statistics for Different Classifications

	Support Personnel	Certificated Positions	Administrator Positions
Protected class	90%	65%	10%
Nonprotected class	10%	35%	90%

As can be observed in Table 4.3, the percentage of protected class persons varies considerably by employee grouping. Protected class individuals are overrepresented in support positions and are underrepresented in administrator positions. Because these data concern only actual employees (as compared to stock statistics), important information is afforded from a policy perspective.

In actual practice, concentration statistics should be compiled also in a manner that reflects career progression within different employee classifications. This involves dividing broad employee groupings in some meaningful ways. For example, the administrator group could be divided according to line and staff positions, as well as according to organizational levels of employees.

More specifically, elementary school principals differ from secondary school principals in some very important ways, and concentration statistics should reflect these ways. Elementary school principals tend to earn lower salaries, to be employed for fewer days during the contractual work year, and to have a different career progression (80 percent of superintendents have a secondary school background). A further refinement of concentration statistics is found in Table 4.4.

Based on these hypothetical data as contained in Table 4.4 reflecting concentration statistics, most of the protected class principals hold elementary principal positions. If, for example, this protected class group represents females, then females are underutilized at the high school principal level. Given organizational advantages associated with high school principals (i.e., workday pay, promotion opportunities) as compared to elementary principals, important recruitment implications exist for this particular group of protected class persons.

Data provided by stock and concentration statistics guide boards of education in formulating systemwide policies for recruitment and selection. This information should be used in determining whether the system will be an equal opportunity employer or an affirmative action employer. It can also be used to guide the development of other policies and procedures that impact recruitment and selection, such as those federal acts listed in Table 4.2.

In addition to mandatory policies directing the recruitment phase of the human resource function, there exist a number of permissive policies. Unlike mandatory policies where a specific stance is required, permissive employment polices require no definitive stance but provide a public school district with options for informing the recruitment process and to legitimizing the recruitment process in light of local school districts' norms and expectations. However, by taking a definitive stance relative to certain permissive topics, school districts can enhance the recruitment efforts and can prevent many future problems with respect to newly recruited employees relative to postemployment expectations on the part of both the school system and the employees.

TABLE 4.4
Concentrations Statistics Reflecting within Group Differences

	Elementary Principals	Middle School Principals	High School Principals
Protected class	70%	50%	20%
Nonprotected class	30%	50%	80%

Permissive Employment Policy and Recruitment

Recruitment is an essential part of a comprehensive human resource plan from a strategic planning perspective. The more today's school boards and school administrators consider the educational problems they are expected to solve, the more clearly they realize that they cannot succeed unless the organization is competently staffed (Marshall & Gerstl-Pepin, 2005). Most all competently staffed organizations rely on an effective and efficient recruitment process to fill either existing or emerging vacancies within a public school district.

An effective and efficient recruitment processes is driven by and is grounded with definitive policy statements relative to certain mandatory as well as to certain permissive issues. To be clear and enforceable, recruitment policies should be written and should be codified in a policy manual, should inform every individual and agency of system standards, and should minimize uncertainties within the employment process for all stakeholders. Without policy guidelines for decisions and actions concerning recruitment activities, inconsistencies that develop will cause dissatisfaction and will defeat the aims of the human resource function in moving a public school district from the current state of operation to a desired state of operation.

In addition to affording direction to a public school district within the recruitment process, policies can be stabilizing. That is, policies provide for the continuity of the personnel process within the public school setting across time. As a managerial technique within the strategic planning process, policies bridge gaps in time through linking the past with the future.

Within the public school setting both policy makers and school administrators relinquish their assignments for various reasons creating voids in leadership and in vision (Cunningham & Cordeiro, 2006). These voids in leadership and in vision are filled by new constituents lacking an organizational history for recruitment practices without the aid of formalized recruitment policies. Formalized recruitment policies provide this history and promote a level of continuity for new leadership as well as for continuing personnel.

For purposes of continuity over time within the recruitment context, policy decisions are needed on certain topics that are unaddressed by the legislative process and warrant special consideration in the direct recruitment efforts on the part of local school districts. Included in Figure 4.3 are some of the most troublesome issues surfacing frequently within the recruitment process at the school district level. For each of these topics as found in Figure 4.3, the public school district is served best when a definitive stance is taken by the school district and when potential employees are apprised about the district's view within the recruitment stage of the employment process through formal policy enactments.

Without exception, all the issues as found in Figure 4.3 have important recruitment implications for the organization as well as for the recruits, and all these issues escape a single definitive recommendation applicable to every school district. What is acceptable in some school districts is totally unacceptable in other school districts. Differentiating between acceptable and unacceptable policy stances within a public school district are the local norms of the community and the philosophies of the boards of education.

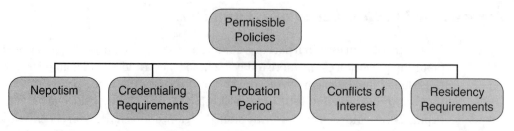

FIGURE 4.3   *Permissive recruitment policies.*

For example, nepotism involves favoring certain types of potential employees within the recruitment/selection process and is most generally associated with immediate family members and more specifically associated with spousal employment in the public school setting. Although in the past antinepotism polices were common, today with many educators having family units comprised of dual-career education professionals, many potential recruits expect as well as need assistance for relocation if they are to relocate.

An antinepotism policy could be a very limiting factor within the recruitment context and may need the attention of policy makers at the local school district level. Although public school districts have been less accommodating in this area, other public institutions (especially universities) have taken a proactive stance. Indeed, it is not uncommon today to find many higher-education institutions that have a spousal employment/assistance policy to facilitate the recruitment of preferred individuals.

In many instances, these policies involve employment within the institution for a significant other. On the other hand, these policies may provide support for the employment of a significant other in a different organization. It is not uncommon for higher-educational organizations to provide economic incentives to other employers through partial salary support for spouses during a defined period (usually one year), and an approach worthy of consideration by some public school districts.

Another policy area that should be resolved within the recruitment context concerns how conflicts of interest are defined in light of local community expectations. It is not uncommon for music teachers to supplement their income by providing private lessons outside the school day or for school psychologists to offer their services on a consulting basis to the community at large. Depending on a particular school district's perspective, such extracurricular activities may or may not be acceptable but any particular stance taken has important recruitment implications for many viable job candidates within a competitive job market.

Even though all individuals need to possess the appropriate credential for their assigned position once employed, whether or not they possess this credential at the time of recruitment and/or selection is within the policy domain. At one time, most all school districts had recruitment policies suggesting that for individuals to be considered within the recruitment/selection process they must be duly certified. For hard-to-find special areas (special education/vocational education students with anticipated graduation dates) or for most any educators recruited from out of state, important recruitment implications exist because many potential job candidates may not have certifications in hand at the recruitment stage of the employment process.

In many instances, school districts have addressed certification issues through employment offers rather than through recruitment policies. That is, employment offers are tendered conditional on candidates obtaining valid certification for a defined position as a condition of ratifying an employment contract. If individuals being recruited and recommended are unable to obtain certification, then the employment offer is invalidated as per contractual offering.

Concerns about residency requirements for employees has waxed and waned in recent times, and "unless forbidden by state law, school boards may require teachers and other employees to reside within the employing district" (Valente & Valente, 2005, p. 158). Underlying this permissive policy perspective is that employees paid in part by the local economy should reside within the specific location. Interestingly, residency policies can be established relative to specific employee groups and need not cover all employee groups.

It is not uncommon for a residency policy to cover only superintendents, but this policy can be expanded to cover other employee groups at the discretion of a board of education. From an implementation point of view, residency policies can be either **proactive** or **retroactive.** For retroactive residency policies, courts have ruled consistently that employees be afforded a reasonable time to comply (usually seven years).

Probationary periods associated with particular positions have important implications for the recruitment process. Although some positions have statutory probationary periods as defined by state legislation with teachers being a point in example (spring notification), most other positions are unaddressed in the legislation and left to the discretion of the school district. As such, public school districts should address this issue via a recruitment policy, and potential applicants should be so apprised at the recruitment stage of the employment process.

Having established certain policy perspectives relative to mandatory as well as permissive issues within the recruitment process, other information is needed early on within the recruitment planning stage from a strategic planning perspective before actual contact is made with potential applicants. To accommodate staffing needs as defined by student enrollment projections (see Chapter 2) and to fill positions as revealed through long-range staffing plans (see Chapter 3), additional information is needed before the implementation stage of recruitment as an operational directive in the field setting.

Information is needed about positions and position requirements for the vacancies to be filled at the recruitment phase of the employment process when following a strategic planning perspective. The strategic planning mechanism used to provide this information is a job analysis, and the medium for communicating this information to potential job candidates is a **job description.** To provide this information for successful strategic planning relative to the human resource function is the focus of the next section of this chapter.

Position and Personal Information for Recruitment

Within this section, a **position** is defined as a collection of tasks constituting the total work assignment of a single employee. To capture these tasks in a meaningful way, information is needed about purpose, requirements, and major job duties associated with positions. Without adequate position information to complement the mission statement, organizational goals, and district objectives, benefits of strategic planning for recruitment can never be fully realized by an educational organization.

To obtain this information within the strategic planning process as needed for the operational directive involving recruitment requires the conduct of a **job analysis.** A job analysis is a managerial technique used for collecting and for summarizing information according to established guidelines. When conducted properly, information from a job analysis serves several other human resource operational directives other than just recruitment.

More specifically, information obtained from a job analysis has important implications for selection of applicants and for assignment of employees. Without valid information about position expectations, selection as well as assignment is an unguided activity. Both selection and assignment require matching the qualifications of individuals to the tasks associated with particular positions.

Job analysis information is fundamental to the operational human resource function involving compensation. Within the compensation context, economic worth is determined largely by positions rather than by the characteristic of individuals holding the position. Individuals can be either underemployed or overemployed for their assigned position, but the value of a position should be fixed in light of defined components revealed through a job analysis.

For the evaluation of individuals through a formalized appraisal process, information from a job analysis is indispensable. Information from a job analysis sets standards and expectations for performance of employees in their assigned positions from an organizational perspective. Without indicators of expected performance, appraisal as a human resource function is a meaningless activity serving only to satisfy statutory requirements as specified either by school policy or by labor contracts.

When conducting a job analysis, it is important to emphasize again that a job analysis focuses on the tasks comprising the job rather than on the person performing the job. Jobs are controlled by the organization and encapsulate specific tasks, while the person performing the tasks can be effective or ineffective, qualified or unqualified, and can change jobs. More specifically, job analysis should be directed to what tasks should be performed, how these tasks should be performed, and why these tasks are performed (Young, 2006).

Job analysis should not be taken lightly or performed unsystematically by those responsible for conducting this important managerial activity. Acceptable techniques and standard procedures should be followed because several of the federal acts listed in Table 4.1 consider job analysis to be a crucial process. In fact, the outcome of many legal challenges involving recruitment, selection, assignment, compensation, and appraisal has been and continues to be decided on the basis of how well the job analysis was performed by an educational organization (HR-Guide, n.d.).

Job Analysis

A formal job analysis should be performed before any applicants are recruited. Written records should be maintained to document the job analysis processes and the procedures used by a school system when performing this administrative activity. At a minimum, these records should describe the procedures used to identify job content and the qualifications of persons who conduct the job analysis.

Several different procedures/sources are used to identify job content for a job analysis. These procedures/sources include interviews, observations, questionnaires, supervisors, publications, and experts (Job Analysis, n.d.). Typically, the more procedures/sources used to assess job content, the richer the information yield and the easier the defense of the job analysis when challenges are made about outcomes from any of the human resource directives as previously noted (e.g., recruitment, selection, assignment, compensation, and appraisal).

Most common among these procedures used to conduct a job analysis are interviews. When the targeted positions exist within an educational organization, interviews are conducted with actual job incumbents. Most generally, a structured interview guide is followed, and actual job incumbents are asked to describe their work tasks.

In other instances involving current positions within an educational organization, a job analyst may rely on observation of actual work behavior performed by an employee(s) rather than verbal reports of job incumbents. Using the observational method for job analysis, the job analyst observes and records the job tasks performed by a position holder. This technique assumes that most job tasks are routine and are performed within the observational period covered by the job analysis. Otherwise, for nonroutine tasks, a time sampling must be employed to capture the noncyclical aspects of particular positions.

Less labor intensive than either the interview protocol or the observational techniques for obtaining information about positions found within the current organizational structure of a school district involves the use of questionnaires to assess job tasks. Questionnaires for assessing job tasks can be constructed at the local school district level or can be purchased from commercial sources. One well-recognized commercial questionnaire is the *Position Analysis Questionnaire* (Heneman & Judge, 2006).

Bridging the gap for job information between existing jobs within an educational organization and/or proposed jobs yet to be staffed within an educational organization is the supervisor. Because supervisors oversee or are expected to oversee the work performed by job holders, supervisors may be the best source of information about job tasks and job requirements. As such, information provided by supervisors provides the source of information for the job analysis.

For many proposed jobs new to an educational organization, still other sources of information may be needed to describe job requirements. One source for this information is published literature describing various jobs and the requirements associated with these jobs. Most notable among these published sources is the *Dictionary of Occupational Titles* (n.d.), which is a well-accepted source afforded great deference relative to jobs and job requirements within the private sector as well as within the public sector.

Another source of information discussed for acquiring information about jobs and job requirements involves the use of experts. Experts are those individuals purported to have knowledge about jobs and job requirements derived from an experiential and/or from a knowledge base. Included among experts are those having held similar types of jobs or those having experience with the different tasks associated with a particular type of job.

If school districts lack either the technical skills with existing employees or the luxury of time required for conducting an adequate job analysis, external agents or agencies may be employed. It is not unusual to hire private consultants or state school boards associations to perform a job analysis. The major downside of this last approach is cost, but, in the long run, this expense may represent a wise use of funds.

When appropriately formulated and when effectively executed, the job analysis should yield 15–25 different job task statements for most jobs (Heneman et al., 2000). After important job tasks have been identified through one or more of the data-collection techniques just described, the next step in the job analysis process is to group different job tasks by common characteristics or dimensions, such as instruction, supervision, communication, and so on. This requires a great deal of theorizing by those who are responsible for conducting a job analysis. "As a rule, there should be four to eight dimensions, depending on the number of tasks statements" associated with a job (Heneman & Judge, 2006, p. 151).

Information, as obtained from the job analysis and as aligned with different job dimensions, is incorporated generally into a job description. Job descriptions should play a very important role within the strategic planning process for all public school districts. Consequently, specific attention is devoted to this very important managerial tool from a strategic planning perspective.

Job Descriptions

Formal outcomes derived from most job analyses processes are job descriptions (Young, 2006). Job descriptions along with mandatory and permissive policy statements provide the informational grist for recruitment from a strategic planning perspective. Individuals as potential applicants as well as educators as actual recruiters need these types of information to be informed participants within the recruitment process.

With respect to information imparted by job descriptions, a specific format is recommended. This format contains different headings with each heading serving a unique purpose. Contained in Figure 4.4 is a depiction of each heading and following is a discussion of the information suggested for the different headings.

Unsurprisingly, the first heading involves listing the job title for the position. However, immediately following the job title should be a set of parentheses encapsulating the number of persons within a particular school district holding this position. This later information can be very informative for certain types of positions within the recruitment process.

For example, if the position is for a supervisor or for a coordinator lacking a universal definition in the public school setting, the number of persons holding this position within a particular school district can be informative to potential applicants. Whether this number is

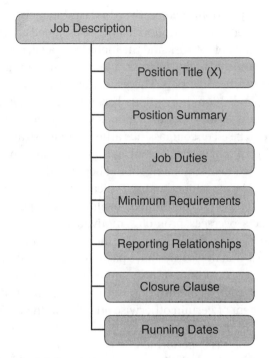

FIGURE 4.4 *Headings for job descriptions.*

one or a larger number conveys important information to a potential applicant about a vacant position. The smaller the number of position holders associated with a particular job, the more prestigious the position is in most instances within the organizational hierarchy.

The second heading suggested for a job description involves a position summary (see Figure 4.4). A position summary should describe the intent of a job in the fewest words possible to avoid confusion and to capture the overall purpose of the position within a particular school district's organizational hierarchy. With respect to an elementary school principal, the position summary could state "Responsible for the organization and operation of an elementary school building."

Heading three, as found in Figure 4.4, represents the body of the job description and should describe the major job tasks performed by a position holder. When describing the job tasks performed by a position holder, certain recommendations are made concerning the construction of the job task statements. These recommendations address the number of job task statements, the wording of job task statements, and the importance of job statements (relevancy and frequency).

The number of job task statements included within the body of a job description should be limited to no more than ten descriptors in most all instances. Each of these statements should reflect a specific dimension as identified by the job analysis with a single exception. This exception is the last statement that should include "completes other duties as assigned."

From an operational perspective, this last statement is very important. First, it prolongs the timeliness of a job description relative to assigned activities. Second, it alerts employees about the fluidity of job task and the inability of a job description to capture all job tasks.

It is not unusual to find job task statements spanning several pages in job descriptions used by many school districts. There are, however, several downsides to this practice. Most notably, expanded job descriptions become quickly dated due to the fluidity needed to meet emerging organizational demands imposed on most position holders and are over-interpreted to be all encompassing rather than illustrative of major job duties.

Wording of job task statements within a job description should be written in present tense. Every job task statement should begin with an action verb describing activities to be performed by a position holder. Typical action verbs used to describe job tasks are su-pervises, administers, coordinates, evaluates, completes, determines, performs, sched-ules, conducts, oversees, promotes, motivates, etc.

Potential job task statements for inclusion in a job description can vary in two important ways, and these ways have particular implications related to the Americans with Disabilities Act. Most importantly, actual job tasks can vary in relevance and frequency. Both of these sources of variation have a potential for influencing the recruitment and the employment of certain otherwise qualified individuals.

Relevance concerns the centrality of a particular job task for a specific position. No doubt, some job tasks performed by position holders are more relevant than other job tasks performed when fulfilling assigned duties. A highly relevant task is one germane to satisfactory performance of a position with or without reasonable accommodations.

In addition to the relevancy of job tasks, frequency of performance for any job task is another issue to be considered when constructing job descriptions within the recruitment context, especially from an ADA perspective. Some job tasks can be highly relevant but performed very infrequently by position holders. As such, not all position holders may be expected to perform these tasks if others are relatively available in the work setting who can perform infrequent job tasks.

To ensure that all job task statements included in job descriptions used to recruit individuals for vacant positions meet criteria addressing relevancy and frequency, an assessment should be performed. Contained in Figure 4.5 is a simple format that can be used to assess the relevancy and the frequency of job task statements before formalizing the job description. Following this format and compiling empirical data about each job task including in formalized job descriptions would serve well public school districts and is highly recommended in light of federal legislation as found in Figure 4.5.

For every vacant job within a public school district, there exist certain *minimum job requirements* expected of applicants at the recruitment stage of the employment process. Collectively, these requirements have been labeled as knowledge, skills, and abilities (KSAs). These KSAs should be described within the job description under the specific heading labeled as minimum requirements (see Figure 4.4).

By knowing these minimum KSA requirements at the recruitment stage of the selection process, applicants can self-select either into or out of further employment consideration. Also, by being apprised of KSAs, organizational representatives can advise

---

Assessment Instrument

Tasks A

How relevant is Task A to successfully performing your job?
_____ Highly Relevant   _____ Moderately Relevant   _____ Not Relevant

How often do you perform Task A when fulfilling your job requirements?
_____ Daily   _____ Weekly   _____ Monthly   _____ Very Seldom

Tasks B

How relevant is Task B to successfully performing your job?
_____ Highly Relevant   _____ Moderately Relevant   _____ Not Relevant

How often do you perform Task B when fulfilling your job requirements?
_____ Daily   _____ Weekly   _____ Monthly   _____ Very Seldom

Tasks N

How relevant is Task N to successfully performing your job?
_____ Highly Relevant   _____ Moderately Relevant   _____ Not Relevant

How often do you perform Task N when fulfilling your job requirements?
_____ Daily   _____ Weekly   _____ Monthly   _____ Very Seldom

---

FIGURE 4.5   *Instrument for assessing relevancy and frequency of task performed by a position holder.*

potential applicants within the recruitment process concerning their viability as a perspective employee. However, the actual definitions of KSAs are often glossed over and afforded little attention within the recruitment process from a strategic planning perspective.

Indeed, minimum requirements as described in job descriptions through well-defined KSAs establish a threshold for consideration of potential applicants within the recruitment process. Because of this gate-keeping function performed by KSAs, minimum requirements as listed in job descriptions have received considerable scrutiny within the employment process from a legal perspective. In light of this scrutiny by federal agencies and courts, several general principles have evolved for assessing the validity of minimum KSA requirements relative to the attraction and to the selection of employees.

One general principal emerging in this body of literature concerns the "least qualified job incumbent." The least qualified job incumbent within a public school district holding a specific position sets the upper level for job qualifications as specified by KSAs. By default, if this person can perform the job effectively as evidenced through continuing employment with a school district, then this person (**least qualified job incumbent**) possesses the necessary knowledge, skills, and abilities for a vacant position.

Another general principle for establishing minimum requirements of a position as described by a job description pertains to the use of proxy measures to capture the intents of KSAs. Proxy measures should not be used in lieu of actual measures of KSAs in most instances, especially if actual measures exist. To illustrate by example, a school custodian may be expected to read at a specified level necessary for following written directions left by the supervisor, but the possession of a high school diploma (proxy) is no assurance of the required reading ability and an inappropriate proxy for screening potential applicants (especially in light of valid tests for assessing reading levels).

Still another general principle—for establishing minimum requirements of a position as described by a job description—pertains to the general as opposed to specific KSA requirements. General KSAs are broad based and reflect competencies, while specific KSAs may be unduly limiting, especially for certain protected groups. It is possible to understand the use of technology for fulfilling job assignments (general) without having knowledge about a specific operating system (Windows or Apple) that can be readily acquired once employed.

Yet another concern addresses those KSAs needed for the vacant position under consideration as compared to those needed for other positions within the organization. To require KSAs beyond a particular position under consideration requires strong evidence for a direct line of promotion (see EEOC Guidelines, Section G). Applicants for a principal's position should not be expected to hold credentials for a superintendent's position unless most superintendents have been promoted from within by a particular school district from the principal's position.

The heading for the reporting relationship imparts valuable information for potential job candidates. This is especially true for staff as opposed to line relationships. In general, the more prominent the immediate supervisor, the more prestigious the vacant position within the organizational hierarchy is likely to be.

Because job descriptions are often overinterpreted, a closure statement is recommended, and this statement reinforces the last job tasks to be performed (see Figure 4.4). This statement should be bolded and should be located near the end of the job description. An example of a closure statement is "This job description contains only examples of the most frequently performed job tasks and should not be interpreted as being all-inclusive of the task to be performed by a position holder."

As a final recommendation for the construction of job descriptions, a running date is recommended. The running date reflects each time a job description has been modified and provides a chronological history for these modifications (e.g., 01/07/92, 05/06/99, etc.). Many disputes arise within a school district concerning information contained in job descriptions because one party may lack the most recent modification or neither party has the most recent job description.

Having satisfied the informational needs involving mandatory recruitment policies, permissive recruitment policies, information about positions (job analysis), and position requirements (job descriptions), school systems should address recruitment incentives as part of the strategic planning process. Recruitment incentives increase the motivation of individuals as applicants to seek employment with a particular school district. Because recruitment incentives vary in cost as well as in viability for particular school districts, a review of possibilities is warranted within the strategic planning process to guide decision making relative to possibilities for enhancing recruitment efforts.

Recruitment Incentives

With the passage of NCLB, the endorsement of ISLLC standards, and the advent of high-stakes testing, the importance of recruitment has emerged as an important operational directive within the strategic planning process to be undertaken by most public school districts. From a strategic planning perspective, an adequate pool of willing and able candidates for vacant positions within the public school setting can no longer be taken as a given by most public school districts (Young, Chounet, Buster, & Sailor, 2005). Potential applicants today as well as in the near future are unlike those in the past from several aspects.

For many individuals once restricted to education as a sole source of employment, their labor markets have expanded in recent times. This is notably true for certain protected class groups, especially females (Young, in press). Today, these individuals have many other opportunities for marketing their skills and for recapturing their educational investments than in the past.

From a demographic perspective, applicants in general are more mobile than in the past. Young applicants are marrying later, are delaying mortgage obligations, and are postponing child-rearing responsibilities to establish professional careers. As such, young applicants are less geographically bound and seek opportunities in the job market with an eye on recruitment incentives.

Older applicants, once a rarity within the recruitment context, are far more commonplace today. Alternate certification routes have been afforded these individuals both by universities and by state departments of education. Almost by definition, older applicants changing careers or entering the education profession later in life are mobile and pursuing choices that may be influenced by recruitment incentives.

To attract viable candidates for vacant positions within the public school setting and to compete with other labor markets for these talents, many school systems have either instituted or reinvigorated proactive programs of recruitment. Functionally, these efforts involve more than offering goodwill on the part of school districts as potential employers. Goodwill, while a constant in every effective recruitment program (Clement, 2006), has been expanded to include certain employment incentives offered to potential job candidates as a condition of their employment with a public school district.

A review of the literature concerning recruitment incentives revealed an informative report by the National Education Association (NEA, n.d.). Within this report, recruitment incentives are analyzed by states as well as by local school districts and are found to be flourishing in many locales. Specific attention is given to bonuses, housing, and educational incentives as a means for attracting able and willing job candidates to meet current as well as emerging human resource demands in the public school setting.

Bonuses represent a one-time payment for "signing on" with a particular school district. As noted in this report by NEA, many types of bonuses are being utilized to attract individuals within the recruitment process with some being as high as $5,000.00, and recent experimental research indicates that educators are receptive to these bonuses (Winter & Melloy, 2005). Included among these bonus options are signing incentives for all new teachers, bonuses for certain subject-area teachers, and bonuses for working in identified school buildings within a district otherwise difficult to staff.

Because of the costs associated with housing and with relocations either to high-cost areas or to less attractive areas, other types of recruitment incentives have been offered by states/public school districts to attract employees. Identified specifically in this report are such incentives as reduced rent, reduced-priced homes, low-interest mortgages, and assistance with closing costs. Some of these incentives come about through school–business partnerships involving banks as well as private sector organizations with little or no cost to a public school district.

Relocation costs are another recruitment incentive used frequently by many public school districts to attract employees. As a recruitment incentive, relocation costs represent a one-time investment on the part of a school district and may cover either in-part or in-total moving expenses. In-part moving expenses are usually defined by a fixed rate, while in-total moving costs can be offset to some extent by prior agreements of the school district with specific moving companies offering a discount to public school districts through formalized agreements.

More common than signing bonuses, housing allowances, or relocation costs is educational incentives provided by states/local school districts as a recruitment enticement for new job candidates. Educational incentives include loans, forgivable loans, scholarships, and tuition assistance. Unlike bonuses involving one-time payments or stipulations for housing agreements, these later recruitment incentives involving educational entitlements are likely to be ongoing both for new, as well as for continuing, employees.

One method used frequently by many school districts as an educational incentive within the recruitment process is fee waivers. In return for providing universities with a readymade worksite and a mentoring professional for student teachers (a current employee), public school districts are provided with fee waivers for their employees rather than any type of cash payment to supervising teachers. Fee waivers can be used as an educational incentive by the school district within the recruitment process through a contractual agreement with institutions of higher education.

Collectively, this interest and emphasis on recruitment incentives suggests that most public school districts should rethink their recruitment program from a strategic planning perspective. Although many school districts may have limited resources for recruitment incentives, other components of the recruitment process become more important. One of these components involves the identification of and capitalization on recruitment sources available to most public school districts.

Recruitment Sources

The major objective of an effective and efficient recruitment program is the generation of a willing, a capable, and a diverse pool of applicants to fill existing as well as emerging vacancies identified by a strategic staffing plan (see Chapter 3). To accomplish this objective requires a well-formulated strategic plan of action on the part of a public school district.

Fundamental to this plan of action is the identification of and the nurturing of specific recruitment sources as part of an overall recruitment plan of action.

From a strategic planning perspective, at least two broad-based recruitment sources exist for attracting a willing, capable, and diverse pool of applicants. One broad-based recruitment source involves those external to the school district. The other broad-based recruitment source is comprised of those employed currently by a public school district.

Neither of these sources (external or internal) of potential applicants for vacant positions should be overlooked or undercapitalized within the recruitment process from a strategic planning perspective. To maximize a school district's opportunities through the infusion of talented individuals filling vacant positions, attention must be continuously afforded to both types of labor markets. Because these labor markets differ in important ways within the recruitment process, specific attention is afforded to each type of labor market.

External Labor Markets

Individuals as potential applicants lacking any formal affiliation with a public school district constitute an **external labor market.** Several recruitment sources exist for identifying a collective pool of external applicants. Some of the most common sources for an external labor market are found in Figure 4.6, are differentiated by the type of positions to be filled, and are somewhat related: (1) certificated or (2) classified.

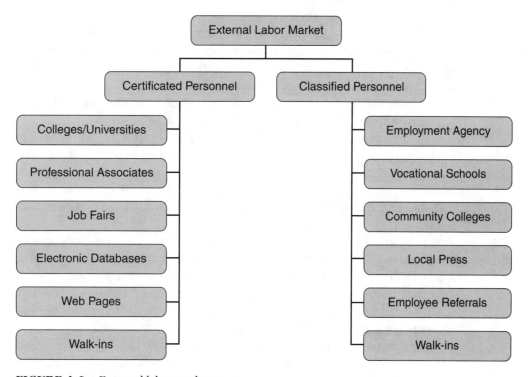

FIGURE 4.6 *External labor market sources.*

Perhaps the most traditional external labor market for certificated personnel is institutions of higher education offering certification programs both for aspiring and for continuing educators. As a labor market, most colleges/universities offer a replenishing supply of potential job candidates on an annual basis. Included among these potential job candidates associated with institutions of higher education are those seeking entry into the profession and those upgrading their credentials for further advancement within the profession.

At most institutions of higher education, each year a fresh group of potential job candidates receive their initial certification for specific focal positions in the field setting. Every year within these institutions, certain individuals upgrade their existing credentials, and other individuals pursue additional certifications. From an external labor market perspective, all sources provide readymade applicant pools awaiting capitalization by a public school district within the recruitment process.

Another traditional external labor market for certificated personnel is professional associations catering to the specific expertise of the membership. Most professional associations both at the state and at the national level provide an external labor market readily available to public school districts. With few exceptions, these associations publish either a journal or a newsletter accepting job announcements for vacant positions, and this recruitment medium is circulated widely among the membership.

Some of these associations provide placement services for their membership. Résumés of potential applicants are collected and are provided to public school districts on request. In most instances, this information is provided to public school districts without cost as a means for serving their memberships.

Given actual as well as anticipated vacant positions by many school districts, **job fairs** are conducted in many locales to attract an external labor market. Structurally, these job fairs are conducted by multiple school districts with each school district sending representatives to recruit external job candidates. As a mechanism for identifying an external labor market, potential job candidates may be recruited and may receive information from multiple districts in one location through a single visit.

More recently, some online databases have emerged that can be utilized by public school districts to identify applicants in an external labor market. Some of these databases are restricted to particular protected groups, while others of these databases contain all applicants without regard to protected class status (see NEA for a listing). Use of these databases for identifying external labor market constituents are without cost to a public school district in most instances.

Many school districts use their web page to attract external applicants for vacant focal positions. For those districts posting a web page on the Internet, it is not unusual to find a link for employment opportunities as a means for attracting an external applicant pool. By following this link as found on many web pages, external applicants can, in most instances, make an online application for specific focal positions, and many public school districts are beginning to rely strictly on electronic applications.

For some certificated positions, especially administrators, fee-based agencies exist for identifying an external labor market. Once limited almost exclusively to superintendents in scope, these agencies have expanded their services to include other personnel, especially building-level principals. Often labeled as "head hunters" within the popular press as well as the professional literature, these agencies maintain an ample pool of individuals from the external labor market.

To support their operations in supplying an external labor market, several types of fee structures exist for private employment agencies. Fees can be based on a fixed amount or on a percentage of the employee's first-year salary. In some instances, the fee is absorbed by the individual, while in other instances, the fee is paid by the public school district.

Not to be overlooked as a means for attracting individuals from the external market are "walk-ins" seeking employment on their own volition. "Walk-ins" visit local school districts in search of employment opportunities. For many of these candidates comprising an external labor market, their job search process is limited due to geographical restrictions.

As noted by Young et al. (2005), some excellent job candidates from the external market have restraints beyond their immediate control that restrict their job search process. For many potential job candidates relying on dual incomes when one spouse is already employed, spousal employment must be considered. Still others may have family obligations (e.g., aging parents or child custody issues), all of which restrict their movement within the external labor market and provide a ready source of external applicants for a public school district.

In contrast to certificated positions, other external labor markets exist for classified positions holding a nonsupervisory status. One primary source of an external labor market for classified positions holding a nonsupervisory status is state employment agencies. These agencies maintain a list of those individuals seeking active employment, and these individuals are readily available, in most instances, for gainful employment.

As a means for receiving unemployment compensation, many individuals list their eligibility with state employment agencies. To receive unemployment compensation, two conditions must exist for this particular group of external applicants. Most importantly from a recruitment perspective of public school districts, these individuals must not have been discharged for reason from their immediate past position, and these individuals must be willing and able to accept reasonable employment offers based on their skills and expertise. Both of these conditions render an external labor market worthy of consideration by a public school district when seeking to recruit certain classified positions.

Because classified employees generally have a restricted external labor market, job advertisements in the local press are often a fruitful venue to be utilized by public school districts. Jobs should be listed in the local press in the classified section of the newspaper and should describe minimum qualifications associated with particular focal positions. This means for identifying an external labor market for classified staff has both practical and political implications for a local school district relative to mandatory policies involving federal legislation (EEOC and/or affirmative action) by announcing job opportunities to underrepresented persons within a relevant labor market.

Like certificated employees pursuing college degrees and/or advance certification, potential classified employees may be attending a vocational school or community college as a method of advancing their professional careers. Their educational training relative to certain curriculums make them particularly viable job candidates for certain positions as found in the public school setting. As such, vocational schools and community colleges are an important external labor market not to be overlooked within the recruitment process from a strategic planning perspective.

Other than "walk-ins" as described for certificated positions, another means for identifying individuals for classified positions is employee referrals. Current employees are connected with an external labor through their community affiliations. To encourage employee referrals for classified positions, some private organizations offer a bonus to existing employees making successful referrals, and public school districts should consider this option as a means for attracting noncertificated applicants.

Internal Labor Markets

Unlike those individuals lacking any formal affiliation with a public school district as found in external labor markets, an **internal labor market** is comprised of those individuals fulfilling job assignments within a public school district. Although the system will probably need to recruit personnel from outside sources, it is also sound policy to promote and to transfer current employees from within the system (Winter, Rinehart, & Munoz, 2002).

With respect to those working at present in a school district, often overlooked is the fact that "current employees are potential candidates for whom the largest amount of job information is available" (Pounder & Young, 1996). Valid information exists about attendance, motivation, and actual job performance of those serving the local school district.

Several different types of current employees exist from which to recruit an able applicant pool for certain types of positions. Most common are those individuals holding a full-time position and having an established record of performance. However, other classifications exist and must not be overlooked from a strategic planning perspective.

Most notable is the realization that current employees can be either a **part-time employee** or a **temporary employee**. Part-time employees generally work the full year but on a prorated basis, while temporary employees work full time but less than a complete work year. For both of these employee classifications, actual as opposed to inferred information exists about their job performance relative to their current assigned job duties.

It should be clearly understood that certain types of positions provide no advancement and that certain individuals are satisfied to remain indefinitely in the same position. However, the general policy of promotion from within to better and more attractive positions is to be encouraged and can be used as an effective recruitment incentive. Internal job incumbents provide a source for generating a viable applicant pool of potential job candidates for filling some vacant positions.

The manner in which positions are filled from the inside depends on the personnel processes that can be used to generate an internal pool of viable job candidates: (1) administrative assignment, (2) position posting, or (3) developmental programs. Under the first method (administrative assignment), personnel within the system capable of advancing to a more desirable and/or higher-level position are identified and assigned by management with the concurrence of the employee.

With respect to the second method for generating an internal applicant pool (position positing), personnel within the system are made aware of vacant positions through internal job postings. In some instances, either by school board policy or by labor contract, internal applicants are afforded preferential treatment within the recruitment process. Those individuals following up on this recruitment mechanism through their own volitions exhibit generally a high level of motivation by seeking new job assignments.

From a strategic planning perspective, many public school districts offer programs of development for existing personnel as a recruitment incentive. This effort, on the part of public school districts, acts both as a recruitment incentive to attract potential candidates and as a source of motivation for those employed. Well-tailored development programs ensure a ready and able pool of internal job candidates for filling vacant positions within a public school district.

As can be ascertained from the previous elaborations, external and internal personnel sources are numerous as well as varied and may be used by a public school district when recruiting potential job candidates from both external and internal labor markets to fill vacant positions as identified within the strategic planning process. The extent to which these external and internal labor markets can be used by a school district depends largely on the school system's recruitment policies and strategic plans. If the recruitment effort is to succeed, it must produce a pool of willing and able applicants well in excess of the number of vacant focal position to be filled; otherwise, a selection process exists in name only.

Obviously, schools with a large numbers of vacancies will utilize different external and internal sources and will employ techniques that differ from those preferred by smaller school systems having a fewer numbers of vacancies. Those educational administrators who operate the recruitment program need to anticipate which sources will provide the greatest number of qualified applicants, how much time and money should be invested, and what methods should be used to attract competent individuals as potential job candidates. To consider all these concerns from an operational perspective involving a strategic planning orientation requires a well-formulated recruitment process.

Recruitment Process

As noted previously in this chapter, action plans and the structure for the recruitment process are derived from the mission statement adopted by a public school district. In effect, the process model is based on the assumption that decisions have been made through strategic planning concerning the number of positions needed (based on student enrollments, Chapter 2) and the allocation of human resources relative to these positions. The operational staffing plan (Chapter 3), which is derived from the strategic planning process, identifies the actions to be taken once the demand for and supply of human resources has been reconciled within the overall strategic plan reflecting the intents of the mission statement.

Although the responsibility for several tasks involved in the recruitment process depends in part on the organizational structure of a school district, at least three features can be identified that characterize the most successful recruitment efforts when conducted from a strategic planning perspective. These features involve formalizing communication between the system and the applicants, establishing an operational budget for funding the recruitment activities, and assessing the effectiveness of this operational directive within the strategic planning process through an auditing process to ensure recruitment goals and objectives are being met in a cost-effective manner.

Formalizing Communication between the System and the Applicants

To be effective within the recruitment phase of the employment process, several different **communication mediums** as noted previously must be used by public school districts to communicate with potential job candidates relative to external and internal labor markets comprising desirable job applicants. For many potential job candidates, their first contact with a particular public school district occurs during recruitment, and this contact shapes, to a large extent, their impressions of a school district as a potential employer. Well known within the general professional literature is the importance of first impressions on the subsequent job choice of applicants (Winter & Morgenthal, 2002).

As noted long ago by a review of this literature, Young and Heneman (1986) found first impressions of applicants to be influential within the job search process, and there are no reasons to doubt these findings today in light of emerging research (Winter, et al., 2005). According to all these researchers, first impressions can be shaped by both formal and informal communication incurred within the recruitment process. Because the most viable job candidates being recruited have options among school districts as potential employers, it is important for school districts to make favorable impressions early within the recruitment process through well-refined modes of communication. In short, public school districts have only one opportunity to make a first impression with potential job candidates and must capitalize on this opportunity if they are to be successful at the recruitment stage of the employment process when competing for the most viable job candidates.

Today, almost all school districts have web pages posted on the Internet as a means for communicating with the public at large. With little effort on the part of a public school district, this electronic mode of communication can be made user-friendly for potential job candidates and can provide important sources of information to these individuals in search of job opportunities. Through the electronic linking process to different sections of a school district's website, basic information about the district's employment policies, recruitment incentives, vacant positions, and application procedures can be made available to those capitalizing on this medium of communication within the job search process. In many instances, today's electronic "surfers" are yesterday's "walk-ins."

Other than web pages as an electronic means of communication with potential applicants, printed brochures represent another mode of communication that can be used by public school districts to inform potential job candidates as well as viable referral sources about employment opportunities specific to a public school district. Although printed brochures are limited in scope of information as compared to web pages, this former mode of communication represents a basic requirement that should be exercised by every school district when attempting to generate applicant pools for filling vacant positions. Indeed, a printed brochure can reach several sources of applicants overlooked by the electronic method of communication.

Not to be underemphasized is the realization that not all potential applicants enjoy a convenient access to the electronic highway. Access to this electronic medium involves hardware and an Internet connection, both of which may be unaffordable by many unemployed individuals who are seeking gainful employment with a public school district. Without these necessary conditions involving hardware and an Internet connection, printed brochures fill a gap between applicants and employers within the communication process otherwise underutilized if a strict adherence is afforded to the electronic means of communication.

Beyond serving as a mode of communication for applicants, printed brochures can provide information to selective referral sources having access to applicant pools. As a tried and a true method for recruitment, printed brochures have and continue to be a favored mode of communication for commercial consulting firms employed to generate applicant pools. It is not uncommon for professors to receive, by U.S. mail, a printed brochure from consulting firms describing a school district, and an accompanying letter requesting the nomination of potential job candidates for vacant positions within the public school district. As such, public school districts would be well advised to follow this lead for attracting potential job candidates through the development and the dissemination of printed brochures describing the specifics of a local school district.

A well-utilized medium for communication between potential applicants and potential employers is a job advertisement. A job advertisement represents an invitation to apply and is published often in both professional and public outlets. Given the popularity of this particular venue as a mode of communication, several research studies have been conducted.

Findings from these studies provide specific directions for a public school district in the search for quality candidates. Importantly, subjects in these studies are educators entertaining a job choice. Effective position announcements identify a specific contact person, address candidates directly ("you should . . ."), and acknowledge applications by a telephone call. Ineffective position announcements identify an office to contact, use impersonal language ("applicant" rather than "you"), and fail to provide a means of acknowledging applications (Winter, 1996).

More labor intensive and costly from an organizational perspective than web-based information, printed brochures, or job advertisements as a means of communication between applicants and school systems is personal contact by district-level employees assigned recruitment responsibilities. Common among the personal contacts used to communicate between applicants and potential employers is the college placement office. Within most institutions of higher education, the placement office provides a centralized location and a ready source of potential job candidates.

Functionally, university and/or college placement offices provide two different methods for fostering communication between potential applicants and employing school districts. One method involves providing interviewing rooms and requiring applicants to sign up for personal interviews with a designated school district at a set date. For some universities and colleges, the utilization of this service by public school districts must be scheduled months in advance and requires considerable coordination within the strategic planning process on the part of a public school district.

The other method utilized by universities and colleges to facilitate the communication process between potential applicants and school districts is a job fair. Job fairs require individuals as applicants to register as a condition of participation, and once registered these individuals are provided access to multiple school districts in a centralized location. However, job fairs initiate rather than conclude the information flow between potential applicants and public school districts within the recruitment phase of the employment process due to contextual constraints.

Public school administrators assigned recruitment responsibilities can capitalize on university and college connections beyond those services provided by placement offices and job fairs. Personal contacts can be made with professors, and professors can serve as *ex official* recruiters for a public school district when relationships are appropriately cultivated by district-level employees charged with recruitment responsibilities. It is not unusual for professors to have organizational recruiters from a public school district as a guest speaker in their classes to explain the recruitment and selection processes utilized by their particular school districts, and all public school districts should capitalize on this marketing activity as a means for attracting potential job candidates.

Personal contacts as just described with college professors should be expanded to include additional stakeholders associated with other external and internal applicant sources as noted in this chapter. For other external sources of applicants, personal relationships should be nurtured with professional association representatives, employment agencies (both public and private), and significant other groups/individuals within the local community having access to potential applicant pools. With respect to internal applicant sources, personal relationships are recommended with unit supervisors as well as with association/union leadership to identify emerging talents. It goes without stating that an open-door policy should be maintained for all employees considering a change in their current job assignment.

To implement the actual recruitment process, an operational budget is required to fund recruitment activities. This budget reflects the school district's economic commitment to the recruitment process. Given this necessity, attention is devoted in the following section to the construction of a recruitment budget that can serve as a format for most public school districts.

Establishing an Operational Budget

Recruitment is not a costless exercise for any public school district. From an economic perspective, recruitment involves paying forward rather than paying back on the part of a public school system. Effectively developed and efficiently executed, recruitment is a wise investment for all public school districts as a method for either replenishing or expanding the current workforce comprising a school system.

Having formalized means and mediums of communication for attracting applicants to fill vacant positions within a public school district, the recruitment activity moves from the planning stage to the goal realization stage of the strategic planning process. At this stage of the strategic planning process, permission must be sought and must be obtained to spend funds allocated for the attraction of applicants to fill identifiable vacant positions as defined by the strategic planning process (see staffing model in Chapter 3). As a precursor to this stage of the recruitment process, a budget must be constructed and subsequently followed by those charged with recruitment responsibilities.

When constructing a recruitment budget, cost consideration should be given to certain line-item expenditures beyond salaries and benefits of assigned personnel. However, the costs of assigned personnel should be a factor in large school districts when the sole responsibility of these persons is recruitment. Barring this exception for large school districts having designed staff devoted exclusively to recruitment, most line items comprising a recruitment budget are found in Table 4.5.

Among these different line-item budget categories as contained in Table 4.5, some items are mandatory, while other items are discretionary. The first six items (brochure, advertisement, mailing, telephone, travel, and reimbursable expenses) represent mandatory recruitment expenses to be incurred by all public school districts. Without this initial level of funding, recruitment is sure to fail.

Other items as contained in Table 4.5 are discretionary but highly recommended as a means for enhancing recruitment efforts of a public school district from a strategic planning perspective. Included among these items are entertainment costs pertaining to paying for meals (not alcohol) of potential applicants and fruitful referral sources worthy of nurturing by a public school district. Because these costs are not normal expenditures for a school district employee, they are labeled as entertainment costs within the recruitment budget.

For special hard to attract individuals (e.g., special education teachers, vocational education instructors, etc.), a ready-made pool of potential applicants exists at professional conventions. Professional conventions charge a registration fee but provide a readily available pool of potential applicants possessing specialized skills in a single location. In many instances, conventions afford employers with recruitment opportunities through job fairs conducted at the convention and charge only a registration fee for this service.

If applicants are recruited at a location off-site from a public school district, an on-site visit may be a necessary condition for consummating an employment contract for many potential employees, especially those having choices among competing school systems.

TABLE 4.5
Categorization of Recruitment Expenses

---

1. Brochure Production
2. Mailing Costs
3. Long-Distance Telephone
4. Recruiter Travel
5. Recruiter Meals & Lodging
6. Entertainment Expense
7. Convention Costs
8. Applicant Travel
9. Applicant Meals & Lodging

Costs incurred by an on-site visit (travel, meals, and lodging) may be absorbed either by the candidate or by the district. For many school districts, these costs are viewed as a wise expenditure of district funds and provide a competitive edge in a tight labor market.

Without an operational budget to support this human resource activity, recruitment is almost doomed to fail. Far too often, many public school districts neglect to fund adequately the recruitment process. However, once funded, the recruitment process and expenditures must be monitored from a strategic planning perspective through an auditing process.

Monitoring the Recruitment Process

From a strategic planning perspective, the recruitment process must be continuously monitored through appropriate audit mechanisms. At least two dimensions of the recruitment process are essential concerns from an auditing perspective. The first dimension is effectiveness, which involves assessing how well the school system's recruitment plans are being achieved and developing courses of action to correct deficiencies. The second dimension is efficiency, which involves assessing recruitment performance against costs and linking strategic aims of the recruitment process with a cost-benefit ratio.

Effectiveness involves making certain that recruitment results are in keeping with established goals. If goals are to be met, then the collection, analysis, feedback, and use of relevant recruitment information is essential. Evaluation is useful to (a) extend information about and understanding of issues, problems, obstacles, and opportunities in human resource planning; (b) assess the strengths and weaknesses of the existing strategy; (c) identify new conditions in the internal and external environments and their potential impact on the human resource function; and (d) consider the interrelatedness of strategy, recruitment, work to be done, skilled personnel to do the work, environments, and fiscal resources.

On the other hand, efficiency involves how well-allocated funds are being expended in the accomplishment of recruitment goals and objectives. Careful accounting of recruitment expenses is essential for providing information about costs/benefits. The costs associated with certain activities and certain sources will reveal that some activities and sources are more productive than others relative to a school system's investments in the recruitment process.

From an efficiency perspective, the system is interested in knowing what personnel sources yield the best-quality personnel and at what cost. It is understandable, for example, that the most satisfactory professionals might not be acquired from the nearest teacher education college. Likewise, it is also conceivable that advertising might provide better secretarial personnel than an employment agency.

After the total recruitment costs have been calculated, unit costs—such as costs per applicant employed—costs per applicant by source, costs by recruiter, costs per contact, and costs per professional employee versus costs of support employees, are some of the indicators that must be analyzed to get a clear view of the total cost of recruitment. Collectively, both effectiveness and efficiency measures are necessary components of a well-designed recruitment program. Based on outcomes from these audit measures, public school districts can direct as well as redirect their recruitment efforts for acquiring an able as well as a willing pool of potential job candidates.

Review and Preview

The theme of this chapter is that an extensive and aggressive program of recruitment is necessary for selecting, assigning, and retaining qualified individuals in every position in the system. To guide the recruitment processes, certain policies and procedures were discussed. With respect to recruitment, a distinction was made between an equal opportunity employer and an affirmative action employer as a mandatory policy stance and was guided by the recruitment contexture of a public school district (stock and concentration statistics). Special attention was afforded to permissive policies that have important implications within the recruitment process.

Germane to the recruitment process is information about positions and personnel requirements. Different methods of job analyses were discussed for collecting information and for the construction of job descriptions. Rules and procedures for constructing job descriptions are outlined relative to the recruitment process. Special attention is given to the knowledge, abilities, skills, and other qualifications of job candidates.

As a means of attracting job candidates to fill vacant positions, many recruitment incentives were discussed. A distinction was made between external and internal labor markets containing potential job candidates. To link theory to practice, several different communication mediums are presented, the budgeting process is illustrated, and auditing criteria are provided.

Collectively, all these recruitment contingencies lead to the next stage of the employment process from a strategic planning perspective. This stage involves the delimiting of the applicant pool to acquire only the most able job candidates for filling vacant positions in a public school district. Like recruitment, selection is a process nested within the confines of policy and governed by well-defined procedures. Within the next chapter, selection is addressed from a strategic planning perspective.

Discussion Questions

1. Is your district an equal opportunity employer or an affirmative action employer? How was this decision made and is this the appropriate tack for guiding recruitment efforts in your school district?

2. How does internal recruiting differ from external recruiting? What is the strategic difference between the two methods?

3. What is the relationship between human resource strategy and recruitment from a strategic planning perspective?

4. Why are permissive recruitment policies important both from a system and from an individual's perspective?

5. What recruitment incentives could best be utilized by your particular school district?

6. Which mediums of communication are used by your district and how could these modes of communication be refined?

7. Which line items would you include in the recruitment budget and what would be your justification?

8. How would you set up your auditing process and what criteria would you use to assess effectiveness and efficiency from an organizational perspective?

Case Study

Assume that you are the new director for human resources in the Sturgis Public School District. This district contains 10,000 students and has a teacher bargaining group. Within the last few years, the district has had an extreme shortage of certain types of teacher candidates. More specifically, the areas are math, science, and special education and within these areas, various applicants have a protected class status.

The school board wants to offer a signing bonus that varies both by areas of specialty as well as by a candidate's protected class status. On the other hand, the Union strongly disagrees and suggests that all teachers need more money, not just a select few. The Union goes even further and indicates that an unfair labor practice will be filed if the board institutes such a practice.

As the new HR director, how would you go about resolving this dispute? What sort of data would you collect? Are there policy issues as well as labor contract concerns? Could this process be justified for other groups within the school district not covered by a labor contract?

References

Age Discrimination in Employment Act. (n.d.). Retrieved July 4, 2006, from http://www.eeoc.gov/laws/adea.html.

Americans with Disabilities Act. (n.d.). Retrieved July 4, 2006, from http://www.usdoj.gov/crt/ada/adahom1.html.

Clement, N. I. (2006). In search of legendary teachers. *The School Administrator, 631*.

Cunningham, W. G., & Cordeiro, P. A. (2006). *Educational leadership: A problem-based approach* (3rd ed.). Upper Saddle River, NJ: Pearson.

Dictionary of Occupational Titles. (n.d.). Retrieved June 29, 2006, from Web site: http://www.nsdc.org/library/publications/jsd/champion234.cfm.

Equal Employment Opportunity Commission. (1978). Guidelines on employee selection procedures. *Federal Register, 35,* 12333–12336.

Heneman, H. G., & Judge, T. A. (2006). *Staffing organizations* (6th ed.). Middleton, WI: Mendota House.

Heneman, H. G., Judge, T. A., & Heneman, R. L. (2000). *Staffing organizations* (3rd ed.). Middleton, WI: Mendota House.

HR-Guide. (n.d.). HR guide to the Internet: Job analysis: Law/legal issues: Court cases. Retrieved July 11, 2006, from the HR-Guide Web site: http://www.hr-guide. com/data/G001.htm.

Interstate School Licensure Consortium. (n.d.). Retrieved July 11, 2006, from the Web site: http://www.ccsso.org/projects/Interstate_Consortium_on_School_Leadership/.

Job Analysis. (n.d.). *Methods and techniques.* Retrieved July 11, 2006, from http://www.job-analysis.net/.

Marshall, C., & Gerstl-Pepin, C. (2005). *Re-framing educational politics for social justice.* New York: Pearson.

National Archives and Records Administration. (1978). *Federal Register, 35.* Retrieved May 28, 2006, from the National Archives and Administration Web site: http://archives. gov/federal_register/.

National Education Association. (n.d). Retrieved June 10, 2006, from http://www.nea.org/ index.html.

No Child Left Behind Act. 2001. (2002). Pub. L. No. 107-110, 115 Stat. 1425.

Pounder, D. G., & Young, I. P. (1996). Recruitment and selection of educational administrators: Priorities for today's schools. In K. Leithwood (Ed.), *The international handbook for educational leadership and administration* (pp. 279–308). Amsterdam: Kluwer.

Section 504 of the Rehabilitation Act. (n.d.). Retrieved July 4, 2006, from http://www.hhs.gov/ocr/504.html.

Valente, W. D., & Valente, C. M. (2005). *Law in the schools* (6th ed.). Upper Saddle River, NJ: Pearson.

Winter, P. A. (1996). Applicant evaluations of formal position advertisements: The influence of sex, job message content, and information order. *Journal of Personnel Evaluation in Education, 10,* 105–116.

Winter, P. A. (1997). Education recruitment and selection: A review of recent studies and recommendations for best practice. In L. Wildman (Ed.), *Fifth NCPEA yearbook* (pp. 133–140). Lancaster, PA: Technomic.

Winter, P. A., & Melloy, S. H. (2005). Teacher recruitment in a teacher reform state: Factors that influence applicant attraction to teacher vacancies. *Educational Administration Quarterly, 41*(2), 349–372.

Winter, P. A., Millay, J. D., Bjork, L. G., & Keedy, J. L. (2005). Superintendent recruitment: Effects of school councils, job status, signing bonus, and district wealth. *Journal of School Leadership, 15*(4), 433–455.

Winter, P. A., & Morgenthal, J. R. (2002). Principal recruitment in a reform environment: Effects of school achievement and school level on applicant attraction to the job. *Educational Administration Quarterly, 38,* 319–340.

Winter, P. A., Rinehart, J. S., & Munoz, M. A. (2002). Principal recruitment: An empirical evaluation of a school district's internal pool of principal certified personnel. *Journal of Personnel Evaluation in Education, 16*(2), 129–141.

Young, I. P. (2006). Job descriptions. In F. W. English (Ed.), *Encyclopedia of Educational Leadership and Administration,* Newbury Park, CA: Sage, S31–S33.

Young, I. P. (in press). Effects of "like type" sex pairing between applicants-principals and type of focal position considered at the screening stage of the selection process. *Journal of Personnel Evaluation in Education.*

Young, I. P., Chounet, P. F., Buster, A. B., & Sailor, S. (2005). Effects of student achievement on satisfaction of newly appointed teachers: A cognitive dissonance perspective. *Journal of School Leadership, 15*(1), 35–51.

Young, I. P., & Heneman, H. G. (1986). Predictors of interviewee reactions to the selection interview. *Journal of Research and Development in Education, 19,* 29–36.

Young, I. P., Jury, J. R., & Reis, S. B. (1997). Holmes versus traditional candidates: Labor market receptivity. *Journal of School Leadership, 7*(4), 330–344.

Young, I. P., Rinehart, J., & Heneman, H G. (1993). Effects of job attribute categories, applicant job experience, and recruiter sex on applicant job attractiveness ratings. *Journal of Personnel Evaluation in Education, 7,* 55–65.

Selection

5

CHAPTER OVERVIEW

Job simulation test
Multiple hurdles model of
  decision making
Objective theory of job
  choice
Personal letters of
  recommendation
Practical significance
Predictor deficiency
Predictor relevance
Predictor variables
Prima facie evidence
Professional letters of
  recommendation
Quadrant analysis
Restricted range
Screening decisions
Selection interviews
Selection ratio
Site-based decision-
  making council
Situational judgment test
Statistical significance
Subjective theory of job
  choice
Work itself theory of job
  choice
Work sample tests

OBJECTIVES

- Amplify the importance of selection.
- Emphasize the interest of applicants within the selection process.
- Examine selection from an organizational perspective.
- Provide a conceptual model for selection.
- Identify components of the selection process.
- Assess the effectiveness and efficiency of specific predictors used to delimit applicant pools.
- Address legal and practical applications of the selection process.
- Use actual field studies for demonstrating validity assessments for the selection process.
- Illustrate different decision models for implementing a selection process in the public school setting.

Purposes, Goals, and Challenges of Selection

Simply stated, the purpose of employee selection is to fill vacant positions in a public school district. Without exception, vacant positions exist in every school system for a variety of reasons and afford school systems with a window of opportunity through selection. Some vacant positions occur because of departing personnel, while other vacant positions are established because of external and internal changes impacting a public school district.

In all school systems, turnovers among existing personnel create selection opportunities for bettering the current workforce. Turnovers can be attributed to retirements, resignations, and nonrenewals of probationary employees. For all these common reasons as well as for some less common reasons (e.g., discharges), the current workforce must be replenished through the selection of new employees to replace departing employees.

Beyond replacement needs for departing personnel, vacant positions exist and must be filled for other causes. New positions are created through growth in student enrollments and through organizational restructuring on the part of a school district. Many public school districts have responded to the mandates of NCLB and to the advent of high-stakes testing by restructuring the existing organizational configuration. Restructuring involves the creation of positions requiring the selection of employees to staff new ventures in organizational design.

Although the need for the selection of employees waxes and wanes somewhat throughout the calendar year, it is safe to state that it is an ongoing activity in every school district. Few months, if not weeks, go by in any school district where selection fails to be exercised as an administrative procedure requiring the time and efforts of educators. Support for this statement can be provided by a review of minutes from monthly school board meetings reflecting personnel changes as a regular item of business on the agenda.

As one of the human resource endeavors listed in Chapter 1 comprising part of the strategic planning process, selection has many goals. One goal is to fill vacant positions with personnel who meet the system's desired qualifications. Desired qualifications for positions and personnel are determined through a job analysis (see Chapter 4) and establish minimum standards for filling vacant positions.

Another goal of selection is to acquire individuals who appear likely to succeed in a designated position. Although individuals may meet minimum qualifications for a particular focal position, they could posses other characteristics that detract from their likely success in an assigned position. Appropriately performed, selection should differentiate among unqualified, qualified, or highly qualified candidates comprising an applicant pool.

Still another goal of selection has economic implications. Selection is far from a costless exercise and has both direct and indirect costs. Direct costs are associated with actual recruitment expenses, while indirect costs involve the time and efforts of those involved with the selection process. To recapture initial costs of both types associated with selection, those selected should be expected to remain with the system for a reasonable period of time.

Yet another goal of selection from a strategic planning perspective has immediate as well as long-range implications from an organizational perspective. Today, more so than in the past, most employees selected to fill vacant positions in a public school district must contribute not only to their immediate job assignment but to the overall vision of the public school district as defined from a strategic planning perspective (see Chapter 1). This level of contribution requires a sustained level of motivation, on the part of newly acquired employees, often ignored by traditional selection systems used in the public school setting.

Indeed, one of the most important human resource challenges facing a public school district is the selection of employees, and this has been long noted in the published literature because "wise selection is the best means of improving the system" (Graces, 1932, p. 62). That is, the effectiveness and the efficiency of any public school district depend largely on the quality of its workforce yesterday, today, and tomorrow. Without an able as well as a willing workforce to execute the schooling process, well-developed strategic plans and best intentions of school officials will be of little value for educating America's youth.

When appropriately executed, selection affords public school districts with a great opportunity to enhance the current state of operation. As an administrative process, selection has the potential to reap benefits for a public school district well beyond the initial appointments of applicants as employees. However, selection is not without its challenges, and the reader must be cautioned against presuming that selection is always perfectly accurate. If selection practices were perfectly accurate, then this administrative process would be characterized by a physical law rather than by different operational theories and organizational processes.

Inappropriately performed, few administrative processes cause as many problems as the selection of employees. Potential applicants can challenge the selection process from procedural and substantive viewpoints. Many challenges can have legal consequences, and most challenges have important public relations implications for a public school system.

Unsurprisingly, how to select the best-qualified candidate for an unfilled position is a perennial organizational challenge for all public school districts. The selection process is fraught with possibilities for serious errors that can be costly to the school system, the community, the taxpayers, and the pupils. However, many of these potential errors can be minimized or eliminated by developing and by applying a selection system based on acquired knowledge that has evolved within the professional literature over several decades.

Based on this literature, the purpose of selection is to fill vacant positions, and the goals of selection are to fill vacant positions with personnel who meet the system's desired qualifications, appear likely to succeed in a designated position, will remain in the system for a reasonable period of time, will be effective contributors to the system at large, and will be sufficiently motivated to fulfill their job assignments at present as well as in the future. To the extent that these challenges are met determines, to a large extent, the effectiveness and the efficiency of a public school district in our ever-changing educational environment.

Traditionally, selection has been viewed largely only from an organizational perspective. However, contemporary thought views selection as a consensual activity incorporating the interests of organizations as well as the interests and rights of applicants. Within this chapter, attention is afforded to the concerns of both parties from a planning as well as from an applicant's point of view.

Selection from an Applicant's Perspective

Often overlooked by many public school districts within the strategic planning process relative to the selection of individuals to fill vacant positions are the concerns of applicants. Applicants, like employing school districts, have a vested interest in the selection process. However, many traditional selection systems used by public school districts to select employees have ignored these concerns, and this oversight has a dampening effect for the selection of new employees from a strategic planning perspective.

Concerns of applicants within the selection process can be viewed from at least two perspectives. One perspective addresses their motivational needs as individuals, while the other perspective pertains to their legal rights as potential public servants. Following is a discussion of both perspectives (motivational needs and rights of applicants) that should be considered when developing and implementing a selection system within all public school districts.

Motivational Needs of Applicants

Underlying the attraction of and the motivation of individuals as applicants is that employment with a particular school district requires the concurrence of applicants as well as employers to consummate a valid employment contract. Like school districts seeking to fill organizational needs identified initially by enrollment projections (see Chapter 2) and authorized through an approved staffing plan (see Chapter 3), applicants have needs also that they seek to fulfill within the job search process. Well documented is that the needs of applicants vary in some definable ways according to existing research (discussed below).

Research addressing the needs of applicants within the educational setting has revealed some homogeneous perspectives that drive purportedly their decision making relative to job choice. Even though these needs are different as per specific theories, there is little reason to believe that one group is better than another group relative to potential job performance of individuals once employed by a public school district. However, knowledge of these findings as revealed through educational research can provide a knowledge base for an effective and an efficient selection process by a tailored yet diversified message of communication addressing certain topics through various mediums of communication within the selection process.

To date, the research literature has revealed three separate theories about the needs of individuals as applicants within the job search process but has failed to reach any definitive conclusions applicable to all applicants from an organizational perspective. These theories differ in some important ways relative to certain constructs purported to guide the decision making of applicants within the job search process. The common constructs for each theory are the orientation of applicants and the needs of applicants for choosing among jobs and public school districts from an individual's perspective.

For example, one of these theories addressing the orientation of applicants is labeled as the **objective theory of job choice**. The objective theory of job choice was developed by Behling, Labovitz, and Gainer (1968) and is grounded within economics. With respect to the objective theory of job choice, individuals, as applicants, are motivated by the economic incentives associated with job opportunities and with school districts. Accordingly, individuals as applicants are viewed as economic beings whose goals are to maximize one's financial standing through job choice.

Of concern to these individuals, from the objective theory perspective, are the economic incentives offered by a public school district. More pointedly, these individuals are sensitive to starting salaries as well as to earning potentials based on additional education, advanced degrees, and potential bonuses (Winter & Melloy, 2005). Fringe benefit programs can be particularly important to some individuals in differentiating among school districts when school districts are viewed as potential employers from the objective theory perspective.

Another personal orientation theory is the **subjective theory of job choice.** As opposed to the objective theory of job choice, the subjective theory of job choice views applicants from a psychological perspective rather than an economic perspective. The subjective theory assumes that applicants have certain psychological needs and use the job search process as a means to fulfill these needs. Judge and Bretz (1992) noted that "individuals who match job or organizational values to their own are more satisfied and less likely to leave the organization" (p. 286) once employed. From the subjective theory of job choice perspective, individuals are sensitive to issues relating to the organizational climate and to the work environment when choosing among competing school districts.

Still another personal orientation theory for individuals as applicants, different from the objective or the subjective theory of job choice, is the **work itself theory of job choice.** The work itself theory describes individuals as rational beings (not economic or psychological beings) in the job search process who seek information about the job tasks associated with potential employment opportunities and requirements (Winter, Ronau, & Munoz, 2004). As such, information about the different job elements, job expectations, and actual job tasks becomes important to applicants during the job search process from the work itself perspective.

The utility of these different theories for the selection process within the educational setting has been assessed in several studies focusing specifically on the perceptions of educators. These studies differ in some important ways that cloud any definitive conclusion applicable to all employee groups but provide insights to those responsible for selecting employees in the public school setting. More specifically, these studies examine the selection decision making of several types of job candidates (teachers or administrators), employ different experimental designs (between subject where each person evaluates only a single theory or within subject where each person evaluates all three theories), and/or use alternate outcome variables to assess reactions toward job opportunities (probability of accepting a job or the attractiveness of a job).

With respect to selection decisions made by teachers, three separate studies indicate that teachers are least influenced by the objective theory concerning the economic incentives and are most influenced by either the subjective factors or the work itself when considering job opportunities (Young, Place, Rinehart, Jury, & Baits, 1997; Young, Rinehart, & Heneman, 1993; Young, Rinehart, & Place 1989). These findings were consistent for females as well as for males and for experienced as well as for inexperienced job candidates. However, experienced job candidates were found to be less enthusiastic about job opportunities in general than inexperienced job candidates.

Perhaps experienced job candidates use a different frame of reference than inexperienced job candidates when evaluating selection opportunities within the public school setting (Van Hoof, Born, Taris, Flier, & Blonk, 2004). For experienced job candidates, they could be either "wiser" buyers within the job market based on past experiences or "conservative" participants by contrasting a known position with an unknown job situation. In contrast to experienced teachers, inexperienced job applicants lacking gainful employment at the time of data collection could compare any job opportunity against continued unemployment with the former condition being perceived as more desirable than the later condition.

Less clear than for teachers are the data concerning school administrators relative to their selection decisions. According to Pounder and Merrill (2001), the single most influential variable for a principal position is the perception about the likelihood of a job offer being extended. These findings indicate that potential principal candidates have a low risk threshold within the job search process and seek opportunity over either working conditions or working environments.

When these researchers controlled for this preference concerning the likelihood of a job offer being forthcoming, other issues surfaced. Like teacher job candidates, principal applicants focused on job task factors associated with the work itself. Most notably, they are concerned about having the ability to manage the school building and to influence student outcomes (Winter & Morgenthal, 2002).

Superintendents, on the other hand, appear to be more economically orientated within the job search process than either teachers or principals. Winter, Millay, Bojork, and Keedy (2005) compared the reactions of aspiring superintendents with actual superintendents relative to potential job opportunities. They found standing superintendents to be more concerned about economic factors (wealth of a district and signing bonuses, objective theory) than aspiring superintendents.

Collectively, these findings from this research stream indicate that applicant selection decisions are moderated by the type of focal position sought (teacher or administrator) as well as by the employment status of the applicant (standing or seeking employment). Depending on these specifics, each theory provides information for writing recruitment messages, developing a recruitment strategy, and communicating within the selection process. By tailoring the communication within the selection process to the specifics of applicants, school districts can capitalize on selection opportunities. In fact, Bretz and Judge (1998) found that "the highest quality applicants may be less willing to pursue jobs for which negative information has been presented" (p. 330). Based on these findings, school districts should trumpet within the selection process those areas in which the district excels within their relevant labor market or at least should stress their strongest suit.

It is important to point out that much of the research addressing these theories assumes that applicants are free agents with unrestricted demands about job choice. In reality, this may not be the case in many situations. According to Young, Chounet, Buster, and Sailor (2005), "many job candidates are faced with personal restraints beyond their immediate control that mitigate their decisions relative to employment offers" (p. 41).

That is, some applicants have personal constraints (e.g., child custody, aging parents needing care) and/or financial constraints (e.g., dual-income families, seeking first professional job, and lacking a financial base). For these later groups of potential job candidates having restricted employment opportunities and rendering them as less than free agents within the employment process, employment rights rather than individual needs may well be more important concerns within the job search process involving public school districts.

Rights of Applicants

The selection process in all public school districts and in most private school districts is governed by constitutional protections, federal enactments, and state legislations (Valente & Valente, 2005) as well as local school board policies. Intent of these governmental actions is to afford certain rights to particular groups of individuals within the employment process. As noted in the previous chapter (Chapter 4), some individuals receive a protected class status within the selection process that prohibits discrimination, at least in part, on the basis of covered group characteristics.

For example, a protected class status is denoted for certain individuals by Title VII of the Civil Rights Act, Age Discrimination in Employment Act, Vocational Rehabilitation Act, Vietnam Era Veterans Readjustment Assistance Act, and Americans with Disabilities Act. Accompanying these federal acts are state-legislated initiatives. More recently, some states have bestowed a protected class status on the basis of sexual preference of applicants (see Chapter 4 for a listing of states).

To exercise the legislative rights afforded by these legislative acts when suspecting discrimination on the basis of their protected class status, applicants must establish only **prima facie** **evidence** of discrimination within the selection process on the basis of protected class status. *Prima facie* is a legal term meaning "at first view" illegal discrimination is likely to have occurred and involves only speculative information rather than conclusive data.

Evidence of *prima facie* discrimination within the selection process is established generally by adherence to a specific doctrine (theory) unique to the legal literature. One doctrine concerns **disparate treatment,** while the other doctrine involves **disparate impact.** "The major difference between these two approaches of allegation rests with the intentions of the employer" (Young & Ryerson, 1986, p. 10).

As an approach for establishing *prima facie* evidence for discrimination within the selection process, disparate treatment addresses specifically the intentions of the public school district and the school district's representatives. Intentions are defined broadly to include both direct and indirect evidence. An example of direct evidence could be a written statement endorsed by a school board.

To illustrate, a school board could have a written policy endorsing the attraction of "young and highly motivated teacher candidates" to complement the current workforce of a public school district (violation of the Age Discrimination in Employment Act). The intentions of a school board are reflected also by job advertisements. For example, it is not unusual for school boards seeking a new superintendent to require previous experience as a superintendent on the part of all viable job candidates for consideration.

Literally, this minimum job requirement assumes that to be a successful superintendent in the focal district requires previous experience as a superintendent in another school district. However, very few females in most states have held a superintendent's position, and this job requirement has a disproportional impact for otherwise qualified females. Thus, *prima facie* evidence of discrimination is provided by such an advertisement.

Indirect evidence could involve only public statements made by important stakeholders (school board members or public school administrators) favoring young candidates over older candidates within the selection process (Age Discrimination in Employment) or experienced superintendents over otherwise qualified job candidates (Title VII of the Civil Rights Act). In both instances involving direct and indirect information, this is what is labeled as the "smoking gun phenomenon" (there is a dead person and the individual holding the smoking gun is presumed to be guilty). This smoking gun phenomenon, as provided through direct and indirect evidence, has long been considered as sufficient for a disparate treatment claim by courts as well as by governmental agencies having jurisdictional authority within the selection process.

Rather than focusing on the intentions of public school districts and their organizational representatives as addressed by the doctrine of disparate treatment is the doctrine of disparate impact. Requirements for the doctrine of disparate impact consider the actions of employers. Actions of employers are assessed in light of outcomes from the selection process regardless of any underlying intentions exhibited or inferred by responsible parties.

School boards and their administrative representatives may well have the best intentions, but the outcomes from the selection process could suggest otherwise. For the doctrine of disparate impact the most common evidence is statistical data. Statistical data are assessed most generally from a disparate impact perspective by **flow statistics.**

Flow statistics consider three types of information. For any particular employee classification, flow statistics reflect (1) the number of applicants, (2) the number of hires, and (3) the **selection ratio** as defined by the percentage rates within a particular employee classification. Contained in Table 5.1 are flow statistics for a high school principal position as compiled across a 5-year period broken down only by sex of applicants (other breakdowns are necessary to address all protected class groups).

An examination of the data contained in Table 5.1 indicates a different selection rate based on the sex of applicants seeking the high school principal position. Clearly, the selection rate for females applying for a high school principal position is less than the selection rate for males applying for the same position within this same time period. Because of these different selection rates, the actions of this public school district are assumed to have a disproportional impact on females and to provide *prima fascie* evidence of discrimination in this particular school district.

Although this may not have been the intention of this particular school district to have such different selection rates based on sex of applicants, evidence of the flow statistics is compelling in light of existing legislation. "A selection rate for any race, sex, or

TABLE 5.1
Flow Statistics for Principal Positions

Principal Positions	Applicant Numbers	Applicant Hires	Selection Ratios
Female	20	1	5%
Male	20	6	33%

ethnic group which is less than (4/5) (or 80 percent) of the rate for the group with the highest rate will generally be regarded by the federal enforcement agency as evidence of an **adverse impact,** while a greater than four-fifths will generally not be regarded as evidence of a adverse impact" (EEOC Uniform Guidelines, 1978, Section 1607.4(D), bold added). Unfortunately, many public school districts fail to collect these data needed to compute flow statistics relative to particular protected class groups.

This omission in data collection for a public school district can have some negative consequences both from a strategic planning perspective and from a legal viewpoint. "Where the user has not maintained data on an adverse impact as required by the documentation section of applicable guidelines, the Federal agencies may draw an inference of adverse impact of the selection process from the failure of the user to maintain such data, if the user has an underutilization of a group in a job category, as compared to the groups' representation in the relevant labor market" (EEOC Uniform Guidelines, 1978, Section 1607.4(D)). However, few if any school districts have a completely representative workforce in all job categories, and selection practices in most school districts are defenseless against disparate impact charges when properly asserted.

Once *prima facie* evidence has been established by applicants applying either the doctrine of disparate treatment or the doctrine of disparate impact, an important legal consequence occurs. The **burden of proof** shifts from those making the charge (applicants) to the employing school districts. That is, school districts must prove that they did not illegally discriminate on the basis of protected class status afforded particular types of applicants rather than applicants proving that the school district did discriminate on the basis of protected class status.

As avenues of defense for charges of discrimination based on *prima facie* evidence, school districts have several options. One option concerns providing evidence of a **bona fide occupational qualification** (BFOQ) relative to protected class status. The other option involves providing data indicating that selection practices and selection processes are job related even though having a disproportional impact on certain protected class groups.

With respect to the BFOQ defense, this approach requires that school districts show a business necessity for excluding particular protected class groups. Omitted specifically from this defense is any protected class groups defined on the basis of race or color (Heneman & Judge, 2006). Even with these exemptions, the BFOQ defense is quite rare in the educational setting, especially in light of reasonable accommodations required by the employer.

One of the few exceptions for a BFOQ in education is chronological age for potential job candidates. Many states have legislated chronological age as a BFOQ for bus drivers. According to this legislation, as presently written in state statues, individuals exceeding a maximum age requirement can be categorically excluded from consideration for a vacant bus driver position. Unlike this exception, for most other positions within the educational setting, a BFOQ is an unlikely defense for public school districts.

However, within the limited confines of most improbable BFOQ's as a probable defense, "nothing contained in any of the legislation prohibits school districts from employing the most qualified candidate if all applicants are treated equitably during the selection process" (Young & Ryerson, 1986, p. 9). As such, the other defense available to public school districts concerns demonstrating that the selection process utilized only preemployment practices and predictors that related to job performance (see EEOC Uniform Guidelines, 1978). Because this later defense has functional advantages for a public school district with regard to the selection of only the most qualified employees, it should be approached from a proactive rather than a reactive perspective in the design of and execution of a selection process used by all public school districts.

Most importantly, this proactive approach involving relating selection processes and preemployment predictors to job expectations is recommended by existing legislation as well as by all those advocating best practices in the public school setting. Specific to this approach is a basic understanding of the components necessary for developing and/or evaluating a selection system used by a public school district. To provide this information is the focus of the following section.

Selection from an Organizational Perspective

Whether a school system is small or large and is located in a rural, suburban, or urban setting, it is easy to make a compelling case for valid selection because a great deal of time, money, and effort is wasted when selection fails to meet either the expectations of applicants or the requirements of public school districts. The impact of poor selection is so serious that the selection process in education has been (Bolton, 1969) and continues to be a critical issue for all public school systems (Young & Marroquin, 2006). No doubt, an effective selection system serves well the interests of all involved stakeholders when properly conceptualized and efficiently executed (Delli & Vera, 2004).

As one of the operational directives comprising the strategic planning process noted in Chapter 1, selection has been reconceptualized over the past few decades. Currently, selection is viewed as a sequential process involving at least two separate but related phases within the public school setting. One phase concerns **screening decisions** focusing on delimiting an initial applicant pool, while the other phase involves **employment decisions** serving as a final hurdle for applicants. These separate but related phases of the selection process have evolved from a sound research stream, and this research stream provides a foundational base for understanding contemporary thought about selection practices in the public school setting.

To recap this research stream from a historical perspective, selection was perceived initially to be an event rather than a process both in early research literature and in actual practice within the field setting. As an event, selection was equated in this literature largely with only the selection interview as a means of acquiring new personnel to meet organizational needs. On reflection of this event perspective in light of current knowledge about employee selection, "Nothing could be further from the truth if the best possible person/job match is to be made" (Heneman, Judge & Heneman, 2000, p. 368).

Altering the perception of selection from an event to a process are several well-grounded studies in the published literature. When selection was considered (inappropriately) as an event in this literature, several different research methodologies were used indiscriminately to examine selection decisions, and these methodologies were assumed to be universal proxies for interview decisions. Included among these methodologies used to investigate selection are the following research protocols used by investigators: (1) paper credentials, (2) video techniques, and (3) experimental simulations.

Paper credentials were used by researchers to create hypothetical applicants simulating data as found in most college placement files. Often included among these data sources are résumés, letters of recommendations, and candidate statements concerning career goals. Within these credentials used to simulate hypothetical job candidates, certain characteristics about applicants (e.g., age, sex, etc.) or applicant qualifications (e.g., experience, GPA's, etc.) are manipulated systematically by the investigator(s) in tightly defined studies. Procedurally, superintendents and principals selected to take part in these studies are requested to evaluate applicants as depicted by paper credentials for a vacant position within their public school district.

To illustrate by example, the first educational study relying solely on paper credentials to study selection decisions of educational administrators was conducted by Young and Allison (1982). Young and Allison created hypothetical teacher candidates through the use of résumés to depict potential job candidates. Within the résumés used to depict hypothetical applicants, all candidate qualifications were held constant with the exception of chronological age for the hypothetical applicant. These investigators mailed credentials of hypothetical job candidates to public school superintendents as well as to high school principals and requested these participants to evaluate the candidates as if they were filling a vacant focal position within their school system.

Evaluations of superintendents and of high school principals for a vacant focal position in their school district were based solely on paper credentials of hypothetical applicants. These investigators found selection decisions to vary systematically according to chronological age of teacher candidates. Although all candidates were depicted as being equally qualified, younger teacher candidates were preferred over older teacher candidates both by superintendents and by high school principals despite rights afforded the later group by the Age Discrimination in Employment Act.

Other investigators of the selection process have used video techniques to explore selection decisions of organizational representatives. Using this research protocol involving video techniques, a **confederate** (job applicant) is videotaped when responding to a preestablished interview protocol. From an experimental perspective, either content of the interview script or characteristics of the applicant is systematically manipulated by the investigator though experimental protocol.

As a point in example, Young and Pounder (1985) varied the chronological age of a job candidate through cosmetic manipulation of the applicant. Content of the interview process was held constant through scripted information, and age of the applicant was manipulated through wigs and cosmetic applications. For the various experimental manipulations, organizational representatives viewed a single condition and evaluated the hypothetical job candidate.

Reactions of persons acting as organizational representatives of a public school district were found to vary according to age of the hypothetical teacher candidate. Younger teacher candidates were preferred over older teacher candidates. However, in reality, the teacher candidate was portrayed by the same person (a confederate) and educational qualifications were held constant in all experimental conditions.

Still different from either paper credentials or video manipulations used to investigate selection decisions is the interview simulation technique. The interview simulation technique includes visual as well as verbal interactions between the applicant and the organizational representative. Functionally, this experimental protocol involves role-playing on the part of both participants (interviewees and interviewers).

The first educational study to use an interview simulation involving only role-playing was conducted by Young (1983). Within this study, structure of the interview format was varied (dyad vs. panel) and participants (administrators and teachers) were assigned at random to specific experimental treatments (dyad vs. panel interview conditions). Administrators evaluated hypothetical job candidates relative to their suitability for a vacant focal position within their respective school district.

Results of this study involving an interview simulation indicate that the structure of the interview protocol can influence selection decisions of educational administrators. Candidates interviewed in panel interviews were more likely recommended for employment than candidates interviewed in dyad interviews. Because applicants in both interview conditions (either panel or dyad) were assigned at random to a specific treatment condition, these findings indicate that interview structure rather than candidate qualifications influence outcomes from the selection process as perceived by educational administrators.

Given these different experimental protocols for investigating selection decisions of administrators (paper credentials, video techniques, and interview simulations), and the assumed validity of these methodologies as a proxy for selection decisions in general, certain methodological studies have been conducted. Unlike existing research holding applicant research protocol constant through relying on a specific simulation technique (paper credentials, video techniques, and interview simulations), methodological studies held constant applicant stimuli and varied research protocols as a means for communicating this information to organizational representatives. That is, what varied is the mode of communication.

For example, Gorman, Clover, and Doherty (1978) compared selection outcomes based either on paper credentials or on interviews, and Young and Pounder (1985) compared selection outcomes based on videotapes with selection outcomes based on simulated interviews. Bolton (1969) manipulated written, audio, and visual information about job candidates. Results of these studies indicate that selection decisions are moderated by type of applicant stimuli presented by job candidates.

When these findings are viewed from the lens of an actual practice perspective in the field setting involving public school districts, some important information is imparted. Mainly, that selection is a process rather than an event and that selection decisions are moderated by the type of applicant stimuli. With respect to the selection process in general and more specifically for teachers as well as other certificated personnel, Young and Prince (1999) captured this realization when they noted the following. "At the screening stage of the selection process, applicants are evaluated on the basis of their paper credentials. . . . At the interviewing stage applicants are evaluated on the basis of their verbal and nonverbal performance in the selection interview" (p. 571).

Further reinforcing the notion of selection as a process involving a screening phase and an employment phase is additional research from the private sector. In the private sector, Cable and Gilovich (1998) noted that the difference between screening and employment decisions is realistic as well as nontrivial and warrants the attention of researchers and practitioners. From both a research and a practice perspective, screening decisions determine who will get job interviews and employment decisions determine who will get job offers (Young & Chounet, 2004).

Although well recognized in research and in practice, the importance of screening decisions and of employing decisions comprising the selection process within the public school setting, at least two modes of decision making exist from an organizational perspective common to each phase of the selection process. One mode involves a top-down perspective involving only administrators and school boards in the selection of employees. The other mode utilizes various stakeholders within the educational domain as defined by **site-based decision-making councils.**

For many school districts departing from the traditional mode of selection, the top-down procedure involving the selection of new employees has changed due to the novel managerial practices involving site-based decision-making councils (Bauer & Bogotch, 2001). In some instances, these changes have been brought about by state legislation (Winter, Millay, Bjork, & Keedy, 2005), while in other instances, these changes reflect local policy preferences enacted by boards of education. At the forefront in legislative, changes relative to the selection of employees is Kentucky where most selection decisions are delegated to site-based decision-making councils involving designated stakeholders (KERA, 1990).

The premise underlying the usage of site-based decision-making councils is that those closest to the work site of a potential employee are best equipped to make selection decisions (Lindle, 2000). In general, site-based decision-making councils are comprised of administrators, parents, and teachers. Collectively, this group determines the outcome of the selection process rather than the traditional model of selection relying almost exclusively only on the decisions of administrators.

Whether or not these changes in the manner by which employees are selected are advantageous to all public school districts is open to question given the current state of knowledge. Interestingly, research has explored the decision making of site-based council members relative to the decisions of administrators for teacher selection outcomes by contrasting these different modes of authority within the selection process (Young & Miller-Smith, 2006). This study indicates that selection outcomes may well be a function of the process used to select employees rather than the credentials of potential job candidates seeking vacant focal positions. Within site-based councils, selection decisions of teachers were more positive than selection decisions of parents and of administrators for equally qualified job candidates.

In light of the incongruence between teachers' perceptions and perceptions of other role incumbents (parents and administrators) on site-based decision-making councils relative to the selection of employees, additional research has been conducted (see Young & Marroquin, 2006). More specifically, two competing hypotheses were set forth to explain the more positive rating of teachers as compared to principals for otherwise equally qualified job candidates: (1) teachers perceived other potential teachers more positively within the selection process because of role congruency (they perform the same duties) and/or (2) teachers perceive other teachers more positively within the selection process because of proximal affiliation (on the same faculty). To test these competing hypotheses, both role congruence (teacher vs. guidance counselor) and role proximity (same building vs. different building) were varied in the same experimental design in this study.

Surprisingly, teachers were found to value guidance counselors more than other teachers (role incongruence) regardless of building assignment (neutral proximity) for potential job candidates. These investigators interpreted these findings as a call for help by teachers in addressing the needs of students in areas other than academic needs (i.e., discipline, personal, etc.) and reacting to federal mandates (NCLB) as well as state initiatives (high-stakes testing). From a selection perspective, these results indicated that different selection models (administrator vs. site-based) may produce different results given the same applicant information and that both approaches warrant additional study within the field setting before a definitive model (administrator vs. site-based) can be endorsed. To endorse one approach over another approach for the selection of employees is without empirical support and may well rest with a political decision rather than with an empirical decision.

Beyond changes in procedures for selecting employees brought about by the reconceptualization of selection from an event to a process and by site-based decision-making councils are other advancements concerning selection as a process. Collectively, these changes in conceptualization as well as in process require some rethinking on the part of school districts. Most notably, when envisioning the selection process from a strategic planning perspective, concerns must be afforded to the contexture of specific school districts. Contexture is important because what constitutes effective performance in one school district does not always translate into effective performance in another school district. Urban school districts, suburban school districts, and rural school districts vary greatly in demands and needs for educational programs as well as types of students served.

Although the content of a selection process should be varied to meet the special problems, needs, and characteristics of specific school systems, certain steps within the conceptualization and the design of a selection process are universally applicable to all school systems. As indicated in the previous chapter, the first steps in effective personnel selection are the development of employment policies and the recruitment of applicant pools. Because both of these topics are discussed in the previous chapter addressing recruitment (see Chapter 4), within this chapter the focus is on selection from a procedural perspective.

Selection from a Procedural Perspective

When viewed from a procedural perspective, the selection process contains two components and the interrelationship between these components. One component addresses predetermined measures of job performance (**criteria measures**), and the other component involves those preemployment predictors used to select employees (**predictor variables**). The relationship between these two components of the selection process determines the effectiveness and the efficiency of a selection system within the public school setting.

Criteria Measures

From a strategic planning perspective, all process models assume that valid measures of job performance exist for a selection system. Without valid measures of job performance for particular focal positions, it is impossible to predict the likely success of an applicant at the preemployment stage of the selection process. That is, actual measures of job performance serve a foundational base for all effective selection systems.

Technically, measures of job performance are labeled as criteria by most selection models. In theory, all jobs contain multiple criteria necessary for defining effective performance on the part of position holders. However, in practice, the identification of satisfactory criteria reflecting actual job performance is a difficult endeavor for many school districts, and an endeavor worthy of considerable attention by those responsible for developing and executing selection systems within the public school setting.

For example, one obvious criterion measure of actual job performance is outcomes from the employee appraisal process used to assess actual job performance of employees and provided by an immediate supervisor. Purportedly, outcomes of the performance appraisal process reflect a supervisor's assessment of a position holder's job performance relative to the execution of assigned duties. However, well-known within the education setting are multiple problems associated with performance appraisal outcomes as provided by supervisors, and problems that render this criterion measure as ineffective for validating a selection system in most, but not all, school systems.

Many of the problems associated with the utility of appraisal outcomes as provided by immediate supervisors for use in the selection process can be attributed to structural restraints associated directly with the performance appraisal system adopted by a public school district. Some performance appraisal systems lack any means of quantification that are useful for defining uniform selection criteria applicable to all employees within a specific classification. Specifically, narrative performance appraisal systems (i.e., management by objectives, portfolios, etc.) produce results unique to an individual, and these results fail to be uniform across positions.

Other performance appraisal systems fail to distinguish among employees relative to any meaningful gradients of job performance necessary for distinguishing between effective and ineffective employees. Rating systems and checklists often suffer from a **restricted range.** That is, employees are evaluated only either as satisfactory or unsatisfactory with almost all employees being classified in the former category.

Support, for these criticisms pertaining to common performance appraisal processes and outcomes as criteria for a selection system, is easily found in the field setting. Within many public school systems, an audit of personnel files in most school districts will reveal data insufficient for valid criteria measures required for developing/evaluating a selection system. Based on such reviews, far too often, performance appraisal processes are designed to satisfy statutory requirements (as per policy or contract) rather than efficiency concerns related to job performance (necessary for selection).

Fortunate, although few in number, are those school districts that have sound performance appraisal systems yielding valid criteria measures for developing a valid selection process. Because of this common deficiency relating to existing performance appraisal systems, other criteria measures and procedures of obtaining these necessary criteria measures are suggested. Specifically suggested by the Uniform Guidelines on Employee Selection Procedures as valid criteria measures are tardiness, absenteeism, and length of service (see Section 1607.14, Subsection 3). As potential criteria measures (tardiness, absenteeism, and length of service) for an employee selection system, these work outcome variables relate directly to some of the selection goals mentioned at the beginning of this chapter.

On reflection, one of the goals of selection noted earlier in this chapter concerns selecting employees motivated to perform their job assignments. If employees are consistently tardy in reporting to work or are frequently absent from work, then these employees lack the necessary motivation for fulfilling their job assignment with a public school district. Another goal of selection indicates that employees should be attracted and employed that will remain with the school district for a reasonable period of time, and length of service is a direct criterion measure of this goal.

Suggested, also, by the Uniform Guidelines on Employee Selection Procedures for obtaining criteria measures for selection systems, is a job analysis. Although a comprehensive job analysis represents a considerable investment of time and energy, it is a wise investment given the importance of selection for the effective functioning of a school district. All too often, this important step in the selection process is omitted and appropriate criteria go otherwise undefined. Unless appropriate job criteria are identified, valid job predictors for an effective selection process are unobtainable, and selection is rendered as a procedural rather than as a substantive administrative process.

Job criteria, as identified through a job analysis and as used for refining the selection process, should reflect the knowledge and skills of position holders required to perform the tasks associated with particular jobs. Knowledge and skill requirements are defined by the Equal Employment Opportunity Commission (EEOC) guidelines on employee selection. The EEOC defines knowledge as "a body of information applied directly to the performance of a function" and skill as an "observable competence to perform a learned psychomotor act" (Equal Employment Opportunity Commission [EEOC], 1978).

In keeping with the goals of selection as described earlier in this chapter, knowledge and skill requirements are important. Knowledge and skill requirements determine who among the pool of applicants possesses the minimum qualifications for a vacant focal position and who among those applying exceed the minimum qualifications. These requirements as defined by a job analysis are a necessary but not a sufficient condition for selection.

An individual without the knowledge and skill requirements for a particular job would be an ineffective employee, but an individual possessing the minimum knowledge and skill requirements for a particular job should be considered only as a viable candidate. For example, a common task dimension for elementary school principals is instruction, which requires both knowledge and skill. To be effective, elementary school principals need both knowledge of learning theory for early childhood and skill for demonstrating teaching in the classroom setting.

To assess the relevance of actual criteria for the important tasks comprising the job(s) under consideration, a content validity analysis is required. Content validity, unlike other types of validity to be discussed, is determined analytically through subject matter experts rather than empirically through statistical techniques. For a content validity analysis, subject matter experts with in-depth knowledge about the position(s) under consideration are used to assess the relationship between actual criteria and required job tasks.

Actual criteria, the knowledge and skill required for effective performance, should be developed for each task dimension comprising focal jobs. The number of actual criteria will vary with the complexity of the task dimension. Some task dimensions may have several different knowledge and skill components, and each of these must be identified.

After the validities of actual job criteria are established through a content validity analysis, the next step is to identify **job predictors** that measure these criteria at the preemployment stage of the selection process. Job predictors are used to assess the competencies of applicants relative to actual job criteria and include "all selection procedures used as a basis for any employment decision" (National Archives and Records Administration, 1978, Section 2B).

Predictor Variables

The actual choice of predictor variables is an extremely important decision for school districts and for applicants. Job predictors are proxies used by management. Functionally, predictor variables are used to assess the probable success of applicants seeking gainful employment with a public school district at the preemployment stage of the selection process.

The number of and the type of job predictors used varies both between school districts for the same position and within school districts for different positions. Some districts use elaborate selection systems with many job predictors, while others use simple selection systems with few job predictors. Depending on the focal position under consideration, the number of and the type of job predictors may vary within a particular school system.

Because the selection of employees to fill vacant positions in the public school setting follows a sequential process involving screening decisions as well as employment decisions, an effective selection system must be attuned to both types of decisions (screening and employing) when identifying potential job predictors for delimiting applicant pools. Screening decisions serve to delimit the initial applicant pool and to determine who among the job candidates will receive further consideration within the employment process, while employment decisions finalize the selection process either by rejecting or accepting certain individuals comprising a final applicant pool of job candidates.

In keeping with the contemporary view of selection being a process rather than an event and with selection involving screening as well as employment decisions, consideration must be given to the identification of predictors at both stages of the selection process. Most predictors used to screen applicants are objective, while most predictors used to employ applicants are subjective. Following is an overview of frequently used potential predictors utilized by most public school systems either to delimit an initial applicant pool or to extend an employment offer.

Predictors for Screening Decisions

Most school districts delimit the initial applicant pool on the basis of information provided by the candidates as part of the application process (Young & Fox, 2002). As part of the application process, applicants submit information about themselves in several forms. In some instances the information is self-reported, while in other instances the information involves external references.

The actual medium used to submit information by applicants for initial consideration is under the control of the school system. School systems should develop policies about application requirements that dictate the type of information acceptable and the type of information used for delimiting an initial applicant pool. Research addressing these different sources for applicant information suggests some sources are better than other sources as potential predictor variables at the screening stage of the selection process.

Application Form

The **application form** is almost a universal source of information collected by most public school districts as part of the employee selection process and is completed either by traditional paper means or electronically on the Internet. As a source of information for identifying potential predictors of subsequent job performance, an application form has several often unrecognized and/or underutilized advantages for guiding the decision making of organizational representatives at the screening stage of the selection process. Most important among these advantages, content of the application form is controlled by the public school district, and the application form yields comparable information about all applicants, seeking a specific focal position.

It is by no means unusual for school districts to have several different types of application forms. Depending on the type of position sought by an applicant, the application form may differ relative to informational requirements. In most instances, application forms within a specific school district should differ for administrators, teachers, and classified positions because of unique informational demands associated with various position classifications.

Beyond the unique information sought for different types of positions, all application forms should have some common elements. Application forms should provide contact information about the candidate, information relating to educational obtainments, information on experiences relating to position requirements, information concerning special skills, a disclaimer statement for indemnifying school systems, and an acknowledgment of truth relative to the information provided. Each of these information sources serves a specific purpose at the screening stage of the selection process.

Contact information provides a means of establishing a communication link between applicants and the school district. Oftentimes, potentially promising applicants are lost during the selection process through a lack of communication, especially those applicants in a transitional stage of life. Recent graduates may be leaving the university setting since applying for a position, and experienced job candidates may be relocating to a new place of residence. At minimum, contact information should be collected in the following categories on all application forms, and many application forms omit some of these contact sources: (1) current address, (2) permanent address, (3) telephone number, (4) cell phone number, and (4) e-mail address. Unless the applicant forms used by a school district have been revisited recently, it is likely that a cell phone number and an e-mail address have been omitted as part of the information requirements.

Important for many jobs in the educational setting are the educational accomplishments of potential job candidates. Educational accomplishments go well beyond awarded degrees. It is important to note educational degrees but it is also important to have information about specific educational achievements/certifications beyond those of awarded degrees.

Application forms should be sensitive to the relevant job experiences of potential candidates. Given that most application forms are sensitive to "like-type experiences" in a similar focal position to the one under consideration, many job applicants have complementary job experiences that could benefit the school district. To avoid overlooking these otherwise qualified job candidates at the screening stage of the selection process, information about job experiences should be broadly requested by the application form to include similar as well as complementary job experiences.

Easily ignored by traditional application forms are special skills of potential job candidates unaddressed by formal degrees. Most notable in our multicultural environment are proficiencies in different languages and knowledge of various cultures having important implications within the work setting. Appropriately designed, an application form can capture this type of information and can inform decision making at the screening stage of the selection process when differentiating among unqualified, qualified, and highly qualified applicants.

The purpose of a disclaimer statement on an application form is to indemnify the school system and its representatives at the screening stage of the selection process. As part of the screening process, school districts should verify previous job experiences and should check reference sources. Decisions made on the basis of this information by school districts and representatives of the school district should be viewed as harmless and so noted on the application form.

Contents of the application form are assumed to be true by the employing public school district. If fraudulent information is provided by job applicants on the application form or if important information has been intentionally omitted (i.e., a previous employment relationship), then school districts should be released from any contractual relationships involving said employee. To provide this outlet in a simple and uncomplicated manner, an application should contain a statement signed by the potential applicant attesting to the truth of information provided (see Table 5.2 as an example).

TABLE 5.2
Waiver Statement for a Public School Application Form

The following waiver contains important legal consequences. Therefore, please read the waiver completely and carefully before signing.

Under penalty of perjury, I hereby certify that all statements made herein are true and correct to the best of my knowledge and authorize investigation of all statements herein recorded. Further, I understand that any false or incomplete statements made may be cause for non-employment or dismissal, if employed. I release and hold harmless all persons and organizations providing any information, references, or data to be utilized by Central Unified School District to determine my qualifications for employment. I hereby authorize the release of any and all such information, references, and data. A photocopy of this authorization may be considered as an original for this purpose. It is understood that if employed, I will be required to submit official transcripts, credentials, TB examination, and loyalty oath. I agree that if employed, I will abide by all policies and procedures established by administration. I also agree that if I am currently under contract with another school district that I will be released from such contract before entering into an agreement with Central Unified School District.

Source: http://www.centralusd.k12.ca.us/.

Beyond these minimum requirements for an application form to be used as a source of decision making at the screening stage of the selection process, certain information should be omitted from this preemployment predictor (Wallace, 2004). Omitted specifically on application forms should be any information infringing on the rights of individuals afforded protection from discrimination in employment based on their protected class status as defined by federal and by state legislation. From an equal employment opportunity perspective, all preemployment predictors should be **facially neutral** relative to protected class status of applicants.

In actual practice, many application forms solicit information that is unrelated to job performance, that is a potential contaminant in the selection process, and that is scrutinized closely by federal agencies. This type of information is of particular concern because research has shown that screening decisions of school administrators are often influenced by factors unrelated to job performance, such as the chronological age of applicants (Young & Oto, 2004), the gender of job candidates (Young, in press), the national origin of individuals (Young & De La Torre, 2006), and the disability status of particular job candidates (Young & Prince, 1999). To reduce these contaminants as a potential influence on preemployment screening decisions, school systems should analyze carefully all application forms, as well as all other types of information requested from job candidates at the screening stage of the selection process.

Although unintentional in many instances by most public school districts, some rights of protected class individuals may be abridged by information requested on application forms. These are rights afforded by specific federal and state legislation through long-established statues. In some instances these informational requests are blatant, while in other instances these informational requests are subtle yet revealing relative to the protected class status of job candidates.

Blatant on some traditional application forms are items pertaining to race, national origin, sex, age, and handicapped status. Information pertaining to race, national origin, and sex is in violation of Title VII of the Civil Rights Act. For age and handicapped conditions, these data are forbidden by the Age Discrimination in Employment Act and by the Americans with Disabilities Act, respectively.

Application forms can require less blatant information but information that can be used to infer the protected class status of some job candidates within the selection process. Sex of applicants can be inferred by requiring a maiden name as part of the information requested on an application form. Maiden names of applicants are requested by some districts to match transcripts with other applicant information sources (i.e., applicant forms, reference information, etc.), but this efficiency attempt on the part of employing school districts should be avoided as a means of protecting the protected class status of individuals at the screening stage of the selection process.

Chronological age of applicants is implied for some individuals by requesting dates of graduation on application forms. In reality, what is important about educational obtainment from an organizational perspective is type of degrees and recentness of educational experiences for potential job candidates. Competencies and not chronological age should be used to delimit an applicant pool at the screening stage of the selection process from an Age in Discrimination in Employment perspective.

Another red flag for differentiating between protected and nonprotected class individuals at the screening stage of the selection process is salary information. Some school districts request information on an application form about either current salary or expected salary. Well-known within the employment context is that protected class individuals receive less salary and have lower salary expectations than nonprotected class individuals, and salary information is a strong indicator of protected class status for applicants and represents a potential violation of both Title VII of the Civil Rights Act and the Equal Pay Act.

Clearly, all public school districts should review the informational requests solicited by their application forms when these forms are used to screen job candidates. Unfortunately, many public school districts have failed to conduct such reviews. Consequently, inappropriate information is solicited from applicants at the screening stage of the selection process.

Once refined, items on the application form can be weighted and scored in a way that differentiates between ineffective and effective applicants at the screening stage of the selection process. Certain items, such as those on related job experience, can be weighted more heavily than other items having less bearing on the positions under consideration (Dessler, 1988). When the items relating to knowledge and skill requirements are appropriately weighted within the screening process, better decisions can be made about potential job candidates at the screening stage of the selection process.

Application forms that are scored can be developed. For example, many positions require a knowledge component to communicate clearly, part of which may involve written expression. The applicant's ability to write, as evidenced on these forms, can be scored for grammar, syntax, and clarity based on their responses to open-ended questions on an application form.

Reference Information

Second only to application forms as a means of delimiting an initial applicant pool of potential job candidates at the screening stage of the selection process for public school employees is reference information. "While it is not very difficult to verify the previous employment of an applicant, it can be rather difficult to verify the quality of his/her previous performance" (Aamodt, Bryan, & Whitcomb, 1993). To assess the work quality of candidates in previous positions or anticipated performance of inexperienced applicants, school systems have used a variety of predictors to obtain reference information addressing probable job success. The two predictors most frequently used to assess probable success of applicants as viewed by reference sources are letters of recommendation and standardized reference forms.

Letters of Recommendation

Research has shown that letters of recommendation influence screening decisions of school administrators at the preemployment stage of the selection process. Of particular concern to administrators is the tone of a letter. Bredeson (1982) varied the tone of letters describing candidate qualifications to be either neutral or positive, and this investigator found that anything less than a strongly positive letter has a negative effect on screening decisions.

Following this line of research, Young and McMurray (1986) manipulated the perceived (not actual) length of letters of recommendation. Within their study, tone was held constant and length was varied. In spite of popular perceptions, the length of letters of recommendation seems to have little influence on the screening decisions of school administrators at the screening stage of the selection process.

As a preemployment predictor at the screening stage of the employment process, some school districts require letters of recommendation to delimit a pool of potential job applicants. Almost always, reference sources/authors of these letters are designated by the job candidates as part of the application process. However, this choice should not be an unguided activity from a human resource perspective.

Directions are needed to determine the type of letters solicited by a public school district. This direction should be provided in the form of a formal policy statement. Depending on the reference source chosen by applicants, letters of recommendation can be broadly classified as either personal or professional and can depart different types of information.

Personal letters of recommendation address primarily the character of the applicant and not the job competencies of the applicant. It is not uncommon for personal letters of recommendation to be solicited from individuals such as elected officials, influential community members, and clergy lacking knowledge about a candidate's professional competencies relative to the focal position sought by a job candidate. In many instances, these sources of recommendation acknowledge their lack of competence for assessing job qualifications and address only the character attributes of the job candidate in their letter of recommendation.

Unlike personal letters of recommendation as provided by well-intentioned parties, **professional letters of recommendation** should focus on the job competencies of the applicant under consideration and come from those with a professional knowledge bearing on a job candidate's potential for a particular job. Sources for professional letters of recommendation provided frequently by applicants are previous supervisors, past college professors, and colleagues having direct knowledge about an applicant's level of proficiency in the job setting. Even with these different sources of potential authors having purported job content knowledge, it is advantageous for a school district to request that letters of recommendation be focused on the particular job competencies of an applicant and be tailored to the specific focal position sought by a job candidate.

Although both personal and professional letters of recommendation are contextually rich in information provided about job candidates, these potential predictors for delimiting an applicant pool at the screening stage of the selection process have several downsides when used to delimit an initial applicant pool. One downside associated with letters of recommendation in general involves the response style of authors providing reference information about job candidates. Another downside associated with letters of recommendation concerns the consistency of information revealed through this preemployment predictor when used to delimit an initial applicant pool at the preemployment stage of the selection process.

Research has shown that letters of recommendation often say more about the source (the author) writing the letter than about the applicant seeking the letter. Interestingly, two letters written by the same author for two different job candidates are more consistent than two letters written by different authors for the same job candidate (Baxter, Brock, Hill, & Rozelle, 1981). Thus, it should not be surprising that letters of recommendation account for less than 2 percent of the variance associated with job criteria when assessed from an empirical perspective (Reilly & Chao, 1982).

Another major downside associated with letters of recommendation is the type of information provided to decision makers. Information obtained by letters of recommendation is specific to an applicant and hampers comparisons among applicants at the screening stage of the selection process. To provide common information about job candidates and to facilitate comparisons of applicants at the screening stage of the selection process, letters of recommendation have been found to be lacking, and many school districts use standardized reference forms rather than letters of recommendation.

Standardized Reference Forms

As a preemployment predictor for delimiting an initial applicant pool, the standardized reference form limits both the amount of and the type of information provided organizational representatives. In so doing, the standardized reference form provides similar information about all job candidates and serves as a common reference point for those charged with delimiting an initial pool of candidates. By having similar information about all job candidates, equitable comparisons among candidates are more likely to be forthcoming than if varied information is provided for each job candidate (see discussion for letters of recommendation).

When designing a standardized reference form for use in the public school setting, several options exist relative to the format of this instrument (Young, 2005). At the basic level, a standardized reference form can be either criterion referenced or norm referenced. Differences between sources of reference rest with the comparison group used by the information provider.

A criterion-referenced form involves rating potential job candidates according to some predetermined standards/content. Typically, a Likert-type rating scale (i.e., 1–5 with higher being better) is used to denote degrees of proficiency relative to specific criteria (specific criteria discussed below). For each criterion contained on a standardized reference form, the referent source rates a perceived level of proficiency for a job candidate relative to an external standard (i.e., a specific criterion).

In contrast to a criterion-referenced form relying on ratings, a norm-referenced form involves a comparative ranking of job candidates. Rather than being evaluated in absolute terms according to each criterion, job candidates are evaluated relative to other individuals known by the reference source. That is, rankings are differentiated according to percentiles (i.e., top 5 percent, top 15 percent, etc.) relative to other individuals known by the reference source.

Beyond standards of comparison (criterion or norm referenced), standardized reference forms can vary in content relative to benchmark criteria. Benchmark criteria contained within a reference varies according to content, and "Content contained within a structured reference could vary according to psychological processes (e.g., motivation/maturity), academic proclivity (e.g., research interest/basic intellectual skills), and/or communication skills (e.g., verbal/written)" (Young, 2005, p. 19). Depending on particular jobs as well as on particular content assessed, validity of this information for informing screening decisions at the screening stage of the selection process can vary within as well as across public school districts and should be assessed by every school district for particular jobs under consideration.

Other Prescreening Indicators

Beyond application forms and reference information, several other sources of information are available about applicants at the screening stage of the selection process to guide the decision making of public school administrators or site-based councils. One of these important sources of information is the academic transcripts provided by potential job candidates and used by many public school districts as part of the screening process. As part of the initial screening process, academic transcripts can be evaluated from several perspectives.

Central to most perspectives for identifying potential job candidates, especially for certificated positions involving teachers and administrators, are quality indicators as reflected by grade point averages. Grade point averages can be differentiated between undergraduate and graduate course work through an analysis of academic transcripts submitted by job candidates as part of the application process. Oftentimes, undergraduate grade point averages are more informative than graduate grade point averages when differentiating among quality job candidates at the screening stage of the selection process.

Undergraduate grade point averages can be viewed from an overall perspective and can be decomposed in several ways to reflect different levels of achievement. From an overall perspective, transcripts reveal a grade point average reflecting efforts spanning undergraduate career accomplishments relative to courses taken and quality points earned. As a potential predictor of academic performance, overall undergraduate grade performance exhibits a high degree of variability for distinguishing among potential job candidates.

Although exhibiting the highest variability (largest standard deviation) as an academic predictor for candidates comprising an applicant pool, overall undergraduate grade point averages, as a potential predictor of future job performance, are challenged frequently from a developmental basis. Well noted within the developmental literature is that many undergraduate students lack direction and focus early in their educational careers, and overall undergraduate grade point averages are insensitive to a "maturing effect" and underestimate the academic proclivity of job candidates. To address this maturing effect from a developmental basis, undergraduate grade point averages can be calculated according to performance in an academic major, to achievements in specific courses, or according to performance in the last two years of undergraduate enrollment.

Typically, graduate course work as compared to undergraduate coursework, as a potential predictor of future job performance, suffers from a restriction in range. For most all individuals, graduate grade point averages are systematically higher, and across applicants, reflect lower standard deviations than undergraduate grade point averages. Given the higher mean ratings and the lower standard deviations, graduate grade point averages are generally less effective for delimiting an applicant pool at the screening stage of the selection process (almost all candidates have a high GPA).

Combining information as contained on college transcripts, information reflected by application forms, and information departed by reference sources are college placement files. For these reasons, many public school districts rely on college placement files to delimit applicant pools as a means for obtaining screening information. The major disadvantage of using college placement files for differentiating among job candidates at the screening stage of the selection is the lack of comparable information provided by different institutions of higher education.

College placement files are generally unique to an institution of higher education and differ across institutions of higher education. Within college placement files coming from separate institutions, different information is collected and is provided to decision makers within the public school setting. Some institutions use criterion-referenced systems and others use norm-referenced systems, while some institutions include candidate statements and other institutions fail to include this information.

As a means for collecting candidate information at the preemployment stage of the selection process, many school districts require potential job candidates to submit résumés as part of the application process. Résumés, like college placement files, vary in content as well as substance. Some potential job candidates use a professional résumé service, while other job candidates rely on less professional sources to depict their qualifications within this mode of communication.

Most recently, some job candidates have attempted to market their skills through the electronic medium as a means for providing information to a public school district at the screening stage of the selection process. Information about self from an applicant's perspective can be and has been provided to school districts as potential employers either on a CD-ROM or via a web page. The utility of these mediums has just begun to be addressed in the professional literature.

For example, Young and Chounet (2004) provided high school principals information about teacher candidates through the traditional method (mailed packets), an electronic method (CD-ROMs), and as posted on a web page. Despite popular opinions about the advantages of electronic information, this national random sample of high school principals preferred by far to receive candidate information through the mail. Candidates using either electronic means of communication for depicting personal information were at a distinct disadvantage at the screening stage of the selection process even though all candidates had identical qualifications. That is, the medium and not the message was an important delimiter for high school principals, in general, when screening job applicants.

For all these alternate sources of information (i.e., CD-ROM, web, etc.) as well as traditional sources of information (letters of recommendation and standardized reference forms), the obtained information can be either confidential or nonconfidential. Whether or not this information is confidential or nonconfidential rests with the applicant and not with the school district. According to the Family Educational Rights and Privacy Act (n.d.), applicants can either waive or fail to waive their access to reference information.

Based on this legislative right, school districts should provide all applicants with this choice prior to collecting any reference information. This choice, as exercised by applicants, should be communicated to reference sources. Importantly, regardless of the choice of applicants (either confidential or nonconfidential), both types of reference information for job candidates must be afforded the same weight within the selection process according to the Family Educational Rights and Privacy Act.

Once the initial applicant pool has been delimited at the screening stage, successful candidates advance to the employment stage of the selection process. At the employment stage of the selection process, candidates are evaluated again on certain predictors. It is these later predictors that are discussed in the following section of this chapter.

Predictors for Employment Decisions

Employment decisions, like screening decisions, serve to delimit a pool of applicants seeking jobs with a public school district. However, the pool of applicants being delimited by employment decisions is comprised only of those candidates surviving the initial screening and advancing to the final stage of the selection process. As such, outcomes of employment decisions determine which job candidates either will be extended a job offer or will be rejected from further consideration by a public school district.

To make employment decisions, school districts use still a different set of predictors for assessing the potential job performance of applicants than those predictors used at the screening stage of the selection process. Most of the predictors used at the screening stage of the selection process rely on written information provided by job candidates. In contrast to the screening stage, most of the predictors used at the employment stage of the selection process rely on verbal presentations and behaviors exhibited by job candidates.

By far, the most frequently used job predictor for assessing verbal performance and behaviors exhibited by job candidates has been and continues to be the selection interview. Few, if any, public school districts fail to use some form of a selection interview at the employment stage of the selection process. Indeed, selection interviews are conducted with classified applicants, teacher candidates, and potential administrators.

Selection Interviews

However, "what many employers fail to realize is that the interview is classified as a 'test' in the Uniform Guidelines and, as such, is subject to the same scrutiny as traditional pencil-and-paper employment tests" (Arvey & Faley, 1992, p. 213). In other words, **selection interviews,** like other job predictors, should be job related and should be subjected to a validity analysis.

As a predictor for employment decisions, the selection interview provides information about job candidates beyond that obtainable with most other job predictors used at the screening stage of the selection process. However, the format of the interview can vary in several ways. Job interviews can be either unstructured or structured. Unstructured interviews are free-flowing, and topics are explored as they emerge during the interview session. Although unstructured interviews provide interviewers with the fewest restrictions and are used frequently as a job predictor, the unstructured interview has been found to be an extremely poor predictor of future job performance because comparable information is not assessed with all applicants during interview sessions (Dipboye, 1992).

A structured interview format eliminates the problem of information incomparability associated with an unstructured interview format. A structured interview format uses a set of prescribed questions, and all candidates are assessed accordingly. At least two distinct formats exist for structured interviews: (1) situational and (2) behavioral.

"The situational interview is based on the theory that intentions predict behaviors" (Maurer, Sue-Chan, & Latham, 1999, p. 168). Intentions are assessed by presenting applicants with a dilemma and by assessing their reactions (Penttila, 2004). For example, candidates for a principal position might be asked if they would start faculty meetings exactly on time or if they would wait until almost all have arrived.

In contrast, the behavior description interview is designed to measure actual past behavior in job-related situations rather than knowledge or achievements (Harris, 1999). Typically a situation is presented (how do you deal with angry parents), and applicants are asked to reflect on previous behavior. For both situational- and behavioral-structured interviews, a scoring guide is used.

In addition to structure, interviews can be either dyadic or panel in design. In dyadic interviews, only one interviewer assesses all job candidates; in panel interviews, more than one interviewer is involved. Recently, many districts have begun to use panel interviews in schools experimenting with site-based management (Young & Miller-Smith, 2006).

Although the choice between a dyadic and a panel interview is far less important than the choice between a structured and an unstructured interview, decisions made about job candidates have been shown to be a function of interview type. Because fewer candidates are recommended for employment when a dyadic interview is used than when a panel interview is used, selection policy should dictate the use of only one interview type when evaluating job candidates (Young, 1983). Otherwise, evaluation of candidates based on their interview performance may be more a function of the type of interview used rather than a function of the actual job qualifications of candidates.

Interviews, in general, can improve greatly by following several simple suggestions as suggested by Payne (2006):

- Aim to allow applicants to demonstrate what they can offer the organization, not to simply confirm expectations or to see how applicants perform under pressure.
- Check on the need for any specific arrangements (e.g., physical access, interpreters, etc.).
- Have questions prepared in advance.
- Ensure consistency and fairness in questioning.
- Focus on the real needs of the job. Do not make assumptions or stereotype individuals.
- The selection committee is entitled to ask applicants whether they can fulfill the requirements of the job (travel, work overtime, perform the physical functions), but such questions must be asked of all applicants.
- It is appropriate to ask people with disabilities whether they require any adjustments to perform the job.
- Allow interviewees time to make their point. Allow silence. Rephrase or clarify if necessary.
- Do not make assumptions about a person's ability to do the job based on physical characteristics.
- Do not ask invasive and irrelevant questions (e.g., Do you intend to have a family?). If necessary, rephrase to gain the essential information you require and ask of all applicants (e.g., Can you commit yourself to the organization for 2 years?).
- Keep records of questions and answers (http://hreoc.gov.au/info_for_employers/best_practice/recruitment.html).

In addition to the above suggestions, Clark (1998) suggested some can and cannot interview questions (see Table 5.3).

TABLE 5.3
Can and Cannot Questions for Interviews

Cannot	Can
Arrest Record	Conviction Record
Religious Affiliations	Limitation on Work Days
Nationality	Languages Spoken
Age or Date of Birth	Dates of Graduation
Nature of Disability	Ability to Do the Job
Martial Status	If Worked under Another Name

Job Simulations/Work Samples

Current research suggests that employee selection can be greatly improved by using predictors with high fidelity (Roth, Bobko, & McFarland, 2005). High-fidelity predictors mirror exactly or as closely as possible the actual job task performed by potential position holders. Although several high-fidelity predictors exist, these are seldom found to be used in the public school setting.

At the lower level of fidelity is the **situational judgment test** (Joiner, 2002). A situational judgment test consists generally of a paragraph describing an event in the work setting. Following this description are four probable outcomes for the situation as described. The applicant is requested to select the best outcome as well as the worst outcome, and to explain the rationale for each choice.

An intermediate level of fidelity is represented by the **job simulation test.** Components of a job simulation test require applicants to perform actual job behaviors in a simulated job environment. For example, an applicant might be required to interact with an angry parent when the parent is being role-played by a current employee.

Content for simulation tests can be obtained from the job analysis process used to identify actual job criteria. For a teacher, a simulation test might involve videotaping a demonstration unit of instruction appropriate for the position; for an administrator, a work sample might involve completing an **in-basket exercise.** The use of simulation tests assumes that inferences associated with traditional job predictors are reduced because the selectors focus on the simulated job behaviors of candidates rather than on more distant proxy measures of potential job performance.

The highest fidelity job predictors for making employment decisions are labeled as **work sample tests** (Heneman & Judge, 2006). Work sample tests involve actually performing the focal position under consideration either in part or in whole. Examples of work sample tests include job tryouts and internships.

Although research in education is limited in the above mentioned areas, some studies have been done. The validity of certain activities for school administrators has been examined in assessment centers (Schmitt, Noe, Meritt, & Fitzgerald, 1984). These initial results appear to be promising, but assessment centers have failed to be capitalized on in the last decade for several probable reasons.

Most importantly among these reasons are efficiency rather than effectiveness concerns. Job simulations require extensive developmental investments on the part of organizations and considerable time requirements for applicants. For both of these reasons, most public school districts rely on traditional predictors for delimiting applicant pools at both stages of the selection process.

Collectively, traditional predictors for both stages of the selection process reflect proxy measures of actual criteria outcomes. To the extent that these proxy measures share common variance with actual criteria measures determines the effectiveness and the efficiency of a selection system used by a public school district. Following is a discussion of this relationship and actual examples taken from the field setting.

Relationships among Criteria and Predictors

When viewed from a process perspective, selection contains two major components necessary for constructing a selection system within the public school setting, and both of these components were discussed in the preceding sections of this chapter: (1) criteria measures and (2) predictor variables. Criteria measures reflect outcomes of the selection process. Outcomes could include selection decisions of organizational representatives, on-the-job performance of employees, and/or behaviors exhibited by employees (i.e., tardiness, attendance). For any specific focal position, multiple criteria measures exist and must be identified as a prerequisite for developing a selection system in a public school setting.

With respect to the second component of a selection system, predictor variables are purported proxies of actual criteria measures that can be assessed for applicants at the preemployment stage of the selection process. Some predictor variables are used by public school districts at the screening stage of the selection process, while other predictor variables are used by public school districts at the employment stage of the selection process. To the degree that predictor variables assess actual criteria measures determines the effectiveness and the efficiency of any selection system used by a public school district.

Graphically, this relationship between only a single criterion measure and a single predictor variable is presented in Figure 5.1 through a Venn diagram. The components of the Venn diagram as contained in Figure 5.1 are as follows: (a) criterion measure, a single outcome from the selection process (Set A), (b) predictor variable, a purported proxy of this criterion measure (Set B), and (c) the intersection of the criterion measure with the predictor variable (Set A∩B). This diagram can be used either when developing an initial selection system or when evaluating an existing selection system from a strategic planning perspective.

These components and the interrelationship among these components are universal to all effective selection systems both from a design and from an evaluative viewpoint. Set A (as contained in Figure 5.1), the criterion measure, consists of one important outcome. This outcome should reflect decisions of organizational representatives, behaviors, and/or processes germane to the effective performance of the job or jobs under consideration.

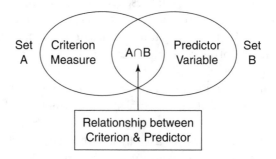

FIGURE 5.1   *Relationship between criterion and predictor.*

The predictor variable (Set B), as contained in Figure 5.1, purports to measure at least one actual outcome associated with either knowledge and/or a specific skill performed by position holders. Predictors may include objective data, such as information imparted by an application form, results from standardized reference forms, and/or academic competencies assessed from transcripts submitted by job candidates. These types of objective predictors are used often at the screening stage of the selection process.

On the other hand, predictors can be based on subjective information. Examples of subjective information include quantified perceptions of organizational representatives about applicants' performance assessed on either the basis of interviews or of simulation exercises. Subjective predictor information is used frequently for employment decisions to delimit a final applicant pool.

Each of these separate but related sets (Set A and Set B) as found in Figure 5.1 helps to conceptualize an effective selection process in the school setting. However, the selection process will be effective only to the extent that the job sets overlap or intersect when applied in the actual field setting (see Set A∩B). Consequently, the goal of effective selection is to maximize the overlap among the sets involving criteria measures and job predictors.

However, the formal relationship between criteria measures and job predictors is seldom assessed by public school districts in the field setting. This omission on the part of public school districts is somewhat surprising because many private sector organizations have been performing such assessments for decades. In actual practice, far too many school systems choose predictors on the basis of untested practices used by other school districts or on testimonies provided by promotional literature.

Underlying this choice of predictors on the basis of usage by other school districts, testimonies, and promotional literature is an assumption of validity. However, federal guidelines address specifically this assumption. "Under no circumstance will the general reputation of a test, its author, or causal reports of a test utility be accepted in lieu of evidence of validity. Specifically ruled out are: assumptions of validity based on test names or descriptive labels; all forms of promotional literature; data bearing on the frequency of a test's usage; testimonial statements of sellers, users, or consultants; and other nonempirical or anecdotal accounts of testing practices or testing outcomes" (Equal Employment Opportunity Commission,1978, Section 1607.8a).

To assess the relationship between job predictors and job criteria, either a **content-related validity analysis** or a criterion-related validity analysis is necessary. The choice between these two different types of validity analyses depends on the characteristics of the predictor under consideration. According to federal guidelines, "A selection procedure based upon inferences about mental processes cannot be supported solely or primarily on the basis of content validity. Thus, a content strategy is not appropriate for demonstrating the validity of selection procedures which purport to measure traits or constructs, such as intelligence, aptitude, personality, commonsense, judgment, leadership, and spatial ability" (National Archives and Records Administration, 1978, Section C1).

Because many predictors used by school districts seek to measure certain traits and characteristics of applicants as defined by the federal guidelines, a **criterion-related validity analysis** is required to assess predictive validity. A criterion-related validity analysis, unlike a content validity analysis, is assessed empirically by statistical techniques, most often a correlation or a regression procedure.

These statistical techniques provide an empirical measure of overlap between job predictors and job criteria (see Set A∩B). This overlap can vary from zero, indicating no overlap, to unity, indicating perfect overlap. In practice, and as depicted in Figure 5.1, the assessed overlap will almost always be far less than unity for any particular predictor of job criteria. This situation is similar to what would be encountered in the field setting. To use an earlier cited example based on an elementary school principal, only part of the knowledge of learning theory (Set B), as assessed from academic course work for early childhood, helps elementary school principals perform effectively in their assigned role when demonstrating classroom teaching (Set A).

The degree of overlap between criteria measures and predictor variables is known as **predictor relevance** (Set A∩B), and the degree to which predictor variables fail to overlap with criteria measures is referred to as **predictor deficiency** (Set B–Set A∩B). In an effective selection system, predictor relevance should be maximized and predictor deficiency should be minimized. To obtain predictors with high relevance and low deficiency is indeed a challenge for school systems.

Unfortunately, most school systems choose predictors on the basis of face validity rather than assessed validity. As a result, many selection systems used by school districts are illegal, counterproductive, and unethical. However, existing selection systems can be improved and effective selection systems can be developed by adhering to this conceptual model, by using current research knowledge about predictors, and by performing additional analyses for predictors. In the following section, attention is directed to these different perspectives through examples obtained from the field setting.

Assessments of Relevancy and Deficiencies

The actual relationship between criteria measures and predictor variables has important legal, practical, and ethical implications for all public school districts. From a legal perspective, this overlap should be assessed statistically. According to minimum federal requirements, "A selection procedure is considered related to the criterion, for purposes of these guidelines, when the relationship between performance on the predictor and performance on the criterion measure is **statistically significant** at the 0.05 level of significance" (EEOC Guidelines, 1978, Section C5, bolded added).

In addition to statistical significance, predictor variables should exhibit a measure of **practical significance,** Practical significance concerns how well a particular predictor improves selection outcomes over baseline conditions. It is possible for a predictor variable to be statistically significant but not practically significant (discussed below).

Beyond statistical and practical significance, other ethical considerations come into play when developing a selection system within the public school setting. Most importantly, predictors should be avoided that have a **disproportional impact** on particular protected class groups. Given these statistical, practical, and ethical concerns for selection systems in the public school setting, attention is afforded to each area and examples are provided that can be used at the local school district level.

Statistical Concerns

Well echoed throughout this chapter is that selection is a process rather than an event. From the process perspective, selection has been defined to include screening decisions and employment decisions. Noted also is that screening decisions and employment decisions are based on separate types of predictor variables and that validity of these predictor variables should be assessed for each types of decision.

To assess the validity of reference information for screening decisions at the preemployment stage of the selection process, Young (2005) provides a format. By following this format, school administrators responsible for selection in a public school district can take theory to practice. In so doing, public school administrators can meet the intent of federal guidelines through an empirical validity paradigm focusing on screening decisions.

For example, Young's study assesses the validity of a standardized reference form, uses a norm-referenced ranking process, and obtains evaluative information provided by reference sources (three for each candidate) nominated by applicants. Content of the reference form contains the following items, most of which are applicable to many focal positions within the public school setting: (1) intellectual ability, (2) educational knowledge, (3) motivation, (4) research ability, (5) maturity, (6) work habits, (7) problem solving, (8) verbal ability, and (9) writing ability. Reference sources nominated by the applicant-ranked candidates' performance on the criteria measures relative to other individuals they have known with "1" denoting a lower 25 percent through "5" denoting the top 5 percent (see Young, 2005, for the actual ranking categories at each level of the 1–5 anchor points).

Contained in Table 5.4 are the rankings and the intercorrelations among these rankings. Most important to note among these data are the high and the statistically significant intercorrelations among reference information provided by referent sources nominated by applicants. That is, considerable redundant information was being collected about the proficiencies of applicants across these chosen criteria, and redundant information fails to serve the applicant seeking consideration, the reference source providing information, or the organization making screening decisions.

As a means for reducing redundant information about applicants and for providing meaningful information about the probable success of applicants at the screening stage of the selection process in an effective and an efficient manner, a regression analysis can be performed. For the regression analysis, the criterion variable in this study consisted of two potential outcomes of each applicant at the screening stage of the selection process: (1) accepted or (2) rejected.

TABLE 5.4
Descriptive Statistics and Correlations among Variables

	Mean	S.D.									
			Descriptive Statistics								
Intellectual Ability	13.36	1.88	1.00								
Education Knowledge	13.22	2.13	.76	1.00							
Motivation	14.09	1.70	.79	.78	1.00						
Research Ability	13.17	2.63	.57	.64	.59	1.00					
Maturity	13.68	1.89	.77	.80	.84	.61	1.00				
Work Habits	13.90	1.76	.79	.81	.90	.63	.87	1.00			
Problem Solving	13.51	2.00	.79	.80	.80	.64	.81	.81	1.00		
Verbal Ability	13.33	2.11	.75	.79	.75	.60	.80	.76	.83	1.00	
Writing Ability	13.02	2.25	.74	.77	.72	.67	.75	.76	.78	.85	1.00

**All correlations are significant at the 0.01 level (2-tailed).
N=243

TABLE 5.5
Statistically Significant Variables Entering the Logistic Regression

	B	S.E.	Wald	df	Sig.	Exp(B)
Research Ability	.377	.083	20.844	1	.000	1.458
Work Habits	−.309	.109	8.065	1	.005	.734
Constant	−.429	1.065	.162	1	.687	.651

Outcomes from the regression analysis indicate that only two of the reference items account for unique sources of variance in screening decisions made by organizational representatives (see Table 5.5) and indicate predictor relevancy (see Figure 5.1). These items, as assessed by referent sources, are research ability and work habits of the applicants (see Set B in Figure 5.1) and are found to account for approximately 14 percent of the variance (see Set A∩B in Figure 5.1) associated with screening decisions (see Set A in Figure 5.1). Given the information imparted by these items, other items contained on the reference form are of little value for guiding screening decisions when attempting to delimit an initial applicant pool and reflect predictor deficiency.

Results of this study suggest important legal implications as well as practical applications for screening decisions based on reference information. By conducting an empirical analysis for the reference information used to delimit an initial applicant pool of potential candidates, organizational representatives are well situated to defend preemployment screening decisions. That is, the predictor variables (reference information, see Set B in Figure 5.1) have a statistically significant relationship (see Set A∩B in Figure 5.1) as suggested by EEOC Guidelines (EEOC Guidelines, 1978, Section C5) with a criterion measure (see Set A, in Figure 5.1) and indicate acceptable measures of predictor relevance.

From a strategic planning perspective, these findings have implications for modifying the content of the reference form. Revealed by these data is the redundancy of reference items contained in the existing reference form and reflect predictor deficiency. With the exception of the two items found to account for unique variance in screening decisions (predictor relevance), other items should be replaced so that additional unique information is acquired at the screening stage of the selection process and redundant information (predictor deficiency) is reduced.

Turning from screening decisions to employment decisions as part of the selection process, other examples exist for assessing the criterion-related validity of other potential predictors for selection outcomes. For a point in example, constructs as measured by a structured interview are assessed (Teacher Perceiver Interview developed by Gallup, Inc.). These constructs are (1) Mission, (2) Investment, (3) Focus, (4) Objectivity, (5) Listening, (6) Empathy, (7) Rapport Drive, (8) Activation, (9) Innovation, (10) Gestalt, (11) Input Drive, and (12) Individualized Perception (see Young & Delli, 2002, for definitions of each theme).

As marketed by the Gallup organization, two versions of this structured interview protocol exist. One version addresses all twelve themes and contains five items per theme, while an abbreviated version assesses only ten of these themes with fewer items per theme. Collectively, these themes represent Set B as found in Figure 5.1 and were assessed preemployment for teacher candidates by trained public school administrators located in the central office.

With respect to criteria measures (see Set A in Figure 5.1), Young and Delli (2002) used postemployment perceptions of supervising principals and attendance data of employees, both of which have been suggested by EEOC guidelines. Most important to note, preemployment predictor assessments made by central office administrators are independent of postemployment criteria measures obtained from separate sources. To assess the relationship (see Set A∩B in Figure 5.1) between preemployment theme assessments and postemployment criteria measures, regression analyses were performed for both versions of the Teacher Perceiver Instrument.

Individualized results from each regression analysis are found in Table 5.6. The relative importance for the different themes vary both by version of the Teacher Perceiver Interview and by criteria measures (principal ratings and attendance data). As a measure of importance, attention should be directed to the Beta Weights.

A summary for the overall regression analyses is found in Table 5.7. As can be observed with these data, the complete version of the Teacher Perceiver is a better predictor than the abbreviated version when all themes are used in the prediction equation. For the complete version of the Teacher Perceiver Interview, 6.25 percent and 5.76 percent of the variance in criteria measures is accounted for with principal ratings and attendance data, respectively, while for the abbreviated version of the Teacher Perceiver Interview only 3.24 percent and .81 percent of the variance is accounted for with respect to these same criteria variables.

Although statistical significance is a minimum necessity from an effectiveness perspective for choosing among potential predictors used to delimit applicant pools, other concerns exist. Beyond statistical significance, potential predictors used by public school districts should have practical significance. Following is a discussion of practical significance as a means for assessing potential predictors from a strategic planning perspective.

TABLE 5.6
Regression Coefficients and Beta Weights for Each Version

T.P.I.	Principal Ratings			Teacher Absentee		
	Theme Titles	Regression Coefficients	Beta Weights	Theme Titles	Regression Coefficients	Beta Weights
Complete Version	Mission	41.765	−0.024	Mission	0.120	0.06
	Investment	−0.147	0.136	Investment	−0.320	−0.16
	Focus	0.821	−0.103	Focus	−0.042	−0.02
	Objectivity	−0.658	0.07	Objectivity	−0.130	−0.07
	Listening	0.396	−0.13	Listening	−0.280	−0.15
	Empathy	−0.727	0.067	Empathy	−0.030	−0.02
	Rapport	0.387	0.238	Rapport	−0.270	−0.15
	Activation	1.319	−0.011	Activation	0.010	0.05
	Innovation	−0.069	−0.054	Innovation	0.320	0.14
	Gestalt	−0.373	0.227	Gestalt	−0.250	−0.16
	Input Drive	1.011	0.007	Input Drive	0.150	0.07
	Ind. Percpt.	0.045	0.120	Ind. Percpt.	−3.650	−0.02
	(constant)	0.693		(constant)	5.810	
Abbreviated Version	Mission	26.980	0.075	Mission	−0.0022	0.00
	Empathy	0.768	−0.255	Empathy	0.2000	0.18
	Rapport	−3.139	−0.104	Rapport	0.2200	0.22
	Ind. Percept.	−1.113	0.002	Ind. Percept.	0.0401	0.05
	Investment	2E−02	0.063	Investment	0.2800	0.22
	Input Drive	0.883	0.181	Input Drive	−0.1200	−0.18
	Activation	1.262	0.265	Activation	−0.1100	−0.14
	Innovation	2.327	0.098	Innovation	106.5000	0.01
	Gestalt	1.034	0.204	Gestalt	−0.0978	−0.07
	Objectivity	3.174	−0.058	Objectivity	0.0965	0.08
	(constant)	−0.810		(constant)	0.6500	

TABLE 5.7
Predictive Validity for Preemployment Composite Interview Scores

	Complete Version (N=124)		Abbreviate Version (N=72)	
	Postemployment Item Theme Composite	Postemployment Absentee Data	Postemployment Item Theme Composite	Postemployment Absentee Data
Preemployment Total Item	.25 (6.25%)[1]	−.24 (5.76%)	.18 (3.24%)	.09 (0.81%)

[1]Note: Numbers represent r^2 as percentage of variance shared.

Practical Significance

Each predictor of job performance used by a school district has a net effect on the effectiveness of a selection system. The net effect of a predictor for a selection system used by a school district concerns the advantage realized by using a particular predictor of job performance as compared to not using that particular predictor. To measure the net effect of each predictor, the job success rates of applicants with and without the use of the predictor must be analyzed.

Success rates of applicants are illustrated in Figure 5.2 by four separate quadrants as defined by Arvey and Faley (1992) and as used in the following examples. These quadrants are determined by establishing the minimum criteria for effective job performance of a position holder (ordinate) and the minimum performance on a predictor required for an employment offer (axis). Because changing the standards of the expected job performance and/or the minimum predictor performance will alter the outcomes, policy makers must consider establishing acceptable levels of performance and cutoff scores.

Each quadrant in Figure 5.2 depicts a specific outcome associated with a particular predictor of job performance: Q1 contains those applicants who were predicted to do well and who did do well; QII contains those applicants who were not predicted to do well but who did do well; QIII contains those applicants who were not predicted to do well and who did not do well; and QIV contains those applicants who were predicted to do well but who failed to do well. Quadrants I and III represent correct outcomes associated with a predictor, while quadrants II and IV represent incorrect outcomes associated with a predictor. Incorrect outcomes are labeled as **false negatives** (Quadrant II) or as **false positives** (Quadrant IV).

Quadrants I and II are used to calculate a **base rate.** The base rate indicates the percentage of persons employed by a district who are successful regardless of their performance on the predictor. A base rate is calculated by dividing the number of successful employees (Q1 + Q2) by the total number of employees selected (Q1 + Q2 + Q3 + Q4) (see Table 5.8).

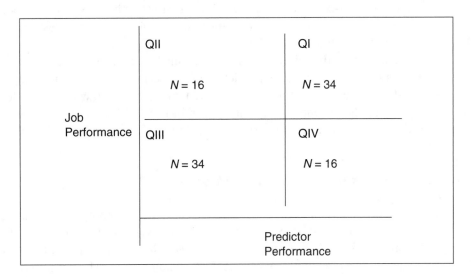

FIGURE 5.2   *Quadrant analysis.*

TABLE 5.8
Base Rate Calculations

Base Rate = (Q1 + Q2)/(Q1 + Q2 + Q3 + Q4)
Base Rate = 50/100
Base Rate = 50%

TABLE 5.9
Accuracy Calculations

Accuracy = (Q1 + Q3)/(Q1 + Q2 + Q3 + Q4)
Accuracy = 68/100
Accuracy = 68%

TABLE 5.10
Calculations for Practical Significance

Practical Significance = Accuracy − Base Rate
Practical Significance = 68% − 50%
Practical Significance = 18%

Quadrants I and III indicate the number of correct employment decisions made by using a particular predictors to select employees for placement in vacant positions. These quadrants provide a measure of **accuracy** for a predictor. Accuracy of a predictor is calculated by dividing the number of correct decisions (Q1 and Q3) by the total number of decisions (Q1 + Q2 + Q3 + Q4) (see Table 5.9).

By converting these numbers to a percentage and by comparing these percentages, the practical significance of a predictor is assessed by the net difference. In this example, the school district could realize a net increase in effectiveness of 18 percent by using this particular predictor of job performance; this net difference provides a measure of practical significance (see Table 5.10).

The steps in the selection process examined so far have emphasized the development and assessment of potential predictors of job performance. The next step focuses on the question "How good is the match?" Stated another way, to what extent do the qualifications of applicants meet the requirements for the positions under consideration and how is this decision made relative to implementation of the selection process?

Implementation of a Selection Process

Rejection or acceptance of an applicant at either the screening stage or at the employment stage of the selection process is a prediction based on information collected using particular predictors of job performance. To operationalize this prediction, two separate decision models can be used at both stages of the selection process. These models involve **multiple hurdles model of decision making** and **compensatory model of decision making.**

According to the multiple hurdles model, all acceptable job candidates must possess a minimum level of competency on specific predictors of future job performance to be viewed as viable candidates. At the screening stage of the selection process, this could include meeting certain certification requirements, possessing a minimum level of academic achievement, and receiving only positive recommendations from reference sources.

For the employment stage of the selection process, all job candidates must exhibit at least a satisfactory level of performance on each predictor to be considered for further consideration. Specific deficiencies noted in a selection interview or in a job simulation could eliminate a candidate from further consideration. Once these minimum hurdles are satisfied, a compensatory decision-making model is used to delimit further the pool of applicants meeting minimum qualifications.

Within the compensatory model of decision making, performances of satisfactory applicants are combined into a composite score. The ideal practice is to place a numerical value on information from each of the several predictors. Raw scores from predictors can be converted into percentile ranks or standard scores so as to be comparable with normative information across all job candidates.

When compiling these scores, different weights can be given to separate predictors. Graphic profiles may be used to portray the results of evaluation. By combining data from application blanks, interview guide sheets, reference and background check forms, tests, and other sources into a profile, the task of relating characteristics of applicants to actual job criteria for vacant positions can be accomplished more effectively.

When all information about a candidate is juxtaposed to the requirements of the position, the selector must compare the two sets of information and predict whether the applicant will perform according to expectations. In various school systems, one employment technique is to place those individuals judged to be qualified for a position on an eligibility list. Before this is done, it is customary to ask each candidate to provide documentation that the certification or license requirements specified by law for a particular position have been met.

Although eligibility is probably defined somewhat differently by various school districts, it generally means that the persons responsible for selecting personnel have designated as suitable for employment applicants who have met established qualifications. The eligibility list should adhere to the employment policy of the board of education (equal opportunity or affirmative action) and should provide a list of applicants, in rank order, who are eligible for appointments as vacancies occur.

In the selection process, it is not unusual to find that some applicants do not meet position requirements. When this happens, several alternatives (which can be explored before deciding to offer employment or deciding to place the individual on the eligibility list) can be considered: (a) delay filling the position, (b) renew the search, (c) provide specific developmental experiences for persons considered to be good risks but who need to improve their skills to fill the position effectively, (d) fill the position temporarily, and/or (e) employ the applicant, but in a different position.

One difficulty in the selection process is the time factor. Many desirable candidates are lost to competing school districts because of the time lag between initial interview and official appointment. Every effort should be made to keep the selection process as brief as possible; in particular, there should be no delay in notifying candidates of their official appointment.

Before the selection process is completed, the applicant and the organization must agree on the terms of employment. It is crucial that both parties completely understand the conditions of employment. Misunderstandings frequently occur about salaries, duties, authority, office or work space, secretarial assistance, collateral benefits, overtime, and extra pay for extra work.

Employment agreements made by telephone should be confirmed in writing. A contractual agreement is essential before hiring is completed. This practice has considerable merit, regardless of how the agreement is made.

Many people develop a negative attitude toward the organization when promises made during the selection period are not kept after the position has been accepted. Therefore, during the final stages of selection, it is good practice to use a checklist containing the terms of employment. This checklist should be designed to ensure that the prospective employee knows the exact nature of the position and its responsibilities, moonlighting policy, compensation structure and its relationship to the applicant's paycheck, terms of the probationary period, collateral benefits, terms of any union or associational contracts in force, and provisions unique to a given position, such as status or status symbols.

Review and Preview

The theme of this chapter is that selection is an ongoing activity in all school districts and seeks to meet specific goals. It was emphasized that selection is both an individual and an organizational activity. Individuals must make decisions about organizations, and organizations must make decisions about individuals.

To guide the selection processes, certain policies and procedures were discussed. A Venn diagram was used to illustrate the relationship among the different components and procedures comprising the selection process. Information concerning several types of job predictors was presented. Methodology was discussed for assessing the statistical and practical significance of particular predictors. Different decisional models for processing information from an implementation viewpoint were discussed relative to multiple hurdles and compensatory processes.

Within the following chapter, attention is given to orienting newly assigned personnel. A differentiation is made between those new to the system and those new to their assignment. For both groups of newly assigned employees, a strategic plan of action is espoused for formulating an effective and an efficient orientation program.

Discussion Questions

1. Within your school district is selection viewed as a process or as an event, and what impact does this perception have for applicants and your school district?

2. From a strategic planning perspective, what attributes of your school district should be communicated to applicants within the selection process? What attributes of your school district would have a negative effect on applicants and how could these situations be modified?

3. What types of job predictors are used to assess applicants in your school organization? What is your perception of the value of each of these predictors? Which predictors do you perceive as most important and which predictors do you perceive as least important?

4. How would you go about setting up a validity paradigm for assessing the predictors used by your school district?

5. Your school organization is hiring a new superintendent. a) What indicators of previous success would you use in assessing the candidates? b) How would you obtain this information?

6. Identify one classified position, one teaching position, and one administrative position within your school organization. What do you consider as a *bona fide* occupational qualifications (BFOQs) of each of these positions?

Case Study

As the human resource director of a public school district, you have received a call from a disgruntled applicant claiming discrimination on the basis of sex. According to this person (a female), her qualifications were just as good as the male who received the job at an elementary school. You contact the principal, and the principal indicates that because both candidates were equally qualified and because the school had no male elementary school teachers, a decision was made to select the male candidate. How would you go about addressing this dispute? What issues and what legal considerations would guide your resolution?

References

Aamodt, M. G., Bryan, D. A., & Whitcomb, A. J. (1993). Predicting performance with letters of recommendation. *Public Personnel Management, 22,* 81–91.

Arvey, R. D., & Faley, R. H. (1992). *Fairness in selecting employees* (2nd ed.). Reading, MA: Addison-Wesley.

Bauer, S. C., & Bogotch, I. (2001). Analysis of the relationships among site council resources, council practices, and outcomes. *Journal of School Leadership, 11,* 98–119.

Baxter, J. C., Brock, B., Hill, P. C., & Rozelle, R. M. (1981). Letters of recommendation: A question of value. *Journal of Applied Psychology, 66,* 296–301.

Behling, O., Labovitz, G., & Gainer, M. (1968). College recruiting: A theoretical base. *Personnel Journal, 47,* 13–19.

Bolton, D. L. (1969). The effects of various formats on teacher selection decisions. *American Educational Research Journal, 6*(3), 329–347.

Bredeson, P. V. (1982). *The effects of letters of recommendation on the teacher selection process.* Unpublished doctoral dissertation, University of Wisconsin.

Bretz, R. D., & Judge, T. A. (1998). Realistic job previews: A Test of the Adverse Self-Selection Hypothesis. *Journal of Applied Psychology, 83,* 330–337.

Cable, D. M., & Gilovich, T. (1998). Looked over or overlooked? Prescreening decisions and postinterview evaluations. *Journal of Applied Psychology, 83,* 501–508.

Central Unified School District. (n.d). Retrieved July 6, 2006, from: http://www.centralusd.k12.ca.us/.

Clark, S. G. (1998). *"Interviewing job applicants: Asking the right questions." West Education Law Reporter.* (128Ed. Law Rep. 939).

Delli, D. A., & Vera, E. M. (2004). Psychological and contextual influences on the teacher selection interview: A model for future research. *Journal of Personnel Evaluation in Education, 17*(2), 137–155.

Dessler, G. (1988). *Personnel management.* Upper Saddle River, NJ: Prentice Hall.

Dipboye, R. I. (1992). *Selection interviews: Process perspectives.* Cincinnati, OH: South-Western College Publishing.

Equal Employment Opportunity Commission. (1978). Guidelines on employee selection procedures. *Federal Register, 35,* 12333–12336.

Family Educational Rights and Privacy Act. (n.d.). Retrieved July 10, 2006, from http://www.ed.gov/policy/gen/guid/fpco/ferpa/index.html.

Gorman, C. D., Clover, W. H., & Doherty, M. E. (1978). Can we learn anything about interviewing real people from "interviews" of paper people? Two studies of the external validity of a paradigm. *Organizational Behavior & Human Decision Processes, 22*(2), 165–192.

Graces, F. P. (1932). *The administration of American education.* New York: Macmillan.

Harris, M. (1999). What is being measured? In R. Eder & M. Harris (Ed.), *The employment interview handbook* (pp. 143–158). Thousands Oaks, CA: Sage.

Heneman, H. G., & Judge, T. A. (2006). Staffing organizations (6th ed.). Middleton, WI: Mendota House.

Heneman, H. G., Judge, T. A., & Heneman, R. L. (2000). *Staffing organizations* (3rd ed.). Middleton, WI: Mendota House.

Joiner, D. A. (2002). Assessment centers: What's new? *Public Personnel Management* (Summer), 1–5.

Judge, T. A., & Bretz, R. D. (1992). Effects of work values on job choice decisions. *Journal of Applied Psychology, 77*(3), 261–271.

Kentucky Educational Reform Act of 1990. H.B. 940, General Assembly, Regular Session, Volume 1.

Lindle, J. C. (2000). School-based decision making. In J. M. Petrosko & J. C. Lindle (Eds.), *2000 Review of Research on Kentucky Education Reform Act (KERA)* (pp. 279–305). Lexington KY: The Kentucky Institute for Education Research.

Maurer, S. D., Sue-Chan, C., Latham, G. P. (1999). The situational interview. In R. Eder & M. Harris (Ed.), *The employment interview handbook* (pp. 159–177). Thousands Oaks, CA: Sage.

National Archives and Records Administration. (1978). *Federal Register, 35.* Retrieved May 28, 2003, from the National Archives and Administration Web site: http://archives.gov/federal_register/.

Payne, J. (2006). Information for employers, best practice: Recruitment and selection, interviewing. Retrieved March 30, 2006, from http://hreoc.gov.au/info_for_employers/best_practice/recruitment.html.

Penttila, C. (2004). Testing the waters: Want to get an idea of how prospective employees perform on the job? *Entrepreneur,* Retrieved May 28, 2006, from: http://www.entrepreneur.com/mag/article/0,1539,312369,00.html.

Pounder, D. G., & Merrill, R. J. (2001). Job desirability of the high school principalship: A job choice theory perspective. *Educational Administration Quarterly, 37,* 27–57.

Reilly, R. R., & Chao, G. T. (1982). Validity and fairness of some alternative employee selection procedures. *Personnel Psychology, 35,* 1–62.

Roth, P. L., Bobko, P., & McFarland, (2005). A meta-analysis of work sample test validity: Updating and integranting some classic literature. *Personnel Psychology, 58*(4), 1009–1038.

Schmitt, N., Noe, R., Meritt, R., & Fitzgerald, M. (1984). Validity of assessment center ratings for the prediction of performance ratings and school climate of school administrators. *Journal of Applied Psychology, 69*(2), 207–213.

Valente, W. D., & Valente, C. M. (2005). Law in the schools (6th ed.). Columbus, OH: Pearson.

Van Hoof, E. A., Born, M. P., Taris, T. W., Flier, H. V., & Blonk, R. W. (2004). Predictors of job search behavior among employed and unemployed people. *Personnel Psychology, 57,* 25–59.

Wallace, J. C. (2004). Personnel application blanks: Persistence and knowledge of legally inadvisable application blank items. *Public Personnel Management, 33,* 331–349.

Winter, P. A., & Melloy, S. H. (2005). Teacher recruitment in a teacher reform state: Factors that influence applicant attraction to teacher vacancies. *Educational Administration Quarterly, 41*(2), 349–372.

Winter, P. A., Millay, J. D., Bojork, L. G., & Keedy, J. L. (2005). Superintendent recruitment: Effects of school councils, job status, signing bonus, and district wealth. *Journal of School Leadership, 15*(4), 433–455.

Winter, P. A., & Morgenthal, J. R. (2002). Principal recruitment in a reform environment: Effects of school achievement and school level on applicant attraction to the job. *Educational Administration Quarterly, 38,* 319–340.

Winter, P. A., Ronau, R. N. & Munoz, M. A. (2004). Evaluating urban teacher recruitment programs: An application of private sector recruitment theories. *Journal of School Leadership, 14*(1), 105–121.

Young, I. P. (1983). Administrators' perceptions of teacher candidates in dyad and panel interviews. *Educational Administration Quarterly, 13,* 46–63.

Young, I. P. (2005). Predictive validity of applicants' reference information for admission to a doctoral program in educational leadership. *Educational Research Quarterly, 29*(1), 16–25.

Young, I. P. (in press). The effects of sex of applicant and sex of principal on screening decisions. *Journal of Personnel Evaluation in Education.*

Young, I. P., & Allison, B. (1982). Effects of candidate age and experience on school superintendents and principals in selecting teachers. *Planning and Changing, 13*(4), 245–256.

Young, I. P., & Chounet, P. F. (2004). The effects of chronological age and information media on teacher screening decisions for elementary school principals. *Personnel Evaluation in Education, 17*(2), 157–172.

Young, I. P. Chounet, P. F. Buster, A. B., & Sailor, S. (2005). Effects of student achievement on satisfaction of newly appointed teachers: A cognitive dissonance perspective. *Journal of School Leadership, 15*(1) 35–51.

Young, I. P., & De La Torre, X. (2006). Superintendents' perceptions about social distance, succession, and "sunset" provisions for Asian, Hispanic, and Native American candidates seeking building level administrator positions: A structural model and an empirical investigation. *Journal of School Leadership, 16*(2), 61–85.

Young, I. P., & Delli, D. A. (2002). The validity of the Teacher Perceiver Instrument for predicting performance of classroom teachers. *Educational Administration Quarterly, 38*(5), 584–610.

Young, I. P., & Fox, J. A. (2002). Asian, Hispanic, and Native American job candidates: Prescreened or screened within the selection process. *Educational Administration Quarterly, 38*(4), 530–545.

Young, I. P., & Marroquin, P. F. (2006). Effects of attraction-similarity, social distance, and academic environment on screening decisions performed by elementary school teachers: An uncharted course. *Leadership and Policy in Schools, 5*(2), 131–153.

Young, I. P., & McMurray, B. R. (1986). Effects of chronological age, focal position, quality of information and quantity of information on screening decisions for teacher candidates. *Journal of Research and Development in Education, 19,* 1–9.

Young, I. P., & Miller-Smith, K. (2006). Effects of site-based councils on teacher screening decisions in high and low performing school districts: A policy capturing study. *Public Policy Analysis in Education, 14*(6).

Young, I. P., & Oto, T. (2004). The impact of principals' screening decisions for Asian, Hispanic, and Native American teacher candidates as viewed from a social distance perspective. *Leadership and Policy in Schools, 3*(4), 295–323.

Young, I. P., Place, A. W., Rinehart, J. S., Jury, J. C., & Baits, D. F. (1997). Teacher recruitment: A test of the Similarity-Attraction Hypothesis for race and sex. *Educational Administration Quarterly, 33*(1), 86–106.

Young, I. P., & Pounder, D. G. (1985). Salient factors affecting decision making in simulated teacher selection interviews. *Journal of Educational Equity and Leadership, 5*(3), 216–233.

Young, I. P., & Prince, A. L. (1999). Legal implications for teacher selection as defined by the ADA and the ADEA. *Journal of Law & Education, 28*(4), 517–530.

Young, I. P., Rinehart, J., & Heneman, H. G. (1993). Effects of job attribute categories applicant job experience, and recruiter sex on applicant job attractiveness ratings. *Journal of Personnel Evaluation in Education, 7,* 55–65.

Young, I. P., Rinehart, J. S., & Place, A. Will (1989). Theories for teacher selection: Objective, subjective, and critical contact. *Teaching and Teacher Education, 5*(4), 329–336.

Young, I. P., & Ryerson, D. (1986). *Teacher selection: Legal, practical, and theoretical perspectives.* Monograph published by the University Council of Educational Administration.

Orientation

6

CHAPTER OVERVIEW

OBJECTIVES

- Stress the importance of the orientation process for socialization of newly assigned personnel.
- Present a planning model for the orientation process.
- Identify goals of the orientation process.
- Focus on ways to help newly assigned personnel achieve the highest level of performance in the shortest period.
- Identify adjustments that are essential for newly assigned personnel to perform effectively.

This chapter expands the human resource function beyond the planning stage where positions were projected (Chapter 2), the staffing formulas concerning how positions are allocated (Chapter 3), the recruitment phase designed to attract an able as well as a willing pool of applicants (Chapter 4), and the selection process used to delimit an applicant pool and to extend an employment offer to the most qualified applicants (Chapter 5). It does so by examining the orientation process as a human resource function for assimilating a newly assigned individual within the position, the school district, and the community at large. The discussion begins with an examination of orientation as it relates to human performance within the position and within the organization.

After discussing the behavioral foundations of orientation for positions and for public school districts, a model of the orientation process is presented. This model examines the activities designed to achieve both a short-range and a long-range orientation strategy that is beneficial to all stakeholders. Questions are posed for content of an orientation program, examples are provided from a policy point of view, design issues are addressed from an operational perspective, and audit mechanisms are illustrated both for monitoring and for modifying an orientation program for newly assigned personnel.

Orientation and Human Performance

Without exception, public school districts as dynamic organizations must contend with personnel changes (Hoy & Miskel, 2005). Each year, employees leave the organization for various reasons (i.e., retirements, resignations, etc.), and new positions may be created to address emerging contingencies (i.e., enrollments, legislation, new construction, etc.). Every year, school districts must recruit, select, assign, reassign, or transfer a number of personnel to maintain continuity of the educational workforce.

Vacancies of all types created through existing staffing needs provide a window of opportunity for a public school district to fulfill system goals as defined by the mission statement (see Chapter 1). Aggressive recruitment, judicious selection, and appropriate assignments of new employees and of existing employees can provide a public school district with several opportunities for achieving system goals and organizational objectives from a strategic planning perspective. Individuals with new skills and knowledge can be brought into the system, while existing experiences and abilities of continuing employees can be capitalized on through reassignments for the benefit of the individuals as well as of the school system.

For some individuals, these opportunities afforded by vacant positions may represent an initial entrance into the world of work for a professional job. These individuals could be young and seeking their first meaningful job assignment or could be mature and having deferred entrance into the workforce until later in life. Individuals comprising either group may be recent graduates of high schools, professional/vocational schools, and/or colleges/universities. However, for all of these groups of newcomers, special orientation needs exist and must be addressed by the human resource function within the public school setting to capitalize on the window of opportunity provided by vacant positions from a strategic planning perspective.

Personnel new to the system are likely to be apprehensive about several aspects associated with their new job assignment and with their new work environment (Heneman & Judge, 2006). Many new employees are concerned about their ability to succeed in an environment unknown to them. Although they may be highly qualified, may have been actively recruited, and may have survived a rigorous selection process, their skills, knowledge, and abilities are yet to be tested in the actual work setting.

Generally, these personnel are unaware of "the way things are done" in a particular public school district. Although they may have general knowledge about their assigned duties as discussed in the preemployment stages of the selection process (see Chapters 3 and 4 addressing recruitment and selection, respectively), they often lack important contextual knowledge necessary for successful performance in a new position. Most new employees know little about the organization's objectives, school and community traditions and taboos, as well as specific personal and position standards which they are expected to meet within a new job assignment.

In light of these uncertainties and of these unknown expectations, many new employees resign voluntarily during their probation period. It has been noted, for example, that the number of first-year teachers who leave the profession is higher than it should be, and that the loss is higher than the profession should sustain. One study indicated that 11 percent of the new teachers left prior to their second year of employment and that this cumulative percentage approaches 30 percent before the fourth year of employment (Ingersoll, 2002).

Other individuals filling vacancies within the public school district may be seasoned veterans of the workforce rather than new entrants to the workforce. Included among these seasoned veterans are experienced employees new to the public school setting, experienced educators new to the public school district, or experienced employees of the district reassigned to a new position. Again, specific orientation needs exist even for the seasoned employees that are different from those orientation needs of new entrants to the labor market.

It goes almost without stating that probably at no other time of employment does the newly appointed or newly assigned employee need more consideration, guidance, and understanding than during their first few months on a new job. Until these individuals become fully adjusted to the work they must perform, to their new work environment, and to their new colleagues, they cannot be expected to give their best effort. If left unmanaged, the feelings triggered by new work assignments can be dysfunctional to employees as well as to the public school district.

To avoid many of the problems encountered with new job assignments, an employee orientation process is needed. More pointedly, the attrition rate for new teachers participating in induction programs is 15 percent, compared to 26 percent for those who had no induction support (Owings & Kaplan, 2006, p. 274). This type of difference between those receiving an orientation and those failing to receive an orientation has important individual and organizational implications for a public school district.

In fact, recent research indicates that orientation programs are particularly important for those new teachers in a low-performing school district. Young, Chounet, Buster, and Sailor (2005) found that new entrants to low-performing districts entered their assignment with a high level of satisfaction but lost this enthusiasm during the first year of

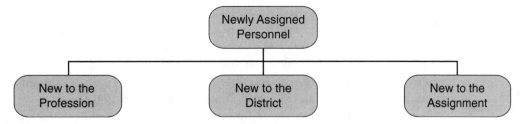

FIGURE 6.1   *Categories of newly assigned personnel.*

employment. However, this same dampening effect was not found for new entrants in high-performing school districts.

A well-planned orientation process is a systematic organizational effort for helping personnel to adjust readily and effectively to new work assignments so that they can contribute maximally to organizational goals and objectives through achieving personal and work satisfaction (Cunningham & Cordeiro, 2006). This definition of an effective **orientation process,** it should be noted, goes beyond the conventional definition of an orientation program. That is, a traditional orientation program has been concerned only with personnel new to a public school system and not necessarily new to their job assignment.

The orientation process, as defined in this chapter, includes all personnel who accept new assignments (see Figure 6.1). This includes personnel new to the profession, new to the system, and new to the position (but not the district). Whether new to the profession, new to the district, or new to the assignment, most personnel seek an organizational environment in which they can find a reasonable degree of security and enjoy satisfaction in their work assignment.

Without important knowledge about their new position, the school district, and the community at large, frustrated employees may withdraw from the work environment. Withdrawal from the work environment takes several different forms, beginning with frequent absences from the work setting. This type of withdrawal as expressed by frequency of absences leads, in many instances, to voluntary resignation by the employee (Batt & Valcour, 2003).

Human resource managers have known for some time that absenteeism and voluntary turnover of newly assigned employees represent an economic loss to the system (Owings & Kaplan, 2006). Investment costs incurred when recruiting, selecting, orienting, and supervising newly assigned personnel are considered a financial loss when these persons are absent frequently or resign voluntarily. These costs can range from several hundred dollars for low-level positions to several thousand dollars for high-level administrative positions (Owings & Kaplan, 2006).

One presumed cause of absenteeism and voluntary turnover is the lack of well-planned orientation practices instituted by the school system. Newly assigned staff members must make so many adjustments before they are assimilated totally into the organization that an effective orientation program is less a luxury than a necessity in modern school systems. Given this necessity, an aim of an effective orientation program is to minimize the strain on the school system's financial and human resource allocations by reducing absenteeism and voluntary turnovers among employees newly assigned to a position.

Indeed, most public school districts have realized the advantages associated with an effective orientation program for newly assigned personnel (Stansbury & Zimmerman, 2002). To imply that educational systems have not been concerned with the problems of the new employee or the newly assigned employee, either in the past or in the present, would be incorrect. Today, however, many excellent programs are in operation in a number of school districts (Massachusetts Department of Education, n.d.).

Some of these orientation programs are based on recent educational reform and restructuring initiatives and include a variety of approaches (see California Beginning Teacher Support and Assessment, n.d.). Depending on location, size, budgetary constraints, regulatory mandates, leadership, and proactive and reactive attitudes to institutional change, the activities within these programs vary. One way to characterize contemporary orientation activity is in terms of five types of programs being used by public school districts to assimilate employees new to their assignment in a public school system:

- University–school system collaboration
- Consortium programs for area school systems
- Districtwide programs
- School-based programs
- Web-based programs

Due, at least in part, to studies of employees new to their assignment and their assimilation within the work setting as well as the community at large, orientation has taken more importance in recent times. Reasons for this importance are well established in the literature through early research on these topics and include the following:

- Individuals change their behaviors when they become members of groups (Michener, Delamater, & Myers, 2004).
- Planned development programs tend to be better than unplanned activities (French, 1987).
- Carefully designed orientation programs minimize disruptive behavior of new employees (French, 1987).
- Orientation programs minimize certain inappropriate interpersonal behaviors on the part of employees newly assigned (Owings & Kaplan, 2006).
- Individuals obtaining alternate certification as teachers benefit greatly from orientation programs (Shen, 1997).

Behavior and the Orientation Process

Existing literature addressing the orientation of new employees contains several synonyms for the process of acclimating new employees to their work environment. These synonyms include such terms as *induction, placement, organizational entry, assignment,* and *socialization.* Each of these terms has been used to define the **assimilation** process by which new personnel are assisted in meeting their need for security, belonging, status, information, and direction in their new position and/or in their new organizational environment.

The orientation process begins in the recruitment stage of the human resource model and ends when the newly assigned employees have made the personal, position, organizational, and community adaptations that enable them to function fully and effectively as a member of the district's staff. It is not uncommon for the orientation program to last the entire first year of employment, especially for persons new to the system (Bergeson, n.d.). For orientation programs covering a considerable period, activities encountered involve considerably more than just making new personnel feel at ease in an unfamiliar environment.

Worth noting is that few, if any, employees begin a new job assignment with all the skills necessary to perform every job task with maximum efficiency. Given this limitation, some investigators have categorized the skills of new employees, for both their position and their work environment, into separate behavioral categories. Luthans and Kreitner (1975) developed four categories to classify the behavioral skills of newcomers in relation to their position: (a) desirable performance-related job behavior, (b) potentially disruptive performance-related behavior, (c) behavior unrelated to performance, and (d) performance behavior deficiencies.

Desirable performance job-related behavior defines the core of responsibilities associated with effective job performance in a newly assigned position. It is those aspects of the job that are germane to organizational goals and the very essence of the focal position for the public school district. Without adequate performance relative to job-related behaviors, individuals are destined to fail in their newly assigned position, and an effective orientation program can reinforce desirable job-related behaviors for newly assigned personnel.

Potentially disruptive performance-related behaviors signal to school administrators important information about individuals in newly assigned positions. These types of behaviors represent acceptable employment practices that have been exaggerated by the employee when fulfilling normal job assignments. Examples of potentially disruptive performance-related behaviors may be either a rigid conformance to performance standards of the newly assigned position ("It is not in my job description") or a lack of flexibility in the employee to adjust to the requirements of the newly assigned position ("This is not the way it is supposed to be performed").

Behavior unrelated to performance creates the least number of problems associated with these behavior indices. Employees new to an assignment may fail to realize all the expectations associated with a position. As such, they may exhibit many behaviors that are unnecessary in the performance of newly assigned duties, and these behaviors may detract from the desired job performance behaviors.

Of major concern are the performance behavior deficiencies by newly assigned personnel. Some of these behavior deficiencies may be attributed to a lack of ability, whereas other behavior deficiencies may be attributed to a lack of motivation. It behooves the school district to discern this differentiation between ability and motivation because each reason for a behavior deficiency has important implications for an orientation program.

By using these behavioral categories to classify the skills of employees newly assigned to positions, certain identified behaviors can be reinforced, modified, or eliminated through what Luthans and Kreitner referred to as a shaping process. **Shaping** is a process by which an employee's behavior is altered through a series of steps involving observation, evaluation, and feedback. For all newly assigned personnel, shaping occurs when the system (a) gathers information about employees relative to desired behavior in their new position, (b) seeks to positively reinforce acceptable behaviors, (c) uses feedback to correct deficiencies in performance, and (d) helps the individual to become part of the organization through day-to-day supervision.

Scope of the Orientation Process

A successful orientation process for employees newly assigned to their position is rooted in an approved **orientation policy** and stems from a formal plan of action developed and implemented by management. By relying on a formal plan of action for designing, implementing, and managing the orientation process, errors of omission are reduced and the orientation process will be sequenced in a meaningful manner. An action plan for the orientation process of new employees should begin by exploring answers to the following questions:

- What are the goals of the orientation process?
- What types of activities are needed to achieve the goals of the orientation process?
- How will orientation activities be sequenced within the orientation process?
- Who will be responsible for specific activities?
- How will different activities of the orientation process be evaluated?
- How will assessment information be used for improving orientation?

A conceptual model for an effective orientation process can provide guidelines for answering these questions in an orderly manner (see Figure 6.2) and can provide an operational framework to guide the development and the implementation of an orientation program. This model, as found in Figure 6.2, shows that the steps of the orientation process include activities associated normally with most administrative tasks when conducted from a strategic planning perspective (determining goals and planning, organizing, administering, assessing, and modifying). These steps, as found in Figure 6.2, should not be surprising because the orientation process is one of the components or subsystems of the human resource function that should be executed by a public school district (see Chapter 1).

The orientation model presented in Figure 6.2 illustrates the kinds of decisions that confront administrators when attempting to assimilate personnel into the system through a formal proactive orientation program. By linking specific questions with certain steps comprising the model, the parameters of an orientation program can be framed in a sequential manner. Within the following sections of this chapter, an outline is provided as to how a school system places into practice the concepts suggested by the aforementioned questions and through the steps reflected within this model (see Figure 6.2).

Determination of Orientation Goals

The overarching purpose of the orientation process is to help newly assigned personnel adjust to their recent assignment and/or to their new work environment with a minimum of difficulties that may stem from this transitional process. However, this purpose will

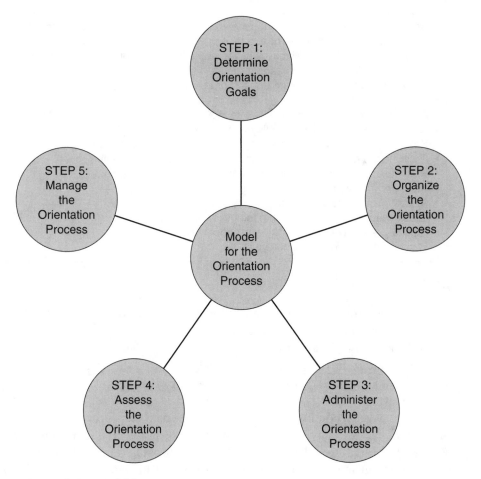

FIGURE 6.2 *Model for an orientation program.*

have little significance for those who plan or implement the process unless the process is translated into specific goals for lending direction to purpose (the first step in the orientation process; see Figure 6.2). Examples of potential goals for an orientation process are presented in Figure 6.3 as suggestions for consideration by a public school district to guide this phase of the strategic planning process (see Figure 6.2).

In addition to the goals listed in Figure 6.3, other potential objectives of a successful orientation process may be identified by assessing the opinions of previous participants of the orientation program (if a program happened to be in existence), reviewing the professional literature addressing orientation programs, and conducting an electronic search for orientation programs. Interestingly, one single website revealed 20 different orientation programs for public school districts that can be used to identify potential

- Assist new employees in acquiring the knowledge, skills, and abilities essential for undertaking a new assignment and for contributing to the system at large.
- Provide new employees with information about the school district's mission, organization, functions, policies, and work requirements.
- Foster organizational commitment and promote job satisfaction.
- Reduce the likelihood of rule violations, resignations, and grievances.
- Address performance problems before they occur.
- Eliminate the gap between employment expectancy and reality.
- Ease the transition from another institution to the current institution.
- Facilitate the reassignment process from within the current institution.
- Promote professional and personal adjustment for new assignments.
- Satisfy regulatory mandates for assigned positions.
- Align system demands with new job assignments.
- Lessen supervisory needs within the new work assignment.
- Emphasize safety requirements within the work setting.
- Minimize anxiety for new employees.

FIGURE 6.3   *Potential orientation goals.*

objectives for an orientation program tailored specifically to a public school district (North Carolina Department of Public Instruction, n.d.).

When designing an orientation program for employees newly assigned to their position, it is important to limit to a manageable number the specific objectives to be addressed in an orientation program. For any single orientation program to accomplish all the objectives found in Figure 6.3 is an unrealistic expectation. In practice, the task for those who develop and implement a successful orientation program is to determine the salience of each objective within their own school system and to link employee and system needs through well-defined goals that can be managed in an efficient manner.

The identification and the selection of goals to be included within an orientation program must be tempered by other aspects of the human resource function. Although orientation should begin at the start of the employment relationship (Heneman, Judge, & Heneman, 2000), those responsible for recruitment and for selection may have omitted important information at this stage of the human resource process or may have addressed this information only at a superficial level during the preemployment period. As such, this information must be covered or revisited in the orientation program when newly assigned employees may be more attuned to information than when they were at the preemployment stage of the human resource process (see Chapters 4 and 5).

Fundamental to the entire orientation process is the formal commitment of the board of education to the objectives of an orientation program. This commitment should be captured in a board policy. Surprisingly, school board policies addressing an orientation program for employees are difficult to find in the public school setting.

However, it is not unusual to find orientation policies for school board members in most public school districts. Unlike the situation found for employees in general, orientation programs for school board members exist in almost every school system and are captured by school board policy. These programs/policies address attendance at

To facilitate the assimilation of newly assigned employees the Sturgis City Public School District endorses the following policy statements:

- Establish lines of authority and responsibilities for the conduct of an orientation program.
- Establish a budget and allocate sufficient funds for the operation of the orientation program.
- Design the orientation program to enhance the ability of newly assigned personnel to move from novice to productive team member.
- Ensure maintenance of ethical standards and integrity in the conduct of the orientation program.
- Monitor the orientation program and assess performance outcomes.
- Embody state-of-the-art practices within the orientation program.

FIGURE 6.4　*Orientation policy.*

workshops performed by the state and professional associations on entrance to their newly assigned duties as public officials and authorize the expenditure of public funds for orientation of school board members.

If the intent of the school system for orientation programs has been formalized in a written document for employees newly assigned to positions within the school system, then the document is found most often in an employee handbook rather than in a school board policy. Because an employee handbook carries less legitimacy than a school board policy, it is recommended that the objectives of an orientation program be committed to school board policy. An example of such a policy that can serve as a starting point for public school districts in the formulation of a policy is found in Figure 6.4.

After a specific set of goals has been defined and after a board policy has been adopted for legitimizing the orientation process, planning moves from goal identification to program organization as depicted by the planning model (see Figure 6.2). Program organization concerns the ordering and sequencing of content for an orientation program. Germane to this phase of the strategic planning process (see Figure 6.2) is the identification of specific content to be addressed in an orientation program for newly assigned personnel.

Organization of the Orientation Process

As has been noted throughout this chapter, a major purpose of an orientation program is to provide newly assigned employees with information needed to become assimilated into their new work environment as productive contributors to a public school system. When this has been done effectively, many adjustment problems can be prevented or at least can be lessened in severity. Although the informational needs of newcomers to a focal position can vary, depending on whether they are recent hires or they are reassigned from within the system, certain areas common to all new employees have been identified in the literature (for a discussion of orientation and of socialization see Heneman & Judge, 2006).

An examination of concerns related to orientation, as noted by recent hires, reveals some common themes that should be addressed by an orientation program within the

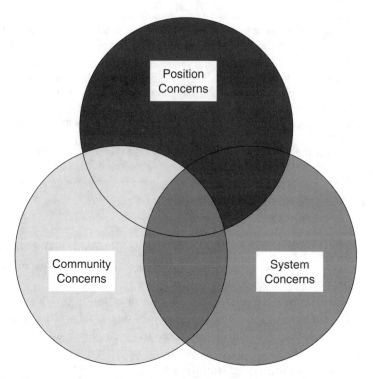

FIGURE 6.5   *Common concerns of newly employed/assigned personnel.*

public school setting. These themes address **position concerns, system concerns,** and **community concerns,** and these themes are interrelated in many ways (see Figure 6.5). As such, these themes provide a broad framework for organizing an orientation program to aid employees in the assimilation of and acclamation to their new job assignments within a public school district (see Step 2 of Figure 6.2).

To embellish this framework with an effective orientation program addressing the concerns of employees newly appointed to their positions, each of these common areas will be discussed in the following sections of this chapter. This discussion begins at the most immediate level of concern for the employee—the new focal position. Then, the discussion moves from the initial level of concern for employees newly assigned through the broader areas of concern for the system and for the community, respectively (see Figure 6.5).

Position Concerns

For any initial employment relationship between an individual and a public school district, a central point of focus for most new employees is the focal position. Although most focal positions have other responsibilities attached outside of the major job functions, such as organizational responsibilities and community expectations (see Figure 6.5), it is the concerns about the primary focal position that dominate the immediate attention of the new job incumbent. Because of the urgency new employees associate with the primary focal position, it is not surprising that the focal position is of major concern to newly assigned employees during the orientation period with a public school district and that these concerns should be addressed early on within an orientation program.

Many concerns related to the focal position may stem from a lack of sufficient information possessed by the newly assigned employee. For new entrants into the labor market lacking appropriate experiences on which to draw, many voids exist within their work repertory for addressing contingencies associated with a new assignment. Although these persons may have mastered many of the technical skills necessary for effective job performance through their formal training, they may lack certain knowledge about the informal aspects of organizational life encountered in an actual workplace.

Experienced employees, on the other hand, accepting new assignments may encounter different ways of doing things. Performing the same job in a different system or performing a different job in the same system may require a different set of skills yet to be mastered. As such, previous learning can interfere with new learning and can influence negatively the on-the-job behavior of experienced employees in a newly assigned position.

The lack of sufficient information about new focal positions and about new responsibilities associated with these positions may be attributed to several causes. Individuals may have been unexposed to the necessary information prior to their initial assignment. Realities of the recruitment and selection processes may have imposed certain time restraints that restricted the information flow between candidates or applicants and organizational representatives.

For example, it is not unusual for recruitment and selection activities for some employees to take place away from the employing school district. Many teachers are recruited and selected at job fairs or through college placement office interviews (see Chapters 4 and 5). Recruitment fairs and college placement offices are far removed from the world of work that successful candidates are to encounter within a public school district, and an orientation program should fill this gap as quickly as possible.

Even when recruitment and selection activities take place within the confines of the school district, these activities may be less than optimal for imparting information about the focal position from a contextual perspective. It is not unusual for many of the recruitment and selection activities to take place when schools are on summer break. During this period, applicants and new employees have little exposure relative to their new job assignment and may approach the new job assignment with hesitation.

Far from being uncommon is that some employees are hired without a specific job assignment at the time of appointment. These types of hires occur when school districts fill slots revealed by staffing projections (see Chapter 3) and assign employees at a later point in time before the beginning of the school year. Without position-specific information at the time of employment, orientation programs fulfill a very important function for newly appointed individuals recently assigned to an actual work site.

An equally likely explanation for the lack of sufficient information is that employees may have failed to assimilate appropriate job information when exposed initially as applicants during the employment process. With both job fairs and college placement offices, interactions between job candidates and organizational representatives are seldom a singular event. Job candidates as well as organizational representatives encounter multiple exposures within these types of employment contexts.

In fact, research that addresses the recruitment and the selection process indicates that applicants tend to blur information they encounter within the employment process (Young, Place, Rinehart, Jury, & Baits, 1999). For truly competitive organizations encountered during the recruitment and the selection process, salient information about districts and job assignments may be very similar across organizations and assignments. Because of this similarity of information across organizations and assignments, individuals, as applicants, may fail to internalize information important for the public school district that they chose to join at the conclusion of the job search process and rely on orientation programs to provide specifics about the employing school district.

To help potential employees differentiate among school districts as well as job assignments and to facilitate the orientation process for those hired, information about the focal position should be dispensed by a school district early within the employment process. Individuals, as applicants, should receive information about focal positions initially through postings of job openings. Interestingly, some research indicates that individuals choose to pursue certain job opportunities over others on the basis of information provided in position advertisements (Winter & Melloy, 2005).

Based on this research, public school districts should afford particular attention to the posting of vacant positions. When possible, content of position postings should be specific as opposed to general, relative to position characteristics (Winter, 1996). By providing specific information about focal positions, orientation can reinforce position information rather than introduce position information for new job incumbents and can satisfy **individual concerns** about positions.

Decisions required by individuals during the recruitment and selection processes can be informed also by using position guides/job descriptions. Position guides are valuable resources in helping new employees become acquainted with their potential job assignments early in the employment process (Young, 2006a). These position guides should not only prevent applicants from accepting positions/job descriptions for which they are unqualified but also should provide information to those responsible for personnel selection and placement so that candidates and positions can be matched effectively within the public school district and lay the groundwork for the orientation process.

Individuals have certain skills they bring to the position and have certain needs they seek to fulfill with the position. Skills are abilities and aptitudes related specifically to fulfilling job requirements. Needs may involve a desire for autonomy, affiliation, or achievement.

Likewise, vacant focal positions have certain requirements and have certain benefits associated with the positions (Young, 2006b). Requirements form the basic necessities for performing successfully in a potential focal position, whereas benefits are derived through such actions on the part of the employee when fulfilling basic job requirements. A match between individual needs and organizational requirements is an integral part of the employment process involving recruitment, selection, and orientation.

After the selection process is completed, the new employee is assigned to a work unit within the organization. When selecting and when placing individuals in new assignments, certain contextual aspects of the assignments must be considered from a human resource perspective. These contextual aspects include the following:

- How well will the individual fit the leadership style of the work unit?
- How well will the individual fit into the work unit's environment?
- Will the newly assigned personnel be accepted by the work group?
- Will the newly assigned personnel accept the work group?

If those responsible for selecting and placing individuals in new assignments ignore these questions, then it should be of little surprise that the recently assigned employees have adjustment problems associated with their new positions. These problems arise when the expectations, values, and goals of new employees are inconsistent with the realities of organizational life (Young et. al., 2005). Unless the selection and placement decisions are sound, new employees will be unsuccessful in new assignments and will lack appropriate **socialization.**

The selection and placement processes overlook frequently these important elements in recruitment, selection, assignment, and orientation: (a) leadership style of the applicant, (b) the persons the applicant will report to, (c) those reporting to the applicant (if the position is administrative), and (d) the structure of the job situation. In the previous discussion of the selection and placement processes (see Chapter 5), it was emphasized that information is the key to making judgments about placing an individual in a position. Management must learn as much as possible about the applicant, and the applicant must learn as much as possible about the position in question if compatibility between applicant and position is to be obtained related to the **organizational culture.**

Without such knowledge about the person and about the focal position, adjustment problems of newly assigned employees likely will occur, can spill over into the work unit, and can cause major disruptions among otherwise satisfactory employees. Widespread dissatisfaction may occur when overqualified or underqualified personnel become part of the work group. No doubt, when members of the work group perceive newcomers as sources of disruption, dissatisfaction becomes widespread in the work setting.

It cannot be emphasized too strongly that improper selection and/or placement can be costly to both the employee and the system and will be uncorrectable even in the best founded orientation program. Placing an incompetent individual in any position or a competent individual in the wrong position often leads to years of grief for the administration, low productivity of the employee, and interference with attainment of system goals. Proactive rather than reactive selection and placement decisions are best for everyone involved in the employment process and can facilitate the orientation of the new employee into a public school system once hired and assigned.

Having addressed the concerns associated with a newly assigned position, other concerns become prepotent. Most notably, newly assigned personnel have concerns about the system. That is, they seek information about how the position and the system interconnect and concerns about the system should be addressed within an orientation program.

System Concerns

Newly hired and/or newly assigned employees seek information about the system as well as about their positions within the system (see Figure 6.5). As noted earlier in this chapter, some of the adjustment problems encountered by new employees are due to a lack of information about the system. New employees need to know about the fringe benefits associated with the position, the support services available to the position holder, as well as the relationship of the position to the organization as a whole and must rely on an effective orientation process to receive this information in a timely manner.

Recent hires, as well as continuing employees with new assignments, often must make decisions during early periods of employment about certain benefit options provided by the system and unique to their new assignment. Depending on whether the new position is administrative, instructional, or supportive, benefit packages may vary because of labor contract restrictions and/or opportunities. Examples of benefit options that may vary by job classification include choosing an insurance carrier, selecting a primary physician, opting for a flexible spending account, selecting a retirement plan, and/or purchasing long-term health care.

The difficulty in choosing among benefit options is compounded for new personnel because these options often have a window of opportunity, which can be either irrevocable or penalty laden. Irrevocable windows require newly assigned employees to choose or to reject the benefit (i.e., defined benefit or defined contribution retirement plan) within a specified time, while penalty-laden windows penalize these employees for accepting a benefit (i.e., long-term health care for assisted living) at a later date in the employment cycle.

To make an informed choice among benefit options with windows of opportunity is difficult for many newly assigned employees. No doubt, most readers can recall the confusions they encountered at this stage of the employment process when presented a menu of items from which to choose. This confusion is only heightened by concerns about mastering the skills needed in the new position, understanding the expectations of the new supervisor, blending with the organization as a whole, and assimilating within the community at large.

Some of the anxieties in choosing among fringe benefits with windows of opportunity can be reduced by providing appropriate and timely information in the orientation process. Providing such information is a major human resource function that should be performed by every school district through a well-defined and a well-executed orientation program. However, this information should inform rather than direct new employees; the ultimate responsibility for choice among benefits rests with the employee, and the employee needs timely information as provided by an orientation program to make an informed decision among benefit options.

Most, if not all, newly assigned employees in schools have certain support functions provided by the system and designed to help them perform effectively and efficiently within their job assignment. However, knowledge of these support systems is assumed, often at the expense of the individual and of the system. Too often within the orientation process, information about support services available to a position holder is overlooked or underemphasized during the early employment period.

For example, newly assigned administrators are confronted many times with situations involving labor-management relations. In the absence of crystal-clear contract language concerning the specific point of contention, these new administrators may be required to provide an interpretation of contract language without any contextual background. Any such interpretation of less-than-clear contract language provided by administrators should be tempered by past labor-management practices within the system. Information about past practices unique to a public school system should be obtainable through the support systems provided by the district and through support systems identified within the orientation process.

Similar to administrators, teachers new to the profession and new to the assignment often are confronted with student-related issues during their induction period. These types of problems and issues surface frequently during this period because students, like teachers, are new to their recent grade-level assignment. With both teachers and students being new to their assignments, adequate orientation of the former is germane to an effective classroom setting and an efficient learning environment.

Some of the issues encountered during the orientation period for teachers are academic, while other issues encountered by teachers are nonacademic. In both cases, a satisfactory resolution of the problem may depend on the district's support system. In many instances, teachers serve as a conduit for students with the district's support systems, and avenues of communication are appropriate, if not essential, content for an orientation program addressing the informational needs of new teachers.

Classified employees encounter problems also requiring assistance from support systems in fulfilling position requirements. Equipment for processing information (clerical), for preparing food (food service), for cleaning buildings (custodians), for transporting students (bus drivers), and for facilitating instruction (instructional aids) may malfunction in the absence of an immediate supervisor. The support systems available to solve problems caused by malfunctions should be known by all classified personnel to prevent loss of time and effort by new employees.

Although a formal orientation program for employees can provide information about available support services, sometimes services and service providers are not linked for newly assigned personnel. And, unless a link is established, new employees may fail to recall what services are available to them when needed and where these services can be obtained. This void in information results in underutilization of support systems by new employees and a loss of productive time for the school system.

To offset these losses, Seyfarth (1996) suggested that services and providers can be linked by having newly assigned employees interview the service providers, and an orientation programs can provide this linkage in an efficient manner. Such interviews, initiated by new employees as part of the orientation process, open channels of communication and allow the involved parties to establish rapport. Putting a face to a service facilitates the orientation process for many employees and reinforces sources of information about support systems available to employees.

In addition to providing information about fringe benefits and support services, every organization should inform members of its purposes, policies, and procedures during the orientation process. Newly appointed staff members want to know, for example, about the mission and the goals of a school system, about the organization and the operation of the system, and about how their position fits into the total picture. They need to know not only the essential components of the system but also how the parts interact and contribute to the success (goal attainment) of the whole—in other words, the context and the culture of a public school system.

Every school system has a unique culture; that is, a set of interrelated values and priorities, norms and expectations, ideas and beliefs (Hoy & Miskel, 2005). This culture, according to Cunningham and Cordeiro (2006), has a variety of useful functions for a system, including (a) establishing standards and shared expectations that provide a range of acceptable behavior for group members, (b) providing guidelines that allow individuals to fit into the group, and (c) setting standards of behavior that facilitate interaction among members and provide a means of identifying with one's peers.

Because each system has a unique culture, employees new to their job assignment often encounter difficulties in the adjustment that takes place between the individual and the organization during initial assignments in a new position. Schools may promote unique beliefs that conflict with those held by new employees (Short & Greer, 1998). Beliefs of new staff members concerning academic freedom; teaching controversial issues; the role of the teacher as a citizen; selection of reading material; and student behavior; as well as their values, traditions, customs, beliefs, goals, appearance, and student discipline may differ considerably from the system's official values and objectives.

From an operational perspective, every public school system should seek to assimilate new personnel by orienting them to the culture of the system. Whether the new staff members will accept or reject the institution's culture, in whole or in part, is not certain but is less certain without a well-designed orientation program (Owings & Kaplan, 2006). However, an awareness of the organizational culture is essential when the inductee is being considered for permanent employment (Winter, Newton, & Kirkpatrick, 1998).

Cultural shaping and reinforcement are important aspects of the orientation process for newly assigned personnel through well defined **orientation goals.** Both at the time when these personnel enter the organization and later on; the system should develop and implement plans for cultural transmission and acquisition by helping newly assigned personnel to understand what the organization expects of its members. Thus, the orientation process provides a timely opportunity to translate system philosophy into cultural reality by describing and interpreting the roles, relationships, and behaviors necessary for individual, unit, and organizational effectiveness as defined by local norms.

Cultural assimilation is to be achieved most likely in an effective orientation process when certain socialization conditions are satisfied. These conditions have been outlined by Wanous (1992) to include the following four-stage framework for the induction of newly assigned personnel:

- Newcomer learns the reality of the work environment.
- Newcomer identifies norms of coworkers and the boss.

- Newcomer makes accommodations between conflicts at the work setting and at home.
- Newcomer accepts norms and realizes that the organization is satisfied with job behavior.

However, not to be overlooked by an orientation program is that all public school districts are not isolated entities. By definition (both physical and fiscal), public school districts are part of a larger community. As such, new employees have concerns about the community that should be addressed in an orientation program.

Community Concerns

The relationship between school systems and their communities is interconnecting and is complementary (see Figure 6.5). The school system has a vested interest in the community, and the community has a vested interest in the school system. The successes of both the school system and the community are linked closely through common interests.

Although there are exceptions to any generality, there are few exceptions about the relationship between school systems and communities. Seldom does one find an excellent school system in an undesirable community. Likewise, seldom does one find an excellent community with a below-average school system.

Because the success of one entity depends largely on the success of the other, school systems should make every effort to strengthen school–community relations (Kowalski, 2004), and an effective orientation program opens this door of opportunity. Research on this issue indicates that effective schools have more contact with parents and the community than less effective schools and that small school districts, like large school districts, must cultivate positive school–community relations (Di Benedetto & Wilson, 1982). Positive community relations programs require efforts by all school representatives so that the local community will be receptive to new employees of the district.

For personnel who are attempting to relocate within the community containing the school district, personal problems may be encountered in this effort that detracts from the on-the-job performance. Common relocation problems include finding suitable housing; arranging transportation; finding educational, religious, cultural, banking, and recreational facilities; and numerous other issues that must be attended to while adjusting to the new environment. The ability to cope with these problems is important to the administration because complete adjustment to the employee's new role will not occur until the anxieties involved in getting established within a new community are relieved.

It is a certainty that newly assigned employees, whether teachers, administrators, or support personnel moving into the community, need various kinds of information. Information on such matters as community geography, economy, government, religious agencies, educational resources, law enforcement agencies, public safety, health conditions, medical resources, recreation facilities, child care, family welfare agencies, and community planning resources is needed to help these newcomers better serve the school system, its clients, and the community (White & Wehlage, 1995).

The school system has a responsibility to increase the public's understanding of education so that the community will be receptive to recent school employees trying to fit into their new environment. What the school staff contributes to these ends depends to a large extent on the staff's understanding of the community. The orientation process gives the administration opportunities to help newcomers adjust to the community, showing them how they can achieve personal objectives and demonstrating how community resources can be used to improve the school system. If the relationship of the community to the school is really as strategic as it is purported to be, then the school system should develop orientation programs to help the staff, especially new members, understand the community and its effect on the school system.

Administering the Orientation Process

Within the previous sections of this chapter, the focus is on the informational concerns of newly assigned employees. For purposes of presentation and of discussion, these issues were classified according to position concerns, organizational concerns, and community concerns. Although these sources of concerns were treated somewhat separately, in reality, much overlap exists with respect to the information needs of new personnel, and this overlap is depicted through a Venn diagram in Figure 6.5.

Because an overlap exists among the sources of informational needs/concerns, these sources of information should be treated as interrelated components within an orientation process. Collectively, information from all sources (position, system, and community) should be integrated and should be ordered in a meaningful sequence within an orientation program for all new employees. This procedure of ordering and sequencing of information within an orientation program is noted by Step 3 of Figure 6.2 as part of the strategic planning process.

Actual content of a particular orientation program should be tailored to the specific needs of the program participants and of the public school district. Orientation needs vary from one system to another and from one year to another within the same school system. Depending on the characteristics of a particular group of newly assigned employees, content and sequence of an orientation program must be revisited on an annual basis.

Even though information needs for new employees may vary among systems and across time, there are certain crucial periods within the employment cycle for all newly assigned employees, and an orientation program must be sensitive to these different crucial periods within the employment cycle. These periods are labeled as the **preappointment period**, the **interim period**, and the **initial service period** for purposes of discussion about the orientation process. A brief description of these periods (to be expanded in the following sections), along with some of the key agents for an effective orientation process during each period, is presented in Figure 6.6.

Preappointment Period

As has been noted consistently within this chapter, the orientation process begins before any initial contact is made between the public school district and potential applicants for vacant positions. Vacant positions to be filled must be identified and authorized, either

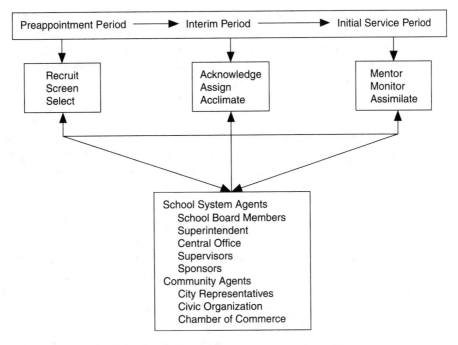

FIGURE 6.6   *Periods of the orientation process.*

through a long-range staffing plan, as described in Chapter 3, or by the exit of current personnel creating new vacancies to be filled for preestablished positions. Regardless of whether vacant positions are created newly or established previously, certain types of information must be compiled for every vacant focal position during the preappointment period of the orientation process.

For every vacant focal position, specific information is needed about the position and general information is needed about the school system. Position information may be obtained through several existing sources within the district. Often, school districts use a well-prepared brochure to inform applicants and employment agencies about the characteristics of the system and the community, the application process, and the names of contact persons within the system (Winter, 1997).

Specific information about the position is presented to applicants generally by a job description (Young, 2006a). Sometimes a job description must be developed for new vacant focal positions; in other instances, an existing job description must be revisited and updated for ongoing focal positions. Far too often, however, dated information is provided to applicants and employment agencies during the preappointment period of the orientation process. As a result of such information, neither the interests of the system nor those of the applicant are served if the position is described poorly or if the qualifications for the position are misrepresented and/or undefined.

The job description should contain up-to-date information about the job and the experiential requirements necessary for satisfactory performance of the position. This information is essential to several involved parties during the preappointment phase of the orientation process. It gives direction to those responsible for recruitment and selection; makes clear to the applicant the qualifications, duties, and responsibilities of the position; and enables placement agencies and recruiters to locate candidates who meet the requirements.

Recruitment brochures provide information about the system and the community. For the system, information should be included about the diversity of the school district, the size of the school district, the number of school buildings, the wealth of the district, the per-pupil spending, and the performance of the district on state-mandated proficiency examinations. Information about the community includes major industries, median home price, number of residents, the median income of residents, the diversity of residents, and the governmental structure of the community.

Sources of information contained in position guides and in recruitment brochures provide topics for exploration within the initial employment interview. Within the initial interview, the organizational representative can give the applicant various types of information likely to be needed in deciding whether to pursue further the employment opportunity. Moreover, during the interview, the applicant is able to ask questions about the position or to get information on a range of relevant issues that may not have been covered by the position guide and the recruitment brochure.

When possible during the preappointment phase of the orientation process, initial job interviews should be held at the actual work site for the vacant focal position or an on-site visit should be provided as part of the preemployment process. By holding either initial screening interviews or affording an on-site visit at the actual work site, individuals as applicants can be exposed to important contextual information about the position, the system, and the community. Exposure to this type of information is the primary goal of the preappointment phase of the orientation process for public school employees and provides the groundwork for the interim orientation period.

Interim Orientation Period

Following the preappointment phase of the orientation process, job candidates enter the interim orientation period (see Figure 6.6). The interim orientation period begins following the consummation of the employment contract. To consummate an employment contract, an offer of employment is made by the school system and the offer is accepted by an individual.

After the employment relationship has been ratified by both parties, certain orientation activities can be accomplished prior to the first day on the job. Although some orientation activities must be tailored to individuals and to work groups, other orientation activities are somewhat constant across individuals and separate work groups, and these constants serve as a foundation for the interim orientation period. The following list presents some of the preliminary steps planned and initiated by the human resource function to help all new employees adjust to the position, the system, and the community at this stage of the orientation process:

- Letters of congratulation and of welcome are sent by the board of education and the superintendent of schools to all newly assigned personnel.

- An experienced employee is assigned to serve as a sponsor for every newly assigned person.
- A written description is prepared for sponsors that explain the aims of the orientation program and the responsibilities of sponsors in the conduct of the orientation program.
- A preliminary conference is held between sponsors and the immediate supervisor of the new employee to confirm the expectations for sponsors.
- A conference between the immediate supervisor and the new appointee is held to discuss the work assignment. The supervisor should avoid giving the new appointee a heavy workload or extra duties (committee assignments) that make it difficult for the beginner to achieve a measure of success in the first year of appointment to a newly assigned position. Whenever possible, assignments should be made on the basis of employee preference and the need to reduce the workload of the employee during the first year of service in a newly assigned position.
- Copies of employees' handbooks, selected board policies, and relevant labor contacts are given to the new employee.
- Conditions of employment are confirmed. The organization makes certain that the newly assigned personnel understand the salary, collateral benefits, extra pay, and other facets of the compensation structure prior to reporting for duty.

By setting in motion during the interim orientation period of the employment cycle many of the activities described previously, several advantages may be realized and many problems can be prevented. Employees will have more time to devote to the information they received prior to reporting to work, and the amount of information imparted after reporting to work will be lessened due to the information received during the interim induction period. As such, some of the anxieties of the employees are reduced, and they are able to cope better on their first official workday.

Within the interim orientation period, the immediate supervisor is responsible for helping the employee adjust to the new work assignment. If possible, an initial meeting between the employee and the immediate supervisor should be scheduled prior to beginning work. This meeting should include interpreting short-range and long-range plans for the coming year, including those for appraising work performance and evaluating progress; acquainting the newly assigned personnel with physical facilities, resources, and support services; and explaining the general policies and work routines of the unit.

Prior to beginning the work year, most school districts have an opening day conference for all employees including those new to the assignment and those preparing for another school year. It is usual for many school districts to require newly assigned employees to report for a day of orientation before the opening day conference. During the orientation day for new employees, presentations should be made by community representatives, informational sessions about the system should be conducted, and a social reception should be hosted by the board of education to close the day's activities.

Activities, as just described, are illustrative rather than exhaustive and any given sequence of orientation activities will fail to satisfy the needs of all school systems. The wide range of orientation problems in different public school districts rule out a prescribed program applicable to all school systems. Each public school system can best achieve the goals of the orientation process by developing and assessing the techniques and activities most effective for particular situations and conditions.

Forms found in Figures 6.7 and 6.8 lend specificity to the foregoing suggestions. These forms illustrate a three-part orientation plan for the time before the newly assigned personnel actually begins work. The following outline is the substance of this plan and can be adopted by any public school district as part of the orientation process:

■ Sessions 1 and 2 cover central administration responsibilities. The intent of these initial sessions is to explain the organization and administration of systemwide personnel policies and procedures applicable to new members (see Figure 6.7).

■ Session 3 covers position and unit-oriented responsibilities. The intent of Session 3 is to acquaint individuals with their responsibilities and to introduce them to their new colleagues. This session is handled by the administrator of the new employee's work unit (see Figure 6.8).

■ Copies of forms are given to newly assigned personnel to acquaint them with the nature and scope of the conditions of employment, constraints that govern their work assignments, and opportunities that will become available during their work year.

■ The newly assigned personnel and the administrator responsible for conducting the session sign the forms; these forms become a component of the new staff member's file.

■ Instructional aids available for orientation sessions are virtually limitless, ranging from programmed materials to filmstrips, slides, tapes, cassettes, records, charts, transparencies, flip charts, videotapes, brochures, booklets, and PowerPoint presentations.

The discussion in this section has addressed certain tasks, procedures, and concerns common to any effective orientation process for newly assigned personnel within any public school district. The focus was primarily on the preappointment period and the interim period of the orientation process (Figure 6.5). However, an effective orientation process goes beyond these two periods to include the regular work cycle of new personnel throughout their probationary period (see Figures 6.2 and 6.5).

Initial Service Period

Orientation responsibilities for new personnel continue beyond the opening of school, as noted in Figure 6.2. Although effective recruitment and selection can improve the quality of applicants and enhance the match among persons, positions, and work environments, both of these human resource functions signal the beginning rather than the end of the orientation process for newly assigned employees (Winter, Keedy, & Newton, 2000). Until the new employee has performed under actual conditions, and until the organization has had an opportunity to appraise the suitability of the newly assigned personnel for the position, orientation is less than complete.

The need for an orientation process to continue after the interim orientation period is based on two facts. First, few newly assigned employees are ready to perform the new

Sturgis City Public School District

ORIENTATION CHECKLIST

DIRECTIONS—This form is part of the orientation process for newly assigned staff members. Listed below is information to be provided as part of the orientation process. Please complete and sign the form.

Name_____

Beginning date of new assignment_____
Probationary period from _____to_____
Location of new assignment_____

Session 1

Check-off acknowledgement
System mission and organizational structure_____
Compensation
        Salary_____
        Benefits_____
        Extra Pay_____
Leaves
        Sick_____
        Personal_____
        Holiday_____
        Vacation_____
Personnel Services_____
Community Relations_____
Code of Ethics_____

Session 2

Review and questions from Session 1_____
Unions Relations_____
Academic Freedom_____
Tenure_____
Promotions_____
Transfers_____
Payroll Deductions_____

All items checked have been discussed_____
Signature of the Employee_____
Date received by the Personnel Office_____

FIGURE 6.7   *Three-phase orientation plan for the Sturgis City Public School District (sessions 1 & 2).*

DIRECTIONS—This checklist has been designed as part of the orientation process of the Sturgis City Public School District. The intent of the orientation program is to acquaint newly assigned employees to the position, school district, and community. This step of the orientation process is one of several planned to help assimilate the employee.

Name of Employee_____

Session 3

Completed

Welcome and introduction to the district   _____

Describe unit organization, objectives, relationship to system   _____

Provided a position guide and discussed content   _____

Explained position performance standards for continued performance _____

Explained the performance appraisal process   _____

Explained conditions of employment

        Hours of work

        _____

        Lunch period

        _____

        Building facilities   _____

        Supplies and equipment   _____

        Parking   _____

        Transportation

        _____

Introduced to colleagues   _____

Signature of the Employee_____

Date received by Personnel office_____

FIGURE 6.8   *Three-phase orientation plan for the Sturgis City Public School District (session 3).*

assignment flawlessly, and second, even the best selection process is fallible. For these reasons, a probationary period for all new personnel is becoming increasingly a matter of institutional policy, and effective orientation processes cover this period of employment.

An effective orientation process for employees newly assigned to vacant focal positions requires mentoring (see Step 3 in Figure 6.2). Mentoring on the part of the immediate supervisor or some other designed personnel is essential for a newly assigned employee during the first few weeks on the job. The timing of such assistance is important because the newly assigned personnel may have trouble understanding the assignment or may encounter difficulty on the job for a variety of reasons.

Within the orientation sequence of activities, conferences should be scheduled as an ongoing part of the orientation process at predetermined intervals. After each conference, the mentor should compile a formal report capturing detailed observations and conclusions derived from consultations, observations, and assessments of actual job behaviors exhibited by newly assigned personnel. Follow-up reports should be submitted by the immediate supervisor to the central administration, which appraises such characteristics as quality of performance, difficulties encountered, and other factors deemed important to the effectiveness of the new employee in a recently assigned position.

Performance appraisal during the probationary period, as one phase of the total performance appraisal process, is designed not only to assist the competent probationer but also to identify the potentially incompetent, marginal, or undesirable employee early on within the employment cycle. Those individuals who fail to perform satisfactorily in one position may be reassigned, given more personal supervision, or provided with intensified training to overcome their deficiencies. Prompt rehabilitation or elimination of unsuitable appointees will save money, time, and effort for the system as well as for the newly assigned personnel.

Assessing the Orientation Process

To monitor the job behaviors of newly assigned employees during the initial service of probationary period, it is necessary to assess the perceptions of both the employee and the immediate supervisor. Contained in Figure 6.9 is an example of a self-appraisal form to be completed by the newly assigned personnel and satisfies, in part, the model requirements as found for Step 5 of Figure 6.2. It is designed to provide feedback to the immediate supervisor on position problems and on progress toward effective role performance as perceived by the new employee.

Complementing the self-assessment form compiled by the employee is a form to be completed by the immediate supervisor. This form is found in Figure 6.10. The form contains the impressions of both parties and is used to inform the central administration about the progress of employees during the probationary period.

Analysis and synthesis of the information obtained from both forms provides the basis for counseling and coaching during follow-up sessions between the newly assigned personnel and the immediate supervisor. Formalizing the methods of collecting information about new employees at the probationary stage communicates an important message. That is, the system has a continuing interest in their welfare, their adjustment to the assigned position, and their contribution to the organization. To capitalize on this interest, an effective and an efficient orientation program must be managed on an ongoing basis and must be revisited on an annual basis.

Managing the Orientation Process

Assessments of new personnel are essential to an effective orientation program (see Step 5; Figure 6.2). The financial and human capital investments associated with recruiting, selecting, and orientating new personnel are considerable for most school systems (Owings & Kaplan, 2006). However, the loss suffered by the system when the newly assigned personnel's service is terminated or when the newly assigned personnel leaves the organization voluntarily warrants the attention of management.

Position Design

Do you have a clear understanding of the expectations your immediate supervisor has for you in your newly assigned position?

Do you have a clear understanding of the goals of the work unit that you have been assigned?

Does you immediate supervisor provide you specific help for improving your performance?

Do you feel that you are well placed in your newly assigned position?

Performance Appraisal

Does your immediate supervisor provide you the necessary information to enable you to assess your current job performance?

How worthwhile was your last performance appraisal in helping you improve your performance?

Summarize the strengths you have demonstrated in performing your assignment during this review period.

Describe the weaknesses you have demonstrated in performing your assignment during this review period.

Development

How much assistance have you been given by your immediate supervisor in planning you career development?

How do you feel about your developmental progress you have made thus far in your newly assigned position?

How confident are you that your career aspirations can be obtained in this school district?

Do you feel that you would be better suited in another job assignment?

Communication

Do you receive sufficient information to perform your role effectively?

Do you receive sufficient information to understand the relationships associated with your position and with the system?

Is your supervisor well informed about your requirements for performing your newly assigned position effectively?

Role Satisfaction

How do you feel about the type of work you are doing in your newly assigned position?

Are there significant observations that you think should be noted about the dimensions of your position (i.e., objectives, position design, organization structure, supervisory process, and/or results obtained) that affect your performance and that should be noted?

How effective do you feel that you have performed in your newly assigned position?

Signature_____ Date _____

FIGURE 6.9 *Self-appraisal form for orientation.*

Name _____ Position _____

Adjustment Progress and Problems	Unit Administrator Comments	New Employee Comments
What progress has been made during this review period? Personal Adjustment? Position Adjustment? System Adjustment? Community Adjustment? What are the obstacles encountered in each of the above areas? What are the milestones achieved in each of the above areas? In what area was the most progress made during this review period? In what area was the least progress made during this review period? What goals should be accomplished by the next review period?		

Signature _____ Date _____ Received by Personnel _____

FIGURE 6.10 *Orientation performance review form.*

In theory, recruitment, selection, and orientation processes should result in the attraction and the retention of the number, kinds, and quality of personnel needed by the system for an effective education program. Periodic assessments of the actual outcomes (Step 5 of Figure 6.2) of these three human resource processes should provide information to minimize turnover costs due to faulty recruitment, selection, and placement. If and when these processes do not lead to the desired results, the system can take corrective action from a strategic planning perspective.

Assessments of the orientation process should focus on several different outcome measures. The most important one is whether the new personnel performed effectively in their assigned position. Because most work assignments have a proficiency curve in which job performance improves over time, the effectiveness of new personnel should be assessed at different times during the probationary period.

It is imperative to determine if the predictions of performance made before selection agree with actual job performance of those employees selected. The ultimate purpose of analyzing the recruitment, selection, and orientation processes is to determine how well the system is succeeding in attracting, selecting, and retaining a competent staff from a strategic planning perspective. An evaluation should reveal what adjustments must be made to achieve these goals.

Because individuals as well as organizations must commit to the employment process, it is important to give special attention to those employees who performed effectively but resigned during the initial service or probationary period. Voluntary resignations of effective probationers may or may not be related to their experiences in the recruitment, selection, assignment, or orientation processes. Exit interviews with these employees can be extremely enlightening to those responsible for managing the orientation process and for refining the orientation process.

Although it is true that much time, money, and talent are invested in recruitment, selection, and orientation, it is also true that person-position mismatches are costly, time-consuming, and counterproductive. To minimize such potential mismatches, ongoing assessment of the orientation process is essential. Without exception, orientation processes must be modified each school year.

Orientation and Human Resource Strategy

Throughout this book, the various functions of a school system (presented in Figure 1.2) and of the human resource processes (shown in Figure 2.1) have been implicitly viewed as interdependent. For instance, recruitment, selection, appraisal, and development are considered to be intertwined. This interdependence among personnel processes should be taken into account in shaping the overall human resource strategy. Thus viewed, orientation, as one of the processes of the personnel function, has considerable potential for achieving the aims of the system, especially in view of the employees' right to be informed, coached, mentored, and assisted in various ways to achieve specific goals.

School systems use many methods to help new employees achieve relative independence as established staff members with personal sets of behavioral determiners. This assistance includes various forms of support designated in the literature by labels such as peer coaching, buddy system, master teacher support, mentor–protégé relationship, and clinical teacher support. The types of staff assistance provided to inductees focus on enhancing their development, depending on the individual's personality and willingness to adjust and adapt to the internal and external aspects of the workplace.

This chapter has emphasized that an effective orientation process serves a number of purposes, including socialization, reduction of personnel anxieties, turnover, and supervisory time, helping individuals to understand themselves, and helping the system to understand new employees. Recent educational reform efforts in the United

States, however, have caused school systems to reconsider the orientation process. Today more than ever, an effective orientation process is a necessity for all functional school districts.

Review and Preview

In this chapter, analysis of newly assigned personnel problems suggests that an effective orientation process is one way that the school system can help new members as well as newly assigned members to assimilate, as well as to enhance their personal development, security, and needs satisfaction. A school system can recruit, select, and assign personnel, but until new employees become fully aware of and adjusted to the work to be performed, the work environment, and their new colleagues, they cannot be expected to contribute efficiently and effectively to the organization's goals. An orientation process is needed to help new personnel resolve community, system, position, and development problems by creating plans to enhance their position knowledge, skills, and behavior. Use of this process indicates recognition of and an attempt to do something about the fact that

human maladjustment is expensive, detrimental to individual and organizational goal achievement, and harmful to the socialization process involving the individual and the system. The orientation process also assumes that the main determinant of motivation is the attraction the position holds for the individual, and that orientation activities designed to enhance the potential for motivated action will result in better performance on the job for newly assigned personnel.

Building on the orientation process is the performance evaluation of employees. Newly hired personnel, newly assigned personnel, as well as continuing personnel seek information about the evaluation system. Information is sought about the purpose and the processes used to establish an evaluation system, and these topics are discussed in the following chapter.

Discussion Questions

1. How does your school district transmit organizational culture to new employees?

2. In school systems, many new employees resign voluntarily during their probationary period. What costs to the school organization are associated with this situation? What can the organization do to reduce the number of new teachers who leave the field after their first year?

3. Who coordinates the orientation process for your school district? Is the orientation process centrally coordinated, or is the process

devolved onto specific work sites? Identify three strengths and weaknesses of an orientation process from each perspective.

4. Respond to the following statement: "A well-designed, carefully implemented recruitment and selection program eliminates the need for an orientation plan."

5. The behavior of a newly assigned person does not appear to mesh with the school organization culture (e.g., violates dress code, eats lunch alone). What should be done with this employee?

Case Study

Using the model in Figure 6.2, describe how each phase is addressed in your school district. What are the advantages and disadvantages associated with each phase in your school district? How would you propose to improve on your current model?

References

Batt, R., & Valcour, P. M. (2003). Human resources practices as predictors of work-family outcomes and employee turnover. *Industrial Relations, 42*(2), 189–220.

Bergeson, T. (n.d.). Teacher assistance program: A model for a year-long induction program. Retrieved July 17, 2006, from the Office of Superintendent of Public Instruction Web site: http://www.k12.wa.us/ProfEd/tap/amodel.asp.

California Beginning Teacher Support and Assessment. (n.d.). Retrieved July 3, 2006, from http://www.btsa.ca.gov/.

Cunningham, W. G., & Cordeiro, P. A. (2006). Educational leadership: A problem-based approach (3rd ed.). Columbus, OH: Pearson.

Di Benedetto, R., & Wilson, A. P. (1982, February). *The small school principal and school–community relations. Small schools fact sheet.* ERIC Digests. Retrieved July 17, 2006, from http://www.ed.gov/databases/ERIC_Digests/ed232798.html.

French, W. L. (1987). *The personnel management process* (6th ed., p. 297). Boston: Houghton Mifflin.

Heneman, H. G., & Judge, T. A. (2006). *Staffing organizations* (6th ed.). Middleton, WI: Mendota House.

Heneman, H. G., Judge, T. A., & Heneman, R. L. (2000). *Staffing organizations* (3rd ed.). Middleton, WI: Mendota House.

Hoy, W., & Miskel, C. (2005). *Educational administration: Theory, practice and research.* New York: McGraw-Hill.

Ingersoll, R. M. (2002). The teacher shortage: A case of wrong diagnosis and wrong prescription. *NASSP Bulletin, 86,* 18–27.

Kowalski, T. J. (2004). *Public relation in schools.* Upper Saddle River, NJ: Pearson.

Luthans, F., & Kreitner, R. (1975). *Organizational behavior modification* (p. 97). Glenview, IL: Scott Foresman.

Massachusetts Department of Education. (n.d.). Induction program. Retrieved July 3, 2006, from http://www.doe.mass.edu/eq/mentor/teachers.html.

Michener, H. A., Delamater, J. D., & Myers, J. D. (2004). *Social psychology.* Wadsworth, CA: Belmont.

North Carolina Department of Public Instruction. (n.d.). *1997–98 model new teacher orientation program grant recipients.* Retrieved July 29, 2006, from the Department of Public Instruction Web site: http://www.dpi.state.nc.us/mentoring_novice_teachers/recipnts.htm.

Owings, W. A., & Kaplan, L. S. (2006). *American public school finance.* Belmont, CA: Thomson Wadsworth Corporation.

Seyfarth, J. T. (1996). *Personnel management for effective schools.* Needham Heights, MA: Allyn & Bacon.

Shen, J. (1997, Fall). Has the alternative certification policy materialized its promise? A comparison between traditionally and alternatively certified teachers in public schools. *Educational Evaluation and Policy Analysis, 19*(3), 276–283.

Short, P. M., & Greer, J. T. (1998). *Leadership in empowered schools.* Upper Saddle River, NJ: Merrill/Prentice Hall.

Stansbury, K., & Zimmerman, J. (2002). Smart induction programs become lifeline for beginning teachers. *Journal of Staff Development, 20*(4). Retrieved July 3, 2006, from http://www.nsdc.org/library/publications/jsd/stansbury234.cfm.

Wanous, J. P. (1992). *Organizational entry* (2nd ed.). Reading, MA: Addison-Wesley.

White, G., & Wehlage, J. (1995). Community collaboration: It is such a good idea, why is it so hard? *Educational Evaluation and Policy Analyses, 17*(4), 23–28.

Winter, P. A. (1996). Applicant evaluations of formal position advertisements: The influence of sex, job message content, and information order. *Journal of Personnel Evaluation in Education, 10,* 105–116.

Winter, P. A. (1997). Education recruitment and selection: A review of recent studies and recommendations for best practice. In L. Wildman (Ed.), *Fifth NCPEA yearbook* (pp. 133–140). Lancaster, PA: Technomic.

Winter, P. A., Keedy, J. L., & Newton, R. M. (2000). Teacher serving on school decision-making councils: Predictors of teacher attraction to the job. *Journal of School Leadership, 10,* 248–263.

Winter, P. A., & Melloy, S. H. (2005). Teacher recruitment in a teacher reform state: Factors that influence applicant attraction to teacher vacancies. *Educational Administration Quarterly, 41*(2), 349–372 and *Policy Analyses, 17*(4), 23–38.

Winter, P. A., Newton, R. M., & Kirkpatrick, R. L. (1998). The influence of work values on teacher selection decisions: The effects of principal values, teacher values, and principal–teacher value interactions. *Teaching and Teacher Education, 14*(4), 385–400.

Young, I. P. (2006a). Job descriptions. In F. W. English (Ed.), *Encyclopedia of educational leadership and administration* (pp. 531–538). Newbury Park, CA: Sage Publications.

Young, I. P. (2006b). Fringe benefits. In F. W. English (Ed.), *Encyclopedia of educational leadership and administration* (pp. 409–410). Newbury Park, CA: Sage Publications.

Young, I. P., Chounet, P. F., Buster, A. B., & Sailor, S. (2005). Effects of student achievement on satisfaction of newly appointed teachers: A cognitive dissonance perspective. *Journal of School Leadership, 15*(1), 35–51.

Young, I. P., Place, A. W., Rinehart, J. S., Jury, J. C., & Baits, D. F. (1999). Teacher recruitment: A test of the similarity–attraction hypothesis for race and sex. *Educational Administration Quarterly, 33*(1), 86–106.

Performance Appraisal

7

CHAPTER OVERVIEW

Multiple-cutoff model
Narrative system
Norm-referenced system
Numerically anchored
  rating systems
Paired comparison
  technique
Portfolios
Probationary employees
Ranking systems
Rating system
Reliability
Self-referenced system
Simple ranking method
Validity
Verbally anchored rating
  systems
Work diaries

OBJECTIVES

- Understand what performance appraisal is expected to accomplish.
- Describe the organizational context of performance appraisal.
- Identify the purposes of performance appraisal.
- Specify a reference source for the performance process.
- Select a model of the performance appraisal process.
- Assess psychometrical aspects for performance appraisals.
- Present a decisional matrix for performance assessment processes.
- Illustrate a procedural model for performance assessment.

Performance Appraisal as a Process

From a system perspective, a fundamental requirement of all effective and efficient public school districts is a functional performance appraisal process for employees. Although the above statement seems to be a given, far too often performance appraisal has been viewed by public school districts as an event occurring at a single point within the work year rather than as a process ongoing throughout the work year, and this viewpoint has many shortcomings in the current era of accountability. Perpetuating this viewpoint of an event as opposed to a process is the general notion that a single performance appraisal system exists that can be readily adopted and easily implemented by any public school district.

If in fact such a utopian system did exist for performance appraisals, then issues related to performance appraisals would have been resolved decades ago within the public school setting. That is, all state Departments of Education would have mandated a single appraisal system for the evaluation of employees and/or educational consultants would have developed a uniform system of employee appraisal applicable to all school districts. Given these unlikely occurrences, what exists in reality are multiple policy decisions, several different evaluation processes, and many procedural concerns that must be interwoven to produce a functional performance appraisal process tailored to a specific public school district.

In light of these contingencies concerning policies, processes, and procedures moderating a functional performance appraisal system for a particular school system, this chapter draws together several streams of thought from a strategic planning perspective. Guiding the developmental process are a series of sequential decisions to be made by policy makers and public school administrators in the formulation and implementation of a functional appraisal process for employees. Contained in Figure 7.1 is a concentric circle for describing processes and procedures in the development, assessment, and implementation of a functional performance assessment process for a specific public school district from a strategic planning perspective.

Within these circles centering on performance appraisal, several different decisions are needed from a strategic planning perspective. Early within the strategic planning process, performance appraisal must be placed in context within the organizational setting. From a contextual perspective, performance appraisal can serve several purposes.

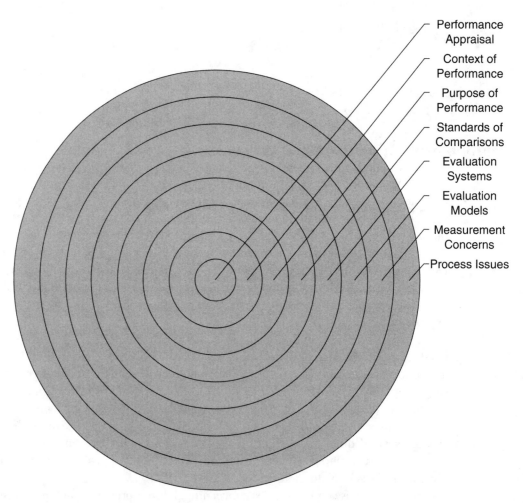

Performance
Appraisal

Context of
Performance

Purpose of
Performance

Standards of
Comparisons

Evaluation
Systems

Evaluation
Models

Measurement
Concerns

Process Issues

FIGURE 7.1   *Concerns underlying the performance appraisal process.*

Purposes of a performance appraisal can be related to compensation, employment considerations, and the development of employees. Depending on the purpose or purposes of a performance appraisal system, different standards of comparison come into play for assessing the job performance of employees. Most importantly, an employee's performance can be compared to the performance of other employees within the organization, to external referent sources as criteria, or to an employee's own level of either past or expected performance in an assigned position.

Each means of comparison for assessing job performance has implications for the type of performance appraisal system used to assess employees. Performance appraisal can involve a **narrative system,** a **ranking system**, and/or a **rating system**. Functionally, these systems of performance appraisal may not always be mutually exclusive within the field setting, but each system has certain strengths as well as weaknesses that must be considered from a strategic planning perspective when adopting and implementing a performance assessment system at the local school district level.

Depending on the type of data collected by any given system of performance appraisal, a specific model of evaluation is suggested. Models of evaluation within the performance appraisal process differ in the manner in which data are availed to the decision maker. Some models focus on specific dimensions of job performance, while other models combine this information into an overall composite measure as an indicator of total job performance.

Undergirding all models of evaluation within the performance assessment context are certain measurement issues. Performance appraisal outcomes must be both reliable and valid to withstand legal challenges and to be meaningful within the educational setting. Finally, certain process issues must be followed in the evaluation of all educational employees, and these processes are tempered by the context of the performance appraisal process.

The Context of Performance Appraisal

Appraisal of employee performance relative to assigned duties, in general, has never been more popular and has never received more attention in the popular press than it has in recent times. Almost without exception, most states mandate the assessment of school districts and/or buildings and of schoolchildren through report cards for organizations and through proficiency tests for students. Indeed, few public school districts and few children have escaped performance assessments in this new era that has placed an emphasis on accountability within the public school setting.

Because the level of performance exhibited by public school districts as organizations and by public school students as individuals depends, to a large extent, on the performance of employees, the focus on performance appraisal for individuals, as employees, has been rekindled. Stakeholders involved with the educational process no longer expect some means of performance appraisal be performed for employees but demand that the assessment of all educational employees be conducted on a continuing basis. This demand on the part of stakeholders is both warranted and expected if the United States is to maintain its global position in the world economy.

Different, however, from the appraisal expectations associated with school districts as organizations and with students as individuals are certain requirements for performance appraisals of employees. Unlike districts as organizations and students as individuals, employees enjoy certain types of legislative protection within the performance appraisal process through due process clauses and property right issues (Valente & Valente, 2005). These different types of legislative protection come into play depending on the purpose of and outcomes for an employee appraisal system.

Purposes of the Performance Appraisal System

Surprisingly, the actual purpose of a performance appraisal system in many public school districts is a mystery to administrators and to employees in many ways. Within many school districts, performance appraisals are nonexistent. Recently, Costa (2004) indicated that only 25 percent of the public school districts conduct performance appraisals for superintendents, and this omission sends a clear message to other employees about the purpose of and the importance for this important human resource activity.

When queried about the purpose of the performance appraisal system used by a public school district, most stakeholders are uncertain about the purpose or purposes served by an appraisal system used by their public school district. Indeed, performance appraisal is viewed by many stakeholders as a statutory requirement rather than as a meaningful administrative process with a specific purpose. This void exists in perceptions among stakeholders due, at least in part, to the lack of a definitive policy statement or of a labor contract specification setting forth a defined purpose(s) for a performance appraisal system/ process at the local school district level.

Without a clear definition of purpose for an appraisal process from either a policy ratification perspective or a labor contract specification, employee assessment becomes an unguided administrative activity in many public school districts. As an unguided administrative activity lacking a specific purpose as defined by board policy or by a labor contract, outcomes from the appraisal process carry little authority within the decision-making context and are largely indefensible when challenged by employees either from a substantive or procedural perspective. Consequently, it should be of little surprise that performance appraisal results are readily dismissed as a valid means for making organizational decisions within the public school setting in order to improve the effectiveness and the efficiency of a public school district.

From a strategic planning perspective, a performance appraisal system for employees should accomplish specific purposes, as designated by boards of education through policy enactments or by a labor contract via bilateral agreements. Mitigating, at least in part, a clear definition of purpose for performance appraisal processes has been past nomenclatures used to describe this administrative activity. Historically, the purposes of a performance appraisal system for educational employees have been categorized grossly as being either formative or summative (Cunningham & Cordeiro, 2006; Webb & Norton, 2003).

This nomenclature involving normative and summative classifications has been found to be too restrictive in actual practice within the public school setting from a development as well as from an applied perspective. For example, a formative performance appraisal system is purported to be process oriented and is designed primarily for the professional development of individuals as employees. In contrast, a summative performance appraisal system is purported to be outcome oriented and is designed primarily for decision making about continuation of employment for individuals. Because these two systems of classification fail to be mutually exclusive in process as well as in practice, these classifications have done more to confuse rather than to enhance the evaluation of employees at the local school district level.

Indeed, the problems associated with developing and administering formative or summative performance appraisal processes are well documented in the professional literature. These terms are not only confusing to policy makers (i.e., boards of education) responsible for approving performance appraisal systems, but also restrictive for administrators responsible for executing performance appraisal systems. The following are some of the more common problems associated with these classifications that have been a deterrent to the school district and a source of alienation for the employees:

- Appraisals focus on an individual's personality.
- Appraisal tools lack reliability.
- Appraisal tools lack validity.
- Raters display biases.
- Ratings and raters are subject to influence by the organization.
- The appraisal system does not apply to all personnel.
- Results of appraisal are not used to promote individual development.
- Appraisal devices do not provide administrators with effective counseling tools.
- Most plans fail to establish organizational expectations for individuals.
- Appraisals used for discipline, salary, promotion, or dismissal are arbitrary.
- Personnel do not understand the criteria on which performance is appraised.
- Performance is unrelated to the goals of the organization.
- Appraisal procedures hamper communication between appraiser and appraisee.
- Appraisal methods fail to change individual behavior.
- Appraisal methods do not encourage the satisfaction of higher-level needs.
- Appraisal models do not complement appraisal purposes.

In lieu of using general classifications such as formative and summative for describing performance appraisal systems, significant stakeholders are served better by using normal descriptive terms for describing the purposes of a performance appraisal system rather than by using traditional nomenclatures as used in the past. In fact, most performance appraisal systems in education can be defined by one of the following purposes: employee compensation, employment continuation, and personal development. Each of these broad purposes has meaningful subdivisions affecting policy and

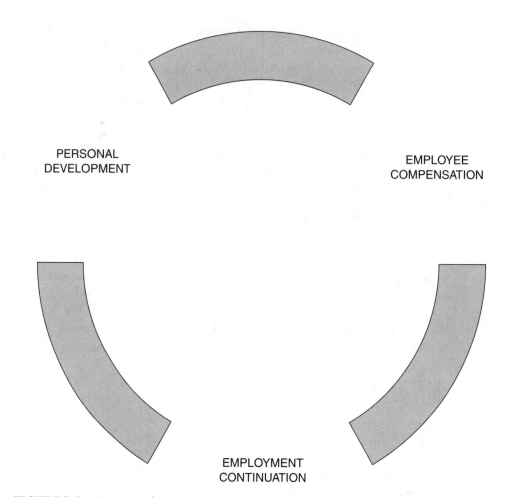

PERSONAL
DEVELOPMENT

EMPLOYEE
COMPENSATION

EMPLOYMENT
CONTINUATION

FIGURE 7.2   *Purposes of a performance appraisal system.*

practice in the execution of an effective performance appraisal system within the public school setting (see Figure 7.2) and should be reconciled from a strategic planning perspective.

Differences within, as well as between each of these purposes, as found in Figure 7.2, are nontrivial with respect to the performance appraisal process. These differences are nontrivial for a performance appraisal process in the sense that separate purposes require different decisional criteria, different evaluation systems, and different models for combining information in a meaningful fashion for guiding decision making from a strategic planning perspective. To place in context each purpose for a performance appraisal, specific definitions are provided for each purpose and serve as a starting point within the strategic planning process for developing an effective and an efficient system of employee evaluation at the local school district level.

Employee Compensation

In some public school districts, outcomes from the performance appraisal process are used to make decisions about an employee's level of compensation for teachers (Kelley, Heneman, & Milanowski, 2002) and for school administrators (Cox, 2006). From the perspective of employees, compensation decisions resulting from performance appraisal outcomes should be differentiated according to the type of compensation decision made on the part of vested authorities. Compensation decisions can be codified several different ways, and each way of codification has important implications for application in the field setting relative to the allocation of compensation: (1) merit, (2) bonus, (3) award, and (4) maintenance.

Decisions about **merit** are performance based and are labeled frequently as pay for performance in the popular literature. With respect to decisions about merit increases, all employees are eligible that exhibit the prerequisite level of job performance necessary to qualify for a merit increase (Young, 2003). In fact, the goal of a performance appraisal process focusing on merit is to increase the job performance of all employees and to motivate all employees toward merit increases.

From an applied perspective, merit systems should be viewed from a cost enhancement rather than from a cost containment perspective. That is, the goal of a merit system is to increase the performance level of all employees. If this goal is accomplished, then all employees would receive a merit increase and the dollar amount for funding compensation obligations is increased proportional to the success of the merit program.

Differentiating merit decisions from **bonus** decisions as the purpose for a performance appraisal system are two considerations. One consideration involves the eligibility of participants for a bonus. Bonuses are restricted in the number of employees eligible to receive a bonus whereas merit is available to all employees.

The other consideration for a bonus concerns the duration of the payments received by an employee. Bonuses fail to be incorporated into the base salary of an employee. As such, bonuses represent a one-time payment obligation on the part of a public school district and not a continuing financial obligation to be continually borne by a public school district as is the case with merit.

These differences in eligibility and in duration have important implications within the performance appraisal context. By being limited in number and in future obligation, bonus incentives can carry higher reward payments than those afforded by merit increases. As a result, bonus incentives can be more meaningful to employees from an intermediate perspective.

Awards, on the other hand, are based on a designated group performance rather than on the performance of any specific individual. A designated group could include all within a specific work site (school building) or some subgroup within a specific work site (academic department or grade level). Compensation decisions involving awards relative to job performance are labeled as "**gain sharing**" within the performance appraisal literature in that all employees enjoy the benefits of performance by being included within a defined group.

Gain-sharing rewards have been differentiated according to personal or professional usage. Personal use involves actual salary that employees can spend as pleased. Professional uses require that employees spend monies that benefit them or their work group professionally (i.e., professional conference or equipment purchase).

Still different are **"maintenance decisions"** based on performance assessment outcomes that focus on the opposite end of the distribution of employee performance. Rather than rewarding superior performance as per merit, bonuses, or awards (when the focus is on the upper end of the distribution of performance), maintenance decisions are designed to defer compensation increases to certain employees failing to perform according to expectations (when the focus is on the bottom end of the distribution of performance). Employees failing to achieve a minimum level of proficiency as assessed through a performance appraisal process receive no salary increase, and employees exhibiting either satisfactory or exemplary performance receive normal salary increases denied low-performing employees.

When the purpose of a performance appraisal process is maintenance, the focus is on cost containment. That is, the purpose is not to spend more money for exceptional performance but to spend less money for ineffective performance. However, differences between maintenance and merit purposes have been blurred often in the field setting at the expenses of both approaches.

Employment Continuation

Another purpose for a performance appraisal system beyond compensation considerations is to provide information for employment continuation decisions about employees (see Figure 7.2). Employment continuation decisions based on performance appraisal outcomes have implications for three employee groups within the public school setting. These groups are probationary employees new to their job assignment, at-will employees with limited term contracts, and continuing employees enjoying property rights.

With respect to the first group, **probationary employees** may or may not be new to the school district. What distinguishes probationary employees from nonprobationary employees is that the former have been assigned newly to positions with temporal performance contingencies attached to the assignments. For some positions (i.e., civil service), the probationary period may be several months; for other positions (i.e., teachers), it may span several years.

At-will employees work at the discretion of the board of education through a limited-term contractual agreement. In most school districts all classified personnel and all administrative personnel are considered at-will employees. Based on the outcomes from their performance appraisal process, these individuals can be nonrenewed, and they lack any appeal mechanism other than procedural violations associated with the performance appraisal process (Lee, 2004).

Having satisfied the probationary contingencies required by a newly assigned position, teachers are considered as **continuing employees** with specified property rights prescribed by legislative enactments (Valente & Valente, 2005). The existence of property rights for teachers places a higher burden on the performance appraisal process than those associated with either probationary employees or at-will employees because employment discontinuation decisions must be based on just cause when property rights are involved. However, despite popular opinion, the mere existence of property rights for continuing employees does not shelter an employee from the scrutiny of the employer and the use of a performance appraisal process for decisions relating to the continuation of employment.

Indeed, continuing employees can be discharged for several reasons when due process concerns have been met by a public school district. Many of these concerns are noted recently by Valente and Valente (2005). Included among these reasons are such causes as incompetence, incapacity, insubordination, unprofessional conduct, and immorality.

Personal Development

Still another purpose of a performance appraisal system is to enhance the job performance of employees independent either of compensation rewards or of employment contingencies (see Figure 7.2). **Development** is, by far, reported as the most common reason by school board members and by educational employees when polled relative to the purpose of the performance appraisal system used by their school district. Underlying this approach involving development of an employee's skill as a purpose for performance appraisal is the general assumption that most employees can improve their on-the-job performance.

To improve the on-the-job performance of individuals as employees, performance appraisal systems can be designed either to identify weaknesses or to pinpoint strengths on the part of an employee. Even though the identification of both weaknesses and strengths focuses on the single bipolar continuum involving development, the focus of each approach is on opposite ends of the same continuum. As such, different standards of comparison and different appraisal techniques are required to maximize the particular opportunity for development, depending on the purpose(s) of the performance appraisal system, and the standard(s) of comparison used to assess job performance.

Standards of Comparison for Performance Appraisal Systems

Performance appraisal should involve assessing a construct (job performance) rather than a single event occurring at one point in time. Within the performance appraisal process, many time samplings of the occurrences of job behavior should be assessed to measure an employee's level of job performance across time. These assessments do not occur in a vacuum but are related to some referent source as a standard for comparison for defining job performance.

In the context of performance appraisal in general, a standard of comparison is defined as the referent source(s) against which the observed or inferred job performance of an employee is compared. Depending on the purpose(s) of a performance appraisal system, different standards of comparison are required to accomplish expeditiously the designated purpose of a performance appraisal system. A particular standard of comparison may be norm-referenced, criterion-referenced, or self-referenced systems, and these different standards of comparison are illustrated in Figure 7.3.

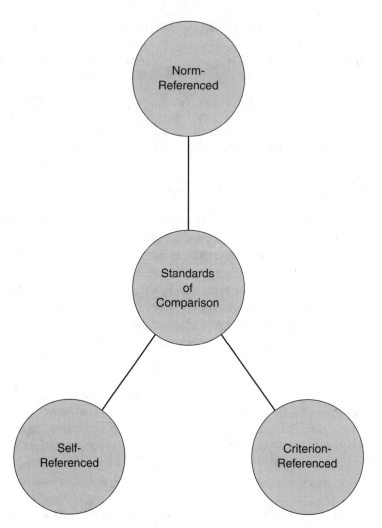

FIGURE 7.3   *Standards of comparison for a performance appraisal process.*

In a **norm-referenced system** for a performance appraisal process involving public school employees (see Figure 7.3), the standard of comparison for the observed and the inferred job performance of an employee is the level of job performance exhibited by other employees holding "like type" positions. By comparing the job performance of one employee to the job performance of other employees holding a like type position, a relative measure of job performance is obtained. The measure of performance is relative in that the job performance of any employee can be categorized as either less than or greater than the job performance of other employees used as a reference standard for comparison.

Norm-referenced performance appraisal systems are useful particularly in certain situations. For example, if the purpose of a performance appraisal system is to determine eligibility for an award (see Figure 7.2), then a norm-referenced system will identify the highest performers within a particular work group. Likewise, if the purpose of a performance appraisal system is to identify particular employees to meet reduction in force mandates (see Figure 7.2), a norm-referenced system will identify the lowest performers within a particular work group.

The major weakness of a norm-referenced performance appraisal system is the inability of this type of system to establish absolute levels of job performance that may be necessary for certain types of managerial decisions. A norm-referenced system allows administrators to determine if one employee's performance is better or worse than another employee's performance, but norm-referenced systems fail to provide adequate insight relative to whether the actual job performance of any employee is satisfactory or unsatisfactory from a absolute standard. Such a distinction between satisfactory or unsatisfactory job performances may not be important if only a few awards exist for a particular group of employees or if only a few persons must be released to meet reduction in force mandates.

To assess the absolute level of job performance for employees, a standard of comparison other than norm-referenced must be employed. The absolute level of job performance for employees may be assessed by using a criterion-referenced standard of comparison (see Figure 7.3). A **criterion-referenced** performance appraisal system designed to assess absolute levels of job performance compares the observed or the inferred performance of an employee against some preestablished standards external to any particular work group.

Preestablished standards are determined by policy rather than by group performance within a criterion-referenced system. The preestablished standards could be a minimum level of acceptable job performance or could be some meritorious level of exceptional job performance. Criterion-referenced systems are particularly advantageous for making continuation of employment decisions and for making merit pay decisions, but entirely ineffective for making either reduction in force decisions or for making award decisions.

More recently, many school districts have been employing **self-referenced** standards of comparison for performance assessments of employees (see Figure 7.3). Rather than relying on the performance of others (norm-referenced) or some preestablished standards (criterion-referenced) for assessing job performance of an employee, a self-referenced performance appraisal system focuses on the job behavior of an individual employee. By focusing on the relative performance of an individual employee across different dimensions of job performance, the relative strengths and the relative weaknesses of an employee can be identified.

Self-referenced systems for performance appraisal are well suited for an individual's development of job skills (see Figure 7.2). Based on an employee's job performance, goals or benchmarks can be established for an individual employee. In some instances, the goals or benchmarks may be remedial addressing a particular deficiency, while in other instances the goals or benchmarks may be enhanced by building on the specific strengths of an employee.

Because a self-referenced system is unique to an individual, a self-referenced system, like other means of comparison (criterion- or norm-referenced systems) has certain weaknesses. Most notably, self-referenced systems fare poorly for allocating rewards among employees. Also, self-referenced systems are largely ineffective for decisions involving a reduction in force.

Functionally, the actual choice of a reference system (criterion-, norm-, or self-referenced; see Figure 7.3) for a performance appraisal process is linked directly to the purpose(s) to be served (compensation, employment continuation, or development; see Figure 7.2). These choices of purposes relate directly to a specific type of evaluation system. Types of evaluation systems that can be used to assess the job performance of employees in a public school setting are addressed in the following section of this chapter.

Types of Evaluation Systems

An evaluation system provides the framework for a performance appraisal process within the field setting. The evaluation system used by a public school district does so by connecting the purpose(s) to be served by a performance appraisal system (employee compensation, employment continuation, or personal development; see Figure 7.2) with the method of comparison (criterion-referenced, norm-referenced, or self-referenced; see Figure 7.3) for assessing employee performance. As such, an evaluation system dictates procedures for collecting information and the format for processing information within the performance appraisal process.

A review of the professional and popular literature will reveal many different types of evaluation systems used by organizations to evaluate the job performance of employees (Heneman & Judge, 2006). Both the number of and types of evaluation systems continue to increase each year. However, at the very basic level, most, if not all, of the evaluation systems can be classified into one of three basic categories relative to the performance appraisal process.

The basic categories are as follows: (a) narrative systems, (b) ranking systems, and (c) rating systems. Differences across these systems have important implications both for evaluation purposes (see Figure 7.2) and for choice of evaluation standards (see Figure 7.3). It is not surprising that, within each of these basic systems, a number of procedural variations exist, and a basic description follows for each system and variations of each system to guide informed decision making from a strategic planning perspective (see Figure 7.4) at the local school district level.

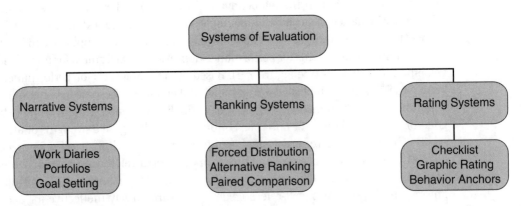

FIGURE 7.4 *Systems of evaluation.*

Narrative Systems

Recently within the public school setting, considerable interest has been directed toward narrative systems as a means for assessing the job performance of public school employees (Peterson, Stevens, & Mack, 2001). Narrative systems of evaluation, when used within the performance appraisal context, are particularly suited for identifying developmental needs (McMillan, 2003). Developmental needs can be isolated either from an individual or from an organizational perspective within narrative systems of evaluation.

The method of comparison utilized by narrative evaluation systems is self-referenced (see Figure 7.3). It is self-referenced because the obtained information is specific to an individual, and the individual's actual job assignment within a public school setting. As such, narrative systems of performance appraisal provide little insight both about the relative level of job performance as compared to other employees (norm-referenced systems; see Figure 7.3) and about the absolute level of job performance as compared to an external standard (criterion-referenced systems; see Figure 7.3).

Narrative systems, when used as a means of performance appraisal, provide employees great latitude within the assessment process because they control the input data used within the performance assessment process. This discretionary aspect has great appeal to employees and increases the likelihood of compliance. Most common among the narrative systems for performance assessments with public school districts are work diaries, portfolios, and goal-setting techniques.

Work diaries are among the oldest method used for collecting information about an employee's job performance (see Figure 7.4). Procedurally, work diaries describe the work tasks performed by an employee, the manner in which these tasks are performed, and the outcomes associated with this performance. This information is recorded in narrative form within a work diary compiled by the employee.

Compilation of a work diary is an ongoing activity throughout the work year. Time sampling within the work year is used to capture any noncyclical components of an employee's job assignment. Within each of the compilation periods, specific incidents of on-the-job behavior are cataloged, enriched with narrative information, and analyzed by an employee in a reflective summary.

When using work diaries as a means of performance appraisal, evaluation is an ongoing process rather than an event. Contents of the work diary are submitted periodically throughout the work year to the immediate supervisor (appraiser). Based on an assessment of the narrative information provided by the employee to the immediate supervisor, a plan of action is developed and monitored as a means of either improving current performance or reinforcing past performance.

Portfolios are, perhaps, the most recent appraisal technique to emerge in the public school setting (Painter, 2001). On inspection of this technique (see Figure 7.4), an obvious conclusion is that portfolios represent a refinement of work diaries. Common to both techniques are basic requirements.

Most notably, work diaries and portfolios allow employees great latitude in the types of information collected within the performance appraisal process. What type of information either included or excluded is largely at the discretion of the employee. However, these techniques differ in some important ways.

A substantial advantage of portfolios over work diaries is the contextually rich information provided by portfolios. Rather than providing descriptions of job tasks as required by work dairies, portfolios contain actual examples of work outcomes. Compiled by the employee, individual portfolios contain samples of the work performed, supporting materials for the work performed, and outcomes attributed to the work performed.

To illustrate some the information contained in a portfolio, specific examples are provided. Teachers might include "artifacts such as lesson and unit plans, attendance records, student work, family contact logs, and documentation of professional development activities" (Heneman & Milanowski, 2003, p. 175). School administrators could include within their work diaries enrollment projections, staffing plans, and employee assignments.

Given this richer contextual information, a more in-depth analysis of job performance can be made with portfolios as compared to work dairies. Portfolio assessment involves a content analysis of the integration of means, methods, and outcomes used by and produced by the employee when fulfilling assigned work duties. Consequently, it is of little surprise that portfolios have replaced largely work diaries as a system of evaluation within the employee assessment process used by public school districts.

Goal-setting techniques represent still another narrative system used by public school districts in the performance appraisal process (see Figure 7.4). As a performance appraisal process, goal-setting techniques carry several labels from an operational perspective. Included among these labels are management by objectives (MBO), administration by objectives (ABO), or education by objectives (EBO).

A major difference for this narrative technique (goal setting) as compared to other narrative techniques (work diaries or portfolios) is a temporal factor. Goal-setting techniques are future oriented rather than reflective. Attention is directed toward what is expected as well as to what has been accomplished.

With the goal-setting procedure, preestablished objectives are identified early within the work year through mutual agreement between the employee and the appraiser (Heneman, 1998). Ideally, the employee and the appraiser develop independently a set of objectives for the employee, and these objectives are commingled and negotiated. Once agreed upon by the appraiser and the employee, fulfillment of the objectives serves as the vehicle for evaluation through a self-referenced system.

Ranking Systems

As a means for performance appraisal, ranking systems are among the most established and the simplest used by organizations to differentiate among employees on the basis of assessed job performance (see Figure 7.4). Within the performance appraisal context, all ranking systems involve comparing the overall job performance of one employee with the overall job performance of other employees. Because of this type of comparison, ranking systems are very effective procedures when the purpose (or purposes) of the performance evaluation demands evaluators distinguish among employees on the basis of their relative as opposed to absolute level of job performance (i.e., norm-referenced; see Figure 7.3).

Examples where the purpose of the performance appraisal process must distinguish among employees on the basis of their relative job performance are compensation awards, reduction in force, or promotion from within the school district, to mention a few. When applied to these decisional situations, ranking systems are excellent choices for educational organizations because these different decisional outcomes require a norm-referenced standard. A norm-referenced standard, however, can be obtained by several different ranking techniques.

One type of ranking technique using a norm-referenced standard is the **forced distribution method** (Scullen, Bergey, & Aiman-Smith, 2005). This technique has been described as somewhat analogous to grading on a curve (Dressler, 1988). Preestablished categories (e.g., exceptional, above average, or average) varying in performance levels like academic grades (A, B, C, etc.) are used to group employees on the basis of relative performance. Within a single grouping, employees are presumed to have equivalent levels of job performance, and between separate groupings, individuals are presumed to have differing levels of job performance.

A major advantage of the forced distribution technique is that the performance appraisal system can be tailored to the specific decisional context of a school district. For example, if the purpose of a performance appraisal is to identify the upper 2 percent of the workforce for economic awards, then the forced distribution method may contain only two categories with the percentage allocations assigned to the categories matching the decisional demands of the organization (i.e., 98 percent and 2 percent). By using only two categories rather than an expanded range of categories, political issues associated with the lowest performers, and with the intermediate performers can be avoided.

By far, the most frequently used ranking technique is referred to as the **simple ranking method.** This technique is norm-referenced and focuses on the criterion of overall job performance. For a particular group of employees, the individuals are ranked according to their overall job performance from the highest performer to the lowest performer within a target group of employees.

When using the simple ranking technique, performance assessments are accomplished generally by having the evaluator or evaluators sort 4- by -6 index cards, with each card listing the name of a sole employee. In some instances, evaluators may have difficulty with ranking employees from highest to lowest relative to their job performance and may render this technique as ineffective. To overcome this problem involving ranking from highest to lowest on the basis of overall job performance, other ranking strategies have emerged within the professional literature.

Rather than rank employees from highest to lowest on the basis of their relative job performance, another strategy is labeled as the **alternate ranking technique.** The alternate ranking technique consists of first identifying the employee with the highest level of job performance, and then second identifying the employee with the lowest level of job performance. Following the identification of the highest and lowest performers, evaluators select the next highest performer and the next lowest performer from the remaining pool of employees being evaluated.

The process of choosing, the next highest and the next lowest among employees, proceeds until the entire pool of employees have been ranked on their relative performance. By choosing extremes from the distribution of remaining employees each time, maximum differentiation is achieved for each comparison. However, problems with the alternate ranking techniques are to occur likely in the middle of the distribution where little variability may exist with respect to relative job performance of the remaining employees.

Problems with the middle ranked groups may not necessarily be an issue for certain decisional situations being faced by an educational organization. If the purpose of the rankings is to identify employees for awards, determine which employees are promoted, or select employees for reduction in force, then middle ranked groups of employees are of little concern in these different decisional situations because middle ranks fail to enter within the decisional context. When even finer differentiation is needed than afforded by the alternate ranking technique, the **paired comparison technique** can be used.

With the paired comparison technique, the job performance of each employee is contrasted to the job performance of all other employees on an individual basis. For every dyadic comparison between the employees, the evaluator must determine if the target employee's job performance is higher or lower than a specific comparison other (ties are not permitted). According to the paired comparison technique, an employee's overall job performance is determined by summing the number of times that an employee's job performance was perceived to be higher than all comparison others job performance.

Although the paired comparison technique provides the maximum amount of information for a norm-referenced system, this system can be taxing with large work groups. The formula for calculating the number of individual comparisons among employees is found in Table 7.1. As can be observed, when the work group doubles in size, the number of comparisons increases exponentially.

To illustrate, a small elementary school district may employ only 10 FTE teachers, and require a total of 45 comparisons $(10(10-1)/2)$. An elementary school building having twice as many teachers requires considerably more comparisons on the part of the principal. Indeed, the number of comparisons required using the pairing technique is 180 $(20(20-1)/2)$.

TABLE 7.1
Formula for Calculating the Number of Required Comparisons

Number of Comparisons = N (N − 1)/2
N = Number of Positions Compared

Rating Systems

By far, rating systems are used most frequently as a means of performance appraisal within the organizational setting (Arvey & Murphy, 1998). In contrast to ranking systems relying on a norm-referenced criterion, rating systems are criterion-referenced. Because criterion-referenced systems rely on an external standard (see Figure 7.3), these types of systems provide information about an absolute level of job performance defined by an external standard.

Several different types of rating techniques exist (see Figure 7.4). These techniques vary in form and in focus. Most popular among the rating techniques are the critical incident checklist, graphic rating scale, and the behavioral anchored rating scale. Underlying the **critical incident checklist technique** is that certain job behaviors are critical to the performance of a focal position. Some of the critical behaviors are important for effective job performance. Likewise, some of the critical behaviors are major contributors for ineffective job performance.

Effective behaviors as well as ineffective behaviors critical to the performance of an employee are gleaned generally through interviews with job incumbents. Job incumbents are asked to provide examples of incidents for job behaviors that are particularly potent for effective or ineffective job performance. These critical incidents are used to develop a checklist that is used subsequently for the assessment of employee performance.

To assess an employee's level of job performance using the critical incidents checklist, the supervisor marks those behaviors that are characteristic of an employee's performance. In most instances, some of the behaviors marked will be positive and some of the behaviors will be negative. An employee's level of job performance is determined by the net difference between the two types of attributes.

In contrast to indicating whether a specific job behavior is either present or absent via a checklist, **graphic rating** scales attempt to measure the degree by which an employee exhibits certain behaviors or traits within the job setting. For a graphic rating scale, the behaviors or traits are distributed along bipolar continuums. Within the confines of each continuum are varying degrees of each behavior or trait reflecting an absolute level of job performance.

Graphic rating scales are anchored directionally either by numerals (e.g., 1–7) or by adverbs. Numerals begin with the number "1" and continue consequently until the maximum interval is reached. In contrast to numerals, adverbs, when used as anchor points, begin typically with "never" and end with "always" or begin with "unsatisfactory" and end with "exceptional."

Because the immediate values associated with graphic rating scales may cause problems of interpretation in practice, more descriptive rating scales have been developed. Foremost among these later rating scales are the **behavioral anchored rating scales** (BARS). BARS are considered by most authorities to be among the best for assessing the actual job performance of employees. Rather than relying on numerals or adverbs as anchor points, BARS use actual job behaviors as descriptors for anchor points throughout the scale range.

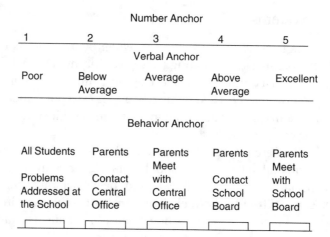

FIGURE 7.5   *Examples of rating scales for principals' handling of student discipline.*

Included in Figure 7.5 are examples of each type of rating scale. Each of these different rating scales purports to measure a principal's ability to address student discipline. Although each scale addresses the full gamut of behavior along a single continuum, each scale provides both the person performing the evaluation and the person being observed with varying levels of definition relative to specific criteria or job behaviors.

On review of the different rating systems, the superiority of the BARS approach is evident. For example, a principal rated either "2" on the numerical rating or "below average" on the verbal anchored approach is provided little specific insight about improving performance other than doing better in the future than in the past. In contrast, a principal receiving the same level of evaluation on the BARS scale realizes that the next step in the improvement process involves keeping parents from meeting with central office personnel.

When constructing rating scales, several issues emerge concerning the structural characteristics of these instruments. Common concerns are the number of points for each scale, polarity for ordering scales, and dimensionality of scales. Fortunately, considerable research exists about each of these concerns, and this information can be used to guide practice in the field setting.

With respect to the number of points for each scale, research has indicated that concerns about either an odd number or an even number of anchor points are not major concerns. Rather, the number of anchor points should be at a minimum of at least 5 and no more than 11. Too few anchor points limit an evaluator's ability to discriminate and too many anchor points require a level of differentiation beyond the cognitive capabilities of the evaluator.

The use of too few anchor points for rating scales is a common problem in the field setting. It is not uncommon to find many school districts that use only two anchor points: (1) "unsatisfactory" or (2) "satisfactory." As a consequence in this restriction in range afforded the evaluator, most all employees receive a satisfactory rating and results of the performance appraisal process convey little informative information about the levels of job performance exhibited by employees.

Rating scales can vary in polarity from being either "positive to negative" or "negative to positive." For example, in Figure 7.5, the polarity is reversed for the verbally anchored and the BAR scales. The former polarity ranges from negative to positive, while the latter polarity ranges from positive to negative.

Early writings (not research) indicate that varying polarity causes raters to pay more attention within the performance appraisal process. Subsequent research indicates that evaluators form a response set early on within the evaluation process and follow this response set throughout the evaluation. Consequently, the polarity of items should be constant within a performance appraisal process regardless of the direction.

Each rating scale should measure only a single concept. Some rating scales found in practice measure more than a single concept. For example, a rating scale might assess "arrives at meetings on time and contributes significant information." This type of scale is labeled as a "double barreled."

That is, an employee can satisfy either one or both outcomes in different degrees. A rating on a double-barreled item confounds the actual level of performance on these different dimensions of performance. Consequently, each scale within a performance appraisal process should address only a single aspect of job performance (i.e., either promptness or contribution), and if both dimensions are important, then two separate items should be used.

Evaluation Models

The literature on performance evaluation indicates that all jobs are multidimensional and have many different dimensions necessary for effective performance. For example, in most school systems, three broad dimensions of job performance are student concerns, district responsibilities, and community relations, and measurement of these dimensions vary depending on the types of focal positions under consideration. These dimensions are overlapping and pertain to all employees (see Figure 7.4), from custodians to administrators, and are necessary to describe how an individual performs assigned duties within the public school setting.

Regardless of the purpose to be served by a performance appraisal system (see Figure 7.2), method of comparison (see Figure 7.3), or system of evaluation (see Figure 7.4), any adequate performance appraisal system must capture these different job dimensions, as found in Figure 7.6, within the decision-making process. To do so, the appraisal system must be sensitive to each dimension of job performance and must process this information in a meaningful manner for managerial decision making. The method used to process these different job dimensions for managerial decision making in an appraisal system will vary depending on the purpose of the system.

At least three different models have been used to process job dimensions for assessment by a multidimensional performance appraisal system: the multiple-cutoff model, the compensatory model, and the eclectic model. Each of these models has a different implication for the performance appraisal system adopted by a school system.

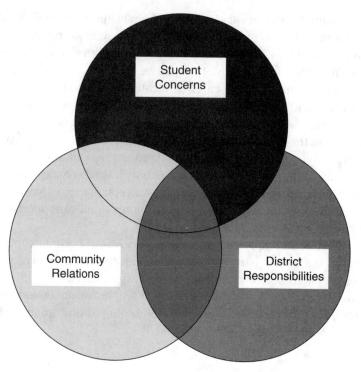

FIGURE 7.6   *Dimensions of performance.*

In the **multiple-cutoff model,** job performance on each dimension is examined separately for every employee (see Figure 7.6), and underlying this model is the assumption that all employees must exhibit at least a minimum level of competency on each dimension of job performance. That is, for every employee, performance on each dimension is viewed in either a relative or an absolute sense depending on the referent source for data collection (norm-referenced, criterion-referenced, or self-referenced; see Figure 7.3). The multiple-cutoff model is particularly appropriate when specific diagnostic information about employees is needed for each dimension of job performance.

With a **compensatory model,** information about an employee's performance on all job dimensions is combined to form a composite measure of overall job performance (see Figure 7.6). Low performance on one dimension can be balanced by high performance on another dimension. Functionally, the compensatory model is somewhat analogous to scoring a test taken by a student.

Test results for students are often reported by a single score, and this score reflects, purportedly, an overall measure of academic performance. Likewise, results from an employee's performance appraisal process can be similarly summarized. However, when job performances across all dimensions are combined, certain strengths and weaknesses on individual performance dimensions may be masked through the use of a composite score to define overall job performance.

The **eclectic model,** as the name implies, combines certain processes of the multiple-cutoff and the compensatory model (see Figure 7.6). In the eclectic model, an initial level of minimum competence is required on each dimension of a multidimensional performance appraisal system. After employees achieve a minimum level of performance on each dimension of job performance (as per the multiple-cutoff approach), appraisal efforts should focus on the employee's performance across all dimensions of job performance (as per the compensatory approach).

Unsurprising, the actual choice for a model of evaluation (multiple cutoff, compensatory, or eclectic) is not a stand-alone decision. Indeed, it a decision that must be guided by previous organizational directives relative to the performance appraisal process. To align all the previously discussed concerns into a schema, a decisional matrix is presented that can be used by policy makers and school administrators in the public school setting when designing a performance appraisal process from a strategic planning perspective.

Decisional Matrix for a Performance Appraisal Process

Previous sections of this chapter address important decisions that must be made with regard to a performance appraisal process in the public school setting. Some of these decisions are policy decisions, whereas others are administrative decisions. Policy decisions are needed that specify the purpose or purposes (see Figure 7.2) that a performance appraisal must serve as related to a mission statement adopted by a public school district.

Once the policy issues have been resolved relative to the purpose(s) of the performance appraisal, several administrative decisions are required. Administrative decisions are needed about the standard of comparison (see Figure 7.3), the method of performance appraisal (see Figure 7.4), and the model for combining information (see Figure 7.6). These later decisions should complement the policy decisions to most expediently accomplish the purpose of the performance appraisal process from a strategic planning perspective.

Contained in Figure 7.7 is a decisional matrix that can be used to guide the decision-making process when designing a performance appraisal process for implementation in for a public school district from a strategic planning perspective. To illustrate the utility of this decisional matrix as contained in Figure 7.7, an example is provided.

Within this example, it was determined by the board of education that the purpose of the performance evaluation is for allocating merit to employees (see AI in Figure 7.7). In this example, the merit performance system is based on a criterion-referenced system of comparison (see BII in Figure 7.7) and utilizes a behaviorally anchored rating system (see CIX in Figure 7.7). The optimal model for a merit system is eclectic (see DIII in Figure 7.7) because it would be embarrassing to award merit for any employee underperforming in a specific area of performance (student concerns, district responsibilities, and/or community relations, see Figure 7.6).

Some reflection on Figure 7.7 indicates that a variety of decisions must be made when developing and implementing a performance appraisal process from a strategic planning perspective. Research and practice indicate that there are limitations associated with any

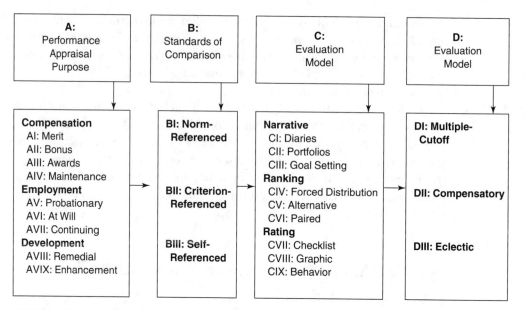

FIGURE 7.7   *Decision matrix for designing a performance appraisal process.*

of these decisions. There are problems, situations, and conditions in every school system that may limit or enhance the use and effectiveness of certain appraisal methods.

However, this model improves on past practice by following the decisional stream as outlined in Figure 7.7, and policy makers as well as administrators will gain a broad repertory about some of the salient issues involved with performance appraisal from a strategic planning perspective. A lack of understanding and of appreciation for these different issues will explain, at least in part, why performance appraisals may have been and continue to be less than satisfactory in many instances. No doubt, this is why Cunningham and Cordeiro (2006) noted that "performance evaluation is one of the hardest jobs in education and one of the most important" (p. 289).

Interestingly, most public school districts do little in the way of assessment concerning a performance appraisal process once constructed. Although performance appraisal processes and procedures represent measurement and are amenable to measurement assessment techniques, these issues are seldom broached in the field setting. As a result of this void, specific attention will be devoted to several measurement issues that determine ultimately the effectiveness and the efficiency of any performance appraisal process from a substantive point of view.

Measurement Concerns of Performance Appraisal Systems

Without exception, all textbooks addressing the performance appraisal process within the educational setting emphasize the importance of measurement issues for performance appraisal instruments and performance appraisal processes. At minimum, the specific measurement issues addressed in these works are **reliability** and **validity**.

Other than trumpeting the importance of these measurement aspects for the performance appraisal process, little guidance is provided to readers relative to actual application in the field setting. This oversight has important implications from an applied perspective. Most notably, a fundamental part of the performance evaluation process has been ignored, and this omission has profound implications for actual practice in the public school setting.

Important within this line of exposition is performance appraisal decisions impacting the property rights of employees. Included among these decisions are issues related to continuation of employment (i.e., discharge), promotional opportunities (i.e., advancement in rank), and salary increases (i.e., merit) as defined by several federal and state legislative acts (i.e., Title VII of the Civil Rights Act). When challenged in light of these legislative acts, the burden of proof for the performance appraisal process rests with the employer and not with the grievant.

Because the burden of proof rests with public school districts rather than with the employee and because most public school districts fail to have this information as part of the defense, the grievant can prevail in many instances from a substantive perspective (Lee, 2004). For these reasons, performance appraisal outcomes have been and continue to be deemed ineffective within the public school setting. To illustrate the procedures and techniques necessary for substantiating a performance appraisal process in the public school setting from a substantive perspective, both the concepts of reliability and of validity are addressed from a contextual point of view using actual data from the field setting.

Reliability Concerns

Most all readers have been exposed to the statement that "reliability is a necessary but not sufficient condition" for any measurement device (i.e., performance appraisal). Underlying this statement are certain mathematical proofs that demonstrate that the reliability of a measure (performance appraisal) sets the upper limit of validity (purpose) for decisions based on outcomes obtained from an assessment process (see Nunnally & Bernstein, 1994). Importantly, if performance appraisal outcomes are unreliable, decisions made on the basis of performance appraisal data can be unenforceable when challenged from a substantive perspective.

Many different types of reliability exist and many different procedures of assessing reliability can be found within the psychometric literature. Depending on the purpose of the process, some types of reliability are more appropriate than others. Within the performance assessment context, reliability is defined most often from a consistency perspective.

Consistency has been defined two different ways with respect to the performance appraisal context: (1) consistency of items comprising the performance appraisal system and (2) consistency of decisions made by organizational representatives on the basis of performance appraisal outcomes. Although these ways of defining consistency, within the performance appraisal context, vary in several meaningful ways, these differences are far from being mutually exclusive. For an effective and an efficient evaluation system, both types of consistency are mandatory.

Consistency of items comprising a performance appraisal system is measured generally by a single coefficient. This coefficient ranges from "0," indicating a complete lack of consistency, to "1.00," suggesting a perfect degree of consistency. The technique used most often to assess this type consistency is Chronbach's alpha.

To illustrate the application of a Chronbach's Alpha with actual field data, a specific example is provided. Within this example involving a public school district from a midwestern state (see Young & Place, 1988), eight dimensions for measuring the performance of teachers were used for assessment: (1) curriculum knowledge, (2) evaluation skills, (3) classroom environment, (4) classroom management, (5) records management, (6) communication abilities, (7) exhibited professionalism, and (8) personal qualities. For assessing each dimension of competency for teachers, multiple items were employed for measuring each dimension.

On each item ($n = 42$) all teachers ($n = 202$) were rated by their principal on a 3-point verbally anchored scale (needs improvement, satisfactory, or strong). Within each dimension a composite score was calculated as a measure of overall performance relative to a specific dimension. Underlying this process for combining scores on particular items is the assumption that items comprising a specific dimension are consistent with the dimension that they are purported to measure.

To test this assumption and to provide defensible data relative to the consistency of the evaluation process from a substantive perspective, a reliability analysis was performed via Chronbach's Alpha technique (see Nunnally & Bernstein, 1994). Results of the analysis are found in Table 7.2. Contained in this table are the specific dimensions (see column 1), the number of items used to measure each dimension (see column 2), and coefficient of internal consistency (see column 3) associated with each dimension.

As can be summarized from the data provided in Table 7.2, some dimensions of teacher performance exhibit higher reliabilities than other dimensions of teacher performance as measured by this particular performance appraisal process. More specifically, the items comprising the dimensions associated with evaluation skills (0.65) and records

TABLE 7.2
Reliability Assessment for Performance Appraisal Process

Performance Dimensions	Number of Items	Coefficient Alpha
Curriculum knowledge	10	0.81
Evaluation skills	3	0.65
Classroom environment	4	0.76
Classroom management	6	0.78
Records management	3	0.66
Communication abilities	4	0.76
Professionalism	6	0.75
Personal qualities	6	0.91

management (0.66) are less consistent than the items associated with personal qualities (0.91) and curriculum knowledge (0.81). In light of this information, certain limitations may be placed on the type of decisions made by this particular school district for teachers especially when these decisions have property right implications (continuation in employment, promotion in rank, and compensation issues).

For decisional outcomes as opposed to decisional processes when assessed from a reliability perspective, a different type of analysis is suggested. Decision outcomes may be assessed via inter-rater agreement. That is, given the same performance data as obtained from a performance appraisal process, what is the agreement between independent evaluators with respect to processing these data?

Agreement, like consistency, can range from no agreement ("0") to perfect agreement ("1.0") across a group of employees being assessed. An example of inter-rater agreement can be found in a study of decision outcomes for teachers in a large urban school district (Heneman & Milanowski, 2003). Within this study, inter-rater agreement was assessed relative to consistency in assessment and to stability of assessment across time.

Consistency was assessed by using two organizational representatives as independent evaluators within the performance appraisal process, and each representative evaluated all teachers independently. One evaluator was a line administrator (principal or assistant principal), while the other evaluator was a teacher evaluator. Teacher evaluators were practicing teachers on special assignment.

Each of these evaluators made decision outcomes based on results from the performance appraisal process. Decision outcomes for teachers being evaluated were the ability to create an environment for learning and for teaching for learning. For these decision outcomes, the authors report inter-rater agreements both within an academic year and between academic years (see Table 7.3)

Results, as reported by Heneman and Milanowski (2003), suggest a high level of consistency for decision outcomes made on the basis of a specific performance evaluation system. It is important to note that this level of consistency is contextually bound. Results are restricted to a particular school district, the method of evaluation, the type of evaluators, and the time period of data collection.

Most importantly, these results (Heneman & Milanowski, 2003) as well as previous results (Young & Place, 1988) pertain to reliability rather than validity. However, reliability, as noted earlier in this portion of the chapter, is a necessary but not a sufficient condition for a performance appraisal system. A sufficient condition for a performance appraisal system concerns validity, and this topic is addressed in the following section.

TABLE 7.3
Agreement of Evaluators Across Time

	Evaluator Agreement 2000–2001	Evaluator Agreement 2001–2002
Creating a learning environment	69%	78%
Teaching for learning	78%	80%

Validity

Issues of validity for a performance appraisal process are concerned with how well the performance appraisal process measures what it purports to measure. Validity issues, like reliability concerns, can be addressed also from a process as well as from an outcome perspective. To illustrate a validity assessment from a process perspective, actual data from the field setting are used.

A review of Table 7.2 reveals that one particular school district assesses the performance of teachers according to eight different dimensions: (1) curriculum knowledge, (2) evaluation skills, (3) classroom environment, (4) classroom management, (5) records management, (6) communication abilities, (7) exhibited professionalism, and (8) personal qualities. Open to question lacking any information pertaining to validity of this particular performance appraisal process is whether or not these are independent dimensions for measuring teacher performance. If in fact these eight dimensions are valid indicators within this particular school district, then several conditions should exist with these data.

More specifically, these dimensions should exhibit both **convergent validity** and **discriminant validity.** Convergent validity reflects the degree to which items comprising a specific dimension correlate with the targeted dimension, and this correlation should be high. On the other hand, discriminant validity measures the degree to which items not comprising a target dimension correlate with another dimension, and these correlations should be low.

Results of this type of validity analysis are found in Table 7.4. Contained in this table are coefficients that differ from regular correlation coefficients. Most importantly, each of the coefficients reported represents an average for a distribution of correlation coefficients.

As can be noted in Table 7.4, all diagonal coefficients are bolded. Collectively, these bolded coefficients reflect how well items comprising a particular dimension of job performance actually converge on that dimension of job performance. More specially, the bolded coefficient for curriculum is 0.51 (see Table 7.4).

This coefficient represents an average of 10 item-total correlations (see Table 7.3 indicating that curriculum contains 10 items). Each item comprising curriculum

TABLE 7.4
Intercorrelations among Dimensions of Teacher Performance

Dimensions	I	II	III	IV	V	VI	VII	VIII
I. Curriculum	**0.51**	0.34	0.19	0.40	0.30	0.33	0.29	0.48
II. Evaluation	0.27	**0.53**	0.20	0.15	0.19	0.17	0.16	0.21
III. Classroom Environment	0.13	0.21	**0.60**	0.07	0.12	0.16	0.17	0.21
IV. Classroom Management	0.32	0.16	0.13	**0.53**	0.12	0.40	0.24	0.43
V. Records Management	0.23	0.26	0.10	0.13	**0.44**	0.10	0.16	0.12
VI. Communication	0.25	0.17	0.15	0.37	0.10	**0.54**	0.40	0.55
VII. Professionalism	0.23	0.17	0.17	0.30	0.19	0.55	**0.49**	0.49
VIII. Personal Qualities	0.33	0.19	0.19	0.41	0.10	0.57	0.39	**0.73**

(n = 10) was correlated with a total composite score of curriculum (n = 1). The average of this distribution of correlations is 0.51, and this average reflects the degree of convergence of these items on this dimension of job performance (i.e., curriculum; see Table 7.4).

Contained in the off diagonals are discriminant validity coefficients. Discriminant validity coefficients fail to be a mirror image on each side of the diagonal because of different item configurations. To differentiate between those coefficients below the diagonal and those coefficients about the diagonal, one group is italicized and the other group is printed in regular type.

For the italicized coefficient involving evaluation and curriculum the result is 0.27 (see Table 7.4). This coefficient was obtained by averaging the correlation of each item comprising the dimension of evaluation (n = 3; see Table 7.3) with the overall composite curriculum rating. Depending on the specific dimensions of job performance under consideration, this process was followed for calculating all italicized coefficients as found in Table 7.4.

Off-diagonal coefficients printed in regular type (above diagonal coefficients; see Table 7.4) are calculated in a different way. The average off-diagonal coefficient for curriculum and evaluation printed in regular type is 0.34. This coefficient was obtained by averaging the correlation of each item comprising the dimension of curriculum (n = 10; see Table 7.2) with the overall composite evaluation dimension.

To interpret these data from a convergent and discriminant perspective, on-diagonal coefficients (convergent-bolded) are compared to off-diagonal coefficients (within a particular roll and a particular column). As can be observed for these data with this particular school district, the validity for assessing communication is suspect. Items purported to measure communication (r = 0.54; see Table 7.4) are equally likely to measure both professionalism (r = 0.55; see Table 7.4) and personal qualities (r = 0.57; see Table 7.4).

Results from this validity analysis have important potential implications for practice within the field setting. For example, if the purpose of this performance appraisal process is to provide information about the continuation of employment for an employee based on poor communication skills, then this decision could be easily challenged from a substantive perspective given the particular configuration of validity coefficients. Similarly, if the purpose of this performance appraisal system is to make merit decisions for employees, it is assumed that the process can distinguish between exceptional employees and all other employees with respect to the different dimensions of job performance when a composite score is used.

The degree to which these assumptions are fulfilled relative to these specific examples is the very essence of validity within the performance appraisal process. Unfortunately, validity studies are seldom conducted in the field setting. Without such evidence it is extremely difficult to defend outcomes from the performance appraisal process in the legal setting when challenged from a substantive perspective. As a result, many of the potential advantages expected of and demanded for performance appraisal processes and procedures are seldom realized in practice, and many of the meaningful managerial decisions are relegated to procedural events (seniority, etc.) rather than to substantive outcomes (job performance).

Turning from substantive issues to procedural issues within the performance appraisal context, the section that follows proposes a general rather than specific model for appraising the performance of school personnel. This model will: (a) address several phases of the performance appraisal process, (b) note some of the organizational and human obstacles to be encountered in establishing the process, and (c) examine the sequential interrelated steps in its implementation. Again, it is worth noting that there is no ideal performance appraisal process. Some of the steps discussed will be appropriate to specific appraisal techniques, whereas other steps will be appropriate to different appraisal techniques.

The Performance Appraisal Process

Within the previous sections of this chapter, the performance appraisal process was examined from a substantive perspective. In-depth attention was provided to the purpose(s) served by an appraisal system (see Figure 7.2), the standards of comparisons used for assessing performance of employees (see Figure 7.3), the particular type of evaluation systems used by an organization within the assessment process (see Figure 7.4), the model of choice for processing this information for managerial decision making (see Figure 7.7), and the measurement issues associated with the development and implementation of a performance appraisal system within the field setting (reliability and validity). To the extent that these issues have been addressed by a public school district determine the probable success for a performance appraisal system when challenged from a substantive perspective.

Other than a substantive perspective, performance appraisal systems can be challenged from a procedural point of view (see Lee, 2004). A procedural challenge focuses on assessment processes rather than on assessment outcomes. To address procedural concerns of the performance appraisal process, certain steps can be taken by a public school district through the development and implementation of a systematic plan of action.

Noted early on and echoed continuously throughout this chapter is the notion that performance appraisal within the public school setting is a process rather than an event and is "one of the most complex and controversial human resource techniques" (Roberts, 2002, p. 1). As a process, performance appraisal should be cyclical rather than linear in function as well as in form. To depict the cyclical nature of the performance appraisal process, a general model is presented in Figure 7.8 that can be used by any public school district and compliance with this model will afford a public school district with a solid line of defense when a procedural challenged is leveled by a disgruntled employee.

Phase 1: Planning and Orientation

Phase 1 of the performance appraisal process consists of a series of steps or activities designed to acquaint or to reacquaint the appraiser and appraisee with the scope,

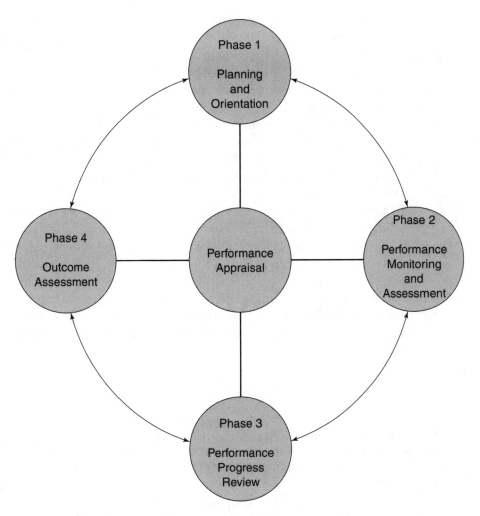

FIGURE 7.8 *Phases of the performance appraisal process.*

intent, procedures, and expectations of the appraisal process and should be performed each year with all employees subjected to the performance appraisal process. This conference should occur early on in the work year and is designed to perform several functions: (a) enable the appraiser and the appraisee to inform and to become informed about the appraisal process, (b) clarify for the appraisee the organization's expectations for the position, (c) elucidate desired levels of job performance, (d) establish future performance expectations, (e) allow the appraiser and appraisee to influence each other in planning the appraisal process, and (f) provide a first line of defense for a procedural challenge. The focus in Phase 1 of the performance appraisal process is on communication.

Communication should be approached as a two-way process whereby the appraiser and the appraisee review jointly organizational purposes, unit objectives, position goals, performance standards, and appraisal procedures. To ensure adequate as well as systematic coverage of these topics, it is recommended that a performance appraisal checklist be prepared, followed, and acknowledged during the preappraisal conference. Far too often, the most frequent challenge of the performance appraisal process from a procedural perspective is the lack of informed information provided the employee relative to job expectations in a timely manner.

Contained in Figure 7.9 is an example of a checklist that can serve as an agenda for a Phase 1 conference. This checklist contains items to be covered and should be acknowledged by the signature of the employee as well as dated. Once completed, the checklist should become part of the employee's personnel file.

Having outlined the process and procedures associated with a performance appraisal process in Phase 1, Phase 2 of the performance appraisal process is entered. Phase 2 is ongoing and involves data collection and data synthesis on the part of the employee as well as the immediate supervisor. In fact, Phase 2 of the performance appraisal process

---

Preapprasial Checklist

The purpose of this checklist is twofold. First, this checklist should serve, at least in part, as a working agenda the preappraisal conference. Second, this form serves as a source of acknowledgment that these topics have been addressed, and this form will become part of your personal file.

Topic Addressed

1. The purpose(s) of the performance appraisal system were described as follows: ***Fill in the blank according to Figure 7.2***.

2. My performance will be assessed according to specific standards of expectation(s): ***Fill in the blank according to Figure 7.3***.

3. The system(s) of evaluation used to assess my performance will be: ***Fill in the blank according to Figure 7.4***.

4. Information obtained from the performance appraisal will be analyzed by a specific model: ***Fill in the blank according to Figure 7.7***.

Signature of Employee _____ Date _____

FIGURE 7.9   *Checklist for a preappraisal conference.*

provides information for assessing current performance, for redirecting future performance, and for acknowledging past successes as well as weaknesses.

Phase 2: Performance Monitoring and Assessment

Following the planning and orientation stage of the performance appraisal process is Phase 2. Phase 2 involves monitoring, assessing, and recording an employee's actual job performance. These activities should be performed both by the employee as well as the immediate supervisor and should be ongoing across the work year.

Although both the employee and the immediate supervisor participate actively in Phase 2, each does so from a somewhat different perspective. The employee performs a self-assessment. Goals of the self-assessment are as follows: (a) to assist the employee in analyzing present performance; (b) to help the employee identify strengths, weaknesses, and potential, as well as to help make plans for improving performance; and (c) to provide information for a progress review conference with the appraiser (see Figure 7.8).

To facilitate the self-assessment process at Phase 2, certain questions should be addressed by the employee. Answers to these questions provide both insights about current levels of performance and likely future levels of performance. Contained in Figure 7.10 is a self-appraisal form that may be useful to many employees at Phase 2 of the performance appraisal process.

---

1. Summarize the overall strengths that you have demonstrated in performing your present assignment.
2. Do you feel that you are well placed in your present assignment? If not please explain.
3. In what areas of your present assignment or in the way you perform your present assignment do you think that you can improve your performance?
4. Do you feel that you have potential beyond your present assignment? What would you suggest as your next assignment?
5. Are there significant facts that you think should be noted about the dimensions of your position that affect your performance and that you think should be brought to the attention of your immediate supervisor, such as:
   Position objectives
   Position design
   Social setting
   Situational factors
   Results achieved

FIGURE 7.10   *Self-appraisal guidelines.*

During this same time period (Phase 2), the immediate supervisor should be garnering ongoing information about an employee's level of job performance. Data collected by the immediate supervisor should be sensitive both to current performance and to future potential of an employee. Of immediate concern is, to what extent are the short-term goals or performance targets being achieved by the employee?

Having assessed the short-term goals, attention is refocused on the long-range goals associated with the position. This aspect of the performance appraisal process is future oriented. The task is to project how well the employee is likely to maintain a course of positive action relative to these goals.

For both observational aspects of the performance appraisal process, detailed records must be compiled. Such records provide the building blocks for subsequent stages of the performance appraisal process. An example of a form that can be used to catalog observations is found in Figure 7.11.

Phase 3: Performance Progress Review

After the self-appraisal form (see Figure 7.10) and the progress review form (see Figure 7.11) are completed by the appraisee and the immediate supervisor, respectively, the next step in the appraisal process, as shown in Figure 7.8, is the progress review conference. The major purpose of the progress review conference is to exchange information between the appraiser

---

Name of Employee _____   Assigned Position _____

  1. What progress has the employee made during this review period?
_____
_____

  2. What progress does the employee perceive has been made?
_____
_____

  3. What areas of performance are strong?
_____
_____

  4. What areas of performance need improvements?
_____
_____

  5. What are specific remedial recommendations?
_____
_____

Signature of Immediate Supervisor _____   Date _____

FIGURE 7.11   *Performance progress review form.*

and appraisee about the latter's performance to date. By providing this type of immediate information to employees in a timely manner, school districts limit another form of a procedural challenge by employees within the performance appraisal context in that information for modifying performance was duly noted.

Prior to the conference, several procedural steps must be completed. Preparation for the conference involves reviewing results of the performance appraisal outcomes. A second purpose of the progress review conference is to clarify viewpoints about the employee's performance. Differing perceptions of the position's goals, responsibilities, authority, and relationships can be identified, examined, and clarified, while obstacles to progress, whether individual or organizational, are topics for discussion and solutions are recommended.

The self-development of the appraisee is a third purpose of the progress review conference. As noted earlier, performance appraisal is designed not only to achieve organizational goals but also to help the individual attain personal objectives, one of which should be performance improvement. It is at this stage of the conference that the appraiser attempts to counsel or coach the appraisee to solve any problems affecting performance.

Another aspect of Phase 3 in the appraisal process is the joint development of an action program for the appraisee based on the progress review conference. The essence of the individual development program may be summarized as follows:

■ Performance appraisal reports should indicate to both the appraiser and the appraisee how well the latter has done in reaching previously established performance and behavior targets.

■ On the basis of the progress review conference (which should make clear both the results achieved and those to be achieved), the appraiser and appraisee come to a common understanding on what performance targets should be reestablished for the next review period.

■ During the period set for the individual development program, the appraiser has primary responsibility for guiding and motivating the behavior of the appraisee to achieve performance targets.

Phase 4: Outcome Assessment

As Figure 7.8 indicates, Phase 4 of the appraisal model is the time for an outcome assessment based on data obtained from the performance appraisal process compiled throughout the work year. This phase of the process is designed to verify the results of the individual development program and to render a final decision in a formal conference. In preparation for and in the conduct of the final appraisal conference, Roberts (2002) suggests several concerns that be taken as a given or often overlooked:

Allow sufficient time between scheduling and conduct of the conference for adequate preparation on the part of both parties,
Reserve adequate time for the conduct of the conference to ensure full discussion of all issues,
Provide a setting that gives the employee privacy and confidentiality, and
Afford the employee undivided attention and avoid any interruptions.

Depending on the purpose of a performance appraisal system used by a particular school system, results of this stage of the selection process can be either closed-ended or looping. If the purpose of the performance appraisal process is to make decisions relative to continuation of employment or for issues related to compensation (see Figure 7.2), then a final decision is made at Phase 4 of the evaluation process. In support of this decision, the immediate supervisor should provide the employee with copies of the preappraisal checklist acknowledged by the employee (see Figure 7.9), the self-appraisal form provided by the employee (see Figure 7.10), and the progress review form completed by the immediate supervisor at the conclusion of Phase 3 of the performance appraisal process (see Figure 7.11).

However, if the purpose of the evaluation process is development, then a different strategy is suggested. This latter strategy involves a recycling of the evaluation process (see Figure 7.8) for the upcoming work year. The goal is to align past performance with future expectations.

As performance standards are reached, the appraisal process is redirected to other areas of performance where improvement is needed. The purpose of diagnosis is to establish continuity and stability in the individual's development program. Concrete plans should emerge for extending the program in areas where certain levels of performance should be maintained while other levels should be enhanced.

Review and Preview

This chapter has provided an overview of the performance appraisal process both from a substantive and from a procedural perspective. Forces were identified that impact traditional appraisal systems and will continue to influence the appraisal systems used by most educational organizations. Specific suggestions were offered for designing and implementing a performance appraisal system in the educational setting.

When designing and implementing, it is important to focus on the purpose(s) of the appraisal system. Certain operational and behavioral concerns that demand specific choices by those who develop an appraisal system were identified. It was shown how the specific purpose(s) of the system requires different means of operational procedures.

Because a universal system for effective performance appraisal fails to exist, several different appraisal methods were reviewed. In each of these methods, at least three different evaluation formats were discussed. Each format was linked to certain appraisal purposes, operational concerns, and behavioral concerns.

A four-phase model for implementing a performance appraisal process was presented. Each phase of the model focused on specific responsibilities and tasks to be accomplished. Finally, it was emphasized that performance appraisal should be part of the ongoing life of an employee rather than an isolated yearly event. As a process, every aspect of this important managerial tool must be continually revisited to ensure that the goals of students, parents, employees, boards of education, and taxpayers are being met.

In Chapter 8 the topic of employee compensation will be addressed. Special attention will be given to criteria used to assess current compensation practices within a school district. Procedures will be presented for establishing new compensation methods.

Discussion Questions

1. As noted in Figure 7.2, a performance appraisal process should serve a specific purpose(s). What purpose does your performance appraisal process purport to serve? How do you research this answer and on what grounds do you support this conclusion (board policy or labor contract)?

2. Performance appraisal does not occur in a vacuum but is related to some type of referent source. What referent source (norm, criterion, and/or self) does your immediate supervisor rely on when assessing your performance? Is the referent source used for assessing performance complementary to the purpose of your evaluation?

3. Several different types of evaluation techniques are discussed in this chapter (narrative, ranking, and rating). What do you perceive as the strengths and weaknesses of each technique?

4. A procedural model for performance evaluation is presented in Figure 7.8. Which phases of this model are followed in your school district? If not all phases are followed, what are the likely advantages as well as consequences?

5. Performance evaluation processes represent measurement and measurement issues are well addressed in the professional literature. How has your school district addressed reliability and validity for the performance appraisal process? If not, why not?

Case Study

An employee has received notice of discharge based on inadequate job performance. This employee has challenged the notice both from a substantive and a procedural perspective. Within this challenge, a claim is made that the performance appraisal process fails to actually measure job performance (substantive) and that this information about inadequate job performance was unknown to this individual prior to receiving the notice. How would you approach this problem? What types of information would you seek? On what grounds would you establish a defense from the school district's perspective?

References

Arvey, R. D., & Murphy, K. R. (1998). Performance evaluation in work settings. *Annual Review of Psychology, 49,* 141–168.

Costa, E. W. (2004, October). Performance-based evaluation for superintendents. *The School Administrator,* 1–4.

Cox, E. P. (2006). Pay performance contract provisions for school superintendents. *Journal of Scholarship and Practice, 2*(2), 31–38.

Cunningham, W. G., & Cordeiro, P. A. (2006). *Educational leadership: A problem-based approach* (3rd ed.). Columbus, OH: Pearson.

Dressler, G. (1988). *Personnel management.* Englewood Cliffs, NJ: Simmon.

Heneman, H. G. (1998). Assessment of the motivational reactions of teachers to a school-based performance award program. *Journal of Personnel Evaluation in Education, 12*(1), 43–59.

Heneman, H. G., & Judge, T. A. (2006). *Staffing Organizations* (6th ed.). Middleton, WI: Mendota House.

Heneman, H. G., & Milanowski, A. T. (2003). Continuing assessment of teacher reactions to a standard-based teacher evaluation system. *Journal of Personnel Evaluation in Education, 17*(2), 173–195.

Kelley, C., Heneman, H. G., & Milanowski, A. (2002). Teacher motivation and school-based performance rewards. *Educational Administration Quarterly, 38*(5), 372–401.

Lee, J. A. (2004, Spring). Factors related to court references to performance appraisal fairness and validity. *Public Personnel Management,* 1–11.

McMillan, J. H. (2003). Understanding and improving teachers' classroom assessment decision making: Implications for theory and practice. *Educational Measurement: Issues and Practice, 22*(4), 34–43.

Nunnally, J., & Bernstein, I. (1994). *Psychometric theory.* New York: McGraw-Hill.

Painter, B. (2001). Using teaching portfolios. *Educational Leadership, 58,* 31–34.

Peterson, K. D., Stevens, D., & Mack, C. (2001). Presenting complex teacher evaluation data: Advantages of dossier organization techniques over portfolios. *Journal of Personnel Evaluation in Education, 15*(2), 121–133.

Roberts, G. E. (2002, Fall). Employee performance appraisal system participation: A technique that works. *Public Personnel Management,* 1–8.

Scullen, S. E., Bergey, P. K., & Aiman-Smith, L. (2005). Forced distribution rating systems and the improvement of the workforce potential: A baseline simulation. *Personnel Psychology, 58*(1), 1–32.

Valente, W. D., & Valente, C. M. (2005). *Law in the schools.* Upper Saddle, NJ: Merrill/Prentice Hall.

Webb, L. D., & Norton, M. S. (2003). *Human resources administration, personnel issues and needs in education.* Upper Saddle, NJ: Merrill/Prentice Hall.

Young, I. P. (2003). The trouble with pay for performance. *American School Board Journal,* Vol. 190, 11(l), 40–42.

Young, I. P., & Place, W. A., (1988). The relationship between age and teaching performance. *Journal of Personnel Management in Education, 2,* 43–52.

Compensation

8

CHAPTER OVERVIEW

Internal consistency
Learning curve
Market assessment
Mixed-rate salary system
Nonexempted employees
Paired comparison
  method
Point method
Ranking method
Rationality
Red circle employees
Relevant labor market
Salary
Simple ranking method
Single-rate pay schedule
Standard of living
  index
Sunshine laws
Supply and demand
Teacher salary schedule
Uniform benefits
Variable benefits
Variable-rate salary
  system
Wage

OBJECTIVES

- Develop an understanding of current compensation practices and problems.
- Provide a model or blueprint for designing the compensation process.
- Analyze the compensable factors that comprise the pay structure.
- Identify external and internal factors that influence pay policies and levels.
- Describe approaches to developing the economic worth of positions.
- Stress the importance of assessing compensation process outcomes.

Employee Compensation: A Perennial Challenge

Employee compensation comprises one of the operational directives listed in Chapter 1 as part of the human resource function performed by public school districts. As an operational directive, compensation is one of the most visible activities performed by a public school district. Indeed, with the possible exceptions of proficiency test scores for students and of report cards for school districts and school buildings, both of which are related less directly but importantly to the human resource function, few other topics command as much interest and as much coverage in the popular press as employee compensation.

Accompanying reports of student achievement, it is by no means unusual for the local press to report the compensation practices of a public school district each budget year and for state databases to contain this information in an easily accessible manner through the web, professional associations, state reports, or at the local school district level. In some instances, this information is disaggregated according to positions as well as to persons. Position information pertaining to salary data includes starting rates, average rates, and maximum rates as well as approved salary schedules, while in other instances personal information pertaining to salary data may reflect the actual rate received by specific position holders, usually central office personnel where position and person are one and the same within a database (e.g., superintendent's salary).

Unlike some of the human resource operational functions, employee compensation for public school districts is public information and is available on request. Access to this information about compensation in public school districts is a right, not a privilege, and cannot be negated either by school board policy or by past administrative practices of a school district. This right is established by federal as well as state statutes.

Overarching federal statutes pertaining to the compensation of public employees are the Freedom of Information Act (1966) as amended in 1974, and the Privacy Act (1974). The Freedom of Information Act requires governmental agencies to make available certain records that are requested by the public, and the Privacy Act was designed to resolve problems relating to disclosure, recording, inspection, and challenges to information maintained by governmental agencies and political subdivisions. Further reinforcing these intentions concerning the compensation of public school employees are state statutes, and these statutes are labeled as "**sunshine laws.**"

To exercise this right relative to the obtainment of information relating to employee compensation, individuals must make only a formal request to a public school district. Based on this request, public school districts are required to comply within a reasonable period of time and to provide this public information about the compensation of public school employees. Failure to do so can result in fines levied against organizations and their organizational representatives.

However, worth noting is that this information about the compensation of public school employees must be provided only in the format used by an organization and assistance in interpreting this information is not required by any federal or state statute. In spite of this statutory limitation, a copy of this information is a right afforded by these legislative enactments. Furthermore, the cost for a copy of this information must be reasonable relative customary charges.

Underlying the interest in and rights for information concerning employee compensation within the public school setting is the impact that this human resource operational directive has for multiple stakeholders. Impacted by employee compensation is the public at large, including those with as well as those without children enrolled in a public school district. Beyond these constituents involving the public at large, employee compensation has important implications for still other stakeholders.

Young, Delli, Miller-Smith, and Alhadeff (2004) have addressed the importance of employee compensation for a variety of stakeholders within the public school setting. According to these investigators, employee compensation practices of a school district have important implications for the public, for the school board, and for the employees. For the public, compensation practices have funding implications related to tax efforts and to their investments in public education either as passive or as active participants within the educational process.

Tax efforts can be viewed both from a state and from a local level as important sources of revenue for funding employee compensation within the public school setting. At the state level, revenue for funding employee compensation is derived from a formula used to distribute monies for employee compensation in the public school setting. Varying across states are the components included within specific formula funding models used to set rates of employee compensation within the public school setting (Owings & Kaplan, 2006).

Included in most formulas are training and experience factors unique to a specific school district. With respect to teachers and other certificated employees (the largest employee groups in a public school system), training and experience are assessed in different ways, both of which have implications for employee compensation from the public's perspective. Some states use the average training and experience for all certificated employees, while other states use an exact measure of training and experience for those comprising a specific school district.

Rates of employee compensation, as established by state funding formulas, are augmented often by local tax efforts on the part of public school districts. Local tax levees can be used to supplement the levels of compensation received by employees of a public school district beyond those granted by the state. As such, the general public is concerned about employee compensation both from a state and from a local level.

Concerned also about levels of employee compensation are school board members. School board members, either elected by public vote or appointed by governing bodies (Cunningham & Cordeiro, 2006), act as guardians of public coffers. As guardians of public coffers, school board members wear several hats relative to the compensation of employees.

At the local school district level, school board members play key roles in the generation of revenue for funding employee compensation and in the distribution of these resources among public employees. To be successful in the generation of levees for employee compensation, school boards must enact and must support legislation at the local school district level. From a distributional perspective, school boards must approve policies and procedures relative to the employee compensation process.

Like the public at large and school board members, employees of a public school district are concerned about compensation. As recipients of outcomes from the compensation process, this operational directive has psychic as well as economic implications. Employee compensation provides both a measure of economic worth for an individual from an organizational perspective (Young, 2006) and dictates, to a large extent, the quality of life enjoyed by a public school employee (Gerhart & Milkovich, 1992).

Most recently, pay satisfaction has been linked to student achievement. Currall, Towler, Judge, and Kohn (2005) surveyed over 6,000 teachers and assessed their satisfaction with pay. Using the Pennsylvania Test of Sentential Learning and Literacy Skills for third, fifth, and eighth graders, they found a significant relationship between pay satisfaction and student achievement.

In view of the implications for the public at large, for school board members, and for public school employees, this chapter views compensation as unfinished business within the human resource function. It provides a perspective on compensation decision making, the goal of which is to solve, effectively and efficiently, compensation issues affecting the community, the school system, and its employees. This perspective includes the components of the compensation process and auditing mechanisms for leading the reader through the steps by which the economic worth of positions and persons is determined, as well as the external and internal environmental influences on this issue from a strategic planning perspective.

Compensation Strategy from a Strategic Planning Perspective

Designing a school system compensation plan starts by considering the link between organizational purpose and **compensation policy.** Organizational purpose focuses on the outcomes to be achieved by the system; strategies are the methods used by the system mission. This perspective, involving the connection between the system mission and strategies, is illustrated in Figure 8.1 and provides the basis for designing a compensation strategy.

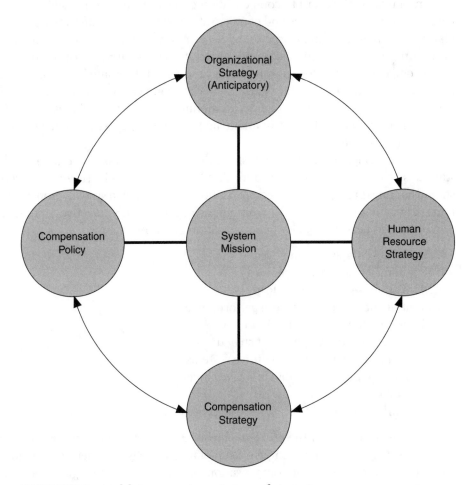

FIGURE 8.1 *Link between system mission and strategies.*

Central to the compensation policy is the mission of the school system. The mission statement, as noted in Chapter 1, should be based on the purposes of the school district. As Figure 8.1 shows, organizational strategy is anticipatory, is future oriented, is concerned with emerging environmental conditions, and is designed to make education a meaningful experience both for students and for employees. Organizational strategy is a set of plans for moving the school system from an existing state to a desired state, thereby achieving the mission of a school district more effectively and efficiently through a strategic planning process.

Mission-oriented guidelines are driven by the interaction between human resource strategy and compensation policy. Human resource strategy addresses the number and kinds of positions needed (see Chapter 2), the skills abilities required for position holders (see Chapter 3), incentives for attracting individuals (see Chapter 4), methods used to select employees (see Chapter 5), processes for orientating employees (see Chapter 6), and systems for evaluating employees (see Chapter 7). Compensation policy indicates the system's intent with regard to compensation obligations and responsibilities. This complex web of human resources and compensation policy, when integrated into a strategic planning framework, can be used to guide the many administrative judgments involved in creating and implementing a compensation strategy applicable to all employee groups.

A compensation strategy may be viewed as a set of interrelated decisions that allocate fiscal resources to change the system's current compensation status to one that will contribute more effectively to the organizational strategy. This includes plans that direct attention and resources to present and to address emerging issues related to compensating school employees.

When developing compensation strategies, one central task of educational administrators is to devise plans for allocating funds to employees for services rendered. This should be done through a formal compensation system. Such a system, properly conceived and fairly administered, helps to promote the organization's objectives and the satisfaction of its members. The goals of compensation planning include:

- Attracting competent employees
- Retaining satisfactory employees
- Motivating personnel to perform
- Creating incentives to improve performance
- Maximizing returns in services for cost
- Designing internally consistent structures
- Maintaining externally competitive systems
- Minimizing union and individual grievances
- Controlling benefit costs
- Ensuring continuity of compensation processes

These goals highlight the problems involved in designing compensation plans. In a school system, an equitable compensation plan is the basic element for employee satisfaction. Without an equitable compensation plan, all other system plans, programs, and processes are weakened.

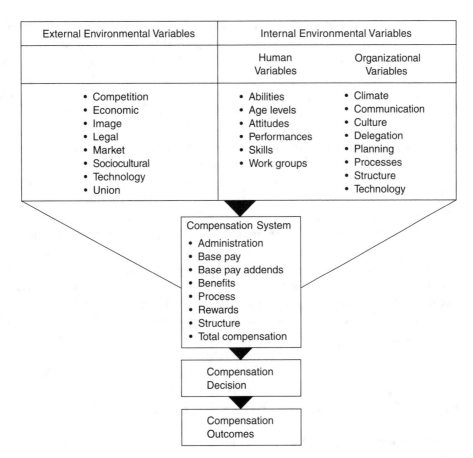

FIGURE 8.2   *Illustration of compensation variables that influence compensation outcomes.*

However, compensation plans and processes, like all human resource plans and processes, are subject to external and internal influences, as shown in Figure 8.2. External influences have a cumulative effect and play a large part in determining the characteristics of a compensation system. Internal influences are generally perceptual and pertain to issues of fairness and social justice.

From an external perspective, any particular school district faces competition for the best talent, and a sound compensation system can provide an edge within this environment. In some instances, this competition may involve other school districts, while, in other instances, this competition may involve private sector organizations competing for the same talent. As noted by Young, Jury, and Reis (1997), school districts can no longer depend on a ready pool of applicants and must compete in the open market for the best talent.

To compete for this talent in the labor market at large and to retain those individuals selected by a system, school districts must have compensation plans that are reasonably competitive within a relevant labor market. Reasonably competitive does not mean that a school district has to be the highest paying but means that the school district cannot be among the lowest paying. This would seem to be especially true for certain individuals viewing employment from an economic as opposed to either a psychological or rational perspective (see Chapter 5 for a discussion of orientations for applicants relative to job choice).

Internal influences important for constructing and for administering a compensation plan are those perceptions harbored by employees. Employees desire a compensation plan that is externally competitive and internally consistent. Externally competitive concerns the perceptions of employees about pay relative to others in like-type school districts and involves the constraints beyond control of a local school district.

On the other hand, internal consistency concerns employees' perceptions about pay relative to other employees within the same school district. From an operational perspective, perceptions of internal consistency are more important than perceptions of external competitiveness relative to the perceptions of employees. Internal consistency pertains to social justice, while external competitiveness has broader equity implications.

To address both external and internal influences on the compensation process within a public school district, attention must be afforded to the total compensation system. The total compensation system can be broken down by subcomponents, and attention is needed for the subcomponents. However, underlying each subcomponent are certain common elements and following is a discussion of the different subcomponents as well as their common elements that comprise a total compensation system.

Components of Total Compensation Systems

The components of the total compensation process found in most school districts can be deconstructed according to different employee groupings. At the basic level, these employee groupings include administrators, teachers, and support personnel. Although these lines of demarcation can be blurred in some school districts, many clear and meaningful differences exist relative to the compensation of employees.

One major difference concerns the authority for establishing compensation procedures and practices within the public school setting. Compensation procedures and practices can be determined either unilaterally by the board of education or bilaterally relative to other parties of interest. Largely differentiating between the unilateral, and the bilateral processes for establishing compensation procedures, as well as practices, is the presence of a union within a public school district.

Another major difference concerns the prerogative for changing compensation procedures and practices at the local school district level. Without a union, the compensation procedures and practices are under the complete control of a board of education. Although boards of education should follow their procedures and practices relative to the compensation of employees, boards retain the right to suspend policies and to act in novel ways when compensating employees not covered by a union contract.

With a union representing the compensation interest of employees, boards of education no longer possess this discretionary authority for suspending past practices. Any changes in past and present practices concerning the compensation of employees represented by a union must be determined bilaterally. The vehicle for bilateral alterations in the compensation practice and process involving employees represented by a union is collective bargaining.

In light of these constraints for developing and for changing compensation procedures and processes in the public school setting, all compensation systems have several common components. One component concerns direct payment as realized by either a salary or a wage. The other component involves other economic benefits awarded employees as part of the total compensation process. Both types of economic incentives consist of several subcomponents, all of which must be considered within the total compensation process.

Direct compensation is defined by the actual dollars paid to employees through preestablished installments in the form of a paycheck. Installments can be paid according either to a work year or to an annual installment for those working less than a full calendar year. That is, a distinction is made between earned income and income distribution. For example, some employees work less than 12 months (i.e., teacher) but receive allocated compensation throughout a 12-month period without any interruption in monthly checks.

Beyond method of distribution, direct compensation can be characterized as either a **salary** or a **wage.** Whether an employee receives a salary or a wage depends both on the method used to calculate the source of the direct payment and on the employee's job characteristics. This difference is defined by the Fair Labor Standards Act of 1938 **(http://www.dol.gov/esa/whd/flsa/).**

In general, a salary is paid to employees who are not covered by the Fair Labor Standards Act of 1938, and these individuals are referred to as "**exempted employees.**" By being exempted from this act, compensation is related to the job rather than to the amount of time worked on the job. Exempted employees are not eligible for overtime pay if the work is performed during their contractual work year for assigned duties.

A wage, on the other hand, is paid to employees who are covered by this act, and these individuals are labeled as "**nonexempted employees.**" Nonexempted employees covered by this act are compensated on an hourly basis. As such, work performed beyond regular schedules of full-time employees not exempted from the Fair Labor Standards Act of 1938 is subject to extra compensation or, in some instances, compensatory time off from the job (see Crampton, 2003).

Within the school setting, administrators, supervisors, and teachers receive salaries and are considered as exempted employees, while custodians, aides, and clerical personnel receive wages and are considered as nonexempted employees. However, certain exceptions can be noted. That is, certain employees otherwise covered by the Fair Labor Standards Act of 1938 may be designated as exempted employees due to the confidentiality of their jobs related to collective bargaining.

At the local school level, confidential employees are determined by state employment relations boards. Guiding their decisions are potential conflicts of interest, given access to certain information bearing on the collective bargaining process. Most commonly exempted and defined as confidential employees are clerical personnel in the business office, and those personnel reporting directly to the superintendent of schools.

The expected salary or wage associated with a particular position is referred to as the **base pay** for said employees. Base pay may be supplemented, however, for all employees, regardless of their status relative to the Fair Labor Standards Act of 1938. Depending on whether or not an employee is covered or exempted from the Fair Labor Standards Act of 1938 determines how base pay can be incremented.

For exempted employees not covered by the Fair Labor Standards Act of 1938, additional effort beyond regular duties is required for supplemental pay. Additional effort usually involves taking on an extra assignment, such as coaching performed by a teacher or by receiving an extended contract for a special assignment by an administration (i.e., summer school). For nonexempt employees receiving a wage instead of a salary, supplements to base pay involve working overtime in the same job or by performing other duties beyond the regular work schedule.

Indirect compensation refers to certain economic incentives received by an employee beyond salaries or wages and is labeled as benefits. These benefits include sick leave, insurance provisions, and retirement incentives and represent a substantial cost for a school district. In fact, benefits usually cost a school district an additional 40 percent beyond the salary or wage paid to an employee.

Benefits play a very important role in the employment process. For many school districts, benefits serve as an incentive to attract potential employees and to retain current employees. Often, it is this form of indirect compensation, rather than direct compensations of salary or wage that gives a school district a competitive edge in the labor market. Because compensation includes both direct and indirect costs, the focus is on each type of payment in this chapter.

Direct Cost

The primary direct cost in a compensation system is the base salary or base wage paid to an employee. This base salary or base wage can generally be ascertained from a pay schedule. Pay schedules vary in several ways both between as well as within school systems.

Schedules can be simple or complex and can have fixed or variable dollar amounts associated with a particular position or with different persons holding the same position. The use of any particular type of pay schedule is based on certain assumptions about the position and about the employees. These assumptions are often overlooked by school districts, resulting far too often in rigid compliance with past compensation practices.

When assumptions underlying a pay schedule are overlooked, many attempted improvements are stymied, and the status quo is maintained. Consequently, several different types of pay schedules are examined in this chapter. These include the single-rate pay schedule, the teacher salary schedule, and the exempted employee salary schedule.

Single-Rate Pay Schedule

An example of a **single-rate pay schedule** is found in Table 8.1. This type of wage schedule is frequently used for support personnel paid on an hourly wage rate. As reflected in Table 8.1, this schedule contains different hourly rates for employees occupying various job classifications (Level I through Level V).

TABLE 8.1
Example of a Single-Rate Pay Schedule

Levels	Hourly Rate
Level I	$15.00
Level II	$16.00
Level III	$16.50
Level IV	$17.00
Level V	$17.50

TABLE 8.2
Example of an Extended Hourly Schedule for Nonexempted Employees

Levels	Step 1	Step 2	Step 3	Step 4	Step 5
Level I	$15.10	$15.20	$15.30	$15.40	$15.50
Level II	$16.10	$16.20	$16.30	$16.40	$16.50
Level III	$16.60	$16.70	$16.80	$16.90	$17.00
Level IV	$17.10	$17.20	$17.30	$17.40	$17.50
Level V	$17.60	$17.70	$17.80	$17.90	$18.00

Each level of a single-rate wage schedule pertains either to a single position or to multiple positions assigned the same level. All positions assigned to a particular level are assumed to have comparable worth to a school system, and all positions assigned at alternate levels are assumed to have different worth to the school system. Because the worth assigned to a position by a school system determines the base rate of pay, an employee must change levels or jobs to increase the base rate when following a single-rate pay schedule.

Table 8.1 shows that a single-rate schedule fails to provide any growth incentives or to reward experience on the job. All employees at the same level receive the same base wage regardless of their education and/or experience. Thus, this type of wage structure assumes a similar organizational worth and an equal base rate pay for all job holders at a particular salary level. That is, the underlying assumption of a single-rate salary schedule is equal pay for comparable work and unequal pay for noncomparable work.

However, many school districts adopt this same assumption but depart from the single-rate wage structure for compensating nonexempted employees. These districts do so by providing increments for on-the-job experience. As such, the wage schedule shares some common characteristics with the traditional teacher salary schedule, but involves nonexempted employees (see Table 8.2) in that steps are incorporated for on-the-job experience.

Teacher Salary Schedule

In contrast to the single-rate wage schedule as used with support personnel is the **teacher salary schedule** (see Table 8.3). With few, if any, exceptions, all teacher salary schedules provide for a growth incentive involving educational obtainment and reward the teaching experience of teachers (Odden & Kelley, 1997). Although the organizational worth of the growth incentive and of employment experience varies considerably among school

TABLE 8.3
Sample Teacher Salary Schedule

Tulare Joint Union High School District
Salary Schedule
2004–2005

Step	A AB + 15	B AB + 30	C AB + 45	D AB + 60	E AB + 60 w/MA
1	$39,515	$39,515	$39,515	$40,779	$44,254
2	$39,515	$39,515	$39,515	$42,389	$45,856
3	$39,515	$39,515	$39,515	$43,989	$47,466
4	$39,515	$39,515	$42,274	$45,593	$49,068
5	$39,515	$40,793	$43,877	$47,194	$50,670
6	$40,015	$42,402	$45,477	$48,804	$52,280
7	$41,631	$44,004	$47,087	$50,398	$53,873
8	$43,227	$45,599	$48,676	$52,002	$55,477
9	$44,829	$47,202	$50,285	$53,595	$57,078
10	$46,438	$48,810	$51,893	$55,205	$58,682
11		$50,408	$53,490	$56,815	$60,284
12		$52,015	$55,099	$58,411	$61,892
13		$53,618	$56,694	$60,020	$63,495
14		$55,218	$58,302	$61,623	$65,096
15		$56,834	$59,905	$63,225	$66,698
16			$60,707	$64,827	$68,308
17			$62,663	$69,266	$72,800

districts across states as well as within states, this type of teacher salary schedule exists throughout the United States and can be found in every state of the union (see Table 8.3).

"Purportedly, this fixed rate structure was developed to eliminate certain inequalities among teachers in a public school district" (Young et al., 2004, p. 390) and has been sustained for decades. Historically, Firestone (1995) noted that prior to the advent of the fixed-rate teacher salary schedule utilized by most school districts today, many inequalities existed among teachers relative to the pay received for the services provided to public school districts. In many instances secondary teachers were paid more than elementary school teachers, and male teachers were paid more than female teachers prior to the adoption of fixed-rate teacher salary schedules.

The growth incentive, reflected in Table 8.3 (see columns) associated with the teacher salary schedule, is defined by the educational achievement of a teacher. Educational achievement may include formal course work, continuing educational units, and/or other approved plans for professional development. Underlying the use of growth incentives to raise the base salary of a teacher is the assumption that additional education increases the teacher's competence on the job. However, "in practice, teachers are often rewarded for taking courses that may have little or nothing to do with the knowledge and skill set needed by the school organization" and represent a weak form of competency-based pay according to Kelley (1997).

Employment experience is another compensable factor common to teacher salary schedules (see rows of Table 8.3). The use of employment experience in determining compensation should be based on the learning curve associated with the job. In some jobs proficiency increases with experience, and salary schedules should reflect this situation by awarding increases reflecting the slope of the learning curve depicting proficiency, but this has not been the practice in education.

Interestingly, little disagreement exists about what counts as appropriate employment experience for teachers. However, there is considerable controversy over the organizational worth of such experience. Depending on whether the teacher is new to the system or an incumbent within the system, the organizational worth of experience may vary within a particular school district relative to board policy or a labor contract.

In theory, the organizational worth of employment experience should be based on the **learning curve** associated with the job rather than on the seniority of a person. Nevertheless, some school districts cap employment experience when placing potential job candidates on the teacher salary schedule. This practice has limited economic value to a school system and restricts the system's ability to compete in the labor market when recruiting experienced teachers.

No doubt, caps on allowable experience for incoming teachers have roots within teacher unions. Teacher unions are concerned more with existing employees than with potential employees (and should be according to their charges). By capping the experience granted potential employees, teacher unions enjoy a strategic advantage within the negotiation process.

Unions are more concerned with salaries paid existing employees, whereas management is concerned with attracting new employees. To attract new employees, school boards must increase entry-level salaries. Moreover, such increases have a rippling effect across all salary levels.

Although most school systems use the traditional salary structure for compensating teachers, some systems are beginning to explore new strategies for compensation. Within some states, these new strategies require the concurrence of union membership and largely build upon rather than depart from the traditional teacher salary structure. Urbanski and Erskine (2000) label these innovations according to performance award programs, National Board for Professional Teaching Standards, and knowledge- and skill-based pay systems.

Performance awards programs focus on a **bonus pay system** for teachers. By definition, a bonus is a one-time, nonrecurring method of reward. As such, a bonus is not incorporated into the base salary of teachers and represents only a single year obligation on the part of a school district.

Bonus systems can be devised either from an individual or from an organizational perspective. From an individual perspective, the bonus is awarded to select teachers based on their personal performance. In other instances, bonus awards are given on the basis of collective performances of teachers, and these awards are labeled as "**gain sharing.**"

Within these types of programs relying on a bonus, teachers receive a supplement beyond base pay awarded via the traditional salary schedule according to their obtainment of preestablished goals. These goals can be linked to student achievement or some other preestablished goals relating to desired outcomes (i.e., student attendance). In some instances, bonuses awarded on the basis of performance may be used by teachers without restrictions (personal use), whereas in other instances, bonuses must be spent for educational improvement of the school (i.e., equipment or learning materials).

Unlike school-based performance awards, other districts have awarded teacher salary increases beyond those attributable to the traditional salary schedule on the basis of acquiring certification by the National Board for Professional Teaching Standards. Underlying this type of award program is the assumption that teachers so certified will exhibit the skills and knowledge necessary for effective performance. In some instances National Board–certified teachers receive a supplement beyond the traditional salary schedule, while in other instances National Board–certified teachers are advanced increments within the traditional teacher salary schedule based on National Board certification rather than on traditional college credits.

To illustrate, in California, the state "provides National Board Certified Teachers (NBCTs) who teach in California K–12 public schools and who opt to teach in a high priority school for four consecutive years with a $20,000 incentive award, to be paid in four annual installments" (**http://www.nbpts.org/about/stateinfo.cfm?state=California**). In addition to the state stipend, some public school districts offer further incentives (see Table 8.4; **http://www.nbpts.org/about/stateinfo.cfm?state5California**).

Still different are the knowledge- and skill-based pay systems for teachers (see Kelley, 1997). Knowledge- and skill-based pay systems assume that education and experience, as awarded by the traditional teacher salary schedule, are poor proxies of their labeled attributes and endorse school district definitions of these attributes (rather than the Board for Professional Teaching Standards). Only by meeting local school district definitions of skill and knowledge can teachers advance through the traditional teacher salary schedule according to true knowledge- and skill-based pay systems.

Research addressing these new innovative pay configurations for teachers is limited at the present to only a few studies. Whether or not these systems offer a new direction for future compensation is unclear. What the research to date does suggest is that performance incentives must be greater than those used by many school districts (Heneman, 1998) and that such pay programs must be enduring (Kelley, Heneman, & Milanowski, 2002). Until further research is conducted that can guide human resource managers, much debate exists in this very important area.

Exempted Employee Salary Schedule

Most **exempted employee salary schedules** found within public school districts pertain to administrators and to supervisors not covered by collective bargaining. Surprisingly, the mere existence of exempted employee salary schedules is the exception rather than the rule across most public school districts. It is not uncommon to find school

TABLE 8.4
Sample Reward Incentives for National Board–Certified Teachers

SANTA MONICA-MALIBU USD: The district pays 50% of the fee up front and reimburses the remaining upon completion. Teachers receive $100 to attend information session, allowed four release days, and once certified will receive an annual $10,000.

districts that lack any type of exempted employee salary schedule on which to base the compensation of administrators and supervisors from a strategic planning perspective.

Within these systems lacking a formal salary schedule for administrators and supervisors, entry-level salaries are negotiated on an individual basis at the time of initial employment. Once employed by a public school district, administrators and supervisors receive uniform annual salary increases each year. Most generally, these increases are determined according to other employee groups, mainly the salary increases awarded to teachers within the public school district.

For those school districts that do have a formal salary schedule for compensating administrators and supervisors, these salary schedules can be categorized by the compensation policies that govern movement through them by employees. Movement through an exempted employee salary schedule can be based on time, performance, or some mixture of time and performance. These different categorizations can be classified along a single continuum (see Figure 8.3).

Anchoring this continuum is a **fixed-rate system** and **variable-rate system.** An intermediate point of this continuum is a **mixed-rate system.** Differentiating among these systems for awarding compensation to administrators and supervisors is the means for advancement within a particular salary schedule.

A fixed-rate salary system for exempted employees is modeled after the basic teacher salary schedule. As such, it has certain commensurable factors, such as education and experience for increasing the salary rate of an employee. An example of a fixed-rate salary schedule taken from the field setting for administrators and supervisors is found in Table 8.5.

In keeping with this type of fixed-rate salary structure, administrators and supervisors have two avenues for increasing their base salary. The employee can acquire additional

FIGURE 8.3 *Exempted employee salary structure schedule continuum for advancements.*

TABLE 8.5
Fixed-Rate Salary Schedule for Administrators and Supervisors

		Step 1	Step 2	Step 3	Step 4	Step 5	Step 6	Step 7	Step 8	Step 9
Level I	PhD (225)	87660	89984	92309	94633	96957	99281	101686	103719	105753
Level I	MA (225)	85522	87790	90057	92325	94592	96860	99206	101190	103174
Level II	PhD (225)	74854	76838	78823	80808	82792	84777	86830	88567	90304
Level II	MA (225)	73028	74964	76901	78837	80773	82709	84713	86407	88101
Level III	PhD (212)	70529	72399	74269	76139	78009	79879	81813	83450	85086
Level III	MA (212)	68809	70633	72457	74282	76106	77931	79818	81414	83011
Level IV	PhD (202)	66293	68051	69809	71567	73324	75082	76900	78438	79976
Level IV	MA (202)	64677	66391	68106	69821	71536	73251	75025	76525	78026
Level V	PhD (225)	68963	70791	72620	74448	76277	78105	79997	81597	83197
Level V	MA (225)	67281	69065	70849	72633	74416	76200	78046	79607	81168

Note: Numbers in parentheses are the days worked.

education and/or can serve another year in the current position. Movement within this type of salary schedule is automatic and is beyond administrative discretion in a fixed-rate salary schedule.

In contrast to the fixed-rate salary schedule system is' the variable-rate salary schedule for administrators and supervisors. This type of schedule, as found in Table 8.6, reflects only minimum and maximum salary rates. Provisions are lacking either for education or for experience in the variable-rate salary schedule.

Movement within the variable-rate salary schedule is based solely on administrative discretion (Cox, 2006). This type of schedule has roots with the pay for performance philosophy (Young, 2003). Increases in base salary for administrators and supervisors within a variable salary schedule can be anywhere between the minimum rate and the maximum-rate salary points and is based on the discretion of the employer.

Still different from either the fixed-rate or the variable-rate schedule system is the mixed-rate schedule. The mixed-rate salary schedule contains certain commensurable factors that are fixed and certain commensurable factors that are variable. Within the example as provided, education is fixed and performance is variable (see Table 8.7).

TABLE 8.6
Variable-Rate Salary Schedule

	Minimum Salary	→	Maximum Salary
Level I	87660	→	105753
Level II	74854	→	90304
Level III	70529	→	85086
Level IV	66293	→	79976
Level V	68963	→	83197

TABLE 8.7
Mixed-Rate Salary Schedule

		Minimum Salary	→	Maximum Salary
Level I	PhD (225)	87660	→	105753
Level I	MA (225)	85522	→	103174
Level II	PhD (225)	74854	→	90304
Level II	MA (225)	73028	→	88101
Level III	PhD (212)	70529	→	85086
Level III	MA (212)	68809	→	83011
Level IV	PhD (202)	66293	→	79976
Level IV	MA (202)	64677	→	78026
Level V	PhD (225)	68963	→	83197
Level V	MA (225)	67281	→	81168

The mixed-rate schedule provides employees with two avenues for increasing their base salary. One avenue is to acquire additional education (vertical), and this acquirement is beyond administrative control. The other avenue (horizontal) is based on job performance and is subject to administrative discretion.

Compensation, as defined by salary schedules, represents only one source of compensation received by employees. Beyond this direct source of compensation, employees enjoy indirect sources of compensation. Because both direct and indirect sources of compensation are a concern from a human resource perspective, the basic notion of indirect cost is introduced in this chapter and is expanded in a later chapter.

Indirect Cost

Another source of economic concern for a school system within the compensation context is the **indirect cost** of **benefits** received by employees as a condition of their employment. A benefit is a form of indirect compensation that does not require additional services beyond those required by a regular job assignment (see Table 8.8). Benefits enhance compensation beyond base pay and incentives and are intended to be dollar free and to focus on a variety of protective arrangements in addition to monetary components afforded by base compensation.

Benefits serve several purposes within the compensation process. From an economic perspective, benefits provide a means of income protection for the employee beyond the direct compensation received. In fact, for many positions, benefits may be more important than salary in that they provide the employee with protection for medical costs when working and provide for income continuity after retirement.

Benefit schedules offered to school employees may be categorized as either uniform or variable. **Uniform benefits** provide the same coverage to all personnel. By contrast, with **variable benefits,** each employee receives the amount of money the system allocates for benefit purposes and may then spend that money any way the employee chooses (often labeled as a **cafeteria benefit plan**).

On the surface, the choice between uniform and variable benefit programs within the total compensation perspective is deceptive. Often overlooked is the **economy of scale.** Fixed benefits are more cost-efficient but may be redundant for certain employees, while variable benefits are less cost-efficient and a fixed dollar amount will purchase fewer variable benefits than fixed benefits.

TABLE 8.8
Examples of Typical Fringe Benefits

Medical insurance	Dental insurance	Vision insurance
Disability insurance	Life insurance	Annuity
Retirement contribution	Flexible spending account	Tuition reimbursement
Personal leave	Sabbatical leave	Sick leave

Criticism is mounting and changes are being initiated in the design and administration of benefits. The following points are illustrative:

- Benefit demands are insatiable.
- Benefit costs reflect 40 percent of total compensation cost.
- Benefits do not depend on performance.
- Benefits are not congruent in two-career households.
- Benefits may not be motivators for performance.

Consequently, the design of compensation plans should involve careful evaluation of existing or proposed benefits in terms of their impact on base salary, incentive compensation, and performance enhancements. Fundamental to the design of and execution of a compensation plan, including direct and indirect cost to an organization, is an assessment of current practices. This assessment involves an audit of the current compensation structure and practices within a public school district relative to established criteria.

Audit of Compensation Structures

Every public school district should perform an audit of compensation structures and practices each year from a strategic planning perspective. An audit of compensation practices should provide information about past as well as about current outcomes of the compensation processes used by a public school district to pay employees. This type of information provides a foundation for informing deliberations among policy makers, for directing future activities relative to compensation practices, and for standardizing communication about compensation practices through uniform auditing indices that link compensation planning to compensation practice as noted in Figure 8.1.

To guide informed deliberations on the part of school board members and public school administrators in the design of and execution of equitable compensation systems for employees possessing external competitiveness and internal consistency, specific aspects of compensation structures and of compensation practices must be considered within the auditing process. At minimum, the auditing process should address three criteria for assessing past and current compensation practices from a strategic planning perspective. These criteria are compression within salary levels, rationality between classification levels, and earning potentials among salary grades.

Compression

As an auditing criterion for evaluating the compensation structures and practices of a school district, compression focuses on the actual economic growth potential of employees within a particular school district. **Compression,** as an auditing criterion, addresses potential economic growth of actual employees within a particular salary level or classification level unique to any particular school district. From a compensation perspective, compression provides one means for assessing the internal consistency impacting the perceptions of employees about the compensation structure(s) utilized by a public school district.

To assess the economic growth potential for a group of employees within a given pay level as per compression, some simple calculations are required. These calculations are based on two measures. One measure involves the actual salary paid the lowest-compensated employee within a particular salary level, while the other measure involves the highest rate of pay associated with the lowest-paid employee's salary range.

For each salary level or pay grade comprising a compensation system within a public school district, the base rate of the lowest-paid employee is divided by the maximum allowable base rate associated with the targeted pay grade within which the employee is assigned. The result of this division is then converted into a percentage. This percentage reflects the actual growth potential associated with a particular pay grade for current employees.

Table 8.9 shows the computations used to assess the compression for a particular pay grade. This table reveals the actual salaries of a group of elementary school principals. In addition to the specific salaries of these principals, the anchor points or salary ranges associated with the pay grade are presented.

Rather than using the minimum beginning salary as depicted by the schedule found in Table 8.9, compression analysis utilizes the minimum actual base rate received by the lowest-paid principal ($297) currently employed by the school district as the divisor. The maximum allowable base rate specified by the schedule ($308) serves as the dividend. After performing the division (maximum base rate/minimum actual base rate) and by subtracting 1 from the finding, the result is converted into a percentage and the degree of compression is obtained for a particular salary level.

The same calculations for assessing compression should be used for each salary range or pay grade (see Table 8.9) within a compensation structure of a particular school district. These calculations reveal the absolute degree of compression for any particular pay grade across all pay levels. The smaller the number obtained by the calculations reflecting compression, the greater the compression exhibited by the compensation system.

Compression can and will vary among salary grades within any particular salary schedule. Within any particular school district, it is not uncommon to find that some

TABLE 8.9
Computational Procedure for Calculating Compression

Minimum								Maximum
255.00	261.00	267.00	280.00	286.00	291.00	297.00	302.00	**$308.00**
Rebecca's Rate	**$297.00**							
Dane's Rate		$302.00						
Karen's Rate		$302.00						
Todd's Rate		$302.00						

Computations

Compression = ((maximum schedule rate/minimum actual rate) − 1) × 100
Compression = ((308/297) − 1) × 100
Compression = .37 or 3.7%

TABLE 8.10
Compression for Different Salary Levels

Salary Level	Position	Compression
Level 1	A. Superintendent	15.00%
Level 2	Sr. High Principal	12.00%
Level 3	El. Principal	3.70%
Level 4	Supervisor	18.00%

salary grades exhibit very little compression, whereas other salary grades exhibit a great deal of compression. An example of variations in compression is presented for one school district in Table 8.10.

In Table 8.10, the salary grade for supervisors shows very little compression, as noted by the actual growth potential of 18 percent. By contrast, the salary grade for elementary school principals exhibits extreme compression, as noted by the actual growth potential of 4 percent. Because the principals in this compensation system have little room for advancement other than through adjustments to their base salaries, elementary school principals are likely to be less satisfied with the compensation system than the supervisors employed within the same school district.

Compression as exhibited by this auditing criterion can be caused potentially by several factors. If the compensation system used with the principals in Table 8.10 awards salary advances based on experience within the district, and if all these principals have been with the district for a long time, then compression may result because of a lack of turnover among this group of employees. Given this possible situation, and if the compensation structure has been maintained appropriately, then compression will be reduced in time by turnover within this group of principals. Replacements for existing employees should have beginning salaries lower than those of continuing employees in a market-driven system. Thus, compression will be reduced by new employees receiving a substantially lower salary than existing employees.

However, a more common cause of compression than workforce stability among this employee group is failure of the school district to update the compensation system for employee groups relative to market values. When a lack of attention has been given to market conditions, beginning salaries, as reflected by an existing salary scheduled, will be too low to attract quality applicants. To be competitive in the external job market for new employees seeking vacant positions, the school district may offer starting salaries that fall in the upper levels of the pay grade or salary range of existing employees.

If new hires receive high salaries within the pay range relative to existing employees, then these salaries encroach on those of long-term employees. This results in compression and produces dissatisfaction among existing employees and violates the notion of internal consistency. As a result of this type of compression, existing employees are likely to question the school board's appreciation for continuous employment in the system and to complain about a lack of economic incentives for advancement.

Educational organizations have used different means to eliminate compression. One mean involves expanding the number of steps in the salary schedule. Functionally, this solution is only short ranged and ineffective.

By expanding the salary range, the general notion of a market perspective is ignored by this correction procedure. Entry-level salaries will still be too low for attracting new employees. Also, continuing employees may be paid more than the market value of their position.

A better solution for eliminating compression than expanding the number of steps in a salary schedule is to update the salary schedule relative to current market parameters. If the salary schedule is realigned with market parameters, both entry-level and continuing salaries will be competitive with the market. However, these realignment processes may be costly when viewed from a single year adjustment, but corrections are seldom inexpensive.

Within the field setting, employees harbor compensation concerns beyond compression relative to a school district's pay practices. Most importantly, employees are concerned about how they are paid relative to how the subordinates they supervise are paid within a district's compensation system. The relationship between supervisor and subordinate pay relationships is captured by another auditing criterion labeled within the compensations context as **rationality.**

Rationality

Another criterion for evaluating compensation structures and practices of a public school district from a strategic planning perspective relative to the compensation of current employees is **rationality.** Rationality addresses the relationship between the salaries of superordinates and the salaries of their subordinates. Underlying rationality as an auditing criterion is the assumption that superordinates should receive higher salaries than the subordinates that they supervise.

With respect to rationality, most school boards and practicing administrators concur with the general principles espoused by the rationality criterion within the compensation context. However, rationality as an auditing criterion can be defined in several ways within the public school setting. Rationality can be assessed either by direct or by indirect supervision with variations in these lines of reporting between organizational representatives.

Although compensation specialists generally agree that rationality assessments should be limited to situations involving direct reporting relationships between superordinates and subordinates, two definitions exist for subordinates in education. One definition favors the superordinate and uses the highest-paid subordinate to assess rationality. The other definition favors the employer and uses a subordinate with like-type qualifications relative to the superordinate for assessing rationality.

To illustrate the difference between these two definitions of rationality, consider the superordinate–subordinate relationship involving an elementary school principal and an elementary school teacher assigned to the same building. For the liberal definition favoring the superordinate, the subordinate chosen to assess rationality would be the highest-paid teacher in the school. In contrast, for the conservative definition favoring the employer, the subordinate chosen for rationality assessment would be a teacher with the same education and the same experience as the elementary school principal responsible for supervising said teacher.

Choosing whether to use the liberal rather than the conservative definition is largely a policy issue for the board of education. However, the choice usually has a substantial impact on the outcome of the rationality assessment for assessing a compensation structure used by a public school district. Consequently, a choice should be made from a policy perspective about the definition of a subordinate before rationality is assessed by a particular school district within the auditing process.

After the definition of a subordinate is selected (like type or highest paid), the length of the work year must be considered when calculating rates of compensation for a rationality assessment. In the present example involving an elementary school principal and an elementary school teacher assigned to the same school building, the principal's work year will almost always be longer for the elementary school principal than for the elementary school teacher. In most public school systems, the elementary school principal's work year extends weeks beyond the students' educational period, whereas for elementary school teachers the work year is only days beyond the reporting period for students.

To control for a work year of varying length between elementary school principals and elementary school teachers within the same school building, each base salary must be converted to a common unit of analysis for rationality assessment. This usually involves using a daily rate of pay. For each position used in rationality assessments, the daily rate is obtained by dividing the base annual salary by the number of days comprising the employee's work year, as specified by the employment contract.

An example of a rationality assessment using actual field data is presented in Table 8.11. These data, obtained from a public school district, involve rationality assessments between line administrators, who directly supervise teachers in this district, and data corrected for length of

TABLE 8.11
Rationality Assessment for Administrators and Teachers

	Current Salary	Like-Type Teacher 2000–01	Actual Difference	Rationality Needs
High Sch. Prin.	$391.00	$306.00	$85.00	$ 0.00
Middle Sch. Prin. A	$386.00	$297.00	$88.00	$ 0.00
Middle Sch. Prin. B	$350.00	$297.00	$53.00	$ 0.00
Elementary Sch. Prin. A	$379.00	$304.00	$75.00	$ 0.00
Elementary Sch. Prin. B	$378.00	$298.00	$80.00	$ 0.00
Elementary Sch. Prin. C	$371.00	$306.00	$65.00	$ 0.00
Elementary Sch. Prin. D	$370.00	$301.00	$69.00	$ 0.00
Elementary Sch. Prin. E	$312.00	$297.00	$15.00	$15.00
Elementary Sch. Prin. F	$311.00	$283.00	$29.00	$ 0.00
Elementary Sch. Prin. G	$306.00	$307.00	$ 1.00	$32.00
Elementary Sch. Prin. H	$291.00	$297.00	$ 6.00	$36.00

the contractual work year of all employees. The assessments are based on the conservative definition of a subordinate using a teacher with like-type credentials as possessed by each line administrator acting as a superordinate for a like-type teacher in their school building.

As Table 8.11 shows, the rationality assessment reveals an inverse relationship between the salaries of some administrators and those of like-type teachers. In this district, administrators responsible for the direct supervision of teachers would earn higher salaries if they were paid similar to like teachers on a per-diem basis. On any given day during the academic school year when both administrators and teachers report to work, administrators earn less money per day than teachers with similar credentials.

The inverse economic relationship between line administrators and teachers shown in this example is not unique to the examples provided. In fact, a survey of over 50 public school districts in a typical midwestern state revealed that the vast majority of those districts had the same problem with respect to rationality assessments involving administrators and teachers assigned to the same school building. As a result, many of these districts reported problems attracting talented teachers from within the district to fill vacant administrative positions.

Violation of the rationality principle often has several related causes. One cause relates to representation of subordinate employees by unions. Another cause pertains to the manner by which managerial employees are compensated.

In many states, unions represent teachers and negotiate their salaries with the school board. Negotiations require an agreement by both sides and have greatly enhanced the economic situation of teachers through a concerted effort. However, administrators, unlike teachers, are seldom represented by a union, and their salaries are determined solely by the school board.

When establishing salaries for administrators, school boards have often used the percentage increase awarded to teachers through negotiations as a guideline for making adjustments to base salaries. This percentage is usually calculated on increases in the base salary of teachers and fails to consider step increases within the teacher compensation system received by teachers. Because of this omission of step increases in calculating the adjustment factor for administrators, any preexisting salary difference between administrators and teachers (rationality) is reduced with each budget year.

Also, many public school districts use a different method for calculating work years for building-level administrators and for teachers. For teachers, their work year is determined by the number of contracted days (usually 180 days ±). For school building employees, their salary is calculated on actual work days failing to consider vacation.

For example, many high school principals are employed for a full work year (typically 260 days). However, these principals receive 20 days of paid vacation. Rather than using the 260 days, some school districts use 240 days, and this decision inflates the daily rate of pay for high school principals relative to the rationality criterion.

Assessments of rationality should not be limited to comparisons between line administrators and teachers. These assessments should be expanded to include the economic relationship for all administrators and superordinate–subordinate reporting relationships within the district. When assessments of administrator–administrator and

TABLE 8.12
Rationality Assessment for Administrators and Highest-Paid Subordinate

Rationality Assessment among Administrators and Subordinate Administrators/Supervisors					
Target Position	Target Salary	Subordinate Position	Subordinate Salary	Actual Difference	Rationality Need
		Dir.			
Ex. Dir. Sch. Improvement	458	Prof. Development	417	41	0
Ex. Dir. Bus. Affairs	412	Maint. & Pt. Oper.	369	43	0
Dir. St. Prog/Learn. Ser.	358	Sup. Early Child.	354	4	32
Dir. Curr. & Inst.	366	C & I Supervisor	369	−3	40
N. High Sch. Prin.	402	AHS. Principal	360	42	0
S. High Sch. Prin	352	Dean	315	37	0
Middle Sch. Prin. Clark	385	AMS Principal	361	23	13
Middle Sch. Prin. Franklin	387	AMS Principal	313	74	0
Middle Sch. Prin. Hayward	391	AMS Principal	332	60	0
Middle Sch. Prin. Roosevelt	385	AMS Principal	375	10	27
Middle Sch. Prin. Schaefer	391	AMS Principal	335	57	0
E.S.P. Emerson	332	AES Principal	327	4	28
E.S.P. Winter Park	365	AES Principal	336	29	5

other superordinate–subordinate relationships are included, the rationality of a compensation structure can be examined from a between-group as well as from a within-group perspective. Contained in Table 8.12 are rationality assessments for school administrators and their highest-paid subordinates as found in one particular public school district.

Beyond actual salary outcomes, employees are concerned with their earning potential from at least two different perspectives. The earning potential of employees can be either internally or externally referenced. From an internal perspective, earning potentials involve comparisons within different employee groups within the same system, while from an external perspective earning potentials are compared to like-type employees in other school districts.

Earning Potentials

Still another measure of equity as assessed from a strategic planning perspective for compensation systems used by a public school district to pay job incumbents concerns the concept of earning potentials anticipated by employees. **Earning potentials** as an auditing criterion differ from compression and rationality in that the focus on the former is on the structure of salary schedules independent of the distribution of employees within a particular salary range. As auditing criteria, compression as well as rationality concern actual, as opposed to theoretical, earning potentials of employees as dictated by a particular compensation system.

Earning potentials associated with particular compensation systems used by a public school district can be viewed from an internal and an external perspective. From an internal perspective, employees of a public school district compare their earning potential to the earning potential of other employees within the same district. For all employees, the earning potential associated with their positions represents a measure of organizational worth (Young, 2006). Lesser earning potentials for specific positions are interpreted negatively, while higher earning potentials are interpreted positively relative to the value of specific positions held by employees.

Functionally, an earning potential is a theoretical construct calculated on the basis of an established salary range. An earning potential is defined by the minimum and maximum base rates that define a particular salary range or pay grade within a salary schedule. Because these minimum and maximum base rates may not reflect the actual base pay received by a specific employee, the term *theoretical* rather than *actual* is used to describe an earning potential. To calculate the theoretical earning potential associated with a particular salary range or pay scale within a school district, some simple computations are required.

Computationally, the calculation of an earning potential involves three steps. First, the maximum allowable salary associated with a particular pay level is divided by the minimum beginning salary (maximum salary/minimum salary) associated with the same pay level. Second, the result from the division is subtracted from 1. And, third, the result of this division and subtraction is then converted into a percentage reflecting an earning potential for a specific level.

An actual example from the field setting involving the earning potential for a group of elementary school principals is provided in Table 8.13. These data reflect a minimum salary rate of $255 per day and a maximum salary rate of $308 per day. The minimum salary is the smallest amount that can be awarded by the school district, and the maximum salary is the largest amount that can be paid to any particular employee.

The theoretical earning potential associated with this pay scale for elementary principals is derived by dividing the maximum rate ($308) by the minimum rate ($255), subtracting 1 from the result, and converting the final number into a percentage (20.8 percent). If the same computations are used for all salary levels within a compensation structure, the theoretical earning potentials can be assessed for an entire compensation structure involving administrators and supervisors in a public school district.

Table 8.14 presents four possible outcomes that could be obtained relative to earning potentials. These outcomes are shown for a constant earning potential across all pay scales (Example A), for a varying earning potential according to pay scales (Example B), for a varying earning potentials inversely with pay scales (Example C), and for earning potentials varying unsystematically among pay grades (Example D). Each example has

TABLE 8.13
Computational Procedure for Calculating Theoretical Earning Potentials

Minimum								Maximum
255.00	261.00	267.00	280.00	286.00	291.00	297.00	302.00	$308.00

1. Theoretical Earning Potentials = ((Maximum Rate/Minimum Rate) − 1) × 100
2. Theoretical Earning Potentials = ((308/255) − 1) × 100
3. Theoretical Earning Potentials = 20.78%

TABLE 8.14
Examples of Elasticity

	Example A	Example B	Example C	Example D
Level 1	25%	25%	10%	25%
Level 2	25%	20%	15%	10%
Level 3	25%	15%	20%	15%
Level 4	25%	10%	25%	20%

certain implications for current and for future compensation practices of a school district when viewed from a strategic planning perspective.

If the theoretical earning potential among pay levels within a school district varies substantially, then the compensation structure is elastic because some pay scales have greater earning potential than others. Whether **elasticity** has a positive or negative effect on compensation practices depends largely on the relationship between the organizational level of pay scales and the size of earning potentials associated with pay grades. Positive effects on compensation practices are most likely to occur either when elasticity does not exist or when it increases according to the organizational level of pay grades.

Lack of elasticity suggests that the theoretical earning potential for employees is a constant percentage throughout the compensation structure (see Table 8.14, Example A). Lower-level employees have the same earning potential as their superiors. An earning potential that is equal or constant across all organizational levels (lacking elasticity) generally has strong appeal to employees and reflects sound compensation practices of a school system.

Elasticity can also have a positive effect when the earning potential increases systematically according to the level within the hierarchy (see Table 8.14, Example B). With this type of elasticity, higher-level employees have greater earning potential than lower-level employees. Underlying this type of elasticity is the assumption that higher-level positions are more difficult to obtain through promotion and require employees to remain within a grade for a longer period of time. To compensate for these limitations, earning potentials increase according to the level within the hierarchy.

The negative effects of elasticity often occur when earning potentials vary unsystematically among organizational levels or vary inversely with levels. Earning potentials that vary unsystematically among levels are a problem often found during an internal audit. Because unsystematic variations usually have no logical explanation, they lead to accusations of favoritism benefiting certain employee groups and reflect poor compensation practices by the school system.

The accusation of favoritism is also made by higher-level employees when earning potentials vary inversely with level. In this situation, lower-level employees have a greater earning potential than those higher up in the hierarchy. At best, this arrangement creates a competitive rather than a cooperative work environment; at worst, it results in a work environment perceived as inequitable.

The negative effects of elasticity can usually be traced to certain compensation decisions made in the past. With unsystematic variation, barring any actions intended to create a privileged group, market competition for certain groups may have required selective adjustments to attract desired employees. If some employee groups receive an adjustment for market fluctuations and other groups do not, the former will have a greater earning potential than the latter.

Elasticity characterized by an inverse relationship between earning potential and organizational level can result from techniques used to update compensation systems. To update compensation systems, school boards can use either a proportional-rate technique based on a fixed percentage or a constant-rate technique involving a fixed dollar amount. The former technique will maintain the status quo with respect to earning potential, while the latter technique will increase the earning potential for lower-level employees.

Collectively, these auditing criteria (compression, rationality, and earning potentials) reflect the **internal consistency** of a compensation system for a public school district involving all employees except teachers. The internal consistency for teacher compensation systems is well established and is differentiated only on the basis of education and experience. To align compensation systems (other than teachers) involving administrators and supervisors for internal consistency is the focus of the following section of this chapter.

Internal Consistency of Compensation Structures

Compensation practices and structures can be assessed according to several different criteria. In the previous section, three criteria were addressed: compression, rationality, and earning potential. Each criterion provides a standard for gaining important baseline information from a strategic planning perspective about certain aspects of compensation systems used by a public school district.

However, these criteria, although informative, are insensitive to another important compensation principle: internal consistency—the relative relationship among all positions within a particular compensation structure. Although the rationality criterion addresses the superordinate–subordinate relationship, it fails to consider the relationships among all other positions comprising the administrator and supervisory ranks.

For example, in most school districts there is usually some disagreement between elementary school principals and assistant high school principals concerning base rates of compensation. Elementary school principals tend to believe that they should be paid more than assistant high school principals; the latter take the opposite position. To resolve this disagreement, as well as similar disagreements involving other positions, school boards have two options.

One option is to consider all positions to be of equal value and to pay all personnel within the compensation system the same base rate, regardless of their position. With this option, elementary school principals would be paid the same as assistant high school principals. However, this option is seldom used and would probably be unsatisfactory both for boards of education and for school district employees.

The other option is to differentiate among positions within the compensation system in terms of organizational value and base salary. That is, some positions would command higher pay than other positions. This is the option generally used for establishing internal consistency among administrator and supervisory positions.

Following this option, salary differentiation within the compensation system should be based, however, on certain principles: positions of similar organizational value should be compensated at a similar rate, while positions of different organizational value should be compensated at a different rate. To determine the organizational value of various positions is difficult but not impossible tasks from a policy perspective.

Some school boards might decide to differentiate among positions with respect to base rates of compensation on the basis of budgetary responsibilities. Because most elementary school principals are responsible for administering a building-level budget, whereas few assistant high school principals are involved in budget administration, the disagreement is resolved. Using the budgetary criterion, elementary school principals would be entitled to a higher base rate of compensation than assistant high school principals.

In contrast to the aforementioned decisional strategy, other school boards might decide to differentiate among positions with respect to time spent performing work for the district beyond the regular workday. Because most assistant high school principals are involved extensively in extracurricular activities after the regular workday, and most elementary school principals are not, again, the disagreement is resolved. Using the extended workday criterion, assistant high school principals would be entitled to higher pay than elementary school principals.

These examples serve both to illustrate a point and to raise an important question. The point is that the solution to the disagreement concerning the base pay of elementary school principals and assistant high school principals depends on the criterion chosen to evaluate the organizational worth of the positions. When the criterion changes for evaluating the organizational worth of positions, the solution changes for resolving the disagreement about positions.

The important question raised by these examples concerns the choice of a criterion or criteria (i.e., budgetary and/or extended day, etc.) to be used for evaluating the positions. Either criterion or multiple criteria are a reasonable choice for a school board. Therefore, the choice is a policy decision rather than an administrative decision for determining the relative worth of positions.

As previously noted policy decisions are required in situations where more than one potential outcome exists and where all potential outcomes are equally appropriate. In these cases, policy decisions depend on the preference of the designated policy group. In turn, the preference for a particular criterion or criteria for assessing the organizational worth of positions depends on the method used to evaluate these positions.

Position Evaluation Methods

Several methods exist for establishing internal consistency relative to organizational worth among positions within a compensation structure from a strategic planning perspective. All methods have some common features while varying in important ways. Common to all methods used to establish internal consistency is a focus on positions rather than on position holders.

Positions rather than position holders serve as the unit of analysis for several reasons. First, positions are established to perform certain tasks within the organization, and these tasks determine the relative organizational value of the positions. Second, the organizational worth of these tasks is independent of their actual performance. Tasks can be performed either well or poorly, but their worth to the school system remains the same. Third, positions are part of the organizational structure and can be changed only by the employer, while position holders can be changed by the whims of the incumbent.

The methods used to evaluate positions differ in complexity. Some methods use only a single global criterion, while others use several different criteria. Although the compensation literature is replete with methods that can be employed to establish internal consistency among positions relative to organizational worth, almost all of them are variants of one of four basic systems: ranking, job classification, factor comparison, and point method.

Each of these systems has been used in education and has been applied to districts with as few as four administrators or as many as several hundred administrators. However, because the systems used most frequently are the ranking and the point methods, the following discussion is limited to these two types of methods.

The **ranking method** is both the simplest and the oldest method used to evaluate the organizational worth of positions. It uses only one global criterion. The criterion is discretionary and should be chosen by a designated policy group.

Some examples of a single criterion are overall organizational worth, impact on children, extended workday responsibilities, and fiscal responsibilities. Because any criterion for evaluating positions has advantages as well as disadvantages, the choice should be made only after these advantages and disadvantages have been thoroughly discussed. This discussion should focus on organizational implications, rather than on particular positions or position holders, in order to reach a consensus about the single global criterion to be chosen.

If a consensus on a single global criterion has been achieved, the next task is to establish the relative worth of all positions in the compensation system. Relative worth, as defined by the ranking method, involves comparing positions with respect to the single global criterion. The comparison process can use one of the following methods: **simple ranking, alternative ranking,** or **paired comparison,** Each method uses a different decisional strategy.

To use any of these methods for assessing organizational worth and internal consistency among positions, a set of 5-by-8 cards is needed. On each card, the title of a single position is recorded. In a particular set of cards, the number of cards should equal the number of positions.

For the simple ranking technique, each person in the designated policy group should receive a single set of cards listing all positions under consideration. Members of the policy group are instructed to work independently and to rank their set of cards according to the global criterion. These ranks should be in descending order.

The first ranking should contain the most important position relative to the global criterion. Ranked second should be the next important position relative to the global criterion. Following this same evaluation process, all positions should be ranked relative to the global criterion.

After each member of the designated policy group has ranked independently all the positions in the compensation study, the ranks across members should be compiled. Initial results of the rankings will almost always reveal disagreements among policy group members; these disagreements should be discussed in a forum. The members of the designated policy group should explain their rankings and question those of other group members. Afterward, the group should once again rank independently all positions under consideration.

Several iterations of independent rankings, followed by discussions, should be performed to obtain a consensus. However, in many situations, no consensus will emerge. If this happens, the simple ranking method should be abandoned, and another method should be used for evaluating the focal positions.

Another derivation of the simple ranking technique is the alternative ranking procedure. This procedure uses the same materials as the simple ranking technique but requires a different decisional strategy. With the alternative ranking technique, policy group members first select the most important position relative to the single global criterion; next, they select the least important position relative to that criterion. This strategy is used with all positions in the compensation study.

The alternative ranking procedure forces maximum differentiation among the positions in a compensation system. Disagreements on internal consistency are most likely to occur with midrange positions. When these positions lead to problems in establishing internal consistency, one other comparison process may be used. This is the paired comparison process, and it involves yet a different decisional strategy.

In the paired comparison process, each position (target position) is compared to all other positions (object positions) in the compensation study. Target positions considered more important than the object position are awarded a plus, and target positions considered less important than the object position are awarded a minus. The organizational worth of any particular target position is determined by assessed net worth reflecting the difference between the pluses and minuses assigned a particular position.

Ranking systems are often used by school systems to establish the internal consistency of positions in a compensation system. These systems have been used to determine the relative ordering of support personnel in a single wage rate schedule and the relative ordering of supplementary assignments for teachers involving extracurricular pay increments to base salary.

In general, norm-based ranking systems are easy to implement, simple to understand, and equitable in application. Thus, employees tend to endorse these systems as a means of establishing the internal consistency of a compensation system. However, the strengths of norm-based ranking systems can be weaknesses when these systems are applied to complex jobs such as those held by administrators and supervisors.

To capture the complexities of administrator and supervisor positions in a compensation system, a criterion-based reference system is generally employed. This system requires a different decisional strategy than a norm-based system. In a criterion-based system, positions are evaluated relative to different criteria rather than relative to a single criterion, as is the case with norm-based systems.

The criterion-based strategy used most frequently to establish internal consistency is the **point method.** This method assumes that all positions in a compensation structure have certain underlying factors or common denominators, such as supervision responsibilities, judgment/discretion, fiscal management, community relations, and involvement with parents.

Factors used in the point method can vary both in degree and in weight. For example, supervision could vary in degree by including direct supervision, indirect supervision, and/or the number of work groups supervised. Degrees of judgment/discretion could be analyzed from either a policy involvement perspective or an organizational impact perspective. In some positions, the organizational impact may exist only for the immediate work site (i.e., assistant principal); in other positions, it may span several work sites (i.e., middle school principal); and in still other positions, it may extend across the entire school system (i.e., chief financial officer).

The outcomes obtained with the point method are related to the factors selected, the degrees used to define factors, and the weight given to each factor. If any alteration is made in factor, degree, or weight, then a different picture of the relative worth of specific positions will be produced. For this reason, the choice of factors, degrees, and weightings is a policy decision rather than an administrative decision.

Once the factors, degrees, and weights have been selected by a policy group, each position in the compensation study is evaluated accordingly. To evaluate each position included in the salary study, several techniques are available. These techniques include an analysis of job descriptions, a written survey, and an interview protocol.

Job descriptions for focal positions included in the analysis can be assessed according to factors and to degrees of factors as defined by the policy group. This approach is efficient, but seldom effective. It assumes that valid job descriptions exist (seldom the case), and omits any personal involvement of employees included in the study.

Position analysis questionnaires can be developed that address the factors and the degrees of factors being considered within the assessment process and completed by all focal position holders. To control either for underreporting or for overembellishing, immediate supervisors for each employee should be required to sign off on their questionnaire. In spite of this safeguard, information is found to be lacking in many instances.

By far, the superior method for obtaining information about factors and the degrees of factors characterizing specific focal positions included in a study is the structure interview method. Within the structured interview method, employees have personal involvement, can express their concerns, and be actively involved in the process. Downsides of this process are time for data collection and personnel expenses associated with interviewers and interviewees.

Because of the advantages associated with the point method, an actual example from the field setting is used to illustrate this technique. To begin the process, a policy group must be formulated to guide the study. The policy group can be the board of education or it can be designated representatives so appointed by the board of education.

Frequently, the board of education fulfills the role of a policy group. However, other configurations are not uncommon. In some instances, a policy group is comprised of school board members, executive-level employees, and representatives of employees covered by the study.

As a policy group, this body has two charges. First, the policy group must identify the criteria to be used for evaluating the focal positions included in the study. Many potential criteria exist (i.e., supervision, judgment, fiscal etc.), and those chosen will produce a specific outcome for the evaluation process.

Second, the policy group should weigh the importance of these criteria relative to local expectations. Although all criteria chosen may be perceived to be of the same value, this is not the typical case. Even when the same criteria are chosen by policy groups from different school districts, a differential weighting of these criteria will yield a unique outcome among school districts concerning the worth of the same focal positions.

Within this working example based on actual field data involving one specific public school district, the policy group is the board of education. This particular board of education chose three criteria to be used to evaluate all positions included in the compensation study: (1) supervision, (2) judgment, and (3) community relations. These criteria were viewed as being of different importance and assigned weights to reflect this value: (1) supervision 40 percent, (2) judgment 40 percent, and (3) community relations 20 percent.

Based on these a priori policy decisions, individual interviews were conducted with each position holder. For each position holder, in-depth queries were made about assigned responsibilities relative to the specific criteria identified by the policy group. In some instances, this assessment involved actual numbers, while in other instances responses were recorded according to scale values.

To illustrate, position holders reported the actual number of employees supervised as documented by signing the employee evaluation form. In other instances, position holders described their community relations involvement associated with their job assignment. For this later criterion, community relations was measured on a Likert-type scale (1–5) with a higher number being more indicative of greater involvement than a lower number.

Results of the interviews yielded different types of measurements. Supervision reflected actual numbers with a large range of values, while community involvement was restricted to a 1–5 range. To render a standard scale of measurement across all criteria, a normalization process is used, and both raw data and standardized data are found in Table 8.15.

As Table 8.15 shows, some ratings have a plus sign and others have a minus sign because all ratings are standardized to a normal curve equivalence (z-score transformation) within each criterion. Within any particular criterion, the average performance of all combined position ratings is zero, and the specific rating of any particular position is given in standard units from the average. To illustrate, positions with large plus ratings (high school principal) involve far more supervision than does the average position in this particular district, while positions with large minus ratings (food service) involve much less supervision than does the average position in the district.

Standardization of ratings allows direct comparison of all positions within any criterion and direct comparison of all positions across all criteria. If certain positions are considered undervalued or overvalued, as reflected by standardized ratings, then ratings within any criterion can be used to help redesign positions from a strategic planning perspective. For

TABLE 8.15
Position Evaluation for Weighted and Standardized Scores

		Raw Scores	
	Supervision	Judgment	Com. Relations
H.S. Principal	60	5	4
M.S. Principal	40	4	3
El.S. Principal	28	3	3
El.S. Principal	24	3	3
A.H.S.			
Principal	16	2	1
Food Service	1	1	1
Maintenance	15	1	1

	Supervision 40%	Weighted Scores Judgment 40% 20%	Com. Relations
H.S. Principal	24.0	2.00	0.80
M.S. Principal	16.0	1.60	0.60
El.S. Principal	11.2	1.20	0.60
El.S. Principal	9.6	1.20	0.60
A.H.S.			
Principal	6.4	0.80	0.20
Food Service	0.4	0.40	0.20
Maintenance	6.0	0.40	0.20

	Supervision	Z-Scores Judgment	Com. Relations
H.S. Principal	1.8	1.5	1.4
M.S. Principal	0.7	0.9	0.6
El.S. Principal	0.1	0.2	0.6
El.S. Principal	−0.1	0.2	0.6
A.H.S.			
Principal	−0.5	−0.5	−1.0
Food Service	−1.3	−1.1	−1.0
Maintenance	−0.6	−1.1	−1.0

example, the food service position is rated low in supervision; this rating could be increased by shifting supervisory responsibility for cooks and servers from principals to food service.

The overall value of positions using the point method is calculated by summing within rows the weighted ratings across all criteria for each position. The overall value of positions, as calculated on the basis of weighted ratings, is used to order the positions in a classification system, and the classification system reflects the internal consistency among the positions relative to the factors, degrees, and weights selected by the policy group. Once established, a classification system should be linked to an identified labor market for assessment from an external perspective.

External Labor Market

Public school systems must compete with other organizations to acquire and to retain employees, at least in part, on the basis of the reward structure of a particular school system relative to the reward structures of competing school systems. To assess the reward structures of other school systems, a **market assessment** should be performed on similar school districts, and these school districts comprise, from a compensation perspective, what is labeled as a **relevant labor market.**

A market analysis requires the identification of a relevant external labor market comprised of similar type school districts for a comparative analysis. In reality, many different potential relevant labor markets exist for comparing the compensation received by public school employees, and each potential labor market will yield unique results for a comparison. Defining a relevant labor market, for any particular school district as opposed to defining the most appropriate labor market for the school district, is a policy/negotiated decision depending on the employee group under consideration.

For all employee groups, the differentiation between a relevant and most appropriate labor market within the compensation context is important and is often a misunderstood construct. The notion of the most important labor market fails to exist in reality within the public school setting. What exists in reality within the public school setting is a relevant labor market and not the most appropriate labor market.

A relevant labor market should be defined operationally by involved stakeholders based on policy considerations. For employees not covered by a labor contract, a relevant labor market is a policy decision exercised exclusively by the board of education. With employees covered by a labor contract, a relevant labor market is determined bilaterally by boards of education and union representatives through the collective bargaining process.

To guide the deliberation process and to identify a relevant labor market for an analysis of compensation practices and outcomes, several different factors must be considered (see Young et al., 2004). Some of the more common factors found to inform decision making about an appropriate labor market are found in Figure 8.4. Underlying each factor are certain basic assumptions about what constitutes a relevant labor market from a policy perspective.

When defining a relevant labor market from a policy perspective, a distinction is made between the target school district and object school districts. The target school district is the school system performing the market analysis. The object school districts are those school systems comprising a relevant external labor market defined by policy considerations.

Geographical location, when used to define a relevant labor market for a target public school district from a policy perspective, includes those object school systems in the immediate physical area. By object school districts being in the immediate geographical area of the target district, a basic assumption is made for defining a relevant labor market, i.e., **supply and demand.** That is, it is assumed that potential as well as existing employees can chose among local school districts within the same geographical area without changing their place of residence.

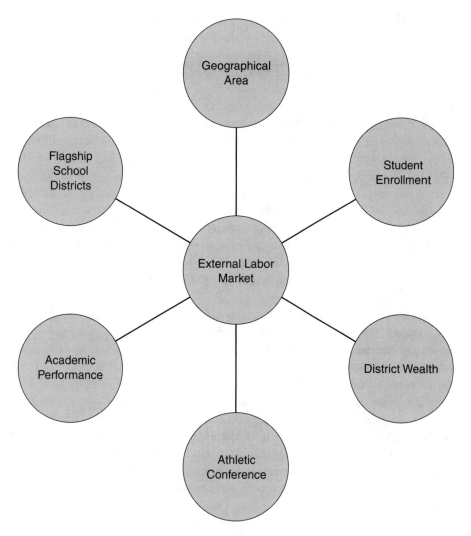

FIGURE 8.4 *Definitions for a relevant labor market.*

With very few exceptions, potential employees as well as current employees can always improve their economic position within the work setting if they are willing to relocate their place of residency. However, relocation involves a substantial cost for individuals. To compete for those individuals unwilling to relocate at their own expense, a target school district must be competitive in compensation with object school districts within the immediate geographical area as captured by the economic principle involving supply and demand.

Another traditional criterion for defining a relevant labor market for a target school district is student enrollment. Underlying this criterion as a means for defining a relevant labor market for a target school district is the economic principle captured by the economy of scale. The economy of scale assumes a direct relationship between size of an organization and the work performed by an organization and its representatives.

Student enrollments are used to define a relevant labor market from an economy of scale that contains districts of similar size relative to the average daily attendance (ADA) of the target school district. Similar size object school districts, as defined by ADA, are assumed to have similar organizational structures and focal positions, comparable to those found in the target school district. Comparable organizational structures and position requirements demand complementary skills and knowledge on the part of employees and define a relevant labor market based on scale of economy.

Still another traditional criterion for defining a relevant labor market for a target school district is organizational wealth or **ability to pay.** Organizational wealth for school districts can be defined in several different ways. From a very broad perspective, organizational wealth can be operationalized either from a revenue potential or expenditure perspective.

From a revenue potential viewpoint, the focus is on relative wealth of school districts. Relative wealth can be determined either by assessed or by real property values. Also, relative wealth may be measured by the income levels of residents comprising particular school districts.

Expenditure data pertains to the manner in which school districts distribute monies. One obvious global measure to be used for defining an appropriate labor market is the per-pupil expenditure of school districts. Similar expenditure data can be obtained for particular employee groups (i.e., per-teacher, per-administrator, etc.).

Depending on the definition of wealth used (acquiring or spending) for defining a relevant labor market with a particular target school district, this factor assumes an appropriate labor market defined by fiscal responsibility. Fiscal responsibility implies that similar resources should dictate a similar economic effort on the part of a target school district relative to equally endowed object school districts. That is, equal financial ability should translate to equal burden when defining a relevant labor market.

Yet another traditional definition of an appropriate labor market is the athletic conference for a target school district. When used to define a relevant labor market, the athletic conference of a target school district has several advantages. An athletic conference is somewhat sensitive to geographical area as well as district size and has general public appeal beyond the first two factors. If residents of a school district are asked to identify comparable school districts that should be used to define a relevant labor market, generally some of the districts in the athletic conference of the target school district are mentioned as a legitimate comparison.

More recently, some school districts have begun to use academic performance of object school districts to define a relevant labor market. With many states legislating standardized proficiency tests, the results of these tests have been used to select object school districts for a market analysis. The underlying assumption here is that similar academic performance should yield similar compensation packages for employees and reflects a **cost-benefit** perspective linking performance to outcomes.

Beyond the criteria mentioned above for defining a relevant labor market, some school districts use other options. Many target school districts select object school districts based on their flagship status within the state as a relevant labor market. Those exercising this option for a target school district view the appropriate labor market from a strictly competitive perspective relative to the object **flagship districts.**

Obvious from the above descriptions of a relevant labor market, any single factor or any combination of factors will define a unique external labor market for a particular target school district. As such, the results of a market analysis are specific to a defined labor market. For this reason, the choice of factors used to define a relevant labor market for a target school system is a policy decision rather than an administrative decision.

After a relevant labor market has been determined by a target school district from a policy perspective involving object school districts, the next step within the compensation process involves a market analysis. A market analysis involves comparing compensation rates of a target school district with compensation rates of object school districts. Following are issues and examples of a market analysis conducted for a particular target school district, reflecting actual data collected from the field setting.

Market Analysis

When conducting a market analysis of compensation data involving a target school district and a relevant labor market comprised of object school districts, several concerns surface. One concern pertains to the number of school districts that should be used to define a relevant labor market. As the size of the labor market increases, the more likely the labor market contains object school districts unrepresentative of the target school district. On the other hand, extremely small relevant labor markets are likely to be unrepresentative of the target school district because of skewed salary data typical of small numbers of object school districts.

More specifically, small labor markets may reflect only the extremes of assigned personnel. The market can contain either the most experienced or the least experienced personnel in their job assignments. As a result, compensation rates are distorted relative to a relevant labor market. To mediate these competing concerns, it is suggested that a relevant labor market contain at least ten object school districts. By including at least ten object school districts in the definition of a relevant labor market, an acceptable distribution of education and experience of position holders is more likely attainable.

Compensation information for those object school districts comprising a relevant labor market may be obtained in several ways, and these ways vary in terms of market sensitivity and in terms of employee acceptance. One method used to collect statistical data about compensation for a relevant labor market utilizes established databases. However, state databases usually report salaries only by specific budget categories (i.e., elementary principals) and are insensitive to the length of work year for employees comprising a budget category. That is, some elementary school principals may work 210 days while others may work 260 days, and many state databases are insensitive to such differences.

Because a valid market analysis of a relevant labor market must control for length of work year for all employees addressed in the survey, many times established databases fall short of providing this level of sensitivity for data collected. To collect data more accurate than provided by general databases maintained by states and associations, a salary survey must be conducted by the target school district. For each of the object school districts comprising a relevant labor market, salary data should be obtained by a target school district for all positions included in the study, each holder of such positions, and the length of their work year.

Within any relevant labor market, the match between all focal positions comprising the object school districts with those focal positions comprising the target school district is a major concern due to potential mismatches. To address this concern about potential mismatches between target and object school districts for focal positions, only select positions are used for a market analysis. These positions are labeled within the compensation literature as "**benchmark**" positions.

Benchmark positions are characterized as those focal jobs exhibiting little variability between the target school district and the object school districts. Typical of benchmark positions for certificated positions are those with line reporting relationships such as assistant principals, principals, and assistant superintendents. Classified positions varying little across public school districts within an appropriate labor market are supervisors for food service, transportation, and facilities/buildings and grounds.

Encompassed within the data collected from individual object school districts should be information about fringe benefits received by employees. Many fringe benefits have important implications for the market analysis. One of many very important fringe benefits to be considered in an assessment is retirement contributions as made by a board of education on the part of employees.

To illustrate the retirement effect on a salary analysis, most state retirement systems require an individual as well as an organizational contribution, and the individual's contribution can be as large as 9.3 percent (see Ohio State Teacher Retirement System, n.d.). If the employer pays the individual's contribution to the retirement system, then the reported annual salary for such individuals will underestimate their annual earnings. Thus, the salary survey must be sensitive to actual as well as earned salary to capture additional benefits awarded employees.

At minimum, this analysis should focus on the base rates of the positions under consideration, the contractual work year for each position, the qualifications of employees occupying these positions, and the amount of money spent for different types of collateral benefits. When information about base rates and the dollar value of collateral benefits is combined, an assessment of total compensation can be obtained.

This assessment provides information about a target school district's performance relative to a relevant labor market from an historical perspective at a particular point in time. To move a target school district from its current mode of operation to the desired mode of operation within the strategic planning context, a market alignment is needed in most instances. A market alignment involves adjusting current compensation practices from a proactive perspective to correct for past practices and to align with future expectations as dictated by a strategic plan of action.

Market Alignment

Depending on the outcome of the market assessment, a target school district may find that the compensation of specific positions is misaligned relative to the relevant labor market as defined by a policy group. Some particular focal positions may be found to be underpaid relative to market values, whereas other focal positions may be found to be overpaid relative to market values. These abnormalities occur with such frequency that they have been given specific labels within the compensation context.

Focal positions underpaid relative to an appropriate labor market are referred to as **"green circles."** Green circle positions identified from a market analysis reflect values being paid current employees of a target school district lower than the minimum salary received by those in the object school district. To eliminate green circle employees, the target school district should increase the compensation of said employees to the minimum rate as paid by target school districts for the like-type positions.

In contrast to green circle employees are **"red circle" employees.** Red circle employees are overpaid relative to the appropriate labor market in that their salary exceeds the value of the position as defined by a relevant labor market. Rather than reducing the pay of red circle employees in order to realign them with the relevant labor market, most public school districts freeze salaries of red circle employees until the cost of living changes exceed their current rate of compensation.

Reasons for green circles and red circles within the assessment process are varied. Green circle employees have been promoted generally from within a targeted school district. Employees promoted internally from within a targeted school district receive generally only minimum salary increases.

Red circle employees emerge often because of job reassignments that involve moving from a higher position to a lower position within the organizational hierarchy. In some instances, employees choose to step down for personal reasons, but retain their current salary. Different is the situation where employees are reassigned by the school district but are allowed to keep their current salary levels.

After corrective actions have been performed both for green circle and for red circle employees, the entire compensation system must be updated for the next school year. This update involves all focal positions included in the study after any realignment of specific positions (green circle and red circle) has been made on the part of a target school district. The focus of an update involves a market adjustment based on the economy at large and not on the appropriate labor market.

Market Adjustment

Unlike the market analysis and the market alignment as a means of assessing and of correcting the compensation structure of a public school district, a market adjustment is future orientated from a strategic planning perspective. A market adjustment is future oriented because it establishes compensation rates for the upcoming school year relative to a particular group of employees. That is, a market adjustment involves the formulation of a new salary schedule for governing the compensation practices of a target school district.

When making a market adjustment for an existing compensation system, a primary concern on the part of a target school district is to protect the purchasing power of employees within their respective economic environment. Underlying the general notion of purchasing power is that employees performing satisfactory in their assigned position should be able to maintain their current living status in light of economic changes in their environment. To so do, employees must receive compensation increases that align with economic changes in their environments.

Economic changes in the environment of employees within any particular target school are captured by a **cost-of-living adjustment (COLA).** In general, a COLA is an index reflecting changes in cost associated with goods and services relative to a geographical area as measured by the consumer price index (CPI) (see Table 8.16).

In contrast to the governmental index reflecting changes in cost associated with goods and services is a **standard of living index** specific to a particular school district. A standard of living index (SOLI) is unique to a particular target school district and can differ from a governmental COLA. As such, the SOLI reflects changes in cost for employees of a target school district and not the general geographical region.

To illustrate, cost for medical insurance may have increased by 10 percent within a specific geographical area. However, if a target school district has and continues to pay an employee's medical insurance, then this cost on the part of a public school district should be deducted from the overall COLA, and a SOLI should be used for establishing future compensation obligations on the part of a target school district. Failure to differentiate between COLA and SOLI on the part of target school districts is a common omission when making market adjustments. Consequently, the notion of total compensation is often inappropriately considered within the strategic planning context.

TABLE 8.16
Consumer Price Index Factors

The CPI represents all goods and services purchased for consumption by the reference population (U or W). BLS has classified all expenditure items into more than 200 categories, arranged into eight major groups. Major groups and examples of categories in each are as follows:

FOOD AND BEVERAGES (breakfast cereal, milk, coffee, chicken, wine, service meals and snacks)

HOUSING (rent of primary residence, owners' equivalent rent, fuel oil, bedroom furniture)

APPAREL (men's shirts and sweaters, women's dresses, jewelry)

TRANSPORTATION (new vehicles, airline fares, gasoline, motor vehicle insurance)

MEDICAL CARE (prescription drugs and medical supplies, physicians' services, eyeglasses and eye care, hospital services)

RECREATION (televisions, pets and pet products, sports equipment, admissions)

EDUCATION AND COMMUNICATION (college tuition, postage, telephone services, computer software and accessories)

OTHER GOODS AND SERVICES (tobacco and smoking products, haircuts and other personal services, funeral expenses) (http://www.bls.gov/cpi/home.htm)

The Total Compensation Perspective

The ideal compensation system will be sensitive to both external and internal factors influencing compensation (see Figure 8.2), eliminate compression between positions within the same pay level (see Table 8.9), establish rationality for superordinate–subordinate pairings both within and between compensation systems (see Table 8.12), address the elasticity associated with theoretical earning potentials across pay levels (see Table 8.14), be sensitive to external market parameters assessed with comparable districts (see Table 8.16), and reflect internal consistency among all positions. However, a perfect compensation system exists more in theory than in practice. In practice, the best compensation system that can be obtained by most school systems is a reasonable system.

A reasonable compensation system is derived from informed decisions based on different sources of information. Beyond the different data sources described in this chapter, a reasonable compensation system must be sensitive both to the fiscal constraints of the school district and to the perceptions of employees in the compensation system.

In most cases, the fiscal constraints of a school district are fixed assets. Regardless of the best intentions of those who develop and administer a compensation system, most school districts have fixed economic resources for a compensation system. Consequently, certain choices or compromises must be made when developing and administering a compensation system for a particular group of employees from a strategic planning perspective.

Perceptions of particular groups of employees about a compensation system vary on two dimensions: procedural and distributive. Procedural perceptions pertain to the methods used to establish the compensation system; distributive perceptions concern the actual economic incentives provided by the compensation system. Both types of perceptions influence the satisfaction of employees in the public school setting.

When considering all sources of data, a balance between system restraints and employee concerns requires certain compromises. For example, it might be determined that rationality can be established and maintained for employees within the same compensation structure (administrator-supervisor pairings) but not for employees in different compensation structures (administrator-teacher pairings). Likewise, it might be determined that internal consistency can be established and maintained among positions within the same compensation structure at the expense of external market sensitivity, as assessed with comparable school districts defining a relevant labor market.

Compromises based on informed decisions will yield a reasonable compensation system for a particular group of employees. Such a compensation system could involve direct costs associated with a fixed-rate salary schedule, with advancement governed by determined factors (education and experience); direct costs associated with a mixed-rate salary schedule, with advancement governed by determined and variable factors (job performance); or direct costs associated with a variable-rate salary schedule, with advancement governed by job performance alone. Depending on the type of salary schedule (fixed, mixed, or variable rate), the economic value of advancements reflected by a salary schedule must be established.

Indirect costs, involving the collateral benefits of a reasonable compensation system, can be either uniform or variable. Uniform benefit plans fail to consider the needs of specific employees but provide a larger return for a fixed dollar amount due to mass purchasing power. On the other hand, variable benefit plans consider the needs of specific employees while suffering from economy of scale.

Because direct and indirect costs interact to influence the total compensation cost of a compensation system, several different compensation models should be developed. These models should be used to conduct economic forecasts that should provide information about each model relative to total implementation costs and total projected costs in subsequent years. Based on the outcomes of the forecasts, a specific compensation system should be adopted.

The resulting compensation system will be less than perfect and should be viewed as a work in progress. In addition, a reasonable compensation system in one district will not necessarily be reasonable in another district. Consequently, the compensation system adopted by any school system should depend on the unique situation of that school system at a given point in time.

Compensation Control and Adjustment

A reasonable compensation system has a short life expectancy. Major components of a compensation system, such as those involving internal consistency, have a life expectancy of about 5 years. Other components, such as those involving base rates and collateral benefits, become dated with each budgetary cycle.

To maintain a reasonable compensation system requires continuous monitoring by those who develop and administer it and this is why compensation was defined as unfinished business earlier in this chapter. At minimum, monitoring involves realigning the compensation structure with the mission of the school district (see Figure 8.1), keeping abreast of external and internal factors impacting the compensation structure (see Figure 8.2), and assessing changes associated with the direct and indirect costs of a relevant labor market.

In assessing how well the actual operation of a reasonable compensation plan conforms to standards, goals, and audits, measures suggested earlier may be used as standards. The ultimate success of a reasonable compensation plan can be judged by the extent to which it attracts competent personnel, motivates them to cooperate voluntarily in achieving the goals of the system, maintains external and internal equity under existing legal constraints and collective bargaining agreements, and results in improved conditions for teaching and learning.

Because the ramifications of any reasonable compensation system are so extensive, checks are required to determine how well compensation plans are reinforcing other plans in contributing to organizational purposes. For example, compensation practices play a key role in determining long-range and operating plans for: (a) recruitment and selection of personnel, (b) appraisal and improvement of performance, (c) design of the organizational structure, and (d) budgeting of expenditures.

The first strategic point considered here is the recruitment and the selection of personnel before assigning them to positions. Every organization, regardless of the nature of its compensation system, should design a recruitment program and a selection plan to attract as well as to screen all applicants for system positions. With the help of position guides, qualifications of applicants can be checked against position requirements to determine how well they are fitted to perform the function and to estimate their potential for advancement. At this point, it should be determined whether the base salaries at each level of the compensation structure are adequate to attract qualified personnel. One test of adequacy is how closely compensation at each level conforms to the relevant labor market. The question to be asked is how much would it cost to replace a current employee with someone else who has the desired qualifications?

The second strategic point concerns performance appraisal after the individual has been assigned. Results of the appraisal, aside from yielding information necessary for making judgments about salary increases, should contribute to plans for the development of employees and for determining whether each employee should be retained in the position, transferred to another position, promoted, or dismissed. Here, the test of effectiveness of the compensation plan is whether it provides for systematic appraisal of personnel performance.

The third strategic point concerns the organizational structure. This area is constantly in need of review and, occasionally, revision. As positions are added, eliminated, or modified, these changes should be reflected in the organizational structure and ultimately in the compensation system and the employee's salary. The criterion for this test of the compensation structure is its congruency with the organizational structure. Clearly, a sound organizational structure is indispensable to both the integrity of the compensation plan and to the workability of the appraisal process.

The final point to be considered, control of expenditures for the compensation plan, is essential. One check on the compensation plan is information relating to its impact on the annual and long-term budgets, such as anticipated salary changes by adoption of the compensation plan, annual cost of the plan, and impact of the plan on the community's tax structure.

In a very real sense, then, controlling the compensation plan is as vital to its success as the design of the structure on which it rests. Information yielded by checking the foregoing points, as well as others not mentioned, can be collected, analyzed, and presented periodically to the board of education so that the final step in the control process—corrective action—can be taken to make certain that the goals of the plan are constantly being achieved.

Review and Preview

In this chapter, an examination of the compensation process and its relationship to the human resource function was discussed from a strategic planning perspective. Although satisfying the monetary needs of school system employees is not the only responsibility of the administration, absence of a sound compensation plan creates human problems that defy easy resolution.

Because the size of the employee's paycheck is related to the satisfaction of both economic and noneconomic needs, the process by which compensation in a school system is determined is crucial to the system's ability to implement an effective human resource plan.

The compensation process presented in this chapter contains various subprocesses, including developing compensation policies, negotiating with unions, establishing the position structure, determining the economic value of positions and position holders, making provisions in the compensation structure for administrative and support personnel, formalizing the compensation plan, and keeping the plan current.

A number of interrelated factors affect an employee's paycheck. These factors include compensation legislation, prevailing salaries, collective bargaining, supply and demand, ability to pay, standard and cost of living, and collateral considerations. Although all of these factors enter into compensation levels established in an organization, one factor or a combination of factors may be more important at a given time than others, depending on the circumstances.

Employment may be viewed as an exchange transaction between the individual and the organization in which each gets something in return for giving something. The employment exchanges between the individual and the system are perceived differently by both parties. One of the major problems in compensation planning is to reach agreements between parties by reconciling the nature of the input–output relationship.

In the next chapter we address certain benefits that enhance the earning power of educational employees. Some of the benefits are related to salaries, while others are independent of salary. Collectively, these benefits improve the continuity of the employment process.

Discussion Questions

1. Discuss the advantages and the disadvantages of the following aspects of pay structures within school systems: incentive rewards and flexible benefit plans.

2. Two criticisms of many educational compensation programs are that they are inequitable and that the salaries do not compare favorably with those of other school systems or other professions. Do these criticisms have any basis in fact?

3. Develop the elements of a pay structure that would provide the kinds of rewards that are important to you and would be acceptable to a public school district.

4. Is there any truth to the assertion that pay based on merit rating is only one of many kinds of incentive options? Do incentives have to be based on a performance appraisal rating?

5. How do unions influence pay practices, directly or indirectly, for those covered and those not covered by unions?

6. In what ways are the compensation practices of public school systems influenced by local, state, and federal governments?

7. Many salary plans include three methods of compensation: (a) automatic increases, (b) pay for performance, and (c) a combination of the above. What are the strengths and weaknesses of each method?

8. Do you agree that experience should be used as a measure of performance effectiveness?

Case Study

As a newly appointed human recourse administrator, you have inherited an administrative compensation system that has been problematic both to the board of education and to school administrators. What steps would you take to rectify this situation? Would you conduct an audit and what criteria would you use for assessing past practices? How would you go about realigning the current positions? Once aligned, what are the concerns with designating a relevant labor market? How would you sell your recommendations to the school board and to the school administrators?

References

California National Board Certified Teachers. (n.d.). Retrieved May 1, 2006, from Website: http://www.nbpts.org/about/stateinfo.cfm?state=California.

Consumer Price Index. (n.d.). Retrieved May 1, 2006, from Website: http://www.bls.gov/cpi/home.htm.

Cox, E. P. (2006). Pay performance contract provisions for school superintendents. *Journal of Scholarship and Practice, 2*(2), 31–38.

Crampton, S. M. (2003, Spring). ADA and disability accommodations. *Public Personnel Management,* 1–10.

Cunningham, W. G., & Cordeiro, P. A. (2006). *Educational leadership: A problem-based approach* (3rd. ed.). Columbus, OH: Pearson.

Currall, S. C., Towler, A. J., Judge, T. A., & Kohn, L. (2005). Pay satisfaction and organizational outcomes. *Personnel Psychology, 58,* 613–640.

Fair Labor and Standards Act. (n.d.). Retrieved May 1, 2006, from Website: http://www.dol.gov/esa/whd/flsa/.

Firestone, W. A. (1995). Redesigning teacher salary systems for educational reform. *American Educational Research Journal, 31*(3), 549–574.

Freedom of Information Act 1966. Retrieved May 1, 2006, from Website: http://www.usdoj.gov/04foia/.

Gerhart, B., & Milkovich, G. T. (1992). Employee compensation: Research and practice. *Handbook of Industrial and Organizational Psychology, 3*(2), 481–569.

Heneman, H. G. (1998). Assessment of the motivational reactions of teachers to a school-based performance award program. *Journal of Personnel Evaluation in Education, 12*(1), 43–59.

Kelley, C. (1997). Teacher compensation and organization. *Educational Evaluation and Policy Analysis, 19*(1), 15–28.

Kelley, C., Heneman, H. G., & Milanowski, A. (2002). Teacher motivation and school-based performance rewards. *Educational Administration Quarterly, 38*(5), 372–401.

Odden, A., & Kelley, C. (1997). *Paying teachers for what they know and do: New and smarter compensation strategies to improve schools.* Thousand Oaks, CA: Corwin Press.

Ohio State Teachers Retirement System. (n.d.). About STRS Ohio. Retrieved December 10, 2006, from Website: http://www.strsoh.org/.

Owings, W. A., & Kaplan, L. S. (2006). *American public school finance.* Belmont, CA: Thomson Wadsworth Corporation.

Privacy Act of 1974. (1974). Retrieved May 1, 2006, from Website: http://www.usdoj.gov/foia/privstat.htm.

Urbanski, A., & Erskine, R. (2000). School reform, turn, and teacher compensation. Retrieved May 1, 2006, from Website: http://www.pdkintl.org/kappan/kurb0001.htm.

Young, I. P. (2006). Establishing the economic worth of teachers: A superintendent's guide for advising school boards. *Journal of Scholarship and Practice*, 2(2), 39–45.

Young, I. P. (2003). The trouble with pay for performance. *American School Board Journal*, 11(1), 40–42.

Young, I. P., Delli, D. A., Miller-Smith, K. A., & Alhadeff, A. B. (2004). An evaluation of the relative efficiency for various relevant labor markets: An empirical approach for establishing teacher salaries. *Educational Administration Quarterly*, 40(3), 366–387.

Young, I. P., Jury, J. R., & Reis, S. B. (1997). Holmes versus traditional candidates: Labor market receptivity. *Journal of School Leadership*, 7(4), 330–344.

PART III

Employment Continuity, Development, Collective Bargaining, and Unionism

9 Employment Continuity

10 Development

11 Unionism and Collective Bargaining

Part III addresses the ongoing relationship between public school districts and the employees through focusing on employment continuity, development, unionism, and collective bargaining. The intent of Part III is to:

- Present an approach for designing, implementing, and assessing the content and process of employment continuity.
- Differentiate between statutory rights and employee privileges within the employment continuity process.
- Address development issues and processes necessary for maintaining an effective and an efficient public school district.
- Identify potential contaminates for assessing the effectiveness of a development process and provide different experiment designs used to assess development programs.
- Increase understanding of three aspects of the collective bargaining system in public education: (a) components of the collective bargaining process, (b) the contemporary collective bargaining issues, and (c) strategic school system opportunities inherent in the collective bargaining process and its managerial implications.
- Examine alternate dispute mechanisms for resolving impasses within the collective bargaining process and differentiate between rights and interest arbitration.

Employment Continuity

9

CHAPTER OVERVIEW

OBJECTIVES

- Portray the relevance of school system culture and system equilibrium to employment continuity and its strategic implications.
- Identify factors that affect employment continuity and discontinuity.

- Present an approach for designing the process and content of employment continuity.
- Stress the potential impact on employment continuity of turnover, absenteeism, tardiness, layoffs, and retirements.

School System Culture and Employment Continuity

From a strategic planning perspective, a major human resource function in the public school setting focuses on the employment **continuity process** for the workforce. Regardless of the size of a school district or the location of a school district (urban, suburban, or rural), the basic building block of all school districts is its employees. Without a capable as well as a committed workforce of employees, effectiveness and efficiency are impossible goals for any public school system (Bolman & Deal, 2003).

Public school employees are immersed in a work environment that has particular characteristics. Collectively these characteristics define loosely the culture of a particular school system (Hoy & Miskel, 2005). The culture of a school system is shaped by attitudes, routines, habitual ways of doing things, behavioral norms, rules of conduct, position requirements, and the network of social relationships within which people work (Sergiovanni, 2006).

Each of these contributors to the culture of a public school district can have either positive or negative impacts on employees when fulfilling their assigned job duties and organizational responsibilities (Sinden, Hoy, & Sweetland, 2004). As such, a major human resource goal from a strategic planning perspective is to maximize the positive impacts and to minimize the negative impacts associated with every aspect of work life. Without specific attention to culture, many of the previously discussed human resource goals will never be fully realized from a long-range perspective.

For example, in previous chapters, attention was devoted to placing the human resource function within the broader context of schooling from an organizational perspective (Chapter 1), assessing human resource allocations reflecting current practice (Chapter 2), and projecting future human resource needs for a desired outcome (Chapter 3). To meet these organizational contingencies necessary for moving a school district from the current mode of operation to a desired level of operation, special consideration was afforded to recruitment of potential applicants (Chapter 4), selection of new employees (Chapter 5), orientation of newly assigned individuals (Chapter 6), compensation of those employed (Chapter 7), and performance appraisal for the ongoing workforce (Chapter 8). On reflection, these later processes focused largely on acquiring and orientating individuals new to the profession or new to their job assignments rather than ensuring their employment continuity once employed and immersed within the organizational setting.

Within this chapter, the focus is on organizational provisions designed to retain personnel and to foster continuity in the services of all personnel. More specifically, in this chapter, processes and procedures for enhancing the work life of employees are addressed from a strategic planning perspective. Attention is afforded to processes and methods by

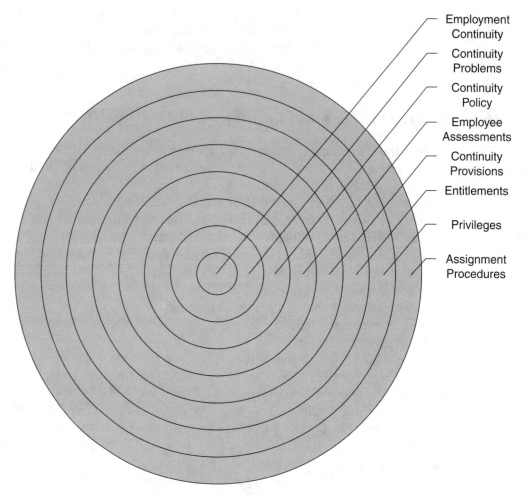

FIGURE 9.1   *Overview of the employment continuity process.*

which such plans can be designed, implemented, and administered that enhance the employment commitment of individuals at present as well as in the future with a public school district (see Figure 9.1).

Problems Associated with Employment Continuity

The importance of systematic planning relative to the continuity of school personnel cannot be overemphasized by public school districts. Even in school systems where the strategic planning concepts are subscribed to and implemented accordingly, things do not always run smoothly and according to plan. As a result of this organizational reality, a sustained effort must be made to keep any organization operating effectively on an ongoing basis.

Indeed, employees have a way of interfering with plans, violating rules, and behaving in other ways inimical to the interests of the organization and, in some instances, the interests of themselves. So long as individuals fill positions in organizations and are required to work with others in satisfying the goals of the organization, there will be interruptions in the workflow (Cunningham & Cordeiro, 2006). Examples of some of the more common problems encountered by public school districts that interrupt the work process include the following:

- Some employees will become physically ill.
- Some employees will become mentally ill.
- Some employees will become obsolescent.
- Some employees will be consistently tardy for work.
- Some employees will need to be absent from work.
- Some employees will have work-connected accidents.
- Some employees will be affected by the physical conditions of employment.
- Some employees will have home-related stresses.

Many of these problems encountered by school districts as complex organizations may stem from or be related to sources of employment insecurities either actual or perceived by the employee. Perceptions of threats about losing one's position, being reduced in status, or forfeiting one's job freedom have existed always in organizations. Real or perceived by employees, the toll of organizational insecurities is immense for the operation and administration of a public school district and has important implications for the human resource function in public school districts.

Because of these reoccurring conditions within the public school setting, a school system must address personnel problems as well as personnel issues from a humanistic viewpoint. Due to the fact that such problems and issues affect two of the district's strategic goals (stability of workforce and organizational goal achievement), the system needs healthy, productive employees continuously on the job who are physically and mentally able to contribute maximally to the work of the enterprise, and who maintain a favorable attitude toward their roles and the environment in which they function. Without such people, the probability of achieving the strategic goals of the system is almost nonexistent.

The nature and scope of provisions for maintaining continuity of personnel service is determined, at least in part, by the system through a strategic planning process. A school system determines, to some extent, what provisions should be made for enhancing continuity of service, what types of programs are needed, and how these programs will be organized and administered. The means by which such plans for continuing employment are designed and implemented fall within the human resource domain under the concept of employment continuity.

The Employment Continuity Process

Keeping the school system staffed continually with competent personnel involves consideration of and action on problems encountered by personnel in the conduct of their assigned duties and assimilation within the overall workforce. The employment continuity process by which the foregoing problems are dealt with varies from, but has much in common with, arrangements for making and carrying out other organizational decisions within the ongoing educational enterprise. In this case, it consists of making a series of decisions about continuity of service, including: (a) what the plans are expected to achieve, (b) what types of plans are needed to realize expectations, (c) who will be responsible for each phase of the program, (d) what the specifics are of each type of program, and (e) how the results of the process will be determined.

Expectations or results that the system intends to achieve from plans for service continuity are both short and long range and include the following:

- Improve the ability of the system to perform
- Enhance the system's work environment
- Prevent and control occupational stress
- Manage personnel costs
- Provide position security for personnel
- Control avoidable absenteeism and tardiness
- Protect the income flow for short-term absentness
- Reduce personnel turnover
- Facilitate change within the system
- Improve individual and system effectiveness
- Prevent accidents
- Maintain position and system performance standards
- Comply with statutory requirements
- Afford opportunities for self-development and renewal
- Establish program limits

Once the goals for maintaining continuity of personnel service have been set forth, implementation by school officials follows. Early in the planning stages, at least two actions are necessary. One of these actions is the preparation of a series of policy statements to guide public school districts in designing and implementing specific programs.

The other action involves a set of specific plans needed to carry out the intent of the policy. This action includes the manner in which personnel continuity programs will be organized and will be administered, as well as the controls essential to the resolution of personnel problems. An example of these intentions for the Sturgis Public School system is illustrated in Table 9.1 by a formal policy adopted by a particular board of education.

The employment continuity policy presented in Figure 9.1 illustrates an approach to reducing undesirable outcomes throughout the continuity process. This policy's intent is to: (a) exercise continuous direction while guiding action and maintaining control over

TABLE 9.1
Employment Continuity Policy

It is the policy of the Sturgis Public School System to

> Provide continuity of personnel employment insofar as this is economically feasible
>
> Control reduction in force on the basis of performance, ability, and length of service
>
> Grant leaves of absence for acceptable reasons
>
> Provide assistance to staff members in maintaining physical and mental health
>
> Strive for an efficient work environment reflective of excellent working conditions
>
> Take proactive measures to prevent work-related accidents
>
> Encourage reassignments to benefit the system and employees
>
> Protect employees against unfair separation from the system
>
> Assist personnel in all areas of career development

the planning and implementation of the process, (b) influence action and conduct of system members regarding employment continuity, and (c) serve as a guiding principle for the growth of the workforce and its organizational entity. The supporting recommendations are provided to interpret and to translate the Sturgis Public School system's continuity policy into more specific operational plans and procedures for implementation in the field setting.

Assessment of Employee Perceptions

A pivotal component underlying the employee continuity process is the perception of individuals about the organization and their jobs (Enomoto & Gardiner, 2006). Strategic planning, as related to the human resource function within the public school setting, must consider these perceptions from a baseline perspective relative to the continuity process. Perceptions of employees may be shaped by labor-management relations, organizational climate, leader behaviors, and job satisfaction facets.

For some school districts, a major concern for the employee continuity process is labor-management relationships. Poor labor-management relationships create a dichotomy for employees. That is, a "we-them" division of commitment emerges, and this emergence fails to reinforce a strong level of organizational commitment and dampens the employment continuity process within the public school setting.

Within many school districts, certain aspects of the human resource planning process pertaining to organizational continuity issues may be embedded within the existing labor contract as a result of prior negotiations. Issues within the existing labor contract that may have been, at one time, under the complete control of management in the design and execution of human resource plans have been restricted by contract language. Information about these restrictions must be considered by the school district when formulating strategic plans that either directly or indirectly impacts the contract contents related to organizational continuity.

TABLE 9.2
Dimensions for Likert's Profile of a School

Profile of a School	
▪ Leadership Processes	▪ Motivational Forces
▪ Communication	▪ Interaction-Influence
▪ Decision Making	▪ Goal Setting
▪ Control Process	▪ Performance Goals

Less tangible than labor contract language are the perceptions of employees as an informational source within the human resource planning process. Employees form perceptions about the organizational climate, leadership behaviors of immediate supervisors, and components of the job. Knowledge of the perceptions is often either taken as a given or overlooked at the expense of the school district when considering continuity as part of the strategic planning process.

To assess these types of reactions harbored by employees impacting the continuity process, formal assessment should be made on an ongoing basis. Information about the internal environment can be assessed through a number of commercial instruments. These instruments vary relative to the focal point of orientation, and the type of employee perceptions assessed.

For assessing the climate of the work environment Sergiovanni (2006) provides information about the Profile of a School (POS) developed by Likert. This instrument purports to measure the climate of a school from eight different dimensions (see Table 9.2).

Similar types of instruments exist for assessing perceptions of employees about school district leadership. One of the popular instruments available to school districts for assessing leadership of all types of immediate supervisors is the Leader Behavior Description Questionnaire (n.d.). Results from the LBDQ provide measures of consideration and initiating structure as perceived by followers.

Leadership characteristics associated with consideration are concerned with the personal interactions between superiors and subordinates, while leadership characteristics associated with initiating structure pertain to an immediate supervisor's organization of the work environment for executing functional directives. Purportedly, these dimensions of leadership are independent with a leader being either high or low on one dimension and being either high or low on the other dimension. From an employment continuity perspective, educators seem to prefer those immediate supervisors that exhibit high scores on both dimensions of leadership.

Reactions of employees toward their jobs and their job environment can be assessed via job satisfaction instruments. Two commercial instruments used to assess the reactions of educators within the public school setting are the Job Descriptive Index (n.d.) and the Minnesota Satisfaction Questionnaire (n.d.). Both instruments provide data that can be compared to national norms.

Incorporating the perceptions of employees about climate, leadership behaviors, and job satisfaction, strategic plans relating to the human resource function must consider anticipated changes within the internal environment (Owings & Kaplan, 2006). A demographic analysis of the current workforce can reveal pending retirements and future growth areas. Current labor market conditions concerning shortages (National Teacher Recruitment Clearinghouse, n.d.) and changes in types of applicants seeking positions within public school districts (U.S. Department of Education, n.d.) make this type of information necessary for effective and efficient human resource planning relative to the continuity of employees once hired.

Due to the specifics associated with any particular school district, a fixed set of answers fails to exist for the type of internal information that is needed in this stage of the planning process. What does exist for any particular school district are some general questions that can be used to guide the collection of internal information at the local school district level. A list of these questions follows:

- Which organizational characteristics promote or impede the system's ability to increase its responsiveness to current and future demands (policies, programs, processes, procedures, practices, rules, and regulations)?
- What is the quality of leadership within the district as perceived by the system's individuals and groups?
- Is the system's division of labor efficiently structured?
- How satisfactory is the current approach for reward structures within the district?
- Does the present leadership of the school district promote change and innovation?
- What are the strengths and weaknesses in each functional area of the school district (programs, logistics, planning, human resources, and external relations)?
- Are the system's values, expectations, and attitudes being communicated effectively to the membership?
- How effective are the system's efforts to bring about an understanding and appreciation of the values, norms, expected behaviors, abilities, and social knowledge needed to carry out position and performance standards, career development, and interpersonal relationships?

Other than the perceptual concerns of employees impacting the continuity process are certain provisional aspects associated with employment. These later concerns involve entitlements and privileges either guaranteed or granted public school employees as a means of reinforcing the employment continuity process. Collectively, entitlements and privileges fall under the general rubric of employment continuity provisions.

Employment Continuity Provisions

Unlike most private sector employees, all public school employees enjoy a number of provisions that promote employee continuity. Provisions promoting employment continuity for public school employees involve certain levels of job security and rewards for continuous public service in the public school setting. In some instances, the provisions

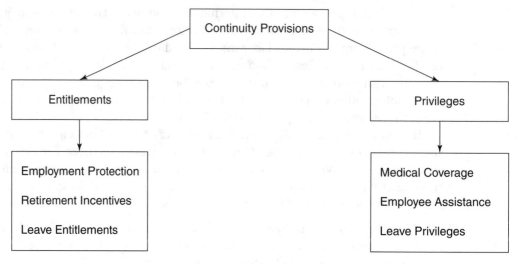

FIGURE 9.2   *Employment continuity provisions.*

are entitlements, while in other instances these provisions are privileges (see Figure 9.2).

Entitlements and privileges differ in several important ways. Most notably, entitlements are guaranteed by either federal or state legislation, whereas privileges are granted by local school districts. However, benefits associated with entitlements and privileges vary in degree across states as well as between/within school districts as to the amount of discretionary prerogative exercised by the school system in the actual administration of the employment continuity provisions.

Entitlements

To enhance the continuity of the employment experience for public school employees, certain legislative acts have been passed by state governments. The intent of these legislative acts is to supplement the employment benefits granted by individual school systems and to provide public employees with a basic level of job security. In most instances, these legislative acts provide employees with a minimum foundation relative to a specified benefit, but allow considerable discretion on the part of school boards in the implementation and administration of said benefit.

Some of these acts are designed to provide public school employees with a certain level of employment protection when fulfilling their assigned duties in a satisfactory manner. Others are designed either to provide employees with rewards for the service rendered to a public school district or to protect the income of employees while working in a public school district. Common examples for each type of employee continuity incentive are discussed for public school employees.

Employment Protection Entitlements

In the broadest sense, employment protection embodies a system designed to provide educators with continuing employment during efficient service and establishes an orderly procedure to be followed for withdrawing this protection. Employment protection clauses have been enacted for teachers and for civil servant employees through specific legislation. For other employee groups, employment protection clauses may be established through written policies adopted by the board of education, labor contracts ratified by the board of education, or inferred through the administrative practices exercised by the board of education.

Salient features of employment protection provisions include the following:

■ Completion of a specified probationary period, construed to mean a temporary appointment during which time the individual is carefully supervised and appraised in terms of ability to render efficient service to the school organization.

■ An orderly procedure for dismissal of personnel. This includes a provision for notifying the individual that services rendered are unsatisfactory, as well as a reasonable opportunity to show improvement before notification of intent to dismiss is given.

■ Notification of the intent to terminate the services of the individual in the event that desired improvement in performance has not been attained. Accompanying this notification is a written notice of the intent to dismiss that details specific reasons for the contemplated action.

■ A hearing before local school authorities that provides an opportunity for the affected staff member to defend them self against the charges.

The implications for employment protection clauses are not always understood by some professionals or by many laypersons. Perhaps this misunderstanding has given rise to the relatively high incidence of litigation on the part of involved parties. In general, employment protection, as defined by legislations, written policies, labor contracts, or administrative practices, is a process rather than an absolute right granted to an employee.

As a process, employees have no inherent right to permanent employment merely because of complying with formal requirements or serving a probationary period during which satisfactory service has been rendered in the eyes of the employer. Employment protection clauses require certain actions on the part of the employer rather than an inert right of the employee to the job. Such actions or requirements on the part of the employer should not be interpreted to mean that the local board of education has no authority to make changes affecting persons who have gained employment protection.

Indeed, the phrase "permanent employment" or a "continuing employment contract" can be misleading and is frequently the cause of many misinterpretations of tenure legislation. If the board decides to reduce the size of the staff because of declining enrollments, then existence of employment protection legislation does not prevent the board from taking such action.

It is generally not the intent of employment security provisions to prevent boards of education from making necessary changes involving personnel. Permanent employment does not mean an absolute absence of change in conditions of employment. If this were so, administrators would be powerless to cope with the day-to-day personnel problems with which they are confronted when trying to manage the public school district.

Worth noting is the differentiation between employment status and job assignment for employees. These terms are not synonymous within the human resource domain as the terms relate to employment security. Employment security clauses address the former but not the latter, and the school board retains the right to reassign personnel at will unless restricted by other sources such as school board policy or labor contract language that forbids such actions on the part of the school board.

Rationale for establishing employment security provisions is multifaceted. Among the more common reasons for employment security clauses are those listed here:

- Security of employment during satisfactory service
- Protection of personnel against unwarranted dismissal
- Academic freedom in the classroom
- Permanent employment for the best-qualified personnel
- Staff stability and position satisfaction
- Liberty to encourage student freedom of inquiry and expression

Legislative activity relating to employment security is defended generally on the basis of social benefit. The state seeks to improve the school system through the instrumentality of employment security, which is designed in part to protect the public and pupils from incompetent employees. Employment security legislation is not intended to establish an occupational haven for the unqualified or unsatisfactory employee.

Much attention has been given to the validity of employment security clauses, especially as these clauses relate to tenure for teachers. Even though many oppose the concept of tenure, all states have some form of tenure legislation for teachers (Valente & Valente, 2005). Although there is widespread discontentment with tenure systems, part of the dissatisfaction arises from the assumption that tenure protects incompetents.

The existence of incompetents in any organization, however, cannot be blamed totally on legislative provisions designed to protect the position security of teachers as well as to protect the school system. Evidence indicates that inaction of school boards and administrators in dismissal and supervisory efforts deserves substantial blame. Tenure systems do not prevent school systems from designing effective appraisal and personnel development processes and do not prevent the administration from taking action against incompetents.

Unions, courts, state governments, and school systems have gone to considerable lengths to provide for personnel security, which is one of the basic psychological needs of employees from a continuity perspective. Tenure for educators, protection under civil service regulations for many classes of noncertified personnel, contracts with seniority provisions, due process, and grievance systems are illustrative of these efforts. Complete security for any individual, however, is an illusion rather than a reality when proper administrative procedures/processes are followed by a public school district.

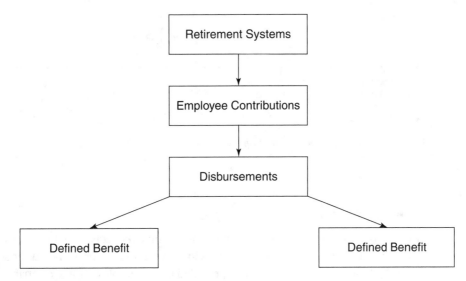

FIGURE 9.3   *Components of retirement systems.*

Retirement Incentive Entitlements

Like employment protection clauses, retirement incentives are another form of entitlement awarded public sector employees by state legislation. With respect to retirement incentives, it is not unusual for states to have three different public employee retirement systems to cover separate groups of personnel employed by public school districts, and these plans share many common aspects (see Figure 9.3). By far, the largest of the retirement systems is the state teacher retirement system (STRS), followed in size by the state employee retirement system (SERS) for noncertified employees, and by the public employee retirement system (PERS) for administrative personnel, respectively.

Functionally, these systems are managed by an independent board that oversees the investments of contributions. Monies from these investment activities fund current retirement amounts received by former employees. To put in perspective this obligation for all states, it is informative to note that the state public employee investment fund in California is the single largest coffer of investment funds in the world.

Although salaries and wages received by educational employees tend to be less than the salaries and wages received by their counterparts in the private sector, the same is not necessarily true for retirement incentives. Public school employees tend to enjoy a retirement system far superior to the retirement systems of most employees within the private sector. Retirement systems falling under entitlement clauses for public school districts can be classified several different ways: (1) employee contributions and (2) disbursement methods (see Figure 9.3).

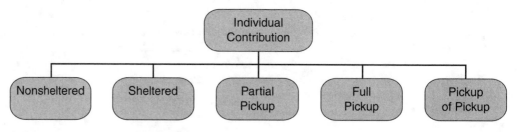

FIGURE 9.4   *Methods of employee contribution.*

Employee Contributions

All state retirement systems for public school employees rely, at a minimum, on two types of contribution. One contribution is provided by the employer or the public school district. The other source of contribution is provided by the employee. The contribution is always a fixed percentage of an employee's annual salary, but this percentage may vary between the employer's contribution and the employee's contribution.

Important to note is that an employee's annual salary has been defined in different ways across states. In some instances, an employee's salary is restricted to only the base amount as found on the salary schedule. Other state retirement systems use a gross salary that includes the base amount as well as any supplemental income received by the employee during the work year (i.e., extended contract, extracurricular assignments, etc.).

Regardless of the way an annual salary is determined across states, all state retirement systems require an individual contribution. Obligations of the individual as an employee can vary in several meaningful ways with each having a different financial implication. Contained in Figure 9.4 are the various methods for an employee's contribution to a state's retirement system.

To illustrate these different methods of contribution for an employee when fulfilling an individual's contribution to a state retirement system, a very simplistic example is provided. Within this example, it is assumed that an employee earns only $100.00 a year and has a 10 percent contribution obligation to a state's retirement system ($10.00). Within the nonsheltered situation (see Figure 9.4), the employee would pay federal and state taxes on the total gross salary of $100.00 and contribute 10 percent ($10.00) of the $100.00 to the retirement system. At the time of retirement, the employee's contributions would be tax free for the retirement funds received.

For the sheltered system of contribution for an employee (see Figure 9.4), the employee would deduct the contribution (10 percent) from the gross salary ($100.00) before paying federal and state taxes. After the deduction, the employee would pay federal and state taxes on $90.00 rather than $100.00. On retirement, all the employee's contributions are taxable at current rates.

Within the **partial pickup** situation (see Figure 9.4), the school district would pay a portion of the employee's contribution (e.g., 1–10 percent) to the state retirement system. The remaining proportion of the 10 percent obligation not paid by the board of education rests with the employee. Although the employer's contribution is sheltered from federal and state taxes, the employee's remaining obligation could be either sheltered or nonsheltered.

A full **pickup** (see Figure 9.4) of an employee's contribution means that the employer pays the total 10 percent of the individual's contribution to the state retirement system on behalf of the employee. This contribution is fully sheltered and benefits received by the employee at retirement are taxable at current levels. Thus, the employee receives $100.00 in annual salary and has an additional $10.00 (10 percent) paid to the retirement system by the employer on behalf of the employee.

Considering that this hypothetical employee made only $100.00 dollars a year throughout the career, the final average salary for retirement would be based on $100.00. However, the employee's actual living wage assumed an annual income of $110.00 because the district was making the 10 percent contribution for the employee. To capitalize on the district's contribution of 10 percent in retirement, the employee would need to have an additional 10 percent of the $10.00 contribution figured into retirement. This process is labeled as a **"pickup of the pickup"** (see Figure 9.4). That is, the employee retires on a living wage of $110.00 rather than an actual wage of $100.00 by having an additional 10 percent of the 10 percent ($1.00) contributed by the employer.

Many school districts use the managerial technique of a pickup as a means to control salary levels. By using the pickup process to pay either part or all of the employee's obligation within the retirement system, the employee's net income is increased because of the reduced liability for that payment. Although overall cost to the school system is increased proportionate to the pickup provision, this type of cost is less visible to the public than changes in cost associated with increasing dollar amounts within the salary schedule.

In addition to the different methods of contribution (see Figure 9.4) for public school employees to retirement systems, alternate methods of disbursement exist for receiving contributions. These methods are independent of the means for contributions on behalf of employees. As such, a discussion is provided for each method of disbursement.

Disbursements Methods

State retirement systems can be defined broadly according to a specific system of distribution for retirement funds. One system is labeled as a **defined benefit** system. The other system is a **defined contribution.**

Most of the state retirement systems are defined benefit systems. Characteristic of the defined benefit retirement system is a constant payout. This payout can be tempered in several ways that alter the amount received.

One way is that it can be paid only to the employee for life, and this method has the highest yield. For a lesser yield, the payout can cover both the employee and the employee's spouse for life. For the later system of payout, an actuarial table is used that considers the life expectancy of the younger party, and payments are adjusted accordingly.

Within the defined benefit system, postretirement income is calculated on the basis of an employee's highest earnings, number of years of contribution, and chronological age of the employee at the time of retirement. Highest earnings have been defined, for the purpose of retirement systems, several different ways. In some states, the highest earnings are based on the last 3 to 5 years, whereas in other states the earnings are calculated on the average of the highest 3 to 5 years.

Another factor that influences the actual payout under a defined benefit system is years of service contributed to the retirement system. To encourage continuity of employment, many states provide employees an opportunity to purchase additional years of service. Purchase clauses, when found in state legislation, can be of two types, and these types are not necessarily independent: (1) "buyback" and/or (2) "buy in."

A buyback clause allows initial contributions previously withdrawn by an employee to be reinstated. For example, some individuals may have worked within the system early in their careers, left the retirement system to pursue other interests (parenting or other vocations), and withdrew their retirement funds. Through a buyback clause, these contributions can be reinstated and used to calculate postretirement income.

In contrast to the buyback provisions is the buy-in option that frequently caps the amount of service eligible for purchase. With the buy-in option, employees may purchase creditable time served with other organizations. Most common examples of allowable purchase are years of contribution in other state retirement systems, service in accredited private schools within the state, and military service.

Beyond the amount of contribution and the number of years for creditable service, the final factor considered by most state retirement systems is the chronological age of the employee. For example, some states allow employees to draw retirement funds as early as 55 years of age (i.e., Wisconsin), whereas other states defer eligibility until an employee reaches at least 62 years of age (i.e., Ohio). Recently, some compensatory models have been used to combine the number of years of service with the chronological age of the employee. Within most states, penalties are incorporated within the calculations for employees meeting minimum qualifications but failing to satisfy maximum qualifications.

To protect the buying power of a retiree, defined benefit systems have a cost-of-living provision. A cost-of-living provision adjusts upward an individual's retirement income to offset inflation.

In contrast to the defined benefit retirement system is the defined contribution retirement system found in some states and offered as an option. "Defined contribution plans require specific contributions by an employer, but the final benefit received by employees is unknown; it depends on the investment success of those charged with administering the pension fund" (Milkovich & Newman, 1996, p. 461). Reasons for the emergence of defined contribution plans in education are twofold.

According to some sources (i.e., National Conference on Public Employee Retirement Systems, 2006) public employees during the 1980s and 1990s witnessed many of their counterparts in the private sector reaping major gains in their retirement portfolios through market increases in stock investments. During these periods, double-digit increases within the same year were not unusual for investments. As a result of their observations, public sector employees campaigned for more discretion in the management of their retirement investments than afforded by a defined benefit plan.

Another problem associated with the defined benefit retirement systems is the lack of portability afforded employees in their professional life. Although employees can change jobs and job locations within the same state, different states have separate plans, and reciprocity among defined benefit plans is either nonexistent or extremely limited between states. To off-set these problems and to quench the investment thirst of public sector employees, many states have initiated defined contribution plans for public school employees.

Today, employees new to a public school district have a choice in many states for deciding which type of retirement system to select. If the employee selects the defined contribution, then the employer contributes a fixed amount to a particular source. The most frequently used source for defined contributions in the public school setting is the Teachers Insurance and Annuity Association (n.d.); however, these sources are constantly expanding to include other investment groups.

Most of the sources of investment used for defined contribution plans provide the employees with investment options. With many employees loosing considerable amounts of their retirement due to a drop in specific stock market investments during recent years, it will be interesting to see how durable the defined contribution plans will be. No longer are these types of plans viewed with the same level of confidence as they were only a few years ago.

Complementing either defined benefit retirement funds or defined contribution plans for some employees in the public sector is the Social Security Act established by the federal government (U.S. Social Security Administration, n.d.). Social Security is a defined benefit plan administered by the federal government and has four types of payments for participants: payments for old age, payments for dependents of workers with disabilities, payments for surviving family members, and payments for lump-sum death payments.

However, the Social Security Act is not universal across states with respect to public school employees. Some states have opted not to participate in social security, and educators in these states have their earnings exempted from the social security tax. In those states where educators fail to contribute to social security (see Ohio and Kentucky, for example), the organizational and individual contributions for defined benefit plans, as well as the organizational contribution for defined contribution plans, are higher in exempted states than in those states where educators participate in social security.

Leave Incentive Entitlements

To enhance the employment continuity of public school employees, certain types of leaves have been developed by state and federal governments. These leaves can be classified as either income protection or job security provisions. Some of these leave provisions pay employees for time not worked, whereas others protect the job security of the employee during time away from the job.

Most states have legislated sick leave provisions for public school employees. Sick leave provisions were designed initially to be an income protection for the employees when they miss work. That is, sick leave was designed initially to protect the income flow of employees from any disruption in the work schedule due to a temporary illness.

Within the public sector, a minimum number of sick leave days are granted to each employee by the state, and these days are administered by the local school district. Actual number of sick leave days granted by the state follows a basic accrual system whereby public school employees earn a specified number of sick days for each month worked. These earned days of sick leave accrue, and unused sick days are carried over into subsequent school years.

Because sick leave days accrue and are carried over, some school districts in conjunction with labor unions have developed a **sick leave bank** for employees (i.e., Westfield Classroom Teachers Association, n.d.). Individuals "deposit" some of their unused sick leave days in a so-called bank. Other employees that lack adequate accumulation of sick leave to cover their illnesses can borrow sick leave days, which must be repaid from sick leave earned in subsequent months or years.

Although the basic purposes for which sick leave may be used are addressed in some state laws, school systems have great latitude in the administration of the sick leave program. School districts can expand the permissible scope for sick leave usage and can develop administrative processes for managing the sick leave program.

To aid in the administration of sick leave programs, some school districts have elected to pay employees for unused sick leave at the end of their career with a public school district. This practice of paying for unused sick leave changes the very purpose of sick leave provisions from an income protection procedure to an income generation procedure. Still other school districts have paid the medical insurance of retired employees by using funds from the purchase of unused sick leave.

However, not all leave entitlements awarded employees compensate individuals for time away from the job. Some types of leaves offer protection for employment but not protection for income. An example of such a leave provision enjoyed by public school employees that protects the job rather than the income is the Family and Medical Leave Act (FMLA).

The Family and Medical Leave Act (U.S. Department of Labor, n.d.), passed in 1993 by the federal government, permits public school employees to take unpaid leaves of absence. These leaves, as ensured by the Family and Medical Leave Act, can be used for certain personal and family reasons: (a) birth of a child, (b) adoption or foster care, (c) serious health problem of a family member, and (d) serious personal health problem. FMLA leaves can be taken for up to 12 weeks per calendar year for qualified employees.

Privileges

Previous sections of this chapter addressed entitlements granted by state and federal governments to enhance the employment continuity of public school employees. Within this section some of the more important privileges that most public school districts use to complement the entitlements extended to employees are explored. These benefits are privileges in the sense that employees lack any statutory rights relative to the benefits discussed in the following sections of this chapter.

Medical Coverage

One of the most important benefits offered to public school employees within the employment continuity process by a local school district is medical coverage. In fact, for many of the lower paid positions in the school system, medical coverage is just as important as salary for attracting and retaining employees. This coverage is especially important for bus drivers and for food-service workers as well as single-wage earners in any job category.

When placing this type of coverage in perspective, in the past, medical coverage was viewed almost as an entitlement rather than as a privilege because most public school districts provided employees with full coverage with no out-of-pocket expenses as a routine way of doing business. Little differentiation was made during this time period between employee coverage for the individual and family coverage for the employee. However more recently, the cost for health care coverage has become one of the most expensive benefits provided to employees of public school districts.

To control these costs associated with medical coverage for public school employees, several steps are taken on the part of human resources. Initially, employees were requested to pay only a deductible each calendar year. Deductibles were fixed costs incurred by the user of the service and paid in full by the employee before the insurance company contributed funds to the provider of health care services.

With medical costs continuing to increase, school boards began to require employees to pay a percentage of their medical premium. Although the family coverage was more expensive than the single coverage, the employee's percentage was usually a fixed dollar amount, regardless of the type of coverage opted for by the employee (individual or family). Recently, however, most school districts changed the way that medical benefits were managed in an effort to reduce the increasing costs associated with this privilege.

School districts adopted many different types of management plans in an effort to control medical costs for employees. Some of the more common plans in existence then and today are the health maintenance organizations (HMOs), the point of service plan (POS), and the preferred provider organization (PPO). Each of these plans has some unique characteristics as well as some common characteristics.

All these plans are very similar and share some common characteristics. One characteristic is that these plans restrict, to varying degrees, the employee's choice of medical providers, and limit the choice of providers to only those preapproved medical professionals. Another common characteristic is that these types of plans require, generally, that the employee pay a co-payment with each visit to the medical provider.

Although employees continue in most school districts to pay a proportion of the insurance cost and to pay a co-payment for each visit to the provider, medical insurance is still an important factor for recruiting and retaining public school employees. In fact, because healthy employees are necessary for the school to operate in an efficient and effective mode, public school districts have become even more proactive in this area. Rather than operating from a reactive position of helping ill employees seek and pay for treatment, school districts operate now in a proactive mode by helping to prevent illness on the part of employees though implementation of employee assistance programs.

Employee Assistance Programs

Knowledge concerning the prevention of certain kinds of health problems affecting employees in their performance of assigned duties and organizational responsibilities has emerged from within the health care industry. In response to this knowledge about prevention, many school districts have taken steps to develop employee assistance programs (Cunningham & Cordeiro, 2006). Underlying the need for such support systems are data indicating more employees than ever before are showing signs of performance dysfunction within the work setting.

Sources of deterioration in work performance stem from both internal and external environmental factors such as changes in work load or work relationships, perceived discrimination, marital adjustment, stressful superordinate–subordinate conditions, and various forms of substance abuse. Organizational consequences resulting from these conditions are numerous and far-reaching both for the school district and for the employee.

Consequences of dysfunction on the part of an employee within the work setting can be exhibited in several ways including personal disorganization, absenteeism, tardiness, increased costs for health insurance, grievance filing, litigation, and, most importantly, erosion of the relationship of the school system to personal well-being. Due to these outcomes, at least three reasons exist for developing effective employee assistance programs: (a) humanitarian considerations that are basic to assisting members in dealing with problems affecting performance, (b) cost-containment-associated remedial actions, and (c) maintenance of performance continuity and strengthening the link between individual and system effectiveness.

With the cost of health insurance premiums rising annually, controlling health-related expenditures has become a key factor for managing the human resource function in the public school setting. Management of the human resource function in public schools involves focusing on reducing insurance claims while increasing the system's ability to develop a viable support system for its members. Regardless of system size, common behavior problems of various kinds are inevitable for employees of a public school system and warrant carefully designed plans to meet the objectives of the human resource function.

Employee assistance programs within the public school setting should include these options: (a) wellness programs, which stress preventive health maintenance; (b) programs focusing on personnel behavior problems that stem from work assignments or work relationships; (c) programs designed to treat personal problems that affect member performance; and (d) any combination of these options. The kinds of and extent of programs offered by a public school district depend on a variety of factors, including program objectives, system size and resources, problem prevalence, and organizational recognition of the existence of a problem and commitment to its resolution. In general, there is a positive relationship between system size and program breadth: the larger the system, the more extensive the number of and types of program services provided.

To design, implement, and monitor an employee assistance program properly, certain issues must be addressed. These issues are brought into focus through questions such as:

■ To what extent have personnel problems been identified that warrant initiation of an employee assistance program (e.g., absenteeism, tardiness, gambling, stressful work-related conditions, personal problems affecting individual performance, and substance abuse)?

■ Of the four options regarding employee assistance programs described previously, which is most suitable as a planning strategy? This issue involves enlisting employee participation in decisions concerning courses of action designed to maintain their well-being as well as that of the system.

Some of the factors considered important to the success of health-related programs include:

■ *Policy:* A policy statement forms the bedrock on which to establish both wellness and assistance programs. Policy is intended to make clear program objectives; board of education commitment; the scope, type, and extent of assistance eligibility (e.g., salaried, hourly, or contingent personnel); and internal and/or external provisions for referral, counseling, and treatment stipulations.

■ *Procedures:* Programs that center on dysfunctional behavior require established procedures. These include such steps as problem identification, referral (by system or by self), diagnosis, intervention, and follow-up.

■ *Sponsorship:* The costs of assistance programs remain a disturbing issue; the extent to which expenses should be borne by the employer, by the union, by the individual, or by a combination of these stakeholders must be determined. Because expenditures for all forms of benefits are reaching new heights, and because more personnel seek or are urged to seek various forms of treatment, cost considerations enter into policy and program decisions. System trends in health maintenance costs and forecasts of health risks are among the types of information that should become part of the system's personnel database.

■ *Education:* Educating all supervisory personnel about procedures for dealing with both wellness and assistance programs is deemed an integral component of program implementation. Program objectives, procedures, confidentiality of information, and forms of treatment and care are examples of program elements about which personnel need to be informed and educated.

■ *Flexibility:* Due to the size range of school systems in the United States, both wellness and assistance programs must be modeled to fit the experiences, conditions, trends, and needs of each system and to the individuals within the system. Need identification is diagnosed through such sources as insurance claims, medical records, surveys, performance appraisal information, and budgetary indicators.

In sum, examination of the contemporary social scene, changing member expectations, and stressful conditions in both internal and external environments leads to the realization that wellness and assistance programs are no longer only theoretical issues. The school system's concern in this regard is how to position the organization and the human resource function so that whatever health maintenance strategies are adopted, they will result in closing performance gaps at individual, group, and organizational levels.

Employee Conveniences

It is an organizational reality that all employees need some time away from their job. This statement is especially true for those employees that work a full work year. To provide for breaks in employment, employees working 12 months receive vacation.

Vacation

Although all school districts award **vacation** for employees working a full calendar year, this means of an employee convenience is often misunderstood and poorly defined by human resource policy/labor contracts. Overlooked is that vacation can be operationalized from several different perspectives when viewed as an employee convenience mechanism for promoting continuity of employment. Contained in Figure 9.5 is a diagram of different concerns that should be resolved and defined from an operational perspective by school board policy and/or encapsulated within a labor contract.

As can be observed in Figure 9.5, a major issue to be resolved initially is the basic purpose of vacation. At least two competing definitions of vacation exist, and these definitions set the tone as well as the direction for other aspects as reflected in Figure 9.5; that is, vacation can be defined either as a refresher or as a deferred economic benefit.

When defined as a refresher, the purpose of vacation is to provide employees a break in their work activities for an extended period of time. Functionally from a refresher perspective, vacation is defined as a period of rest between periods of work. By being afforded an authorized absence from duties and responsibilities, employees will less likely experience "burnout" and more likely return to their assignment with renewed levels of motivation.

In contrast to the refresher definition for vacation is the view that vacation is a deferred economic benefit. As a deferred economic benefit, vacation is a reward for continuous service and is vested with the employees. Depending on the purpose of vacation as adopted by a school system (refresher or deferred economic benefit), implications are implied about the acquisition of vacation.

Acquisition of vacation pertains to the manner by which this employee convenience is earned (see Figure 9.5). It is not unusual to find that vacation is earned only after a minimum service requirement has been met (for example, employees must work at least 6 months), whereas in other instances, vacation accrual begins on employment. A minimum service requirement is reasonable from a refresher perspective but makes less sense when vacation is defined as a deferred economic benefit.

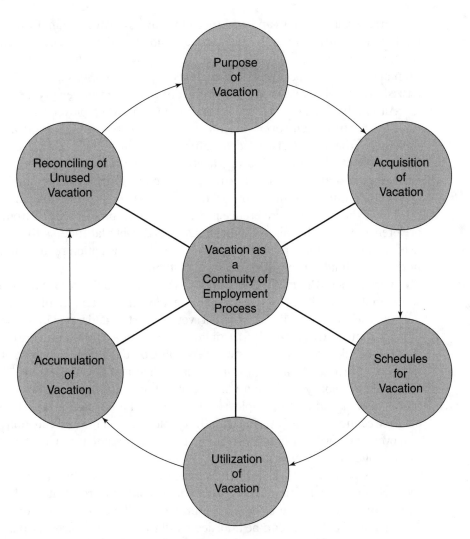

FIGURE 9.5 *Different decisional components for vacation procedures.*

Closely related to acquisition of vacation is the type of schedule for determining the number of vacation days allocated to employees (see Figure 9.5). Vacation can be allocated according to either a fixed- or to a variable-rate schedule. A fixed-rate vacation schedule provides all employees with the same number of days and is in keeping with the refresher perspective (all employees need the same time off), while a variable-rate schedule rewards continuous service by increasing the number of vacation days according to length of service (i.e., those working 5 years earn 15 days and those working 20 years earn 20 days; deferred economic benefit rewarding continuous employment).

Earning vacation days and using vacation days is always an administrative concern for public school districts. Because vacation is an employee convenience rather than a statutory right, different methods of utilization come into play when administering vacation from a human resource perspective. These methods of utilization (see Figure 9.5) can be characterized as being either an **employer preference** or an **employee preference** process.

Although all vacation is used at the discretion of the employer, various degrees of latitude exist between employer and employee preference processes. From a strict employer preference, the school district determines when vacation is used. For example, some school districts determine that all vacation will be used during the month of July and early August, and during this time the public school district will be shut down.

Lending utilization more toward the deferred benefit perspective than the refresher purpose is the employee preference provision. Utilization of vacation from the employee preference perspective allows individuals considerable latitude as to when vacation is used. Usually employee preference processes for using vacation require only a reasonable notice and a final approval by the school system.

Regardless of the method for utilizing vacation (employer or employee preference), some employees will not be able to capitalize fully on their allotment of vacation days. As a result, the issue of accumulation (carryover) must be addressed by school board policy or labor contract (see Figure 9.5). Guiding the issue of accumulation are different stances that can be taken by a school system, depending on the adopted purpose of vacation.

If the purpose of vacation is a refresher, then it is not unreasonable to have a no-accumulation policy because a window of opportunity has been missed by the public school district and by the employee. However, if the purpose of vacation is viewed as deferred economic benefit vested with the employee, then unused vacation should be carried over. Carryovers of unused vacation, however, present another set of decision issues from a policy/labor contract concern.

The issue of carryover for unused vacation concerns the means and methods of reconciling unused time (see Figure 9.5). Of concern are a rate and a value factor. Unused vacation can be afforded a prorated rate (each carryover day is worth only 50 percent of a day) or can be afforded a full rate. From a refresher point of view, the full worth of a carryover has been diminished through a missed opportunity, whereas from a deferred economic benefit perspective the worth of a day is equivalent regardless when it is used.

With the exception of certain central office personnel and certain support staff, most public school employees work less than the standard work year followed by employees in the private sector. Many of the employees that comprise a public school district's workforce have work schedules that follow closely the school calendar for students or extend the basic school calendar for students by a specified number of days or weeks. Although variations exist among school districts, the calendar followed by most students will average approximately 185 days across the nation.

Because most of the public school employees work less than the standard work year (260 days), most school employees fail to earn vacation. Without vacation time many school employees may encounter difficulty in managing certain aspects of their personal lives that require attention during their scheduled work times. To address these contingencies, public school districts have developed certain types of leave provisions in an effort to facilitate the employment continuity process for employees.

Leaves

These types of time-off provisions are a privilege rather than a legislative right and are designed to protect the income flow of an employee when the work schedule is disrupted temporally through no fault of the employee. As such, school districts should have great latitude in the development and administration of these types of leave provisions. However, far too often, school boards and school administrators have forfeited the school district's authority with respect to these types of leave provisions either through poorly written polices or inappropriate concessions at the bargaining table.

The most common mistake made by school boards and by school administrators in this area of human resource management is to develop in policy or agree to in contract a single leave procedure that purports to cover the array of contingencies that employees may encounter during their work year. This single leave provision is labeled generally as "**personal leave**" and is applicable to a wide range of situations. To qualify for global personal leaves, employees must satisfy generally only regulatory provisions.

A review of many policies and contract provisions reveals several common regulatory provisions governing the usage of global personal leave procedures. Examples of the regulations are as follows:

- Employees must apply a specified number of days before the leave.
- Leaves cannot be taken the day before or the day after a holiday.
- Leaves cannot be taken either the first week or the last week of the school year.
- Leaves cannot be taken the last day of a grading period.
- Leaves cannot be taken if a certain percentage of the employees at a work site are to be absent.
- Leaves cannot be taken to pursue other employment opportunities.

If an employee satisfies the regulatory conditions, then personal leaves are granted by management, usually without question. By following only regulatory provisions for granting personal leaves, school administrators relinquish managerial prerogatives that have an important administrative and economic implication for a public school district. Time away from the job by employees has profound operational and economical implications that should be controlled whenever possible.

However, regulatory requirements, as cited previously, defeat, in many instances, the basic purpose of leaves as a means of enhancing the employment continuity process for employees. Events occur within the lives of employees that fail to fit within the confines of such regulations. Failing to satisfy regulatory requirements, employees are ineligible for personal leaves.

In contrast to this singular approach for personal leave as practiced by many public school districts, it is advocated that personal leave be decomposed and that several different types of leave be made available to employees. By decomposing personal leave into

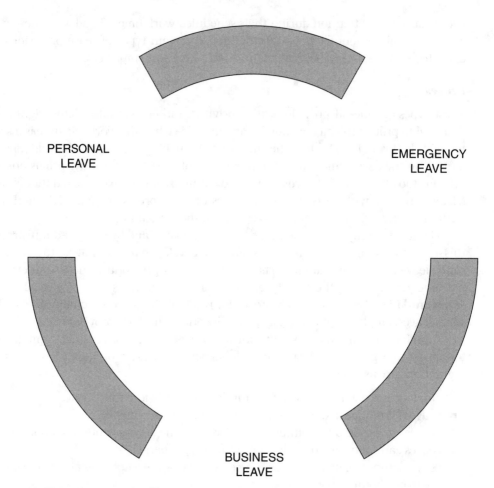

PERSONAL
LEAVE

EMERGENCY
LEAVE

BUSINESS
LEAVE

FIGURE 9.6   *Potential leave provisions for employees.*

different types of leave provisions, more latitude is granted the employee in the use of leaves and more authority is granted the employer in the operation of a public school district. Following this diversification, personal leave can be decomposed to include the following three categories (see Figure 9.6) rather than a single category: (a) **emergency leave**, (b) **business leave**, and (c) personal leave.

Emergency leave should be requested only in specific situations by employees. Situations warranting emergency leave are those that require an employee's immediate attention and failure to afford such attention would result in irreparable harm. Examples of incidents requiring emergency leave are broken water pipes in the home or a noninjury automotive accident involving the employee or an immediate family member.

To qualify for a business leave, employees must be involved in some type of economic transaction. An economic transaction involves situations where each party stands either to loose or to gain something of economic value as a result of the interaction. Some common examples for a business leave with public school employees are closing on a house or settling an estate.

Personal leave, within the proposed scheme of leave provisions, is more narrowly defined than typically found in most school districts. That is, personal leave is defined as a nonrecurring event that is somewhat unique to an individual. Examples of situations where personal leave would be appropriate include graduating from an educational institution or attending the wedding of an immediate family member.

By decomposing a global personal leave provision into more specific types of leave provisions, several advantages can be realized in the employment continuity process. Most important, individuals as employees will have greater liberty in using leave and will be less restricted by the leave process than some employees utilizing global personal leave provisions governed by regulatory provisions. Equally as important is the ability of school administrators to manage more efficiently and effectively the educational organization with separate leave provisions than with a single strictly regulated leave provision.

Administrative Processes for Employment Continuity

School districts as employers can develop and administer certain processes and procedures that enhance the employment continuity of employees in their assigned duties and organizational responsibilities. Foremost among these processes and procedures are mechanisms that allow employees the opportunity to change positions within the organization. Employees can move vertically or horizontally, and these moves can be initiated by the employee or by the employer.

Movement within an Organization

Individuals accept employment with a public school district for many reasons. Among these reasons is the need for gainful employment that will yield compensation for services rendered that can be used to fund a certain level of life's pleasures. Once the need for gainful employment is satisfied, other needs may become potent for some employees.

Among these other needs that may become potent is a desire to change work assignments within the public school district. A desire to change work assignments can be attributed to several reasons, both psychological and economical. Employees may seek novelty within the work environment, may seek avoidance of an unpleasant working situation, and/or may seek to improve their organizational status within the public school district.

School employees, like any other employees, are not exempt from the psychological phenomenon of burnout. Working at the same job for many years can result in levels of performance that are less than the employee is capable of performing. Seldom do

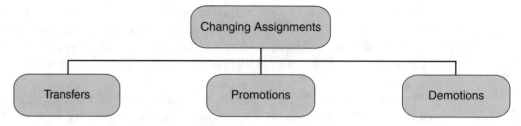

FIGURE 9.7   *Administrative procedures for altering job assignments.*

dysfunctional employees fail to know what to do, but lack, in most instances, the motivation to perform at their capacity in assigned duties.

What may have been a desirable work environment for some employees upon entrance to the school district workforce could have changed. School districts are dynamic entities and evolve over time. Both leadership changes and work group composition changes can alter what was an ideal working situation into one that is no longer desirable for some employees.

Still other employees may desire to enhance their position within the organization. These employees may have been underemployed on their entrance into the workforce of a school district or may have upgraded their job skills after being employed by a school district. In either situation, this group of employees seeks to capitalize on their occupational skills through obtaining a higher-level position within the public school district.

Regardless of the reasons underlying the desire for employees to seek different work assignments within a school district, it behooves the organization to provide means for employees to satisfy their desires. Public school districts that ignore these needs are likely to experience turnover rates in excess of those normally expected in the operation of a school district. Many of the employees electing to leave a public school district because of restricted opportunity are likely to be the type of employees that the school district should retain within the workforce.

To retain satisfactory employees desiring changes in work assignments, school districts can develop several different policy/procedures (see Figure 9.7). These provisions provide employees with a means for changing their immediate work environment while maintaining their continuity of employment with a public school district. Through changing their immediate work environment, satisfaction and performance on the part of the employee may be enhanced.

Transfers are linked closely to one aspect of human resource planning: the need to shift position holders within the system to staff vacancies, to place personnel in positions in keeping with their interests and abilities, and to correct staffing errors in the current workforce. The term *transfer*, as used here, refers to the horizontal movement of personnel from one position, office, department, or school to another position, office, department, or school within the same school district. Movement involved with transfers is horizontal generally and may or may not involve increases in responsibilities and/or compensation for the employee.

In general, transfers are initiated either by the administrative staff (involuntary) or by the employee (voluntary). Because of the implications associated with transfers, transfer of personnel is an important aspect of school administration for enhancing the work continuity process for many employees. Indeed, transfer provisions deserve more attention from a policy standpoint than is usually afforded by most public school districts to this important administrative process.

When formulating a transfer policy for a public school district, certain issues must be addressed. To help in addressing these issues, a series of questions are proposed for consideration by those responsible for developing and implementing a transfer provision. These questions include the following:

- What forms of employee transfer will be recognized in the system's transfer policy (employer initiated and/or employee initiated)?
- What criteria shall apply in evaluating employee transfer requests?
- What contractual considerations are involved in employee transfer?
- What arrangements exist to consider personal reasons of employees who request or refuse transfer?
- What are the reasons for making involuntary transfers?

Answers to these questions should be addressed in the transfer provisions of a public school district and should form the framework of a transfer provision. By addressing these issues in board policies and in labor contracts, many potential problems can be avoided. Most important is that transfers should be encouraged whenever they are in the interest of the individual and in the interest of the system, and that transfers are a valuable administrative process for improving staff development and flexibility.

A related, but somewhat different, administrative process for changing the employment status of individuals within the workforce is **promotion.** Promotion is taken generally to mean vertical movement for employees within the organization, whereas transfer is taken generally to mean horizontal movement for employees within the organization. Most often, promotions involve changes in compensation and in job duties that seldom accompany transfers.

Throughout this text, the importance of designing and implementing a proactive human resource strategy has been stressed. One aspect of this strategy is getting the right people into the right positions. An administrative mechanism for facilitating this strategy is sound promotion polices and procedures.

Promotion policies and procedures should be shaped to advance individuals who have the abilities, skills, attitudes, and commitment to enhance organizational efficiency and effectiveness. Under this arrangement, promotions are bestowed on those who meet and exceed minimum performance standards. Promotion criteria are needed for helping to identify people whose strengths are needed to achieve position and system aims and to place such individuals where their strengths can be exercised fully to the advantage of the individual and the school system.

A major issue for promotion, like for transfer, is the potential impact of seniority on promotion decisions. Promotion policy should avoid practices that place a priority on seniority when filling a vacant position. Seniority should become an issue only when candidates for promotion are equally qualified relative to the vacant position requirements; otherwise, promotion decisions should be made on the basis of merit.

Although policies of the school board and labor contract procedures for transfers and for promotion require considerable planning on the part of school boards and system administrators, the contingencies addressed in these types of reassignment provisions are more easily dealt with than those required of still another type of reassignment provision encountered by most school districts. This last type of reassignment provision is demotion. **Demotion** is a special type of reassignment that involves moving to another position that commands less salary, is lower in status, has less responsibility, offers fewer privileges, and/or affords less opportunity than the current position of an employee.

Demotions, like transfers, can be either voluntary or involuntary. Voluntary demotions are sought by the individual, while involuntary demotions are initiated by the school district. Depending on the initiating source for demotions, different processes and procedures may be evoked.

Individuals seeking to be demoted do so for several reasons. It is not uncommon for certain service employees to seek a lesser job to obtain a more accommodating work schedule, especially if the latter schedule adheres more closely to that followed by their children. Central office clerical personnel may seek building-level secretarial positions to have summers off when their children are home.

Other personnel may have accepted promotions only to find that the newly assigned position fails to fulfill previous personal expectations anticipated with a reassignment. It is not unusual for newly assigned assistant principals to desire to return to a former teaching position after the first year of administrative service. In large school districts, some employees may desire to obtain a work assignment closer to their home than their current higher-level assignment that requires greater commute time to the primary work location.

When employees seek actively a demotion for personal convenience, employees should accept fully all consequences of the reassignment. If the new position commands less salary than the previous position, then the employees should be expected to take a reduction in compensation. However, when the change in job assignment involves involuntary demotion, other factors may come into play.

Involuntary demotions can happen for any number of reasons. Declining enrollment may require that certain school buildings be closed and that school personnel be reassigned. For some personnel, the reassignment may involve an involuntary demotion. An involuntary demotion for administrators is likely when other principalships are unavailable within the school system.

Some other position holders may encounter an involuntary demotion as a result of an organizational realignment. Results from organizational studies may reveal that certain positions have been overclassified and overcompensated. When such results surface through no fault of the employee, the school district may have certain obligations to the employee that fail to exist when demotions are sought on a voluntary basis.

From the standpoint of the public school system, one of the most important aspects of involuntary demotion is that appropriate procedures for such action are established and adhered to scrupulously. For many individuals, work is the most important element in their lives. To be subjected to an involuntary demotion is, to most persons, a rejection, a crushing blow, one that is likely to generate the severest kind of antiorganizational behavior.

For certain employees that have performed faithfully and effectively, involuntary demotions may not be the appropriate action if certain responsibilities of such individuals can be shifted temporarily to other positions. Other alternatives include transfer to a less demanding position without loss of pay or status or providing incentives for early retirement. Such solutions are preferable when they can be arranged without interference with system operations and without creating role inequities that may lead to conflict.

Whatever the reasons for an involuntary demotion, the decision should be based on clear procedures and processes. Given adequate school board policies and labor contract provisions, the system is in a sound position to use involuntary demotion appropriately. At minimum, an involuntary demotion should include: (a) informing the employee of the intent to demote; (b) providing options, where feasible, such as transfer to a position of lower status, responsibility, and salary readjustment; (c) endeavoring to negotiate a settlement acceptable to both parties; (d) formalizing and informing the individual of the reasons for demotion; (e) notifying concerned parties of the official starting date; and (f) prescribing new position responsibilities.

Review and Preview

This chapter stresses the importance of employee continuity both from an individual and from an organizational perspective. Employment continuity is viewed as a process rather than as an event, and specific attention is afforded causes as well as consequences associated with the employment continuity process. When approached from a strategic planning perspective, the importance of policies and processes are discussed relative to application and to implementation.

To provide a broad base for promoting the employee continuity process, a differentiation is made between entitlements and privileges. For each of these means for enhancing the employment continuity process, specific examples are provided as well as detailed. Accompanying these examples are certain policy concerns that must be dealt with either through policy or labor contracts.

As outlined in this chapter, the process for maintaining continuity of personnel service stresses the need for a projected course of action based on a series of decisions relating to what the plans for personnel continuity are expected to achieve, such as types of plans needed to realize expectations, and program organization, administration, and control. Expectations or results that the system derives from plans for service continuity are both long and short range and include improvement of the system's ability to perform its mission; improvement of individual effectiveness; and improvement of the system's physical, psychological, and organizational environments.

In the next chapter, attention is directed to the collective bargaining process from a human resource perspective. An overview is provided about unions and collective bargaining. Various stages of the collective bargain process are discussed with attention being afforded to common contract terms and different types of impasse procedures.

Discussion Questions

1. Most school systems follow the state allocation for sick days that provides for a limited number of authorized days of absence. Some employees use all of these days, whereas others rarely use one day. Given these outcomes, what are some of the advantages and disadvantages of forming a sick day bank?

2. Within most public school districts personal leave is used as an income protection to ensure a continuous flow of salary for an employee due to a temporary absence. Often restrictions are placed on the use of personal leave. How is personal leave defined in your school district? Does your district's definition fulfill the employment continuity needs for employees, and what are some of the restrictions? What are the advantages and disadvantages of using different types of leaves (personal, emergency, and/or business) rather than a single leave provision (personal)?

3. Vacation can be defined as a "refresher" or as a "deferred economic benefit." How is

vacation defined in your school district? Given the specific definition either used or implied by your school district, how consistent is the flow from the purpose to other aspects (acquisition, schedule, utilization, accumulation, and/or reconciliation)?

4. Employee assistance programs are viewed as devices that aid in cost containment and in the maintenance of organizational effectiveness. How is it possible to gauge the effectiveness of these programs, and what types of assistance programs are available in your district?

5. Employees often become stagnate in their current job or wish to change their current job for a variety of reasons. At least three mechanisms exits: transfers, promotions, and demotions. How are these mechanisms used in your district and what are the issues/problems associated with each approach?

Case Study

Assume that you are a Human Resource Administrator for a public school district. When providing an orientation for a new employee, David Wag, the topic of retirement plan choice is discussed. Because David has a choice of choosing either a defined benefit or a defined contribution plan with a window of opportunity, he relies on your advice.

Within the conversation, David indicates that his fiancé will soon be completing her degree in education from a different state. Although the marriage seems eminent, it is unclear where they will reside after being married. Which plan would you advise, given the uncertainty? What are your concerns about contribution? What type of information would you provide him in making the decision before this window closes? Would your advice be different if the sex roles were reversed?

References

Bolman, L. G., & Deal, T. E. (2003). *Reframing organizations: Artistry, choice, and leadership (3rd ed.)*. San Francisco: Jossey-Bass.

Cunningham, W. G., & Cordeiro, P. A. (2006). *Educational Leadership: A problem-based approach (3rd ed.)*. Boston: Pearson.

Enomoto, E. K., & Gardiner, M. E. (2006). Mentoring within internships: Socializing new leaders. *Journal of School Leadership, 16*(1), 34–60.

Hoy, W. K., & Miskel, C. J. (2005). *Educational administration: Theory, research, and practice (7th ed.)*. New York: McGraw-Hill.

Job Descriptive Index. (n.d.). Retrieved July 23, 2006, from Web Site: http://www.bgsu.edu/departments/psych/JDI/.

Leader Behavior Description Questionnaire. (n.d.). Retrieved July 23, 2006, from Web Site: LBDQ, http://www.cob.ohio-state.edu/supplements/10/2862/1957%20LBDQ.pdf.

Milkovich, G. T., & Newman, J. M. (1996). *Compensation* (5th ed.). Boston: Irwin McGraw-Hill.

Minnesota Satisfaction Questionnaire. (n.d.). Retrieved July 23, 2006, from Web Site: http://www.psych.umn.edu/psylabs/vpr/msqinf.htm.

National Conference on Public Employee Retirement Systems. (2006). Retrieved July 23, 2006, from Web Site: http://www.ncpers.org/.

National Teacher Recruitment Clearinghouse. (n.d.). Retrieved July 23, 2006, from Web Site: http://www.recruitingteachers.org/channels/clearinghouse/.

Owings, W. A., & Kaplan, L. S. (2006). *American public school finance*. Belmont, CA: Thomson-Wadsworth.

Sergiovanni, T. J. (2006). *The principalship: A reflective practice (5th ed.)*. Boston: Pearson.

Sinden, J., Hoy, W. K., & Sweetland, S. R. (2004). Enabling school structures: Principal leadership and organizational commitment of teachers. *Journal of School Leadership, 14*(2), 195–210.

Teachers Insurance and Annuity Association. (n.d.). Retrieved July 23, 2006, from Web Site: http://www.tiaa-cref.org.

U.S. Department of Education. (n.d.). Retrieved July 24, 2006, from the U.S. Department of Education Web Site: http://www.ed.gov/index.jhtml.

U.S. Department of Labor. (n.d.). *Family and Medical Leave Act of 1993*. Retrieved July 24, 2006, from the U.S. Department of Labor Web site: http://www.dol.gov/dol/topic/benefits-leave/fmla.htm/programs/handbook/fmla.htm.

U.S. Social Security Administration. (n.d.). Social Security Act of 1935. Retrieved July 24, 2006, from the Social Security Administration Web Site: http://www.ssa.gov.

Valente, W. D., & Valente, C. M. (2005). *Law in the schools*. Upper Saddle River, NJ: Merrill/Prentice Hall.

Westfield Classroom Teachers Association. (n.d.). *Article XIV—Sick leave bank*. Retrieved July 1, 2006, from the Westfield Classroom Teachers Association Web Site: http://www.wwcta.org/.

Development

10

CHAPTER OVERVIEW

OBJECTIVES

■ Develop an awareness of the importance and extensive implications of staff development for achieving system goals for human resources.

■ Consider internal and external conditions that influence staff development programs.

■ Illuminate key elements in the staff development process from a strategic planning perspective.

■ Stress the importance of organizational development policies and procedures that enhance attainment of individual, unit, and system aims.

■ Identify alternate explanations for development outcomes other than those attributable to development efforts.

■ Present different assessment designs for use in evaluating development efforts at the local school district level.

Development

Development as it pertains to the human resource function within the public school setting involves enhancing the knowledge, skills, behaviors, attitudes, and opportunities for those involved with any aspect of the schooling process. Included in this definition are school board members, full-time employees, part-time employees, and temporary employees. To enhance the services of these groups from an individual and from an organizational perspective, this chapter emphasizes the administrative process by which plans for development of human resources are conceived, implemented, managed, as well as evaluated, and a model is used to guide the discussion of the process through which plans for organizational, group, and individual development are designed and assessed from a strategic planning perspective.

More specifically, this chapter addresses development from a process as opposed to a content perspective. "Schools are inundated with programs, plans and tools for staff development and training, but amid all the flurry, they should assess their current state, coordinate resources, and create strategic, systematic plans for growth" (Partee, 2001). As such, attention is afforded in this chapter initially to the steps involved in establishing a development process rather than the content of any specific development program. Following this line of presentation, consideration is provided to methods and means for evaluating the outcomes of a development program through illustration of different data-collection designs, and the discussion of factors potentially influencing the evaluation process.

Development by Design

Without a doubt, development is a concern for every public school district, and "educators recognize that training is critical in helping schools to achieve the high standards that are expected of them" (Cunningham & Cordeiro, 2006, p. 294). However, the development efforts of a public school district can be either haphazard or systematic in conception, in implementation, and in evaluation. Systematic development efforts occur only by design and require a well-conceived plan of action on the part of a public school district.

In this chapter, development activities for all individuals throughout their involvement with a public school district are addressed through **in-service education.** All individuals affiliated with a school district can benefit from a focused program of appropriate development activities for their current role or for an anticipated new role within a public school system. Individuals addressed in this chapter include members of the board of education, school administrators, teachers, classified staff, and temporary employees.

By including all individuals in a formal development program designed to enhance the performance of their current role or their anticipated new role sends a distinct message to employees throughout a public school system. This message is that development is an important organizational activity and that development is expected of all individuals, not just specific groups of employees (Hirsh, 2004). Through leading by example in the development process, school board members provide one of the most influential means of endorsement for professional development programs in a school system by conveying the message that no group is exempted from development and that all groups should be included in the development process.

Like school board members as participants in the development process, school administrators benefit from a well-designed development program (Sparks, 2003). For many practicing school administrators, new technologies have emerged since their formal education and since their basic certification requirements have been satisfied (Sergiovanni, 2006). Most notably, few practicing administrators have received any training in forecasting methods (see Chapter 2) or in the construction of staffing plans (see Chapter 3), both of which are necessary for administering the human resource function in a public school district from a strategic planning perspective and require development efforts to update managerial skills.

Many teachers within any public school district were appointed prior to the advent of high-stakes testing. As such, these individuals may lack the necessary skills for deciphering test results in a meaningful manner and for tailoring their teaching strategies for improving the performance of students. Development programs provided by a district can fill in this gap in knowledge and expertise for many public school teachers (Richard, 2004).

Classified employees have not been exempted from an ever-changing work environment. They are confronted with new technologies and with new health concerns in their assigned duties. Computer technology used once only by a select few in the school district has become common practice for most classified positions, and issues associated with hazardous material as well as blood-borne pathogens are important concerns for classified employees in the conduct of their job assignments.

Temporary employees serving as substitutes or filling in on a short-term basis need development. For many of these individuals, their formal education and/or past job experiences may be limited, and their levels of knowledge/skill development is lacking relative to current standards and to job expectations. However, many of their job responsibilities are similar to regular full-time employees, and they require the attention of a public school district within the development process.

During the working careers of all individuals within a school district, employees experience many changes that impact the operation of the school system and that impact the fulfillment of their job responsibilities. This is especially true in the 21st century. In fact, for many employees, school reform has been the rule rather than the exception since the 1980's due to the publication of *A Nation at Risk* (U.S. Department of Education's National Commission on Excellence in Education, 1983) over 25 years ago, and reform requires a continuous plan of development.

Changes altering the way schools are administered may originate from external sources, internal sources, or some combination of these sources that impact the way business is conducted within the public school setting. External changes impacting the way schools are administered can stem from emerging research findings, international comparisons with selected countries, federal agendas modifying the school process, state mandates establishing new standards, and changing community expectations at the local school district level. Internal changes altering school administration and reinforcing the need for development activities can come from priorities of the board of education, desires of the central administration, and needs of individual employees.

Management of change within the school setting to meet emerging needs requires a systematic plan for developing employees and school officials. Development of school employees and school officials should be an ongoing process and should consider immediate as well as advanced career stages and needs of individuals. To maintain the momentum necessary for an effective development process focusing on career stages and needs of individuals, certain tasks must be addressed continuously by those charged with development responsibilities in a public school setting.

Following are some of the more important tasks that must be addressed continuously by administrators of a public school district when attempting to execute an effective and an efficient program of staff development at the local school district level:

- Assessing how effective current staff development programs are for improving individual, unit, and system performance of role incumbents.
- Highlighting ineffective and inefficient development activities for improvement or elimination in a staff development program.
- Designing and shaping development programs to attain strategic human resource goals and objectives as stated in the strategic plan of a school district.
- Linking other processes of the human resource function such as recruitment, selection, orientation, and performance appraisal to the staff development process.
- Viewing staff development as an important vehicle for career development plans.

- Considering the strategic importance of changes in the internal and the external environments that impact staff development activities of a public school district.
- Establishing a planning agenda that anticipates rather than reacts to the changing development needs of individuals.
- Basing the staff development program on the assumption that the needs of a specific school are paramount and critical to any development endeavor; thus, avoiding the temptation to clone other development programs.
- Upgrading the investment in staff development activities in areas found to have the greatest impact on performance improvement related to the strategic plan of a public school district.

Creating a master plan that identifies high-impact development activities, anticipates outcomes, and achieves optimal results is a must for an effective public school system. In fact, many of the characteristics for goals of effective staff development programs have been identified through extensive research about this topic. These characteristics, as listed below, are associated with promising professional development programs within the public school setting:

- Goals identify teachers as central to student learning yet include all other members of the school community.
- Goals focus on individual, collegial, and organizational improvement.
- Goals emphasize and enhance the intellectual and leadership capacities of teachers, principals, and others in the school community.
- Goals reflect the best available research and practice in teaching, learning, and leadership.
- Goals enable teachers to develop further expertise in subject content, teaching strategies, uses of technologies, and other essential elements in teaching to high standards.
- Goals promote continuous inquiry and improvement in the daily life of schools.
- Goals are planned collaboratively by those who will participate in and facilitate the development.
- Goals require substantial time and other resources to be accomplished.
- Goals are driven by a coherent and long-term plan of action derived from a strategic planning process.
- Goals are evaluated ultimately on the basis of their impact on teacher effectiveness and student learning, and this assessment guides subsequent professional development efforts (U.S. Department of Education, 1998).

Obstacles to Development

Development, one of the processes within the human resource function, has not escaped criticism from several sources. Commission reports (Interstate School Leaders Licensure Consortium, n.d.), reform initiatives (No Child Left Behind, 2002), and the popular media have criticized staff development efforts in school systems. These criticisms are based on international comparisons, state-mandated proficiency test results, and escalating district operating budgets.

- Allocating staff development resources without knowing what, if anything, has been derived from the experience.
- Rejecting the concept of staff development as a tool for leveraging human resource strategy.
- Viewing staff development as an end in itself rather than as a means to an end.
- Initiating unguided and unorganized staff development programs.
- Disregarding the need for professionalizing internal change agents.
- Giving precedence to individual development rather than linking individual, group, and system development.
- Taking for granted that there is a close fit among programs, individual, and group needs.
- Minimizing the importance of validating job relatedness of staff development activities.
- Offering tuition reimbursement programs without any linkage to system needs.
- Disregarding needs assessment when funding self-nomination development plans.
- Assuming that correcting staff development problems will solve major organizational problems.
- Lacking models to analyze whether programs produce changes, whether changes are the desired ones, and whether changes meet target needs.
- Viewing conference attendance as vacation time and as a hiatus from position demands.
- Failing to identify specific objectives of the staff development process before implementation.
- Emphasizing program activities rather than facilitating the learning of desirable behaviors.
- Failing to centralize control over cost of staff development programs and activities.

FIGURE 10.1 *Factors contributing to ineffective staff development.*

For many school systems, criticisms of development efforts for employees have merit. Indeed, development efforts in some school systems have been and continue to be a series of haphazard isolated events unrelated to system goals and represent inefficient use of public funds (Dickenson, McBride, & Lamb-Milligan, 2003). Some of the most common factors contributing to ineffective staff development efforts by public school districts are listed in Figure 10.1.

Awareness of the most common problems associated with staff development attempts can benefit greatly those responsible for staff development activities within the public school setting. The problems listed in Figure 10.1 can be used to assess the current operation of staff development programs and activities in a school system. Once problems within the staff development program have been identified, corrective measures can be taken to align staff development activities with the strategic plans of a particular public school district.

Underlying many of the problems, as listed in Figure 10.1, is the absence of any systematic attempt to link staff development efforts to the strategic plans of the school system (Partee, 2001). This problem can be attributed, at least in part, to the tendency to view

- Each individual is a part of a whole—every individual action has consequences for the system as a whole.
- To change the outcomes of an organization, one must change the system, not just its parts.
- Organizations must focus on the root causes of problems and long-term goals and consequences, not the symptoms.
- Effective change occurs by understanding the system and its behaviors, and working with the flow of the system, not against it.

Effective staff development for a systems approach includes:

- Training in the concepts, values, and specific tools of systems thinking.
- Ongoing processes that involve all segments of the organization in a dialogue so that there is collective rather than individual staff development.
- A focus on the application of the beliefs and tools of the system in the context of day-to-day workings of schools and the school system.
- Questioning and examining underlying assumptions and beliefs.

FIGURE 10.2   *Key principles of systems thinking.*

staff development as a series of isolated events rather than as a continuous program of development. Using a systems approach to staff development can solve many of the problems that are found in Figure 10.1.

A systems approach for linking staff development efforts to the strategic plans of the district has been suggested by Asayesh (1993). Asayesh's approach uses the concept of systems thinking (see Figure 10.2). Systems thinking is a planning tool for dealing with various organizational problems that are difficult to resolve by the temporary application of isolated practices.

A major benefit of applying a systems approach to staff development is that this methodology enables human resource planners to consider both the internal and the external dimensions of organizational behavior in the design and the execution of staff development programs in a public school district. School systems acquire substantial resources from external sources, are regulated externally, must satisfy a host of external interests, and are subject to various forces over which they have little control. Thus, systems theory embraces the view that organizational effectiveness depends on the ability to adapt to the demands of the external environment and to shape the culture of the internal environment to meet external demands in an efficient and effective manner through a continuous development program.

Staff Development Domain

Providing systematic means for the continuous development of skills, knowledge, problem-solving abilities, and attitudes of system personnel has been a cardinal professional tenet of all organizations for centuries. Education has been no exception to this tenet.

Considerable efforts and numerous resources have been and continue to be directed toward the improvement of educators as professional employees within the public school setting.

For example, many states have passed laws requiring staff development activities for certificated personnel. Some states require these individuals to obtain a master's degree within a specified time period following initial certification by the state department of education, and other states have required individuals to complete an approved plan for staff development as a condition of continuing employment. Failure to satisfy these regulatory requirements involving staff development often renders an individual ineligible for future certification in these states.

Almost without exception, states have codified in-service education expectations for employees by designating a minimum number of days that must be devoted to in-service activities each year. Initially, in-service education was restricted to teachers and other certificated personnel; later on, it has been expanded to cover all employees in the school system. According to most state codes, failure to perform in-service activities is grounds for employee termination.

Accompanying state-mandated requirements for development activities have been certain historical trends. Political action in the late 1970s resulted in the creation of federally supported teacher centers as a means of upgrading staff development programs (DeLuca, 1991). In the 1980s, state legislators and local school administrators viewed staff development as a key aspect of school improvement efforts. Most recently, this trend has been reinforced by President Bush's initiative of No Child Left Behind (U.S. Department of Education, 1998).

When staff development for educational organizations is viewed as an integrated activity from a systems perspective, staff development can be linked to those processes designed by the system to attract, retain, and improve the quality and quantity of staff members needed to achieve desired goals. Staff development is vitally linked to human resource planning because, as the reader may recall from previous chapters, a sound human resource plan calls for:

- Improving the job performance of all employees
- Developing key skills of personnel selected to fill anticipated vacancies
- Promoting the self-development of all employees to facilitate need satisfaction
- Identifying and developing individuals in each employee group who have the potential to be promoted

Staff development, as considered within this chapter, includes both informal and formal approaches to the improvement of effectiveness on the part of individuals in their assigned positions. As illustrated in Figure 10.3, this involves both short-term and long-range activities; each activity has different objectives, involves different levels of personnel, and addresses a variety of ways for conceptualizing and organizing the staff improvement function. In effect, staff development is the process of staff improvement through approaches that emphasize self-realization, self-growth, and self-development.

Development includes those activities aimed at the improvement and the growth of abilities, attitudes, skills, and knowledge of system members for both current and anticipated assignments. Figure 10.3 indicates that staff development includes various

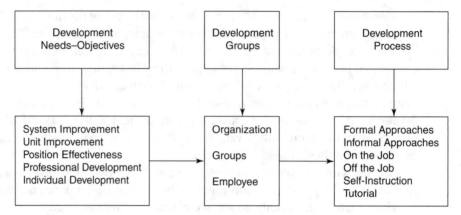

FIGURE 10.3   *Typology for personnel development.*

situations in every public school district and calls for some form of individual or group development. The following statements are illustrative:

- Development requires interrelationships among system, unit, and individual goals and has implications for the design and implementation of development programs.
- Development includes all school personnel within the public school system.
- Development entails meeting two kinds of expectations: (a) the contribution of the individual to the school system and (b) the rewards anticipated by the individual in return.
- Development involves all activities designed to increase an individual's ability to work effectively in an assigned or anticipated role.
- Development is focused on two kinds of activities: (a) those specifically planned and administered by the school system (formal approaches) and (b) those initiated by personnel (informal approaches).
- Development is concerned with values, norms, and behaviors of individuals and groups.
- Development is designed to serve the following purposes: personal growth, professional development, problem solving, remedial action, motivation, upward mobility, and job security.
- Development programs initiated by the system are aimed at educating individuals above and beyond the immediate technical requirements of their position.
- Development programs sanction activities related to practical and position-oriented needs, as well as to longer-range purposes focused on full development of the individual.
- Development encourages career-long staff development for all personnel as an organizational necessity.
- Development activity has been evaluated judgmentally rather than empirically in the past.
- Development has failed to capitalize fully on existing knowledge and theory regarding staff development.

- Development programs have been subjected to an array of fads and fashions that have not been based on a sound process development model (such as human resource objectives) or carefully designed, administered, and tested experiences.
- Development is a powerful tool for affecting individual, unit, and system change.

Improvement of employee performance calls for a variety of approaches to modify and to enhance the behavior patterns of individuals and of groups to maximize organizational effectiveness. A framework by which efforts are systematized to deal with the many development problems arising continually in school systems, both individual and group, is referred to as a process model. The section that follows presents a comprehensive development process model consisting of sequential and interrelated phases for an effective and efficient staff development process.

Staff Development Process

Staff development activities in educational organizations have changed substantially over the last two decades. Beginning as a group of unconnected, isolated events, staff development has become one of the key human resource functions in a school system. Some of the changes in staff development that have evolved over time are presented in Figure 10.4.

Many of these changes associated with staff development, as listed in Figure 10.4, stem from certain inferences about labor markets and certain views about career stages for individuals as employees. From a labor market perspective, boards of education are beginning to view staff development as an ongoing process rather than as a periodic event and have taken note of the emerging reality for human resource planning. This emerging reality reflects a dramatic shift taking place in the workforce of this country; a shift that affects every employer in America, not just educational systems.

No longer are traditional labor pools as readily available for recruitment and selection (see Young, in press). Growth of the pool of workers is slowing, and the workforce is diversifying. Because of these changes, recruiting and retaining knowledgeable personnel have become extremely difficult for all organizations.

Recent research addressing the recruitment and selection of employees indicates that this problem is likely to continue in the near future for educational organizations (Prince, 2002). What was once a captive pool of potential educational employees fails to exist in today's market. Many of those who once would have chosen education as a career have other viable options in more lucrative labor markets.

One way of identifying and maximizing the talents of existing labor pools is by viewing development activities from **career stages** within the educational setting and using this view as a means for enticing applicants to consider a public school district as a career option. In the professional literature and in the work world, increasing attention is being devoted to the relationship between career stages and staff development programs. Three descriptions of career stages for employees of a public school district are presented in Figure 10.5.

It is important to stress that staff development occurs over time, goes through several stages, cuts across a wide range of development issues, and includes changing positions

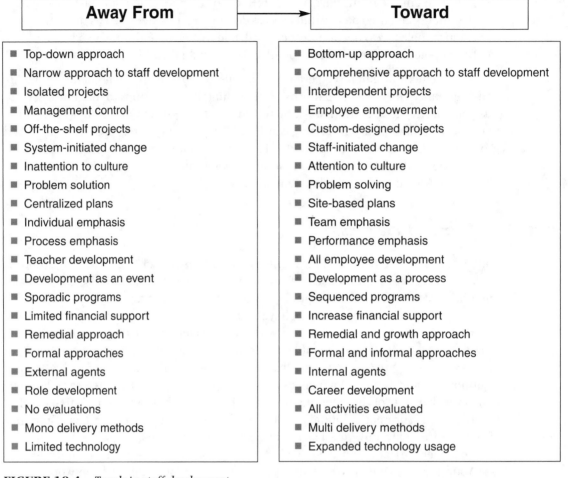

Away From	Toward
■ Top-down approach	■ Bottom-up approach
■ Narrow approach to staff development	■ Comprehensive approach to staff development
■ Isolated projects	■ Interdependent projects
■ Management control	■ Employee empowerment
■ Off-the-shelf projects	■ Custom-designed projects
■ System-initiated change	■ Staff-initiated change
■ Inattention to culture	■ Attention to culture
■ Problem solution	■ Problem solving
■ Centralized plans	■ Site-based plans
■ Individual emphasis	■ Team emphasis
■ Process emphasis	■ Performance emphasis
■ Teacher development	■ All employee development
■ Development as an event	■ Development as a process
■ Sporadic programs	■ Sequenced programs
■ Limited financial support	■ Increase financial support
■ Remedial approach	■ Remedial and growth approach
■ Formal approaches	■ Formal and informal approaches
■ External agents	■ Internal agents
■ Role development	■ Career development
■ No evaluations	■ All activities evaluated
■ Mono delivery methods	■ Multi delivery methods
■ Limited technology	■ Expanded technology usage

FIGURE 10.4 *Trends in staff development.*

and personal needs of employees. Traditionally, some organizations have viewed these career stages as found in Figure 10.5 only from a vertical perspective. From this perspective, individuals enter the organization (early career), refine and master initial job skills (mid-career), and move up the hierarchy through a series of promotions during their term of employment (late career) with a public school district.

However, career stages involving only vertical movement may have little appeal today for many employees in school systems. For some positions requiring certification (e.g., teacher, psychologist, librarian), incumbents have invested several years in specialized training and have established an identity with a professional group. To move vertically within the school system would require further study in a different subject matter area and professional affiliation with a different professional group.

Further complicating vertical movement of employees within a public school district, unions representing certain employees have made substantial economic gains through

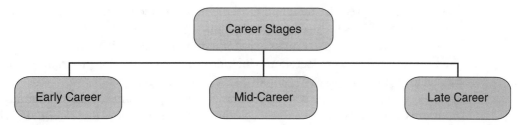

FIGURE 10.5 *Career stages for employees.*

collective bargaining with boards of education. These economic gains have often exceeded those of entry-level management and supervisory personnel. For mid-career employees to use vertical movement for career progression would often result in less economic benefits than those enjoyed by employees at the top of the career ladder in their current bargaining unit position.

Management and supervisory personnel have career needs, as do all employees of a public school district. Although some of these individuals occupying managerial and supervisory positions may have cleared successfully some of the hurdles associated with vertical movement confronting their subordinates, other supervisory and managerial employees may be relegated to the same position or to the same level within the organization for many years. These employees, like all others, have career plateaus and career needs that must be addressed through a staff development program.

Overlooked by many is that the single largest employer in most communities is the school system. School systems are, however, pyramidal in structure, and the number of opportunities near the top of an educational organization is small relative to the number of employees that may seek higher-level positions through promotional opportunities. Therefore, even if most employees sought vertical movement as a means of career progression, only a few of these employees could be accommodated within their current school system.

To protect their initial investments in recruitment and selection, as well as to keep effective employees in their current position or in similar positions at the same organizational level, innovative school systems have changed their ideas about career stages within the staff development process. These farsighted school systems now view career stages from a horizontal as well as from a vertical perspective. Effective staff development programs include ways to enrich and revitalize the work life of all employees, including those seeking vertical as well as horizontal advancement.

Research and practice addressing career stages from both vertical and horizontal perspectives suggests many implications and raises several considerations, including the following:

■ When staff development becomes a policy commitment, this commitment signals that the system is willing to provide continuing improvement opportunities for personnel. These opportunities may relate to career goals, career counseling, and career paths; information about position openings; and various forms of development programs, some of which address special needs such as problems relating to outplacement, preretirement and retirement, and choices confronting mid-career staff members as well as those who have developed physical disabilities.

■ Many types of opportunities exist for enhancing career development. The development process model should include decisions to develop programs most suited to specific groups comprising a school district's workforce.

■ Recognizing that the pool of talent is decreasing, organizations throughout the nation are broadening their roles regarding staff development and retention. (This is especially true in the cases of women and minorities.)

■ Emerging questions relating to the design of career development programs include the following: What are the system's ambitions for the career stages of its employees? Does the system have sufficient mechanisms in place to support career development? In an era of increased competition for personnel, what career plans are best designed to retain and to improve current as well as future staff members?

■ Opportunities may exist to include particular development incentives such as sabbaticals, tuition grants, research accounts, or flexible working assignments that have the potential to enhance the pursuit of careers within the system.

A **development process** model provides a framework to facilitate the systemization of development activities and to resolve some of the issues concerning staff development activities. An example of a process model for development activities that could be used by school systems is presented in Figure 10.6. This model contains four phases, each of which requires certain decisions and actions by those responsible for establishing and implementing development activities at the local school district level.

Phase 1: Diagnosing Development Needs

The initial step in the process model (see Figure 10.6) is diagnosing development needs of a public school district's workforce. **Development needs** are defined as a discrepancy between the actual level of functioning and the desired level of functioning. The purpose of a staff development process is to reduce the discrepancy between actual and desired levels of performance.

Development needs vary according to source, and sources include the individual, the group, and the organization. McGehee and Thayer (1961) identified these potential sources of development needs over 40 years ago. Since that time, according to Scarpello, Ledvinka, and Bergman (1995), these sources of development needs have become and continue to be an accepted standard for most development processes and models used today by the majority of public and private organizations.

Development needs of the individual focus on the person as an employee. These needs may be attributed to **skill deficiency,** skill obsolescence, and/or motivation to perform. A skill deficiency occurs when individuals lack knowledge or the basic skills necessary to perform their work in a satisfactory manner. Without knowledge and skills, these individuals fail to know how to achieve satisfactory performance in their current work assignment and require skill enhancement.

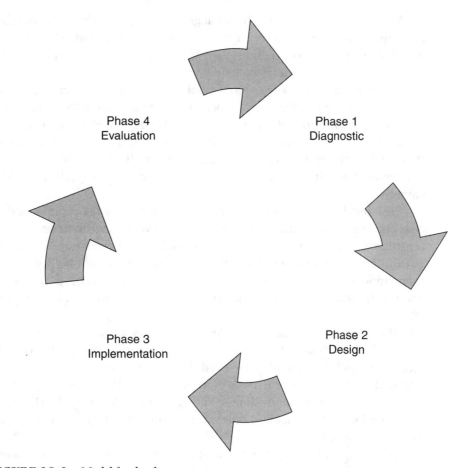

FIGURE 10.6 *Model for development process.*

Skill obsolescence occurs when the individual's skills and knowledge become out-dated. New developments may alter the way work should be performed. Persons experiencing skill obsolescence know what work to perform but lack skills or knowledge to perform the work according to best practices.

In some cases, the individual may know what to do, as well as the best way to do it, yet may still fail to perform at an optimal level, as defined by organizational standards. In this situation, the employee may have a **motivational deficiency** (Farber & Ascher, 1991) rather than a skill or knowledge deficiency. A major cause of motivational problems in employees who fail to perform optimally is attributed often to be burnout.

In addition to variation in sources of development needs (individual, group, and organization), these needs vary by content. Seyfarth (1996) identified two content areas for development needs: **technical needs** and **structural needs.** However, this classification of content omitted consideration of the **affective needs** of employees in educational organizations, and in many instances, affective development needs are the most important within the public school setting.

Technical needs stem from technological advances that can enhance the way work is performed. Today, more than ever, technological advances have changed the way educational organizations conduct business. Manual systems for management have been replaced by automated systems for management.

Today, most school systems have online accounting procedures for administering and for monitoring public school expenditures at all levels of the organization. Likewise, information about students, both personal and academic, is readily available through automated systems. Consequently, efficient school systems have incorporated many of these technical advances into their operation, and the incorporation requires extensive development activity on the part of an organization to change the attitudes and skills of employees.

Structural needs address the manner in which the work is performed. Many school districts have begun to experiment with alternative management strategies involving decentralized decision making such as site-based management (see Young & Miller-Smith, 2006). These new strategies for decision making alter substantially the way work is performed and may require considerable development efforts on the part of employees if success is to be attained by using different management strategies to accomplish traditional job tasks.

Affective needs pertain to employees' attitudes toward and perceptions about the work and the workplace. Often overlooked as appropriate content for a development program by school districts, affective needs have long attracted the interest of the private sector. Many times, affective needs of individuals are the cause of dysfunctional behaviors such as absenteeism, tardiness, and grievances (Markley, 2001). Development efforts have focused erroneously only on the symptoms of dysfunctional behavior rather than on its causes.

In keeping with the systems view of development, potential needs diagnosed in this phase of the development model may have internal or external origins. Internal development needs may be due to program initiatives, performance assessments, or opinion polls. External causes may include current events, government agencies, and research and development outcomes.

Development needs (technical, structural, or affective) may surface at various levels (organization, unit, or individual), at different times, and for various reasons (internal or external). Personnel shortages may occur, legislation may be passed requiring new programs, or information may be compiled that indicates certain types of skill deficiencies. Consequently, every development need is likely to be subjected to some form of priority analysis to determine if it should be included in the staff development plan currently in operation.

Before development needs are translated into program designs, several questions pertaining to planning need to be examined. Among these are the following:

- Is there a consensus that a need exists?
- How important is the need in terms of system priorities and resources?
- Can the need be met through system action?
- What is the probability that satisfaction of the need will be cost effective?

Underlying this discussion is the premise that ongoing diagnosis of system development is an essential management task. These diagnoses identify which needs are important to individual, group, and organizational effectiveness, and which ones are faddish and unnecessary. Also, these diagnoses pinpoint the content area of development needs as technical, structural, and/or affective.

Phase 2: Designing Development Plans

In the design phase of the planning process (see Figure 10.6), considerable effort is devoted to issues related to the format of a staff development program in a public school district (see Figure 10.6; Phase 2). Format within the design phase of staff development refers to the way program elements are translated into program specifics for execution. Format components of a development program are content, methods, location, participation, implementation, and evaluation.

These format components are incorporated into a structural model contained within Figure 10.7. Each of the elements contained within the structural model has several subsets. Following is a discussion of each component of the structural model that must be addressed in the design phase of a development program for employees.

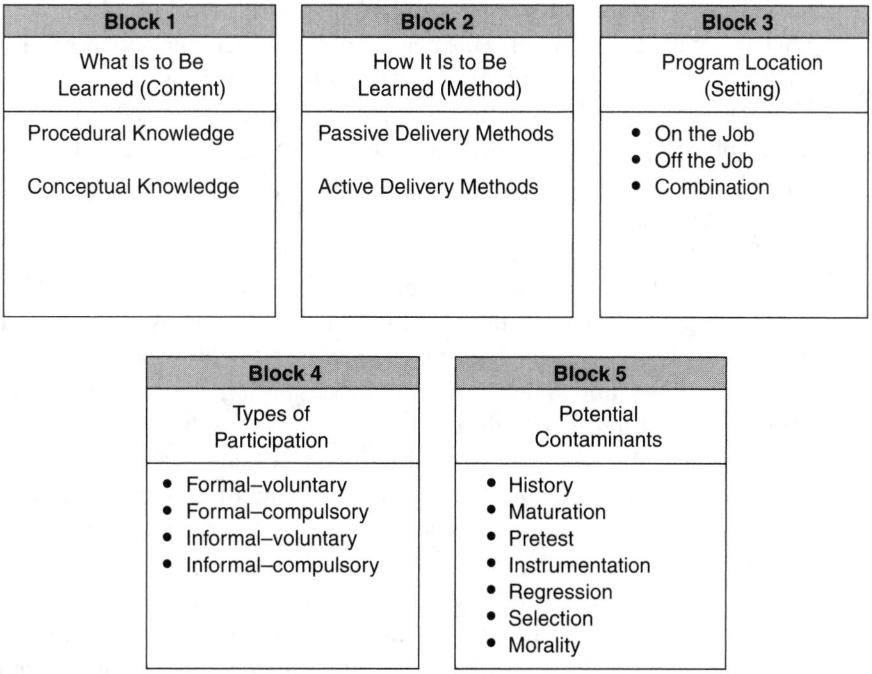

Block 1	Block 2	Block 3
What Is to Be Learned (Content)	How It Is to Be Learned (Method)	Program Location (Setting)
Procedural Knowledge Conceptual Knowledge	Passive Delivery Methods Active Delivery Methods	• On the Job • Off the Job • Combination

Block 4	Block 5
Types of Participation	Potential Contaminants
• Formal–voluntary • Formal–compulsory • Informal–voluntary • Informal–compulsory	• History • Maturation • Pretest • Instrumentation • Regression • Selection • Morality

FIGURE 10.7 *Structural model for designing development formats.*

Program Content

Within the design phase of a development program two types of learning must be considered when identifying program content for staff development (see Block 1 in Figure 10.7). One type of learning that must be considered pertains to theories, concepts, and behaviors, and the other type of learning that must be considered relates to the application of theories, concepts, and behaviors. Both types of learning are necessary for content of a development program to transfer from the program setting to the job environment of participants (Richardson, 2003).

Firestone and Pennell (1997) suggested that these types of learning involve acquiring both **procedural knowledge** and **conceptual knowledge** about program content delivered through a staff development program. According to these investigators, procedural knowledge is acquired by mastering the content of a development program. Content acquisition of procedural knowledge is, however, only part of the learning process that employees need for application of program content within the job setting.

On-the-job application of the content of a development program requires conceptual as well as procedural knowledge. Conceptual knowledge represents a higher level of learning than procedural knowledge. To acquire conceptual knowledge, individuals must be able to internalize the information presented in a development program and to apply this information in the work setting.

Far too often, development programs and activities in public school systems have focused on procedural knowledge and have neglected conceptual knowledge in the design phase of staff development. This neglect occurs when participants are treated as passive learners and are given content but little contextual information about applying program content within the job setting. Because conceptual knowledge is often ignored in the design phase of the development program, the most common criticism offered by program participants is that the content of staff development programs is not relevant to their actual job setting.

To bridge the gap between conceptual and procedural knowledge, Richardson (2003) offered several suggestions. These suggestions involve identifying the links between content and application for transfer, setting the stage for transfer through discussion, using content-appropriate examples for participants, reflecting about transfer opportunities as well as obstacles, and applying information as obtained from the development activity as soon as possible in the actual work setting.

Although procedural knowledge may be all that is necessary for certain development activities or certain elements within a development activity, most development efforts require both types of knowledge for an effective development program. The key task of program designers, at this phase of a staff development process, is to decide which type of knowledge is needed to achieve the particular program objectives and how all elements of a planned development activity can best be learned as well as can best be applied by participants. This decision has important implications for other components of the framework in Figure 10.7.

Program Methods

Block 2 in Figure 10.7 addresses the methods used to present the content of development activities to participants. The method to be used in a particular program format or in a particular element of a program will depend on a number of factors. These factors include the objectives of the program, number of personnel involved, cost per participant, availability of personnel to conduct the program, availability of learning aids, and learning ability of program participants.

All potential methods for delivering a staff development program can be effective in certain situations. Effectiveness of any particular staff development program will depend on the learning conditions, including what is to be learned and the type of knowledge to be acquired. Especially important within this phase of program design, according to research, is the relevance of a particular method for attaining a specific organizational goal as noted within the strategic plans of a school district.

Many methods for conveying development information can be used when designing development programs and activities for public school employees, and these methods have advanced beyond the "set and get" modality (Dickinson et al., 2003). The most effective methods rely on a variety of procedures and processes. Some of these procedures and processes for effective staff development are passive, while other methods are active.

Passive delivery methods rely heavily on individuals as self-directed learners. Within passive delivery methods, the content of development programs and activities is communicated largely by a single method. Passive learning techniques commonly used by school systems include conferences, academic classes, and independent study.

Conferences have been and continue to be a mainstay for development programs and activities involving personnel at all levels of the school system. Most conferences focus on a single topic and are of short duration. In communicating the content of development programs and activities, conferences are particularly effective in increasing the employee's procedural knowledge about certain topics or issues but are less effective in communicating conceptual knowledge to participants.

With the recent emphasis on distance learning in colleges and universities, academic classes are becoming a viable development option for many school districts when relying on passive methods to present contents of a staff development program. Academic classes can cover a broad range of topics and can take many weeks to complete. Class assignments can be designed to enhance both the procedural and the conceptual knowledge that employees need to transfer the content of development programs and activities to the work setting.

Independent study, as a passive teaching technique, has an advantage over conferences and classes. The content can be tailored to the specific needs of the individual and of the work assignment. Selected readings and programmed instruction can often reduce the difference between actual and desired levels of performance as assessed earlier within the development process.

In contrast to passive techniques, **active delivery methods** for development programs and activities require behavioral as well as cognitive responses from participants. With active methods of delivery for staff development, participants are given opportunities to apply the knowledge, skills, and/or behaviors they have been exposed to during the staff development process. Common examples of active methods for delivering development programs and activities with public school employees are role-playing, simulation, and coaching.

Role-playing allows individuals to apply certain knowledge, skills, or behaviors in a protective environment away from the actual work setting. Using this method for presenting staff development content, program participants can either role-play their actual job assignment and/or can role-play the counterpart to their actual assignment in the organizational setting. Both roles reinforce actual learning but do so from different perspectives.

When playing a **congruent role** with an actual job assignment, the procedural knowledge of the program participant is strengthened. Knowledge, skills, and behaviors are reinforced. By assuming the role of their counterpart (**incongruent role**), individuals may gain a better understanding of their own organizational role from a contextual perspective by viewing activities through the lens of the other person rather than from a self-perspective point of view.

Like role-playing, **simulations** are removed from the actual job setting of an employee and provide a protective environment. Simulations involve role-playing but embellish the contextual environment in which roles are played. Thus, simulations are one step closer to the actual job assignment of an employee than found typically in a role-playing situation.

Within simulations, considerable attention is given to mimicking all those salient aspects of the work setting through the usage of real data and actual props. With this development technique for delivering staff development content, employees are required to perform or to exhibit the actual skills and behaviors required by their current position or by an anticipated position. This technique gives them an opportunity to develop and to refine certain job skills and behaviors in a protective setting where errors as well as omissions are expected, are identified, are critiqued, and are corrected.

Coaching involves acquiring and developing job skills and behaviors in an actual job situation as opposed either to a role-playing or to a simulated job setting. With this technique, individuals practice the knowledge, skills, and behaviors under the tutelage of an accomplished mentor in the work setting. Mentors advise and instruct as well as provide modeling behavior, performance assessments, and critical feedback designed to promote the development of employees in their current or anticipated position (Middle Web, 2002).

As previously noted, the choice between a passive or an active method for delivering content in development programs or activities depends on many contextual variables. One method of presentation is not necessarily superior to other methods of presentation, and each method of presentation must be evaluated within the constraints of the development program at a particular school district. Again, it must be emphasized that effective development programs and activities utilize more than one of these techniques for enhancing the job skills of employees within a particular school system.

Program Location

The program setting for staff development, as indicated in Block 3 of Figure 10.7, can be located on the job, off the job, or some combination of these locations (DuFour, 2004). The choice among these options for location of staff development depends largely on the resources of the school system. Resources that may impact the delivery of development programs within a particular school system include instructors, facilities, funds, time, and materials.

One key question incurred during the planning phase of staff development is where can the most competent instructor be found? The search for a competent instructor to lead staff development efforts may extend to colleges or universities, regional education agencies, commercial enterprises, private consultants, and/or personnel within the system. Because the school system's funds and facilities are usually limited, some organizations share instructors, facilities, and materials in the staff development process as a means for controlling costs associated with this important human resource function.

Another problem associated with development programs is the need to free personnel from their assigned organizational duties to participate in development programs and activities. The organization must subsidize the time of these personnel in the form of paid leaves of absence, time off with pay, or time off during the school day without extra pay. Lack of funding for release time has been and continues to be a major deterrent to the improvement of development programs for employees at all levels within the school system.

Still another issue associated with the location of staff development activities involves the administration of development programs and activities. Each program format, if it is to succeed, involves an administrative process that includes planning, organizing, directing, coordinating, and evaluating. These processes call for a combination of data, competence, and participation, which must be provided by the system to ensure an effective and efficient program for staff development.

Answers to many of the format issues require alternative ways of viewing development programs and activities that involve a combination of locations. This suggests that staff development programs and activities must be diversified. Diversification can provide new and exciting alternatives to traditional staff development activities for all educational employees.

One relatively new method for diversifying traditional locations and for delivering staff development activities within the public school setting involves using computers to establish professional networks. Professional networks connect a number of individuals, both inside and outside the school system, who have a common interest and a common identity. Professional networks focus on a single topic (reform movement, subject area, etc.), support a number of activities (workshops, conferences, etc.), provide ongoing discussion, and give participants opportunities to lead as well as to participate in the staff development process (Lieberman & McLaughlin, 1992).

Another relatively new method for diversifying traditional locations of staff development programs involves collaboration between school systems and outside agencies. Partnerships are formed in which development activities and resources are shared by the organizations. Initially conceived as university–school agreements focusing on instructional issues involving teachers (Holmes Partnership, 1987–1997), collaborative efforts have been expanded to include other types of organizations and all categories of personnel.

Program Participation

Approaches to staff development programs and activities are listed in Block 4 of Figure 10.7 and are classified as either voluntary or compulsory. Both types of participation may be either formal or informal, depending on the staff development's objectives. Examples for each type of participation and each type of program follow:

- **Formal-voluntary** system: conducts an informational seminar for technology users.
- **Informal-voluntary** system: awards a budgetary allowance to teachers for personal and professional development.
- **Formal-compulsory** system: conducts a seminar about new state mandates for public school districts.
- **Informal-compulsory** system: establishes a deadline for personnel to meet certification requirements. Individuals are free to choose among various approaches to meet the requirements.

Depending on whether a staff development program is formal or informal as well as whether a staff development program is voluntary or compulsory has implications for participation of public school employees. Public school employees have both professional demands and personal demands that must be managed in their everyday lives. Today, more than ever, public school employees must contend with dual family careers and single-parent responsibilities, both of which can influence participation in staff development activities.

Formal staff development programs tend to have a fixed schedule of events. Informal staff development programs tend to have a flexible set of activities. The choice between these two types of programs must be afforded employees of a public school district if the ultimate goals of staff development are to be realized in an effective and an efficient manner.

Voluntary staff development programs may require public employees to preregister and be subject to enrollment caps imposed by physical limitations. Compulsory staff development programs are more restrictive than voluntary staff development programs and may be disruptive to the work setting or the personal life of employees. Although the latter type of staff development program may be a necessity in some instances, these instances can cause undue hardship for certain public school employees.

Examination of these forms of participation leads to two inferences about approaches to personnel participation in staff development activities offered by a public school district. The first inference is that uniformity in the design of development programs and activities is neither feasible nor desirable for most public school districts. A second inference is that program format planning calls for great flexibility in meeting the development needs of various types of personnel through providing a variety of locations for staff development activities.

Potential Program Contaminants

The last step in the design phase of staff development involves considering specific contaminants that may influence the outcomes from a staff development process in ways other than intended by the developers (see Block 5 in Figure 10.7). These contaminants have been overlooked within the staff development process by many school districts. In the past, the emphasis for most school districts in staff development has been placed on processes and procedures for administering the staff development activities rather than on assessing outcomes obtained from development activities (Champion, 2002).

Far too often, little thought has been devoted within the development phase of the staff development process to evaluation. Without an adequate evaluation of staff development activities, it is impossible to determine if these efforts are fulfilling the goals of a strategic plan as set forth by a public school district (Hirsh, 2004). In the absence of a formal evaluation, the outcomes of development efforts may be difficult, if not impossible, to assess in any meaningful manner, either from a remedial or from a proactive vantage point of view by a public school system.

It is not only likely, but is quite probable, that outcomes from many staff development activities may be due, at least in part, to contaminants other than those associated with the staff development activities. Many of the factors that can influence potentially the outcomes of a staff development program have been identified by Campbell and Stanley (1963). Because these factors have important implications for assessment of development programs and activities in the work setting, each factor should be considered when designing an assessment process for a staff development program.

By considering the factors described by Campbell and Stanley when designing the evaluation component of a staff development program or activity, important planning information can be realized by a public school system. Although these factors will be treated independently in this discussion, in practice, these factors may interact and may have a combined influence on the assessment of outcomes associated with development programs or activities. These contaminants include history, maturation, pretest, instrumentation, regression, selection, and mortality.

History, as the term implies, concerns the knowledge, skills, and behaviors that individuals bring to the staff development process within the public school setting. Most staff development issues involve refining and enhancing current knowledge, skills, and behaviors about specific topics/content rather than introducing the topics/content to participants for the first time. This is particularly true when development activities address vogue topics, covered by media complementing development efforts.

For example, vogue topics for staff development include drug abuse among students, single-parent households, and discipline/violence in the school environment, to mention only a few. For each of these topics, participants have a baseline knowledge repertoire. The goal of an effective and an efficient development program is to expand the current knowledge base of participants beyond the existing repertoire.

To determine if this expansion has been accomplished through development efforts, the assessment procedures must consider the history of participants within the evaluation process. By ignoring the history of participants within the assessment process, outcomes from the evaluation of development efforts may well overestimate the effectiveness of a particular development activity. That is, redundant information may have been presented in a development program, and redundant information represents a poor usage of tight fiscal resources in this important area.

Beyond the history that employees bring to the development process, the knowledge, skills, and behaviors of all employees change over time as part of the employment experience. This type of change is labeled as **maturation** within the evaluation literature.

More specifically, maturation concerns developmental changes experienced by employees due to the normal assimilation process and not to any development efforts on the part of a public school district.

Appropriately designed development activities should accelerate this change and should shape this change in a positive manner for knowledge, skills, and behavior. Development programs and activities designed to acclimate new employees may appear to be effective when, in fact, a certain level of adjustment should be expected to occur normally without the benefit of staff development activities. Consequently, one of the goals of development is to increase the knowledge, skills, and behaviors of employees beyond those expected by the normal maturation process.

To assess the history of participants and their current level of maturation relative to knowledge, skills, and behaviors, many times a **pretest** is administered by those responsible for development efforts in a public school setting. A pretest is administered prior to the execution of any development activity to acquire baseline data about participants relative to history and to maturation. These data, as obtained from the pretest, are used to assess net gains in knowledge, skills, and behaviors of those taking part in the development activity by comparing initial results to posttest results.

However, well documented within the evaluation literature is initial deficiencies in knowledge, skills, and behaviors as detected by pretesting may sensitize participants to certain content areas that might go unnoticed during a training program in the absence of a pretest. Because of information gaps detected by a pretest, certain content areas may become important for employees taking part in development programs or activities due to a pretest exposure of voids in current knowledge that would have gone unnoticed without the use of a pretest, and outcomes from a development process could be more a function of the pretest than a function of the development effort.

Core to all evaluation processes for a development effort in the public school setting is the measuring instrument used to assess outcomes from the development process. Within the evaluation process, it is assumed that the calibration of a measuring instrument remains constant across individuals as well as across time. Changes in the measuring instrument either across time or across individuals unrelated to development efforts are known as an **instrumentation.**

Overlooked by many evaluation processes for development efforts in a public school setting is that the measuring instrument for assessing development outcomes is an individual. No doubt for many development activities the measuring instrument for assessing the success of development efforts is the immediate supervisor of those employees taking part in the development activities. If the proficiency of this supervisor in measuring the success of development efforts improves through practice during the staff development process, changes in employee performance may be attributable to the improvement in the supervisor rather than to the content of the development activity.

Many staff development programs are remedial and attempt to rectify deficiencies in knowledge, skills, or behaviors of existing employees relative to their on-the-job performance. By definition, these employees perform less well than their counterparts within a public school district. Because their current performance is well below average, their performance can only improve (rise toward the mean) if they are to remain employed by a public school district.

Improvements for low-performing employees taking part in a remedial development effort may be attributed to **regression** toward the mean rather than any content of a development activity. Regression to the mean occurs when employees are selected for development programs or activities because of their extremely poor performance on certain measures (job performance, absenteeism, etc.). As a result of regression toward the mean level of performance, remedial programs often appear to be effective when effectiveness is due to the regression phenomenon rather than due to the content of a development program. For an effective and an efficient development program, improvements must exceed those expected by regression to the mean.

Participation in development programs and activities can be either voluntary or compulsory (see Block 4 of Figure 10.7), and these differences involve the **selection** of participants. Voluntary participants self-select particular development efforts based on their perceived needs and/or interest in the topics under exploration. These types of participants (voluntary) generally bring a high level of motivation and of goal orientation to the development effort and will, in most instances, perform well.

In contrast to voluntary participants, compulsory participants typically are less motivated and are less goal orientated about the development effort within the public school setting. Development programs and activities that appear to be highly successful with voluntary participants who have sought out this development initiative on their own volition may be disastrous with compulsory participants, even when the content and methods of these programs and activities are the same for both groups of employees. Thus, any generalization of program success as derived from an evaluation process must be tempered by the manner through which employees were selected for participation.

Attendance to development programs and activities within a public school district are seldom 100 percent of the anticipated involvement. Some individuals will fail to show up, and other individuals will depart before the completion of the program. Those that drop out of a development program or activity represent a **mortality** rate, and the mortality rate can distort the results of evaluations for development efforts.

Mortality can be caused by several factors, some related to the program and some related to other events. Many development programs and activities require a great deal of time and effort on the part of participants. If participants are allowed to drop out, an assessment of the knowledge, skills, and attitudes of only those who remain in the program may provide a distorted view of the program's effectiveness. Assessments should include both those who drop out and those who complete the program.

All of the factors described may influence assessments of development programs and activities and may provide misleading information to those responsible for developing, implementing, and evaluating these programs and activities within the public school setting. Although not all of these factors may be pertinent to all development programs and activities, some of the factors can influence every staff development program and activity within the public school setting. To control or to assess the impact of the factors mentioned, consideration must be given to these factors in the design phases of staff development processes as these processes are addressed in the evaluation phase of the staff development process.

Prior to discussing Phase 3—as found in Figure 10.6—which involves implementing development programs and activities in a school environment, certain issues should be recapitulated. The specifics of each program format for staff development, as discussed in Phase 2, need to be summarized and disseminated for review, formalization, and implementation. A form for linking program formats to development objectives is shown in Figure 10.8.

This form emphasizes, prior to implementation of staff development activities, that each development program should be reviewed for links among program formats, program objectives, and strategic goals of the organization. By analyzing the items contained in the form, human resource planners can determine whether development objectives have been translated into specific operations and whether the program format is capable of achieving the objectives of the program and the strategic goals of the system in an effective and an efficient manner. The analysis should reveal gaps to be filled and revisions needed before development plans are implemented in the actual work setting.

Phase 3: Implementing Development Programs

Reexamination of the model in Figure 10.6 indicates that completion of Phase 2 (program design) leads to Phase 3 (implementation of development activities). Phase 3 occurs when the design of the program is shaped into an operational structure and when the planning activities are put into operation. At this time, Phases 1 and 2 are meshed to link together individual, unit, and organizational goals as contained within the strategic plans of a school district.

In the implementation phase of the development process, several types of human resource decisions are required. The persons responsible for developing and implementing the process must determine the timing and the sequencing of development activities and events within the staff development process. These decisions are incorporated into an operational structure known as the assessment design.

The assessment design of development programs or activities determines the protocol for program administration. Most importantly, the assessment design dictates which employees will be exposed to certain program components and activities, as well as when these program components and activities are to be administered. The answers to these questions have profound implications for Phase 4 (evaluation) of the development process.

Assessment Design

The assessment design provides the framework within which development programs and activities are carried out by a public school system. Public school systems use several types of designs when administering and when evaluating a staff development activity. These designs vary both in complexity and sensitivity to those factors that can potentially confound the assessment of development programs and activities (history, maturation,

DEVELOPMENT PLANNING FORM

1. Title of Program _____

2. Program purpose:

   System Improvement _____   Unit Improvement _____

   Position Effectiveness _____   Professional Development _____

   Individual Development _____

3. Specific program objective(s):

   Disseminate Information _____   Develop Skills _____

   Alter Organizational Climate _____   Change Attitudes _____

   Enhance Problem Solving _____   Career Development _____

4. Target audience:

   Administrative and supervisory _____

   Instructional personnel _____

   Classified personnel _____

   Temporary personnel _____

5. Level of learning:

   Simple _____ Complex _____ or Highly Complex _____

6. Type of learning:

   Procedural _____ Conceptual _____ and/or Behavioral _____

7. Program scope:

   System _____ Building/site _____ or Individual _____

8. Type of participants:

   Voluntary _____ or Compulsory _____

9. Anticipated number of participants _____

10. Program methods:

    Self-Instruction _____ Tutorial _____ and/or Group Instruction

11. Program setting:

    On the Job _____   Off the Job _____ Combination _____

12. Program needs:

    Funds _____   Facilities _____   Materials _____

    Equipment _____   Personnel _____

13. Contact person _____

14. Assessment design:

    Case Study _____, Pretest _____, Control Group _____, Other _____

15. Outcome measures (criteria):

    Participants' Reactions _____, Participants' Knowledge _____,

    Participants' Behaviors _____

16. Outcome Intent: In what way will the system, unit, or employee change as a result of this development effort?

FIGURE 10.8 *Development program planning format.*

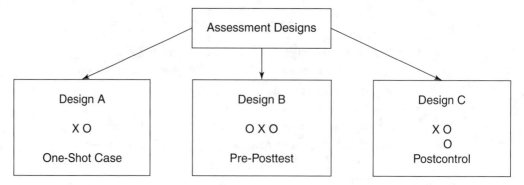

FIGURE 10.9   *Assessment designs.*

pretesting, etc.). Choosing among assessment designs is a major human resource task in Phase 3 of the development process (see Figure 10.6).

Assessment designs used most frequently for staff development programs and activities in public school districts are shown in Figure 10.9 (see Campbell & Stanley, 1963). In these designs employed by public school districts for assessing the effects of staff development programs and activities, two symbols are used to denote the implementation and assessment of program activities. The first symbol, "X," represents the actual staff development program or activity, as executed in the development setting, and the second symbol, "O," represents an outcome assessment associated with that particular program or activity following the presentation of the development program/activity.

Design A, as found in Figure 10.9, is used most frequently by public school districts for assessing staff development activities in the educational setting. This design is labeled as a **one-shot case study.** In a one-shot case study, participants take part in a staff development program or activity as denoted by "X." After taking part in the staff development activities, the program or activity is assessed at the conclusion of the development efforts with the participants as noted by "O."

Although educational organizations use often the one-shot case study to evaluate staff development activities, this design is an extremely poor choice for the implementation phase and for the evaluation phase of the staff development process. With a one-shot case study, it is impossible to determine what effects are attributable to the development program or to the staff development activity and what effects are attributable to outside factors (history, maturation, selection, etc.) rather than to program content. Even when participants perform exceptionally well on the assessment following presentation of staff development content or development activities, several viable alternative explanations exist for these findings that renders one-shot case studies as extremely questionable at best.

Because this design (design A) is insensitive to any previous knowledge, skills, and behaviors possessed by the participants, these participants could have well possessed the knowledge, skills, and behaviors addressed in the development effort prior to their participation either through history or through maturation. Depending on the measuring instrument, on the participant selection process, and on the participation rate, other viable explanations exist for evaluation results obtained from a one-shot case study. In short, Design A is almost entirely ineffective for evaluating development efforts even though it is the most frequently used design within the public school setting.

To provide information about the prior level of performance/knowledge of participants in development programs or activities (controlling for history, maturation, and selection), Design B is used with an even a lesser frequency than Design A in the public school setting for assessing development efforts. This design (Design B) is labeled as a **pre-posttest design.** With the pre-posttest design, participants are assessed prior to the staff development program or activity and are assessed, again, immediately after they complete the staff development program or activity.

When the two assessments are compared, a measure of program or activity effectiveness is obtained through a discrepancy analysis involving pre- and posttest comparisons of assessments. The pre-posttest design is slightly superior to the one-shot case study because the pre-posttest design provides baseline data on participants taking part in the staff development activities. However, the pre-posttest design may sometimes pose problems for several reasons.

A major problem with the pre-posttesting design is the sensitization of participants to their voids in knowledge, skills, and behaviors to be covered by a development activity. With respect to the regression phenomenon associated with remedial development efforts, the pre-posttest is insensitive because regression effects cannot be separated from program effects (i.e., all participants are assessed at two different times). Instrumentation could be a likely explanation due to a practice effect across pre-posttesting, and mortality is also a concern unless all participants are assessed.

Substantial improvements over the one-shot case study and the pre-posttest design can be achieved by using Design C in Figure 10.9 when implementing and when evaluating staff development activities in the public school setting. Design C, as found in Figure 10.9, is a **posttest control group design.** In this last design, as found in Figure 10.9, some participants receive the development program or activity and others do not (at least not at the time of assessment). Both groups are assessed at the same time at the conclusion of the staff development activities.

A posttest control group design, when properly constructed, provides an extremely effective framework for implementing and evaluating staff development programs and activities in the public school setting. By using a proper control group for comparison, many potential factors other than those attributable to the development effort can be addressed in this type of design. Specifically, the posttest control group design either assesses or controls for such factors as testing, selection, regression, history, instrumentation, and mortality.

Those designs presented in Figure 6.9 are only some of the designs used frequently to implement and assess a staff development program in the public school setting. Other designs and other options exist, and those responsible for implementing development efforts must make an informed choice based on the potential factors in a given situation. The design chosen specifically for staff evaluation influences the implementation phase of the development process as well as the evaluation phase of staff development.

Phase 4: Evaluating Staff Development Programs

Development efforts of public school districts have been criticized often for failing to focus on significant individual or organizational needs, attacking the wrong problems, or attempting to solve the right problems with inappropriate staff development techniques. It should be noted: (a) that in some school systems, evaluation fails to take place at all, (b) that evaluation occurs frequently to human resource planners as an afterthought within the staff development process, and (c) that evaluation of development activities in many school systems serves only a procedural requirement and fails to impart substantive information. The development process introduced in Figure 10.6 includes Phase 4 (evaluation) as the last step in the development process model for a public school district.

If the evaluation phase of a staff development process is omitted, then feedback is lacking to identify and to correct program defects, information is unavailable to enhance decision making, and a sound foundation is lacking for improving the total staff development effort within a public school district (Mizell, 2003). There are many constraints and many obstacles to overcome in evaluating staff development programs. In addition, there are varying viewpoints regarding the necessity for, approaches to, effects of, and values derived from evaluation of school district efforts within the development process.

Nevertheless, it is generally held that staff development requires a sound evaluation based on appropriate data (Lowden, 2005). There is also considerable agreement that awareness of important factors in the evaluation phase makes it possible to avoid useless evaluations and to derive information that will be helpful in directing development planning. In this connection, key considerations in the evaluation of staff development programs are outlined in Figure 10.10.

Purpose of the Evaluation:	What is to be evaluated (Employees, Content, and/or Application)?
Type of Evaluation:	Quantitative or Qualitative?
Criteria for Evaluation:	Reactions, Knowledge, Behaviors, Attitudes?
Assessment Design:	What type of assessment design will be employed?
Methods of Data Collection:	Observation, Interviewing, Questionnaire, and/or Supervisor Ratings.
Presentation of Data:	How will data be recorded, analyzed, presented, and interpreted.
Outcomes:	What will be the audience for the evaluation results?

FIGURE 10.10   *Evaluation considerations.*

It is worth emphasizing that program content (what to deliver) and program methods (how it should be delivered) are critical decisions in the design and evaluation of staff development programs in the public school setting. The learning process by which new behaviors (skills, knowledge, abilities, and attitudes) are acquired involves practicing those behaviors so that those behaviors result in relatively permanent change and enhance the performance of public school employees. The types of questions used to determine whether a development project has succeeded include the following:

- Participant impact: What has the project done to change the behavior of the participant?
- Position impact: Did the participant's performance in the work setting improve?
- Organizational impact: In what ways and to what extent did the development efforts contribute to attainment of organizational goals and objectives?

These questions bring into focus the need to specify carefully the objectives of a staff development program and to identify criteria by which to measure the objectives sought by a public school system. If the objectives are unclear, it will be difficult to choose or to develop appropriate measuring techniques and to judge whether the intended results were achieved by the school district's efforts.

Rational decisions can be made with greater conviction when there is some basis for determining whether improvement programs have been or will be an effective and an efficient means for improving the knowledge, skills, and behaviors of public school employees. There are many questions relating to the extent to which knowledge, skills, attitudes, work behavior, and organizational impact have changed. In addition, informed stakeholders will want to know whether changes in these variables are due to the staff development program or due to some of the extraneous factors previously discussed (history, maturation, pretesting, instrumentation, regression, selection, and/or mortality). An analysis of Figure 10.10 leads to these observations:

- The evaluation process is complex and extensive. Sophisticated knowledge is needed to initiate, implement, and coordinate all of its facets.
- The evaluation phase requires knowledge, skills, attitudes, and position behaviors to improve the system's evaluation capabilities.
- The purposes of evaluation constitute the "engine" that pulls the evaluation "train." Evaluation methods, criteria, criterion measures, as well as collection and refinement of data derived from evaluation, inform future development efforts.

This section on the evaluation phase of staff development is concluded by suggesting that nurturing an organization's human resources is a primary leadership responsibility to be undertaken by all public school districts as part of the strategic planning process. This requires an organizational investment of considerable time, money, and talent to solve major evaluation problems. These problems—either by design or by default—have been seriously neglected and will become even more critical in light of social change, technological development, and public concern about the quality and effectiveness of the nation's schools.

Review and Preview

This chapter has stated that the school system that embraces the policy of continual development has important strategic advantages. Key ideas of this thesis include the following:

- School improvement through personnel development is best accomplished within individual schools and school systems. Traditional practices do not generate effective staff development programs.
- The staff development process includes identifying needs, establishing program objectives, creating plans to achieve the objectives (including teaching methods), and evaluating program outcomes.
- Staff development includes individual, group, system, and board member development.
- Major factors to be considered in the assessment of personnel needs are the external and internal environments, the school system, positions, position holders, position-person matches, position context, and work groups.

- Cues for designing programs can be derived from system policy, research and practice, value trends, career stages, and the external environment.
- Formal development program design includes program content, methods, setting, participation, and resources.
- Criteria for evaluating staff development programs include the participant, position, work group, and organizational impact.

In Chapter 11, attention will be devoted to the collective bargaining process within the public school setting from a human resource perspective. Discussion is provided about the formation of unions, the construction of bargaining units, and the collective bargain process. Different types of impasses are identified and attention is afforded to impasse resolution procedures both when negotiating and when administering a labor contract. Ground rules for negotiations and contents of labor contracts are analyzed from different perspectives.

Discussion Questions

1. You have been given oversight of the development program for a small school district. What information will guide your decisions on the content of the staff development activities that you will implement?

2. What is the relationship between staff development and strategic planning?

3. What external factors influence the direction of staff development in your school organization? What inner factors influence that direction?

4. You oversee employee development for a school organization. What are the

implications of career stages on the staff development program you implement?

5. Consider the in-service education that you have undertaken in your career to date. What have been the strengths of this activity? What are the weaknesses of the processes you have encountered?

6. Development activities can be targeted to the individual, the group, or the organization. Give three examples of activities at each of these levels.

Case Study

Your school district uses the one-shot case study approach to evaluate development activities. More specifically, participants of development activities "show up" and participate. At the conclusion of their participation, they are administered an evaluative questionnaire to capture their reaction according to policy. What are the problems with this approach and what are some of the viable explanations for the outcomes obtained with this approach? How would you address these problems within the political context of your school district? What types of opposition would you likely incur and from whom? Design a plan of action.

References

Asayesh, G. (1993, Fall). Using systems thinking to change systems. *Journal of Staff Development, 14*(4), 8–140.

Campbell, D. T., & Stanley, J. C. (1963). *Experimental and quasi-experimental designs.* Chicago: Rand McNally.

Champion, R. (2002). Taking measure: Map out evaluation goals. *Journal of Staff Development, 23*(4). Retrieved June 29, 2006, from Web site: http://www.nsdc.org/library/publications/jsd/champion234.cfm.

Cunningham, W. G., & Cordeiro, P. A. (2006). *Educational leadership: A problem-based approach* (3rd ed.). Columbus, OH: Pearson.

DeLuca, J. R. (1991, Summer). The evolution of staff development for teachers. *Journal of Staff Development, 12*(3), 45.

Dickenson, G., McBride, J., & Lamb-Milligan, J. (2003). Delivering authentic staff development. *ProQuest Innovation.* Retrieved July 1, 2006, from Web site: http://www.findarticles.com/p/articles/mi_qa3673/is_200310/ai_n9332108/.

DuFour, R. (2004). Leading edge: The best staff development is in the workplace, not in a workshop. *Journal of Staff Development, 25* (2). Retrieved June 29, 2006, from Web site: http://www.nsdc.org/library/publications/jsd/dufour252.cfm.

Farber, B., & Ascher, C. (1991, July). Urban school restructuring and teacher burnout. *ERIC Clearinghouse on Urban Education, 75.* Retrieved August 14, 2002, from the Eric Clearinghouse Web site: http://ericweb.tc.columbia.edu/digests/dig75.aspcoran.

Firestone, W. A., & Pennell, J. R. (1997). Designing state-sponsored networks: A comparison of two cases. *American Educational Research Journal, 34*(2), 237–266.

Hirsh, S. (2004). Putting comprehensive staff development on target. *Journal of Staff Development, 25*(1). Retrieved June 29, 2006, from Web site: http://www.nsdc.org/library/publications/jsd/hirsh251.cfm.

Holmes Partnership. (1987–1997). *Origins of the Holmes Partnership.* Retrieved August 14, 2002, from the Holmes Partnership Web site: http://www.holmespartnership.org/origins.html.

Interstate School Leaders Licensure Consortium (n.d.). Retrieved July 11, 2006 from Web site: http://www.ccsso.org/projects/Interstate_Consortium_on_School_Leaderships.

Lieberman, A., & McLaughlin, M. W. (1992). Network for educational change: Powerful and problematic. *Phi Delta Kappan, 73,* 673–677.

Lowden, C. (2005). Evaluating the impact of professional development. *The Journal of Research in Professional Learning.* Retrieved June 29, 2006, from Web site: http://www.nsdc.org/library/publications/research/lowden.pdf.

Markley, M. (2001, August 15). Districts taking new steps to stem teacher turnover. *Houston Chronicle.* Retrieved August 14, 2002, from the Houston Chronicle Web site: http:// www.chron.com/cs/CDA/story.hts/topstory/1006096.

McGehee, W., & Thayer, P. (1961). *Training in business and industry.* New York: Wiley.

Middle Web. (2002). *Some teacher mentoring resources*. Retrieved May 23, 2002, from Web site: http://middleweb.com/mentoring.html.

Mizell, H. (2003). Facilitator: 10 refreshments: 8 Evaluation: 0. *Journal of Staff Development, 24* (4). Retrieved June 29, 2006, from Web site: http://www.nsdc.org/library/publications/jsd/mizell244. cfm.

No Child Left Behind Act 2001 (2002). Pub. L. No. 107–110, 115 stat. 1425.

Partee, G. L. (2001). A strategic approach to staff development. *National Association of Secondary School Principals*. Retrieved July 1, 2006, from Web site: http://www.findarticles.com/p/articles/mi_qa4002/ is_200102/ai_n8929783/.

Prince, C. D. (2002, January). *The challenge of attracting good teachers and principals to struggling schools*. Retrieved August 13, 2002, from the American Association of School Administrators Web site: http://www.aasa.org/issues_and_insights/issues_dept/challenges_teachers_principals.pdf.

Richard, A. (2004). School-based. . . . or not. *Journal of Staff Development, 25* (1). Retrieved June 29, 2006, from Web site: http://www.nsdc.org/library/publications/jsd/richard252.cfm.

Richardson, J. (2003, October/November). Building a bridge between workshop and classroom. *Tools for Schools*. Retrieved June 29, 2006, from Web site: http://www.nsdc.org/library/publications/tools/tools 10-03rich.cfm.

Rowand, C. (n.d.). Teacher use of computers and the Internet in public schools. *Education Statistics Quarterly, Elementary and Secondary Education*. Retrieved July 11, 2006, from the National Center for Education Statistics Web site: http://nces.ed.gov/pubs2000/quarterly/summer/3elem/q3-2.html.

Scarpello, V. G., Ledvinka, J., & Bergman, T. J. (1995). *Human resource management: Environments and functions*. Cincinnati, OH: South-Western College Publishing.

Sergiovanni, T. J. (2006). *The principalship: A reflective practice perspective*. Boston: Pearson Education, Inc.

Seyfarth, J. T. (1996). *Personnel management for effective schools*. Boston: Allyn & Bacon.

Sparks, D. (2003). Significant change begins with leaders. *National Staff Development Council*. Retrieved June 29, 2006, from Web site: http://www.nsdc.org/library/publications/results/res10-03spar.cfm.

U.S. Department of Education. (1998, September). Improving professional development practices. In *Promising practices: New ways to improve teacher quality*. Retrieved July 1, 2006, from the U.S. Department of Education Web site: http://www.ed.gov/pubs/PromPractice/chapter6.html.

U.S. Department of Education's National Commission on Excellence in Education. (1983). *A nation at risk*. Retrieved July 1, 2006, from the North Central Regional Educational Laboratory Web site: http://www.ncrel.org/sdrs/areas/issues/content/cntareas/science/sc3 risk.htm.

Young, I. P. (in press). The effects of like-type sex evaluations within the labor market for principals. *Personnel Evaluation in Education*.

Young, I. P., & Miller-Smith, K. (2006). Effects of site-based councils on teacher screening decisions in high and low performing school districts: A policy capturing study. *Public Policy Analysis in Education, 14*(6).

Unionism and Collective Bargaining

11

CHAPTER CONCEPTS

Agency shop
American Federation of Teachers (AFT)
Appropriate bargaining unit
Arbitration
Certification bar
Closed shop
Consent agreement
Contested election
Contract bar
Decertification
Declaratory ruling
Election bar
End run
Exclusive representation
Fact finding
Fair share
Final offer arbitration
Good faith bargaining
Grievance procedure
Ground rules
Illegal
Impasse
Impasse procedures
Interest arbitrator

Item-by-item arbitration
Labor contract
Local Educational
   Association (LEA)
Make whole procedure
Mandatory
Master agreement
Mediation
Mediator
Meet-and-confer model
National Education
   Association (NEA)
National Labor Relations
   Board (NLRB)
Negotiations
Open shop
Parent organizations
Permissive
Prenegotiation
   preparation
Procedural denial
Quickie strike
Ratification process
Redress sought
Rights arbitration
Scope of bargaining
Self-representation
Showing of interest
State Education
   Association (SEA)
State Employment
   Relations Board (SERB)
Strike
Substantive denial
Sympathy strike
Timeliness
Uncontested election
Wall-to-wall bargaining
Wild cat strike
Zipper clause

OBJECTIVES

- Overview the historical basis and attendant developments of 20th-century collective bargaining in public education in the United States.
- Portray the importance of the human resource function in coordinating, systematizing, and administering the collective bargaining process.
- Indicate why teacher unions should be a dynamic part of resolving public education problems in the 21st century.
- Depict the elements of a model for the collective bargaining process.

Historical Perspective

Collective bargaining is an organizational process for diversifying decision making within the public school setting from a unilateral **self-representation** to a bilateral mode of other representation. Prior to collective bargaining within the public school setting, all human resource decisions relative to the organization and operation of a public school district were at the local level largely within the preview of a local board of education. As a result of collective bargaining being implemented in the public school setting, many human resource decisions require the concurrent agreement between school boards and labor unions.

Indeed, a polling of school board members, public school administrators, and employees will indicate that few other organizational phenomena have influenced the practice of human resource management in public school districts more than the advent of collective bargaining in education. Collective bargaining has changed the entire scope of human resource management in public education in many ways. What was once a unilateral decision-making process on the part of management has changed to a bilateral decision-making process requiring the concurrence of unions for managing many employee groups through **negotiations.**

When viewed from a historical perspective, collective bargaining within the public school setting is an evolving process that has spanned several decades. Early within the public school setting, collective bargaining followed the private sector model. More recently, some very important differences have emerged between private and public sector collective bargaining practices, and these differences have had and will continue to have implications for the practice of human resource management in public school districts.

The single most notable difference between private sector and public sector collective bargaining is the enabling source for this administrative activity. Within the private sector, the enabling source for collective bargaining is the federal government. For public education, the enabling source for collective bargaining is the state government.

Because collective bargaining within the private sector is a federal concern, a single law, standardized procedures, and administrative rules exist that govern totally the collective bargaining process across all states. These regulatory provisions transcend state boundaries and cover all types of unions within the private sector (truckers, mine workers, agricultural employees, etc.). Oversight of all collective bargaining in the private sector falls under the same legislative act and is administered by a single regulatory agency, the **National Labor Relations Board** (**NLRB; http://www.nlrb.gov/).**

Unlike the consistency for collective bargaining within the private sector, considerable variations exist for collective bargaining within the public sector. In some instances, states have authorized collective bargaining for public school districts through the passage of specific legislation, whereas in other instances, states have failed to enact legislation pertaining to collective bargaining in the public school setting (for a complete listing of all state employment laws see State Employment Relations Laws, n.d.). Since the first enabling act was passed by Wisconsin in 1959, 34 states have passed similar enabling legislation, whereas other states lack enabling legislation for collective bargaining in the public sector (American Federation of Teachers, n.d.).

Of those states passing enabling legislation, many variations exist concerning the practice of collective bargaining within the public school setting. For example, some states have established **State Employment Relations Boards (SERBs),** similar to the NLRB to administer the public sector bargaining laws. Within these states, collective bargaining issues related to recognition, negotiations, and impasses are dealt with in a systematic manner by a single agency.

In contrast, some states have passed enabling legislation for collective bargaining but have failed to provide for a regulatory agency. Without a regulatory agency for administering the collective bargaining process, parties are left to their own means for resolving conflicts stemming from the collective bargaining process. To resolve difficulties/ disagreements, public school districts within these states must rely either on the court system or some mutually agreed upon dispute resolution process (American Federation of State, County & Municipal Employees, n.d.).

States without enabling legislation for collective bargaining may still have collective bargaining in the public school setting but do so without the benefit of statutory rights. For those latter states failing to sanctify collective bargaining, collective bargaining is viewed as a privilege rather than a right. It is a privilege in the sense that collective bargaining exists only because the school board agrees to extend the bargaining process to the employees.

Without the existence of enabling legislation for collective bargaining, employees fail to enjoy any basic rights relative to the collective bargaining process other than those rights granted by the local board of education. The general notion of extending the privilege of collective bargaining to employees has expanded beyond the scope of existing legislation in several instances. To illustrate, certain school districts in Wisconsin and Ohio have extended bargaining rights to managerial groups exempted from the public sector bargaining laws within these states. More specifically, school districts in Milwaukee, Wisconsin, and in Toledo, Ohio, afford collective bargaining rights to principals and to managers even though these groups have been excluded specifically by state legislation within the respective states (see Milwaukee Public Schools, n.d. and Toledo Public School, n.d.).

As a result of the growth of collective bargaining in general, school boards and human resource administrators have become increasingly cognizant of the need for continuing education relating to collective bargaining in the public sector to keep abreast of rapidly changing conditions and to learn how to deal more effectively with the organizational impact of collective behavior. This phenomenon, considered to be one of the most significant legal developments in the 20th century, has forced school systems to master collective bargaining procedures, just as school boards and school administrators have learned to master other organizational problems imposed on them by a world in transition.

School boards and human resource administrators are rapidly gaining greater sophistication and acquiring those skills essential to cope with numerous complex issues posed by unions. The initial collective bargaining movement in education found school boards and human resource administrators unprepared generally to engage in the collective bargaining process. With the passage of time, however, there has been increasing awareness by school officials that the application of collective bargaining techniques to school personnel problems requires boards and administrators to adjust to new and changing roles in order to establish conditions of employment for personnel under their jurisdiction.

Purpose Perspective

Collective bargaining is defined as a bilateral process through which elected representatives of school personnel meet with representatives of the school system to negotiate an agreement defining the terms and conditions of employment covering a specific period of time as encapsulated within a **labor contract.** The following information identifies important purposes and elements of the transactional relationship by which conflicting demands and requirements of both parties are reconciled within the collective bargaining process. It is useful to review these propositions and to show their relevance to the human resource function before going on to a discussion of various steps in the conduct of the collective bargaining process.

Worth noting is that the employees of school systems seek representation by a union for many reasons. These include economical, psychological, political, and social reasons. The major goal of unions is to maximize opportunities and security for their membership, including a higher standard of living, financial protection, position security, employment rights, opportunity for advancement, maintenance of individual integrity, and attainment of status and respect warranted by members of any profession.

A major objective of the administration of a school system is to operate the system effectively and efficiently in the public interest and to maintain the authority and the rights it needs to accomplish these purposes. In contrast, unions seek to restrict unilateral decision making by the board of education and to modify decisions so that outcomes are in accord with the needs and desires of the membership. Many times these differences encroach on the prerogatives of each party and must be reconciled through the collective bargaining process.

The collective bargaining process in the public sector is influenced by a variety of interests that are portrayed graphically in Figure 11.1. The contract ultimately agreed to by both parties will be the result of the combined interaction of various forces, factors, and conditions. Over the years, the judicial, union, media, administrative, students, governmental, economical, and public have become acutely interested in, drawn into, or have attempted to influence the settlement of disputes between employees and employers in the public sector.

Collective bargaining goes beyond the willingness of a board of education to hear from, listen to, or to be consulted regarding conditions of employment. The willingness of a school board to hear from, listen to, or to be consulted about conditions of employment for an employee group follows a **meet-and-confer model** rather than a collective bargaining process. The meet-and-confer model requires only that the board of education listen to the demands of employees rather than react to their demands.

Meet-and-confer models are common in public school districts. For example, most school districts have an administrator association with representatives that meet and confer with boards of education about the desired benefits for administrators each year. At the basic level, a meet-and-confer model is a precursor to the collective bargaining process but without the binding characteristics.

In contrast to the meet-and-confer model, the collective bargaining process requires codetermination of the terms and conditions of employment, which, when mutually agreed to, bind both parties to those terms and signals the end of individual relations and

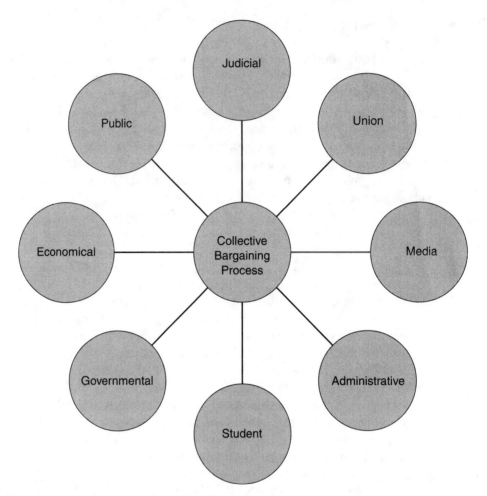

FIGURE 11.1   *Forces influencing the collective bargaining process.*

the beginning of group relations between employee and employer. Often, the collective bargaining process involves new and emerging responsibilities for the system, modification of the administrative structure, extension of the human resource function, and different styles of leadership to deal more effectively with emerging employer–employee relationships, the new work ethic, and changing criteria for individual effectiveness in the world of work. Collective bargaining in the public sector gives the public employee the right to participate through a chosen representative in the determination of policies and practices that affect terms and conditions of employment.

Often overlooked is the fact that collective bargaining imposes restrictions on the system, the union, and the employee. Unilateral action is prohibited on the part of all stakeholders. The system must bargain with the official bargaining unit and not with individuals as employees. Once organized, employees forfeit their rights as individuals to negotiate with the school board and school administrators and delegate this right to their chosen bargaining agent.

Existence and acceptance of the collective bargaining principle by a school system does not imply abandonment of the twin objectives of organizational efficiency and effectiveness so legislatively charged to a local school board. The investment that a system makes in its human resources is considerable. As such, the system should focus its attention on controlling costs and maximizing the productive contribution of each of its members in exchange for the system's investment in pay, benefits, opportunities, and position-related satisfactions.

A major goal of collective bargaining is to establish a sound and stable relationship between the system and the chosen representative of the employees. Only by participation of both parties in the resolution of disagreements and by good faith on either side in yielding to reasonable demands can this end be achieved. Adherence of the board to its responsibilities to constituents is an essential ingredient of harmonious personnel relationships.

The Regulatory Anatomy of Bargaining

Public employment practices within each state are shaped by specific labor laws and are enforced by different administrative agencies and by various court rulings. The structure of the regulatory anatomy governing union–school system employment relations, the policies by which they are shaped, the manner in which legislation is enforced, and the judicial interpretations of such policies are of primary importance to the human resource function in the public school setting from a strategic planning perspective. Knowledge of each authority is a necessity for the effective human resource manager.

It is important to understand the organizational structure of unions, recognition processes for unions, bargaining unit characteristics, **impasse procedures** used to resolve disputes, and strike provisions provided by different states (see Figure 11.2).

Union Organization

From an organizational perspective, most unions within the public school setting are not stand-alone entities. In general, public school unions are tiered and involve **parent organizations** both at the national and at the state levels. Contained in Figure 11.3 is the general organizational structure for most unions found in public school districts.

These tiers are national level (nea), state level (sea), and local level (lea) (see Figure 11.3). In most instances for teachers, the national organization is either the

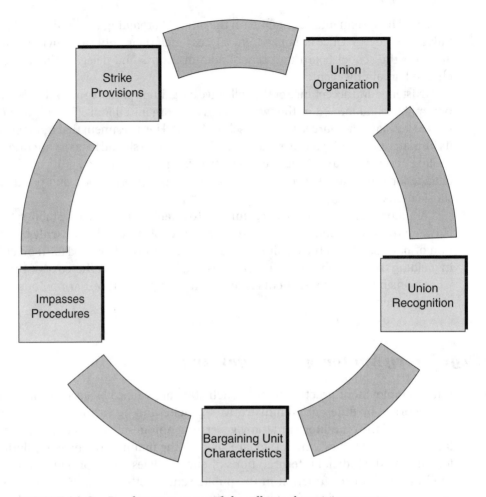

FIGURE 11.2   *Regulatory anatomy of the collective bargaining process.*

American Federation of Teachers (**AFT**; **http://www.aft.org**) or the **National Education Association** (**NEA**; **http://www.nea.org**). Each of these national organizations has a counterpart labeled as the **State Education Association (SEA)**, and each **SEA** counterpart has many **Local Educational Associations (LEAs).** For the many other school district employees who are not teachers and who are also organized for the purpose of collective bargaining, similar municipal employee structures exist for exclusive representation by parent organizations (American Federation of State [national level], County & Municipal Employees [state level], and local affiliates [school district level]).

Several advantages are associated with the tiered model involving parent organizations used by unions when negotiating with boards of education. Most important is the

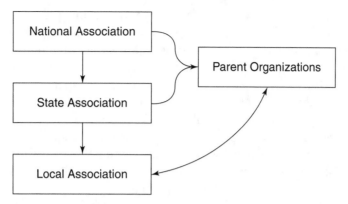

FIGURE 11.3 *Organizational tiers of public school unions.*

expertise available to a local education association within the negotiation process. National and state organizations will supply drafts for contract items, advise about negotiation processes, and in some instances, provide an on-site consultant for a local association.

Union Recognition

To duly represent the interests of employees, unions must be recognized by a formal authority(ies) (see Figure 11.3). Recognition of a union is, however, not always a one-time process. That is, employees must always authorize an initial union, but employees may wish to change their union affiliation once organized.

Several methods exist for authorizing a union to represent employees. These methods include a petition signed by employees, a membership list reflecting employees' affiliation with a professional association, or a formal election voted on by employees. For initial certification of a union to represent employees, each of these methods has been and continues to be used.

Other than initial representation, employees of a public school district may wish to change their union affiliation. A change in union affiliation can occur in two different ways. One way concerns a **decertification** whereby employees revert from union representation to self-representation.

The other way involves changing the affiliation with parent organizations. That is, employees being represented by NEA may wish to be represented by AFT or vice versa. To consider a change involving either decertification or alternate representation, a formal petition is required.

A formal request is evaluated typically by two criteria: (1) **showing of interest** and (2) **timeliness.** Underlying the showing of interest criterion is the general notion that any contemplated change must be endorsed by a simple majority of the employees represented. Functionally, this criterion prevents small groups from attempting to alter the status quo operation through a likely unproductive challenge.

Timeliness as a criterion for evaluating a formal petition to change the status quo is judged according to three criteria. One criterion is a **contract bar.** If a current labor contract is controlling and is valid (not expired), then this contract may contain a provision that prohibits any consideration for a change in status. For example, a labor contract may state via a contract bar, "the parties agree that changes in affiliation may not be considered during the duration of this contract."

Another criterion for evaluating the timeliness of a request for changes in affiliation is a **certification bar.** A certification bar is defined by state legislation and affords an elected union the opportunity to represent employees without any challenges during a specified period of time. Certification bars are controlling generally for the immediate two years following initial certification of a union.

Still another criterion for evaluating the timeliness of a request for changes in affiliation is an **election bar.** An election bar exists only by state statute, and if present, will be found as part of the public sector bargaining law. Usually an election bar prohibits any consideration for change in the status quo (initial certification, decertification, or alternate representation) if a valid election has been held in the last two years.

Given that both the criterion for showing of interest and the criterion of timeliness have been satisfied, an election is usually held. If the election is to determine potential initial or decertification and involves choosing between only a single representative or self-representation, this type of election process carries a specific label. It is labeled as an **uncontested election.**

When more than a single union is vying to represent employees, the process is referred to as a **contested election,** and contested elections are far from being uncommon within the public school setting. The National Teachers Association (NEA) has made a concerted effort to represent all employees within a school district including teachers as well as noncertificated employees (i.e., clerical, bus drivers, etc.). When a single labor organization (i.e., NEA or AFT) represents all public school employees within a specific school district (albeit through separate labor contracts), this type of representation is labeled within the labor literature as **"wall-to-wall" bargaining.**

Bargaining Unit Definition

Without exception, all public sector bargaining laws adopt the principle of **exclusive representation,** for employees. Employees being represented by an exclusive agent are referred to as members of a bargaining unit. It is common for state bargaining laws to exclude certain groups of individuals, such as managers, from representation and to use the term **appropriate bargaining unit** for those being represented. An appropriate bargaining unit is one that has been certified by a state employment relations agency or mutually agreed to both by labor and by management, and one that recognizes the fact that a perfectly construed bargaining unit fails to exist in practice.

The composition of what constitutes an appropriate bargaining unit varies considerably within the same state. What is an appropriate bargaining unit for one school district is not always an appropriate bargaining unit for another school district. To illustrate, one particular school district may determine that school psychologists be part of the teacher bargaining unit, whereas a neighboring school district may exclude school psychologists from a teacher bargaining unit.

Although all employees comprising a bargaining unit must receive the same level of representation by an exclusive representative, formal membership in parent organizations is strictly voluntary in the public sector. Unlike the private sector where employees can be required to join parent organizations and to maintain in good standing as a condition of employment, public school employees have a choice. Unions in the private sector are known as "**closed shops**," whereas unions in the public sector must be at a minimum "**open shops**" but may be "**agency shops.**"

An open shop has a bargaining unit comprised of both members of the parent organization and nonmembers of the parent organization. In an open shop, nonmembers fail to have any financial obligation to the union and fail to pay any type of membership dues. However, this lack of financial obligation does not diminish this group of employees from equal representation.

Because union representation is not a costless exercise, many states allow for agency shops. Within an agency shop, nonmembers of the labor organization must pay their "**fair share**" of the cost associated with negotiating and administering the labor contract. Costs associated with fair share are always less than the dues paid by full-fledged members of the union.

Specifically prohibited by agency shop is the usage of fair share funds for supporting the political ideologies espoused by the local association or parent groups. All revenue obtained from fair share must be spent on the negotiation and administration of a collective bargaining agreement. Without exception, agency shop is permissible and not statutory and must be negotiated between management and labor at the local school district level.

Once recognized, a labor union must represent the interests of all bargaining unit members within the collective bargaining process. Because the interests of labor and of management often conflict, the collective bargaining process may be halted. To resolve conflicts between labor and management within the collective bargaining process, certain impasse procedures/processes are brought into play.

Impasse Procedures

Collective bargaining is a bilateral decision-making process involving school boards and representatives of employees. Both of these parties are charged with making good faith efforts to reach a contract covering the terms and conditions of employment for a bargaining unit. Despite the best of intentions, disagreements may occur within the bargaining process.

When these disagreements cannot be resolved at the local school district level through collective bargaining, an **impasse** exists. Within the bargaining process, an impasse exists when either labor or management perceives that no further progress can be made toward reaching an agreement. An impasse can occur either when one party refuses to negotiate a specific item proposed by the other party or when both parties fail to concur about the disposition of an item being negotiated.

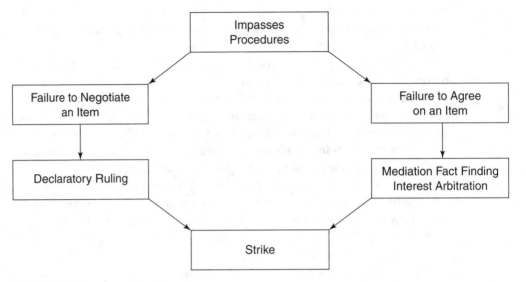

FIGURE 11.4   *Overview of impasse processes.*

To resolve these types of stalemates, most public sector bargaining laws address impasse procedures (see Figure 11.4). Depending on the type of impasse halting the collective bargaining process, different remedial steps are taken. Given these different avenues of dispute resolution, both types of impasses are discussed (see Figure 11.4).

As part of the collective bargaining process, both labor and management bring items to the bargaining table that they wish to be incorporated ultimately within the final labor contract. To consider these items as part of the final labor contract, both parties must agree that the content of the proposed items are within the legitimate scope of bargaining. Although potential items for collective bargaining may be classified several ways (**illegal**, **permissive**, or **mandatory**, to be discussed later), only mandatory items are required to be negotiated.

Mandatory subjects of collective bargaining include those items that pertain to terms and conditions of employment, wages and fringe benefits, other working conditions, and those items impacting these employment contingencies. If either party perceives a proposed item for bargaining to be outside this mandatory range, then that party can object to negotiating said item. When the party proposing the item perceives it to be a mandatory subject of bargaining and fails to withdraw their proposal from the bargaining table, an impasse is reached.

In states having a state employment relations board, this type of dispute is adjudicated by an employee of the state employment relations board. Procedurally, a hearing is conducted where both labor and management present their stance about the deposition of the disputed item. Following this hearing, the state employment relations board employee will issue a **declaratory ruling** (see Figure 11.4).

The declaratory ruling will indicate whether or not the disputed item is a mandatory subject of bargaining. A determination of a nonmandatory status removes the item from the bargaining table and excludes the disputed item from the collective bargaining process. If the item is found to be a mandatory subject of bargaining or to impact a mandatory subject of bargaining, the item or the impact must be negotiated, respectively.

To illustrate h___ ___ndatory item of bargain can impact working conditions, an example is pr___ ___xample, consider a labor proposal that contains content about hirir___ ___e) and supervising teacher aides (mandatory impact on wo___ ___ling would likely require the bargaining of only the s___ ___ hired.

Althou___ ___nay be determined to be a mandatory subject of___ ___ins to the process and not to the outcome. T___ **od faith** the disputed item. Good faith, howev___ ___reach a mutual agreement about the content___ ___ith is defined by intentions as well as efforts to r___

f___ ___l agreement on an item being negotiated, a dif
___ ___11.4). This latter type of impasse is concerned
___ ___ses. The goal for resolving an impasse concerning
___ ___ labor contract that contains the disputed item.
___ ___ining the disputed item(s), different types of impasse
___ ___than involved with a declaratory ruling. These proceau___ **nding**, and **arbitration** (see Figure 11.4). Persons performing___ ___differ in roles as well as in responsibilities, and the amount of pressure b___ ___arties in dispute increases as the process moves from the mediation phase to th___ ___tion phase of the dispute resolution process.

Mediators are mo___ often employees of the state employment relations board. Because either party can declare an impasse and can request the services of a mediator from the state employment relations board, the first task to be resolved by the mediator is to determine if an actual, as opposed to a perceived, impasse has been reached. It is by no means uncommon to find that the negotiation parties disagree on different aspects of the items under contention and that an impasse fails to exist when assessed by a mediator.

Lacking a consensual disagreement between labor and management on the same aspects of an item being bargained, the mediator will fail to certify an impasse and will direct the parties to continue the negotiation process. Only after an impasse has been certified will the mediator begin the mediation process. The purpose of mediation is to assist and not to supplant the collective bargaining process.

Once the mediation process has begun, the mediator seeks either to "jump start" the bargaining process again by resolving certain hurdles or to facilitate an agreement between labor and management about the content of a disputed item. Mediators are defined often as being goal driven and value free because their aim is reconciliation at the expense of either party. To promote movement between labor and management and/or to obtain an agreement between labor and management, mediators must create doubts and must suggest face-saving alternates.

COUNCIL ROCK SCHOOL DISTRICT

David M. Bollinger
Director of Human Resources
and Staff Development
The Chancellor Center
30 N. Chancellor Street
Newtown, PA 18940
Phone: 215-644-1022
Fax: 215-644-2366
Email: dbollinger@crsd.org

In the event that mediation is unsuccessful and the parties remain at impasse, the dispute mechanism process moves to the second stage of the dispute resolution process. The second stage of the dispute resolution process is labeled as fact finding (see Figure 11.4). A fact finder may be an employee of the state labor relations board or an outside party. In some states, a fact-finding panel is used where labor appoints one member, management appoints one member, and the state employment relations board appoints one of its employees.

Given the label afforded this level of the dispute resolution process, fact finding is a misnomer. Within the fact-finding process a formal hearing is conducted and the facts of the dispute are presented by each party. Whether or not these facts are valid rests with the challenges provided by the opposing party, and no attempt is made to verify any data outside the scope of the hearing other than recapped in a brief submitted by labor and by management.

A major difference between mediation and fact finding is the issuance of a formal report. This report will summarize the facts as presented and will provide specific recommendations relative to the items of disagreement (for actual examples, see Fact Finding Reports, n.d.). However, the fact-finding report in most instances is only advisory to the parties of dispute.

Even though the fact-finding report is only advisory, it does create winners and losers through reflecting the opinions of a third party neutral about issues of dispute. Unlike mediation that produces no formal report, outcomes from the fact-finding process may stimulate a restarting of the bargaining process. In the event that the fact-finding report fails to resolve differences or stimulate new bargaining activities, the third stage of the dispute resolution process is entered (i.e., interest arbitration).

Interest arbitrators are, in most instances, private parties and are not employees of the state labor relations board. Within states having a state employee relations board, a pool of potential arbitrators has been preapproved, and a list can be provided on request, following the fact-finding process. For states failing to have a state employment relations board, similar services may be obtained from the American Arbitration Association (AAA; n.d.).

Typically, a list of potential arbitrators, as provided either by an SERB or the AAA, will contain only five names. To obtain a specific arbitrator, a multistage elimination process is used. First, one of the parties in dispute (either labor or management) will strike a single name, and the other party will strike a single name from the remaining list. Following two strikes by both parties, the remaining person will serve as the interest arbitrator.

Strike-offs made by each party are or should be well researched. For each potential interest arbitrator, a case history should be compiled. It is important to know how many times each person has served as an interest arbitrator, what items were addressed within each interest arbitration conducted by these persons, and how many times each potential interest arbitrator has sided with labor and with management.

Once chosen, the interest arbitrator will begin the arbitration process. It is not unusual for the arbitrator to begin the dispute resolution process with an attempt to mediate the dispute. In the event that mediation is successful, the arbitrator will issue a **consent agreement** that describes the resolutions mutually agreed upon by both labor and management.

When mediation conducted by an interest arbitrator is unsuccessful and fails to produce a consent agreement, a formal arbitration hearing will be conducted. Following this

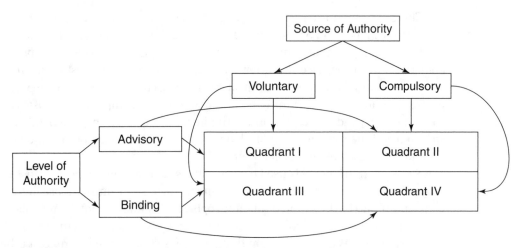

FIGURE 11.5 *Sources and levels of authority for interest arbitration.*

hearing, an interest arbitrator will issue a final report. This report will outline the items of dispute and will render a final decision about these issues.

The process as well as the report will be tempered by certain restraints under which the interest arbitrator works. Many different types of interest arbitration exist in the public sector collective bargaining environment. Contained in Figure 11.5 is a figure depicting the different combinations impacting the interest arbitration process.

An examination of Figure 11.5 reveals that interest arbitration is influenced both by the source of authority and by the level of authority. The source of authority can be either voluntary (see Quadrant I and Quadrant III) or compulsory (see Quadrant II and Quadrant IV). Voluntary authority rests with the mutual agreement of both labor and management to use the interest arbitration process for settling disputes. Compulsory authority for interest arbitration is statutory. Many state public sector bargaining laws require public school districts to submit to interest arbitration when an impasse is reached within the collective bargaining process pertaining to the content of an item being negotiated.

The level of authority for interest arbitration can vary also in two different ways (see Figure 11.5). These ways of variation pertain to the level of force associated with an interest arbitrator's recommendations. An interest arbitrator's recommendations can be treated either as advisory (see Quadrant I and Quadrant II) or as binding (see Quadrant III and Quadrant IV).

Advisory interest arbitration demands only that both labor and management consider the recommendations of the arbitrator. Recommendations of the interest arbitrator can be either accepted or rejected following Quadrant III. If the recommendations are rejected, then the parties must continue the negotiation process or labor must **strike.**

Binding interest arbitration requires that the recommendations of the arbitrator be accepted by both parties. As such, the recommendations of the arbitrator are incorporated within the new labor contract. When formulating these recommendations as required by binding arbitration, several options exist for an interest arbitrator.

Some states require interest arbitrators to choose only among the items of dispute submitted by labor and by management. That is, the interest arbitrator can choose some of the union's proposals and can choose some of the management's proposals. This choice among proposals is at the complete discretion of the interest arbitrator.

Other states allow interest arbitrators more discretion within the dispute resolution process. An interest arbitrator can choose among the competing proposals or can construct an independent resolution for the items of dispute. The independent resolution should blend the strengths of both labor and management proposals and eliminate the weaknesses associated with each proposal.

Still a different model is used by some states. This model is labeled as a "**final offer**" model. Within the final offer model, the interest arbitrator must choose in totality either all the proposals of the union or all the proposals of management. When following the final offer model a "win all-loose all" situation prevails, and underlying this method of interest arbitration is the assumption that all proposals submitted to interest arbitration by each party will be realistic as well as competitive (for examples of actual decisions see Final Offer Arbitration Decisions, n.d.).

When interest arbitration fails to resolve disputes between labor and management within the negotiation process, unions can strike. Striking is considered both as the final means and as the ultimate means for resolving labor disputes. As a dispute resolution mechanism, strikes may take several forms.

Strike Provisions

In addition to the interest impasse procedures for resolving an impasse during the bargaining process, some states provide the employees with the right to strike. The right to strike is addressed by state bargaining laws and differentiation is made within these laws between legal and illegal strikes. Interestingly, even when employees utilize their right to strike and perform a legal strike, they can be discharged by the board of education for failing to fulfill their contractual duties.

The general definition of a strike is that it is "a temporary work stoppage by a group of employees to gain concessions from the employer." Two components of this definition are worth elaboration. The first is the use of the word *temporary* within the definition.

Temporary implies that strikes are short term in duration. The goal of a strike is to bring about immediate actions on the part of an employer through the withholding of services by an employee group. Underlying this goal is the assumption that an employer is unable to conduct business in a satisfactory manner without the essential services of those going on strike.

A second component within the definition of a strike concerns the use of the word *employer*. Although an employer is always the object of a strike, the employer in question may not necessarily be involved directly within the labor dispute promoting a strike. In fact, the definition of an employer determines, in many instances, the type of strike sponsored by a labor organization.

One type of labor stoppage executed by public sector employees is a "**wild cat**" **strike.** A wild cat strike is a work stoppage not authorized by state legislation, a parent labor organization, or the labor contract. The employer involved in a wild cat strike is always the active party within the negotiation process.

A strike can be either announced or unannounced. An announced strike provides the employer with a window for resolving labor disputes, and some state statutes require that an intention to strike be filed in advance of any concerted action on the part of a labor union. However, some strikes are unannounced and are called "**quickie strikes**."

The purpose of a quickie strike is to catch the employer completely off guard and to force immediate concessions. For example, bus drivers may bring students to school and then go on a quickie strike. Their goal is to resolve labor differences in time to take the students home.

Even in situations where the labor relations between a union and the school board are harmonious, a strike can still occur. This last type of work stoppage is known as a **sympathy strike.** A sympathy strike occurs when an uninvolved union goes on strike to support an involved union in an effort to show a concerted labor front for all unionized employees.

Given the regulator anatomy of the collective bargaining process as depicted in Figure 11.2, and the discussion of the components comprising this figure (union organization, union recognition, bargaining unit characteristics, impasse procedures, and strikes) (see Figure 11.4), attention is now directed to how these aspects fit within the human resource function in education.

Collective Bargaining and the Human Resource Function

An examination of the relationship between the regulator anatomy of the collective bargaining process and the human resource function in the public school setting reveals consistent overlaps. Both collective bargaining and human resource management address economic as well as noneconomic decisions that have considerable significance for the system, personnel, clients, and community members. As such, the human resource function should be designed to facilitate the collective bargaining process from a proactive rather than a reactive perspective.

A proactive perspective requires human resource administrators to approach the collective bargaining process from an organizational as well as from an individual point of view. From an organizational point of view, human resource administrators must be concerned with protecting the interests of the organization so that established goals are met and promoted as provided by opportunities arising within the collective bargaining process. To satisfy needs of individual staff members and to create a framework conducive to goal achievement on the part of individuals as employees, the human resource process must address separate but related concerns and obligations.

The proactive thrust on the part of human resource management requires coordinating the collective bargaining process by maintaining a diligent focus on bargaining goals and negotiation strategies from a strategic planning perspective. Monitoring of activities within the collective bargaining process is necessary to ensure, as much as possible, outcomes from the bargaining process are aligned to strategic plans of the school district and facilitate goal achievement at all levels of the public school district. When coordinating the collective bargaining process from a human resource perspective, management must set aside antiunion sentiments, must remain in a problem-solving mode, and must approach collective bargaining from a good faith effort.

Another function within the collective bargaining process served by the human resource approach involves data collection, data analysis, and data management. Data must be collected, refined, stored, retrieved, and analyzed for many different topics negotiated within the collective bargaining process (see Chapter 2). Only by using current and relevant data can serious omissions within the collective bargaining process be avoided by boards of education and can functional agreements between management and labor be obtained in the collective bargaining process.

At the conclusion of the bargaining process and following the **ratification** of the master contract/labor agreement both by labor and by management, the human resource office/assignment assumes much of the responsibility for administering the contract across the school year. With only very few exceptions, contract language must be interpreted for those at the school building level and certain management personnel must be in-serviced with each new labor contract. For purposes of continuity, part of the contract administration process involves keeping records about the existing contract and developing strategies for upcoming negotiations involving successor contracts.

As a process, collective bargaining is interrelated with other processes included in the human resource function. Human resource planning (see Chapters 2 and 3) is a primary area of concern for collective bargaining because planning influences the future organizational structure, suggests the number of positions needed by a school system, the rules for promotion from within, transfers, staff curtailment, and the nature of the work performed. Similarly, matters pertaining to salaries and wages as well as fringe benefits are of prime concern to both labor and management within the bargaining process (see Chapters 8 and 9).

In attaining and in sustaining the goal of a competent and an adaptable workforce within the collective bargaining process, bargaining unit members are regarded as the school system's core constituency. If there is one overarching reason for the operation of the human resource function within the public school setting, it is to contribute to the generation of strategies and practices to improve the quality of work life for employees and the attainment of system goals. This means exerting effort, through collective bargaining and other processes, to make the school environment more acceptable to those who render system service. Fundamental to this effort is consideration of those aspects of the collective bargaining process unique to public education.

Collective Bargaining Developments in Public Education

To understand the current direction, key issues, and continuing problems in the evolution of collective bargaining in public education, it is helpful to review some of the salient developments that have occurred over the past decades. These changes are noteworthy and include the following:

■ A majority of states now permit collective bargaining for local and state government personnel, the laws for which generally follow the format of laws governing private sector bargaining.

■ Membership in national organizations for educational personnel (e.g., the National Education Association and the American Federation of Teachers) has increased significantly, as have their resources and political influence with respect to collective bargaining.

■ National organizations that have focused almost exclusively on certificated personnel in the past have expanded recruitment efforts to include noncertified school personnel through a wall-to-wall agenda.

■ Negotiated agreements between school boards and teaching personnel as well as between school boards and noncertified personnel have become a standard operational process within the public school setting.

■ Growth of unionization and collective bargaining in the public sector has been accompanied by a substantial increase in strike activity as a means of dispute resolution.

■ Movement toward unionism for school administrators has been spurred by: (a) a concern that school boards are bargaining away the rights of middle level school management, (b) fluctuating enrollments creating an unstable work environment, (c) the desire of administrators for greater employment security through union representation, and (d) economic pressures for a competitive standard of living relative to other collective bargaining groups.

■ Development of and promotion for statewide, regional, council, multilevel, and multilateral collective bargaining as solutions to personnel issues in education.

■ The scope of negotiations, whether the subjects are mandatory or permissive bargaining issues, continues to be controversial within the public school setting. Major trends in teacher agreements include provisions relating to compensation, grievance procedures, school calendar, class hours, class size, supplementary classroom personnel, evaluation of teachers, assignment of teachers, transfers, reductions in force, promotion, in-service and professional development programs, instructional policy committees, student grading and promotion, student discipline and teacher safety, and federal programs.

■ Using a dual strategy of collective bargaining and political action, organized teachers have secured contractual gains locally and simultaneously have achieved political success at higher levels of government. Although these gains are neither total nor universal, teachers have acquired a number of noncompensation items that limit the flexibility of school management and increase the cost of public education. At the same time, collective bargaining has emerged as a tool for remedying decades of low salaries and arbitrary treatment by school officials.

■ One emerging pattern immediately discernible is the continually strengthening pressure for citizen involvement in the entire public school collective bargaining process.

■ Collective bargaining has a significant impact on the allocation of resources in school districts. The link between inputs and student outcomes, however, is less than direct but promoted by the collective bargaining process.

Union membership, once organized, seldom decertifies a bargaining agent and reverts to self-representation. The resulting influence of unions within the public school setting in the United States must be regarded as substantial and as growing. Its power goes beyond union membership at a single school district. Union tactics and negotiated contracts are emulated across the nation; federal, state, county, and municipal governments are helping to shape employment relations in education through following models set forth within the private sector.

The Collective Bargaining Process

The text that follows considers the actual steps in the collective bargaining process by which the board of education and the authorized negotiating unit for employees move from prenegotiation activities through the collective bargaining process to obtain a **master agreement.** The framework in which the content of this section is presented is based on a model of the collective bargaining process illustrated in Figure 11.6. This model depicts the bargaining process as embodying three phases: prenegotiations (Phase 1), negotiations (Phase 2), and postnegotiations (Phase 3). Although the discussion that follows focuses on the various facets of prenegotiations preparation (Phase 1), reference will be made to the interrelationship of each phase to the entire bargaining process.

The terms *collective bargaining* and *collective negotiations* are employed interchangeably in the literature. For purpose of exposition, the term *bargaining*, as used here, refers to the total bargaining process, one phase of which is negotiations. At-the-table activities, as well as those directly relevant to them, are viewed as negotiations.

Prenegotiations Planning

Prenegotiations planning (Phase 1 in Figure 11.6) is a continuous activity within the collective bargaining process. It begins, for a successor contract, during the negotiation phase for the current anticipated contract being discussed at the bargaining table. Many items and issues discussed for inclusion in one contract are revisited and/or refined for inclusion when negotiating subsequent contracts.

One of the major reasons for the now generally recognized need for increased negotiation planning time is the complexity and the number of issues to be negotiated. Although economic issues (such as salaries, wages, retirement, leaves of absence, group insurance, extra pay for extra work, and compensation incentives) once constituted the core of bargaining processes, noneconomic issues (such as organizational justice, performance appraisal, nonteaching functions, and class size) have become equally important to union members in recent times and have continued to surface within the collective bargaining context. In many instances, these latter areas of concern may be just as expensive as actual economic items because of the restrictions they may place on the ability of school boards and of school administrators to manage the school district on an ongoing basis.

Responsibility	Phase 1 Prenegotiations Period —to—	Phase 2 Negotiations Period —to—	Phase 3 Postnegotiations Period —to—
Board of school directors	Creates planning committee and bargaining team. Identifies internal responsibilities and relationships. Approves alternate proposals to be designed and costed.	Approves all variances from negotiations plan. Ensures that all issues are resolved at the required levels. Reviews contract prior to approval.	Ratifies agreement. Incorporates agreement elements into official budget. Directs chief executive to communicate agreement details to appropriate parties.
Chief executive	Coordinates all planning responsibilities. Ensures that preparations are proceeding systematically. Prepares for possible strike. Keeps board informed about negotiations proceedings.	Serves as board liaison agent to planning committee and negotiations team. Coordinates all system activities related to bargaining process.	Coordinates communication of contract details to administrative staff. Coordinates implementation of contract.
Bargaining planning committee	Prepares bargaining strategy and negotiating plan for board review and adoption. Advises board on personnel plans related to negotiations.	Counsels with negotiations team on actual or anticipated negotiations problems, impasses, and disagreements. Appoints ad hoc committee(s) as needed.	Records experiences concerning planning and negotiating the agreement.
Bargaining team	Identifies strike issues for board. Establishes negotiations strategy and tactics.	Continues bargaining process in accordance with planning guidelines.	Communicates short- and long-term implications of contract (chairperson submits written report).
Professional negotiator	Assesses union motivation, strategy, and goals for impending negotiations. Counsels board on impact of union proposal in relation to system goals. Provides analyses of strengths and weaknesses of current contract. Counsels and drafts contract language on request.	Conducts bargaining process in accordance with board objectives. Focuses negotiations on problem solving. Counsels on request. Ensures that all contract items are in legal compliance. Advises board on third-party utilization.	Evaluates and submits in writing report on all aspects of various negotiations (within 45 days). Reviews contract for omissions, errors, and ambiguities. Counsels board regarding contract infractions and disputes about contract interpretation.

FIGURE 11.6 *Collective bargaining process time structure.*

(continued)

Responsibility	Phase 1 Prenegotiations Period —to—	Phase 2 Negotiations Period —to—	Phase 3 Postnegotiations Period —to—
Director of business affairs	Provides comparative data on system's standing regarding economics, benefits, and other issues. Assesses impact of settlement costs of optional plans.	Evaluates union proposals relative to settlement costs. Renders general support service to negotiations item.	Transforms agreement into budgetary items. Administers fiscal aspects of agreement.
Director of personnel	Prepares strike manual. Provides current and historical information pertinent to planning. Prepares negotiations handbook. Reviews prior grievance and arbitration decisions.	Furnishes negotiations team with relevant information concerning key issues. Prepares press releases as directed by chief executive.	Records experiences concerning administration of agreement (disputes, infractions, and court decisions).
Secretary	Renders secretarial service to planning committee and negotiations team. Develops minutes, records, and reports for negotiations team.	Provides support service to system negotiations personnel.	Prepares official negotiations documents to be stored in information system.

FIGURE 11.6 Continued

In addition to the initial costs associated with traditional benefits enjoyed by school personnel, the relative cost of many of these same benefits has increased substantially due to inflation. Many of these benefits were awarded initially only to the working employee but have been expanded to cover family members and significant others through the collective bargaining process. Little doubt exists that the list of benefits provided for school personnel will multiply as the number of and types of benefits increase for employees in general (see Chapter 9).

Recently, many social issues related to education are being addressed at the negotiations table, especially those involving student testing, integration, decentralization, transfer of teachers to inner-city schools, and community control of local school attendance units. Accordingly, the need for sophistication at the negotiations table, based on extensive and careful preparation, is no longer debatable for boards of education; time is needed to gather facts, relate facts to issues, decide strategy, and complete budget planning before contract settlement. Those boards of education that fail to plan from a strategic perspective will forfeit many of their managerial rights unknowingly at the bargaining table, and to facilitate the planning process certain prior planning provisions should be acknowledged.

Prior Planning Premises

Planning premises are listed below to stress the importance of developing a system of plans and a planning process that will: (a) strengthen the relationship between collective bargaining and contract administration and (b) lead to an organizational planning culture that methodically pulls together all of the strands of collective bargaining, which when entwined will lend substance to system purposes, direction, and the future generation of effective educational programs and services (see Figure 11.6). Planning premises include the following:

- *Premise 1*—A public school district's information system should be designed to facilitate effective strategic planning for collective bargaining.
- *Premise 2*—Political, governmental, technological, economical, and legal factors that affect the administration of modern educational organizations are rather complex and not readily resolved by simple, short-range plans.
- *Premise 3*—The collective bargaining process encompasses a group of activities with considerable potential for exploring the broad range of opportunities and strategies to move the system from where it is to where it ought to be.
- *Premise 4*—A collective bargaining planning structure is an effective mechanism for implementing the strategic aims of the system.
- *Premise 5*—One of the objectives of prenegotiations planning is to generate plans for (a) development of new programs and services, (b) improvement of existing programs and services, and (c) divestment of nonproductive programs and services.
- *Premise 6*—A collective bargaining policy serves as a guide to thinking, discretionary action, and decision making, and provides a common premise for action and policy implementation.
- *Premise 7*—The organizational right to engage in public bargaining is a long-standing public policy in the United States since 1959.
- *Premise 8*—Responsible players in collective negotiations include three parties—employees, employer, and government. Each engages in protecting and promoting its fundamental objectives.
- *Premise 9*—Gaining a thorough knowledge of the board's statutory powers and duties, and of laws and regulations that apply to bargaining, is an indispensable obligation of the board (National School Boards Association, 1996).
- *Premise 10*—Cultivate sources of expertise and seek these sources as needed throughout the negotiation process to promote the interest of all stakeholders.

Organization for Negotiation

In the preceding section, the planning aspects of collective bargaining were discussed from several perspectives. Illustrated were activities that relate to the assembly, summary, and organization of information needed by the policy committee and the negotiating team. Concurrent with or prior to these planning activities, a decision is needed to determine what agents will represent the system in negotiating with the association representing bargaining unit employees.

Before representatives of both management and labor sit down at the negotiations table, it is essential that the school system organize activities relating to collective bargaining. Decisions are needed to determine what work is to be done, what mechanisms are needed to perform the work, and what the rules will be for individuals delegated to do the work. As outlined in Figure 11.6, one conceptual approach to a collective bargaining organization consists of two mechanisms: a planning committee and a negotiations team. The functions of each group will be examined in turn within the following sections of this chapter.

The Planning Committee

One approach for reducing the number of and the complexity of potential collective bargaining issues is a central committee that develops recommendations for consideration by the board of education. A major function of this committee is to advise the board on systemwide personnel matters related to collective bargaining such as compensation, security, promotion, transfer, and other working conditions. A second function of this committee is to advise the board with respect to strategies and tactics that could be adhered to in collective negotiations sessions.

The collective bargaining planning committee is one mechanism for strategic planning. It can recommend what proposals the system should make, identify and analyze proposals unions are likely to make, and suggest alternatives to both union and system suggestions. Controlling for this committee is that the system is interested in judging proposals on the merits of their contribution to the strategic aims of the total operation.

Strategic plans will be affected by a variety of factors, including resources of the school system and attitudes of groups who influence plans (unions, boards of education, communities, and administrative personnel). The strategic plan in negotiations really boils down to how the system intends to treat the human resources in its employ. If properly planned, it can be advantageous to all parties.

The planning committee may include representatives from the board of education, the chief executive, line and staff administrative personnel (such as principals, supervisors, and assistant superintendents), legal counsel, and professional negotiators or other consultants. No single model can be suggested for the planning committee. As a generalization, however, it should be noted that the board of education, the immediate superintendency team, and administrative extensions of the superintendency should have representation on the planning committee.

The Negotiating Team

Much attention has been devoted in the literature to the issue of who will represent the board of education at the negotiations table. An adequate answer to this question requires the consideration of many factors. What might be an appropriate answer for a small school district may not be the same answer for a large school district; likewise, what might be an appropriate answer for a school district with a stable union–management relationship may not be the same answer for a school district with a hostile union–management relationship.

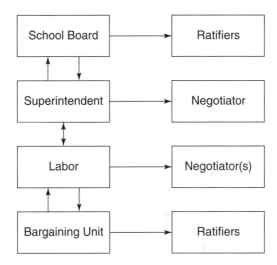

FIGURE 11.7 *Model A for collective bargaining.*

Following is a discussion of several different ways that the negotiating team for a school board may be operationalized. All these ways are in common usage within the public school setting. Most importantly, each way of constructing a negotiating team has certain advantages as well as disadvantages.

Contained in Figure 11.7 is the most common model used by public school districts for negotiating a labor contract. According to Model A as found in Figure 11.7, the interest of the board of education within the collective bargaining process is reflected only by the superintendent at the bargaining table. The superintendent provides input to the board of education as well as receives direction for activities at the bargaining table.

Implied by Model A is that the superintendent is an extension of the board of education rather than a representative of the school district at large. Functionally, this model places the superintendent in an adversarial role with the core contingencies of a school district because of potential competing interests between labor and management. It must be kept in perspective that the role of a negotiator (superintendent in this instance) is to represent the interests of the employer and not to mediate differences between the employer and a labor union within the collective bargaining process.

Given the fact that most school districts within the United States are relatively small, another predominant managerial collective bargaining team is one comprised of the superintendent and school board members (see Figure 11.8, Model B). When adhering to this model as the designated negotiating team, it is important to limit the number of board members participating at any one time to be less than a quorum. If a majority of school board members participate in a particular negotiation session, items agreed to within that particular session may by default be ratified because of the majority presence on the part of school board members.

A major advantage of Model B is that a concerted front for the board of education is represented at the bargaining table. Interest of both the administration and the school

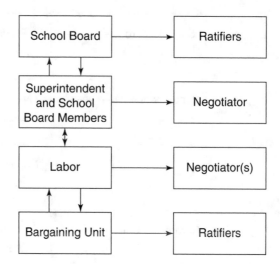

FIGURE 11.8   *Model B for collective bargaining.*

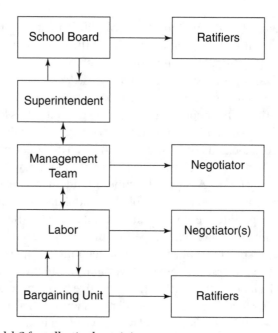

FIGURE 11.9   *Model C for collective bargaining.*

board are represented by a concerted team rather than by a single individual as was the case in Model A. By their mere presence at the bargaining table, school board members increase the legitimacy of the collective bargaining process and decrease the probability of an **end run** between an appointed negotiation representative (see Model A, Figure 11.7) and the school board.

Another common model for a managerial negotiating team consists of using administrators from within the district (see Model C, Figure 11.9). Ideally such a negotiating team would be comprised of administrators with job assignments in the business area, student personnel area, curriculum area, building-level assignment area, and human resource area. An advantage of this model is that it preserves the board members' roles as ratifiers of the final contract but includes the input of the superintendent.

According to Model C, all team members should be knowledgeable about the organization and operation of the school district. Different areas of expertise can be brought to bear on specific contract proposals being discussed at the bargaining table. Major disadvantages associated with Model C are the time required for bargaining activities and an external knowledge about the bargaining climate within the state.

Because collective bargaining requires time as well as expertise, still other districts employ the services of a professional negotiator to represent the school board at the bargaining table (see Figure 11.10, Model D). The advantages associated with a professional negotiator are many and include experience with all phases of collective bargaining as well as knowledge about external market conditions. Major disadvantages include expenses associated with services rendered and with being absent from the system when the contract is being administered.

Regardless of the particular team designated to represent the school board, there are certain prerequisites. These include the following:

- Understanding the operation of the system, and all its ramifications
- Possessing the knowledge to conduct negotiations within the established legal structure
- Understanding the needs of personnel groups and the ability of the system to satisfy those needs

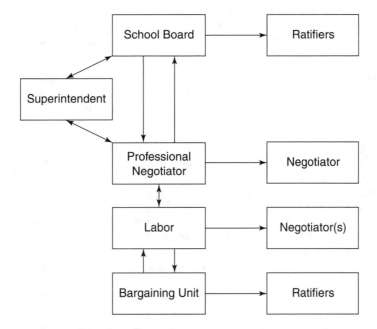

FIGURE 11.10 *Model D for collective bargaining.*

- Discerning trends in personnel policies and procedures
- Possessing the ability to retain the confidence of the system and to make decisions on its behalf

Shaping the Human Organization Through Contract Design

By considering the collective bargaining process as a series of stages, one can identify several aspects of Phase 1 (**prenegotiation preparation**, see Table 11.6) where opportunities exist to develop plans for enhancing both individual and organizational effectiveness. To capitalize on these opportunities, consideration must be given to the existing contract and to the anticipated contract. A vision is needed to guide the school system from where it is to where it should be.

During the time period when the system operated under the existing contract, many changes are likely to have occurred. Board members, administrative staff, and bargaining unit members may have changed, and these changes may be compounded with other changes in the internal and external environment existing when the original contract was ratified. Effective planning in this phase of the collective bargaining process requires consideration of and anticipation for effects of these changes on the upcoming bargaining process.

An actual critique of the existing labor contract can be facilitated greatly through the use of a questionnaire. The intent of the questionnaire is to secure facts as well as opinions regarding the functional operation of the existing contract. Contained in Figure 11.11 is an example of some of the questions for which responses may be sought.

Reactions to the existing contract should be assessed from a variety of stakeholders. At minimum, these stakeholders include school board members, management-level staff, members of the planning committee, and members of the bargaining team. An analysis of these responses provides the initial gist for the bargaining planning process.

Prior to formulating any formal reaction to the existing contract based on the information provided by the stakeholders, the school board should request that the bargaining agent for the employee group submit an initial set of proposals for the new labor contract. Receiving this set of proposals from the bargaining agent affords the school board a strategic

---

A. Are there clauses in the present contract that need modification?
B. What are the reasons for the needed modification? What information has led you to make a recommendation for modification?
C. Has the labor agreement achieved those goals the school system expected to achieve as a result of its formulation and ratification?
D. Is evidence available to indicate a violation of terms of the current agreement?
E. What difficulties have been encountered in administering the agreement?
F. Have important items been excluded from the current agreement?
G. Does the present agreement permit the flexibility required to administer the school system effectively and efficiently?

FIGURE 11.11   *Questionnaire for assessing current contract provisions.*

advantage within the upcoming bargaining process. That is, the school board will possess knowledge about what the labor union desires before they reveal what they have to offer.

Such knowledge is particularly important when formulating a negotiating strategy— important in that those areas of managerial prerogatives that failed to be addressed within the confines of a labor contract remain under the exclusive control of the school board. Consequently, it is to management's advantage within the collective bargaining context to limit the scope of bargaining and to retain those rights not restricted by a labor contract.

Determining the Scope of Bargaining

The **scope of bargaining** is determined by the types of issues actually negotiated at the bargaining table by the representative of the employees and the negotiation team of the school board. As such, the scope of bargaining is determined, at least in part, by the counterproposals that the school board offers to the union prior to entering the actual negotiation process. Management's initial set of counterproposals should be based on an analysis of the initial contract critique and on an evaluation of labor's initial set of proposals.

Initial proposals submitted by the union for the anticipated labor contract can be evaluated according to three criteria. These criteria originated from the private sector and have been adopted almost universally by the public sector bargaining laws. The criteria are mandatory subjects of bargaining, permissive subjects of bargaining, and prohibited subjects of bargaining.

Mandatory subjects of bargaining are those items that, if requested by either party, must be bargained. Generally, these subjects include hours, wages, and working conditions and/or issues that impact these items. In addition to these basic items, certain states, such as Ohio, have expanded this list to include as mandatory items of bargaining those items in the existing labor contract regardless of the item's former status.

Permissive subjects of bargaining include those items that both parties must agree to bargain if such items are to be actually negotiated at the bargaining table. Examples of permissive items might be the use of district facilities or district equipment for union activities (buildings for meetings, copying equipment, etc.), assignment of teacher aides, classroom changes, and so on. If either party refuses to negotiate a permissive item, then that item is ineligible as a topic for the bargaining table.

Prohibited subjects of bargaining involve those items that, if encapsulated within a labor contract, are unenforceable. These items involve issues beyond the lawful authority of the employer (e.g., revealing student records to unauthorized sources) or items that impact the legislative rights of employees (e.g., discriminatory hiring). In some instances, prohibited subjects have been declared by state legislation, such as in Minnesota where student class size is declared a prohibited subject of bargaining and becomes unenforceable even if included within a ratified contract.

In addition to using the legislative classifications involving mandatory, permissive, and prohibited subjects for evaluating proposals submitted by a bargaining agent, other schemes for evaluating these proposals exist. Proposals submitted by a bargaining agent can be evaluated according to organizational concerns, individual concerns, and general concerns. Each of these concerns can provide the board of education with valuable insight when designing a negotiation strategy for upcoming contract talks.

Organizational concerns pertain to those proposals that benefit primarily the bargaining agent. By being able to use school facilities (e.g., buildings for meetings) and school equipment (e.g., copying machines and the mail system for communication) in the conduct of official union business, the administrative cost is decreased and the communication efficiency is increased for the bargaining agent. Whether or not employees are required to pay their fair share (agency shop) for representation has implications for the size of the bargaining agent's coffers.

Individual concerns focus largely on economic items within the proposals. Most important are issues related to the amount of and rate for actual pay. Less important than actual salaries, but still important for individuals, are the levels and types of benefit packages available to them.

General concerns are less of a priority either to the organization as a bargaining agent or to the individual as an employee. Examples of general concerns include personalized parking places or "dress down" days. Although certainly a pleasure to have, individual concerns are unlikely to generate much opposition within the bargaining process if management refuses to negotiate these items.

To determine exactly which items the school board desires to incorporate within its initial proposals to the bargaining agent, both the legislative and functional classification categories can be used to define a negotiation strategy and to restrict the scope of bargaining. Contained in Figure 11.12 is a 3 x 3 matrix whereby each item from the bargaining agent's proposals can be classified. By following this classification, considerable insight can be gained and a plan can be designed to address one of the most difficult aspects of the collective bargaining process.

Indeed, the scope of bargaining has been an issue fraught with conflict throughout the history of public sector bargaining. At the core of the matter is the question of bargaining scope, especially as it pertains to noneconomic issues. Unions have sought to extend their sphere of influence into the policy role of organizations by insisting that the scope of negotiations include items traditionally considered to be organizational prerogatives.

It is not uncommon for unions to submit proposals pertaining to the curriculum, the instructional system, the performance appraisal system, and staff development. Expanding the scope of bargaining to include educational policy issues (especially those that are

	Union Concern	Member Concern	General Concern
Mandatory			
Permissive			
Illegal			

FIGURE 11.12   *Item classification scheme.*

not conditions of employment) is unwise on the part of management. However, in far too many instances, school districts have forfeited the right to manage by bargaining important topics that should not have been discussed at the bargaining table.

Contract Negotiations

After the initial proposals for the school board have been formulated through prenegotiation planning (see Figure 11.6), the collective bargaining process is ready to advance to Phase 2. It is within Phase 2 where the actual give and take of bargaining a master agreement between the school board and the employee group begins. As can be observed within Figure 11.6, a series of events takes place within this phase of the collective bargaining process.

During the initial meeting between the designated representatives of both management and labor, two major events should transpire. First, management should present the school board's initial set of proposals to the bargaining agent of the employees. Time should be allotted for management to discuss the rationale underlying each proposal, point out the strengths as well as the weaknesses within the current operation addressed by the proposals, and explain how the proposals complement the strategic plans of the district.

Focus of the initial presentation is to present and not to negotiate. Actual negotiations should commence at a later stage (discussed later). This presentation is designed to impart information and to answer questions about the school board's position relative to the anticipated contract.

Second, the other order of business in the initial meeting between the parties is to set two specific calendar dates for subsequent activities. The first of these two dates establishes a cut-off point beyond which no new item may be introduced into the bargaining process. This date should allow the union enough time to review management's initial set of proposals and to recast, if necessary, the proposals presented to management prior to the initial meeting of the parties at the bargaining table.

It is important that management enter into the bargaining process only after it is clear what items are to be bargained. By establishing the actual scope of bargaining prior to beginning table negotiations for the anticipated contract, important parameters are set for the negotiation process. Without knowledge of the true scope of bargaining, management enters the negotiation process at a disadvantage.

A second date sought in the initial meeting between labor and management involves the starting time for actual negotiations to begin. This date should follow the first date and should allow management sufficient time to modify the school board's initial proposals and to address any new content, if necessary. It is during this second meeting that the actual negotiations between the school board representatives and the employee representatives actually commences.

Within the second meeting between the representatives for labor and for management the major goal is the establishment of ground rules. **Ground rules** are formal procedures and processes by which the negotiation process is governed. As such, ground rules should be agreeable to by both parties, committed to writing, and signed by both parties.

Ground Rules

1. Location of bargaining sessions.
2. Starting time for bargaining sessions.
3. Duration of bargaining sessions.
4. Agenda for bargaining sessions.
5. Status of bargaining sessions (open or closed).
6. Size of bargaining teams.
7. Caucuses for the bargaining process.
8. Method of record keeping.
9. Tentative agreements (TA).
10. Order of the ratification process.
11. Press releases.

FIGURE 11.13   *Ground rules governing the collective bargaining process.*

Some of the most common issues addressed by ground rules are found in Figure 11.13. As can be observed within this figure, ground rules cover the entire bargaining process from beginning through ending. In the event that problems develop during the negotiation process, the ground rules will be controlling where applicable.

Given the importance of ground rules for the collective bargaining process, attention is devoted to each of the issues found in Figure 11.13. In some instances ground rules are established easily, whereas in other instances ground rules may take weeks to resolve. Disagreement about ground rules occurs for several different reasons.

A major concern for the location of the bargaining sessions rests with access to information within the actual collective bargaining process (see Figure 11.13). Management's preference for location is to have all bargaining sessions conducted at the central office. By being conducted at the central office, management has ready access to personnel files and other system data that have immediate implications for ongoing discussions within the collective bargaining process.

To offset this strategic advantage afforded to management, unions will often propose alternate sites. Included among these suggestions is either a union office (if one exists) or a rotation among school buildings. Both of these options reduce the strategic advantage of management when compared to the central office location.

As a compromise for the location of bargaining session, a neutral site is often chosen. Churches, civic organizations, and hotels may have conference rooms that could be used by a public school district. In most instances, the facilities can be acquired without any cost.

When the actual bargaining session will be held is part of the ground rules (see Figure 11.13). Unions will request that bargaining be conducted during the workday and substitutes be provided for bargaining team members. In contrast, management will most likely want bargaining sessions to follow immediately the end of the school day for students. A typical compromise is to hold a bargaining session in the evening, and this compromise is common with school board members holding outside jobs (see Model B, Figure 11.8) that prevent them from meeting during the day.

Independent of location and of time is the duration of bargaining sessions. Bargaining sessions can be either open ended or time specific. An open-ended bargaining session is terminated by the mutual agreement of both parties, whereas a time-specific bargaining session has a defined time parameter.

Most unions will propose open-ended sessions as a means of facilitating the collective bargaining process through extending the bargaining time. In contrast, it is to management's advantage to have set time limits. Set time limits promote proactive bargaining and limit posturing on nonproductive areas.

For every bargaining session, management must be well prepared. Preparation requires considerable research on items to be discussed at the bargaining table. This level of preparation requires a preestablished agenda for guiding bargaining sessions (see Figure 11.13).

To establish a preestablished agenda for any collective bargaining session, ground rules should set parameters about what is to be negotiated. Frequently ground rules will specify that at the conclusion of one bargaining session, the agenda for the next bargaining session be established. It is extremely important that only those items listed on the agenda be discussed because these are the items that should have been thoroughly researched, and strategic errors within the negotiation process can be avoided by adhering strictly to a preestablished agenda.

Bargaining sessions can be either open or closed (see Figure 11.13). An open session allows any party of interest to observe actual contract negotiations. In contrast, a closed session limits actual contract negotiations to only those members comprising the bargaining teams.

Although some states require that all negotiations be conducted in open sessions, most states delegate this decision to the bargaining groups at the local school district level. Within these later states, if the groups cannot agree to an open session, then the session will be closed. Because management represents the public via the school board, it is often advantageous to propose an open session.

As noted, closed sessions are limited to those that constitute a bargaining team. Without any limiting parameter as specified in the ground rules (see Figure 11.13), a bargaining team may be either a committee or the group at large. For some important issues (i.e., salaries), unions may invite their entire membership as part of the bargaining team to observe the initial offer of management (albeit a conservative offer of management) as a means to solidify bargaining unit members.

This problem can be avoided from a proactive perspective by limiting the size of the membership team (see Figure 11.13). However, size should not be confused with composition. That is, it is not important as to whom, but as to how many, and the composition may change but not the number at the actual bargaining table.

During the collective bargaining process, each bargaining team may need to meet privately and away from the bargaining table. The mechanism for satisfying this need is a caucus. Indeed, a caucus can serve several proposes: (1) discuss a strategy, (2) show consideration for a proposal, (3) emphasize a concession, and/or (4) draft/modify a proposal.

However, in many instances, caucuses have been used to delay the collective bargaining process. For these reasons, procedures governing caucuses have often been included with ground rules (see Figure 11.13). Issues to be resolved in ground rules include the authority for calling caucuses, frequency for requesting a caucus within any bargaining session, and the allowable duration of a single caucus.

Record keeping of the negotiation process is often addressed in ground rules (see Figure 11.13). Several potential methods have been and continue to be used. These include tape recording the sessions, using a professional stenographer, or delegating this responsibility to each bargaining team.

Surprising to most novices to the collective bargaining process is the level of depth required for bargaining session records. Bargaining session records need only to capture major issues and objections and not necessarily who said what and when. For this reason, a favored way is to allow each party to keep their own records.

During the actual negotiation process, proposals and counterproposals for specific items are submitted and evaluated by labor and by management. These proposals can be evaluated as stand-alone items or can be evaluated as a package containing more than one item. To acknowledge agreement at the bargaining table level, a tentative agreement (TA) process is used (see Figure 11.13).

Ground rules for the collective bargaining process should set forth if tentative agreements are either on an **item-by-item** basis or involve packaging of items. A tentative agreement requires both parties to sign and to date the agreed upon proposal(s). Once agreed on and certified by a tentative agreement, this information is set aside and is not revisited during the bargaining process.

After the bargaining table representatives have tentatively agreed to all proposals, the entire package of proposals is submitted for approval. This approval process, labeled as ratification (see Figure 11.13), requires a majority approval by both constituents. Constituents for management are the school board members and constituents for labor are the bargaining unit members (see Figures 11.7–11.10).

Ground rules should specify the order of the ratification process. It is extremely important from a human resource perspective that the union ratifies the proposals before the school board considers the entire package. If the school board ratifies the proposals first, then the union is signaled that the school board is willing to make, at a minimum, the concessions afforded the union in the current package.

The collective bargaining process in many public school districts is of great interest to the community at large. The local press is quick to capitalize on this interest and will publish an ongoing report in the local newspaper. The source for this information is provided by management and/or the union.

To control the type of information appearing in the press, ground rules may be used (see Figure 11.13). Ground rules can specify that all press releases be jointly approved by management and the union. A violation of this agreement, as reflected in ground rules, is an unfair labor practice and reflects bad faith bargaining.

Having presented and discussed many of the important issues governing the collective bargaining process at the local school level, attention is directed toward an overview of some of the important content negotiated. Content of a labor contract is addressed from several different perspectives. Included among these perspectives are areas dealing with organizational security, compensation, and working conditions, as well as individual concerns.

Contract Content

The new labor contract ratified by the school board members and by the bargaining unit personnel stipulates certain terms and conditions of employment that will exist over a specified period of time. Most labor contracts consist generally of three functional categories, each of which serves a specific purpose: (a) organizational security, (b) compensation and working conditions, and (c) individual security. Each of these divisions of the agreement will be discussed in the following text.

Organizational Security

One of the first steps in collective bargaining is to settle the scope of recognition to be afforded bargaining units representing teachers or other personnel in the school system. Security clauses in agreements covering personnel groups negotiating with the school system may include such matters as the description of the bargaining unit, duration of the agreement, degree of recognition of the union or of the association, avoidance of discrimination based on union membership, permissible union activity on school premises, and access to school executives by union officials.

Prerogatives of the school system in the agreement are intended to affirm the rights the system must have to discharge the administrative functions with which it is entrusted. Protective clauses in agreements reserve for the system discretion in such personnel matters as size of staff, position content, teaching or work schedules, promotion, transfer, discipline, dismissal, staffing assignments, appraisal, and leaves of absence. In addition, the system may demand clauses stipulating protection of personnel from union intimidation, exercise of good faith in the use of privileges granted, restraint in publishing false or misleading information about the system, and a **zipper clause** that ensures that negotiations will not be reopened for a specified period of time.

Compensation and Working Conditions

Central to any agreement negotiated collectively between two parties are compensation and working conditions for bargaining unit members. The school system, under the terms of the agreement, agrees to provide certain remunerations and to establish working conditions for employees in exchange for specified services. Capturing these concerns are clauses addressing salaries, wages, collateral benefits, class size, consultation in setting school calendars, lunch and rest periods, adequacy of physical facilities for teachers, transfers, teacher planning time, protection of teachers from physical assault, nonteaching functions, control of student behavior, school closings at noon before holidays and vacations, academic freedom, and recruitment of unqualified personnel.

Individual Concerns

Clauses in the agreement that cover the security of an individual member are designed generally to protect the employee against arbitrary treatment from the school system, the union or association, other personnel or personnel groups, and community groups. This type of security is of as much concern to the system as to the individual or the bargaining agent. Protection against arbitrary acts by the system is provided by a **grievance procedure.** Likewise, protection of the individual against arbitrary acts by the union or association is provided by clauses covering the right of an individual to belong or not to belong to the union and to be free from intimidation by the union.

Contract Administration

Following the ratification of the labor contract by bargaining unit members and by school board members, Phase 3 (see Figure 11.6) of the collective bargaining process is entered. Much of the work in Phase 3 rests squarely with the human resource function in the public school setting.

Because each new labor contract contains changes of the previous labor contract, system personnel working with bargaining unit members must be apprised of these changes. To apprise appropriate personnel of the changes, human resource administrators conduct workshops. Within these workshops, hopefully, before the implementation date of the contract, information is contextualized for administrators and supervisors about new changes and past problem areas.

After the agreement has been ratified by both parties, each party has a responsibility to make the contract work. Although the rights and obligations of both the system and the union are specified, disputes are certain to arise over the meaning of the language in the agreement, as well as over methods employed to implement the contract. Because numerous disputes arise from the interpretation or application of contractual language, care should have been taken to use language that will minimize misinterpretation.

In spite of the care taken when drafting the agreement, it is likely that problems will arise in the interpretation and/or application of items within the agreement. When problems do arise, the contractual means designed for their resolution is the grievance procedure. A grievance procedure provides a systematic process for resolving disputes arising from the administration of a labor contract.

Grievance Procedure

The purposes served by a grievance procedure are many. From a proactive perspective, one purpose of the grievance procedure is to provide a vehicle for problems to be expressed rather than to be repressed. That is, the grievance procedure serves as a relief valve.

As a relief valve, a grievance procedure promotes two-way communications between labor and management. As such, seeds may be planted for fostering a harmonious labor–management relationship. From a reactive perspective, another purpose of the grievance procedure is to provide functional guidelines for resolving disputes arising from contract administration.

Functional guidelines for a grievance procedure are encapsulated within the labor contract. Indeed, the right for a grievance fails to exist beyond the language of a labor

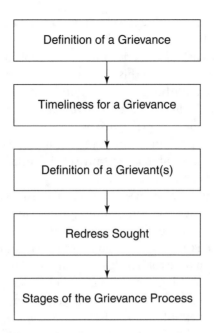

FIGURE 11.14   *Components of a grievance process.*

contract. Contained in Figure 11.14 is an overview of the issues that should be defined by contract language relative to the grievance process.

A grievance can be defined as a claim or an allegation relative to the violation, misinterpretation, or misapplication of contractual terms within the agreement. The difference between a claim and an allegation can have a bearing on where the burden of proof rests. A claim is less defined, whereas an allegation shifts the burden of proof clearly to the party filing the grievance.

Within the definition portion of a grievance in a labor contract, further specifications should be provided. Most pointedly, the grievant should be required to identify the specific article and page number for the article under contention. A clear definition of the problem area will facilitate the resolution process.

Grievances should be addressed in a timely manner (see Figure 11.14). A lengthy time between the purported infraction and the filing of a grievance serves neither labor nor management well. Psychologically, the issue will only fester across time, and practically, the facts of the disagreement will fade in the memories of the involved parties.

Given the psychological as well as the practical problems associated with timeliness, a sound labor contract will establish a window of opportunity for filing a grievance. A window of opportunity can be either time specific or knowledge specific. A time-specific clause in the contract will dictate that a grievance must be filed within a certain number of days or weeks after the disputed violation. Typical time-specific clauses indicate that the grievance must be filed within 10 working days or two weeks following the alleged infraction.

Rather than anchoring the window of opportunity for filing a grievance to the actual occurrence of the purported violation, some contracts open the window of opportunity based on knowledge of the grievant. For example, the contract may state that the grievant has 10 days from when this information was known or when this information should have been known. Without any definition of time for filing a grievance within a labor contract, the period for filing a grievance remains open.

The party filing a grievance warrants definition within a labor contract (see Figure 11.14). A grievance can be filed by a single individual, by a group of individuals, or by the organizational representative of the union. Filing rights are associated with the authority to police the labor contract.

A labor contract may specify any or all the above mentioned combinations of parties for filing a grievance. Even in instances where individuals are afforded the right to file a grievance, this right does not demand automatic representation by the union. Unions are charged with making decisions about representation within the grievance process that serve best all employees of a bargaining unit and not necessarily any specific employee at the expense of the collective bargaining unit at large.

Some labor contracts allow for group grievances. Group grievances are applicable when the same purported infraction affects more than a single individual. By allowing group grievances within the contract language, the goal is to expedite the grievance process rather than treating each grievance addressing the same cause as a stand-alone issue.

It is by no means uncommon to find contract language that permits only the labor union to file a grievance. This does not lessen the labor union's obligation to represent employees. However, representation is defined by listening to an employee's or to a group of employees' concerns and evaluating these concerns in light of the total bargaining unit (representation requires only consideration and not adjudication).

Regardless of how the definition of a grievant is determined within contract language, another important issue is the type of **redress sought** from the grievance process (see Figure 11.14). The type of redress sought can be either within or outside the authority of a school district. A redress can be vague involving such terms as *fairness* or *equity*, or it can be specific relative to definable outcomes.

In general, the type of redress sought should not be punitive and should not involve the disciplining of other employees. Disciplining of employees is a management decision and not a labor decision from a contractual point of view. Redress should be approached from a **"make whole" principle** where wrongs are righted and inequities are corrected.

Typical grievance procedures have "a series of stages that must be followed, and each of these stages is monitored by the human resource administrator (see Figure 11.14). Most grievance processes begin with an informal stage. At the informal stage, an attempt is made to resolve the issues through an open discussion involving the parties of dispute.

If the discussion between the parties of dispute fails to satisfy the grievant(s), a formal stage of the grievance process is entered. Depending on the size of a public school district, the formal stage of the grievance process may vary in levels of consideration. At minimum, the process in totality will include a district decision, a school board decision, and perhaps the decision of a third independent party (to be discussed).

Decisions at each level may vary in several ways. One way of variation is to grant the grievance. If the grievance is granted, then the process terminates because the grievant is awarded the redress sought.

The other way of variation involves denying the grievance. A grievance can be denied from different perspectives. One perspective is a **procedural denial,** whereas the other perspective is a **substantive denial.**

If the grievant fails to follow the grievance process as outlined in the master contract, then management can issue a procedural denial. Leading the causes of a procedural denial is the failure of a grievant to meet time factors associated with filing the grievance or with appealing unsatisfactory decisions at the different stages of the grievance process in a timely manner. Other than timeliness, the second most common reason for a procedural denial is the aggrieved party's failure to follow each stage of the grievance process as specified in the labor contract.

Independent of the procedural denial is the substantive denial. A substantive denial indicates that the content of the grievance is inappropriate. The content of a grievance could be inappropriate for several reasons.

In many instances the content of a grievance could be outside of the collective bargaining contract even though it might be a legitimate concern. Even if it is a legitimate concern within the context of the labor contract, the type of redress sought may not be appropriate. The redress sought could be either punitive or could exceed the lawful authority of the school board, both of which conditions would warrant a substantiate denial on the part of a public school district.

An appeal of either a procedural denial or of a substantive denial at both the district level and the school board level can be addressed by a third party neutral if provided by contract language. This third party neutral is an arbitrator. The type of arbitration conducted for grievance procedures is **rights arbitration** as opposed to interest arbitration (i.e., settling a contract) discussed earlier in this chapter.

Unlike interest arbitration mandated by certain states (compulsory), rights arbitration is always voluntary. It is voluntary in the sense that rights arbitration must be negotiated at the local school district level. Because rights arbitration is voluntary, it can be either advisory or binding.

Interest arbitrators may or may not be agents of a state employment relations board. Within those states having state employment relations boards, employees of the agency are the ones used most frequently. However, available to all boards are rights arbitrators from the Federal Mediation and Conciliator Service on a no-cost basis.

To resolve disputes in violation, misinterpretation, or misapplication of contractual terms within the agreement, rights arbitrators issue a ruling. This ruling may grant or deny the grievance. Depending on whether this ruling is advisory or binding, a resolution is provided with varying levels of force.

From a human resource perspective, bargaining and administering the contract is an ongoing activity. During the life of a labor contract, the human resource administrator is monitoring and appraising constantly the effects the contract has on fulfilling the goals of the strategic plan. Monitoring and appraising includes several activities:

- Recording and reporting to the superintendent of schools progress and problems encountered in administering the contract
- Interpreting the agreement for the administrative staff
- Recording experiences concerning the administration of the meeting with union representatives to examine ways of improving the administration of the contract and proposing new items for successor contracts.

Review and Preview

The collective bargaining process is rooted in the private sector model but has expanded in several different ways. Most notably, parallels were drawn between the National Labor Relations Board and state employment relations boards. Within this chapter attention was afforded to the organizational structure of public sector unions, union recognition processes, bargaining unit characteristics, impasse procedures, and strikes.

Different types of bargaining models were presented for designing a management team, and advantages as well as disadvantages were discussed for each model. A connection was made between the collective bargaining process and the human resource function within the public school setting. Outlined were several premises driving this relationship.

Ground rules governing the collective bargaining process were listed and discussed from a human resource perspective. Examples of broad content items contained within a collective bargaining agreement were presented. To administer the collective bargaining agreement, salient issues involved in the grievance process were described.

Discussion Questions

1. What do you see as the advantages associated with an open shop and an agency shop? If you had a choice between an open shop or an agency shop, which type of shop would you prefer and why?

2. Describe the characteristics of an effective negotiating team. Several different negotiating models were presented in this chapter (see Figures 11.7–11.10). Which model is used by your school district, and what is the justification for the present model? Which model should be used by your school district?

3. Compare and contrast each of the following impasse procedures: mediation, fact finding, and arbitration. What are the unique aspects of each dispute resolution phase?

4. Do you think interest arbitration should be voluntary or compulsory? Given your preference, do you support advisory or binding interest arbitration?

5. What differentiates between a procedural and a substantive denial of a grievance? What are some examples of each type of denial in your school district?

Case Study

Assume that you are a newly employed human resource director in your school district and that you are appointed as the chief negotiator (see Model C, Figure 11.9) of the bargaining team. One of your first tasks is to negotiate an appropriate bargaining unit for teachers. What employees would you include and what employees would you exclude (i.e., regular teachers, substitute teachers, part-time teachers, temporary teachers, adult basic education teachers, attendance teachers, guidance counselors, and school psychologists, to mention a few)? How would you support your proposal for an appropriate bargaining unit?

References

American Arbitration Association. (n.d.). Retrieved June 10, 2006, from Web site: http://www.adr.org/.

American Federation of State, County & Municipal Employees. (n.d.). Retrieved June 5, 2006, from Web site: http://www.afscme.org/.

American Federation of Teachers. (n.d.). *Collective bargaining: Are teacher unions hurting American education?* Retrieved June 5, 2006, from the American Federation of Teachers Web site: http://www. aft.org/teachers/index.htm.

Fact Finding Reports. (n.d.). Retrieved June 5, 2006, from Web site: http://www.serb.state.oh. us/sections/research/WEB%20FACTFINDING/_FACT%20FINDING%20LIST%20HYPERLINKED2.pdf.

Final Offer Arbitration Decisions. (n.d.). Retrieved June 5, 2006, from Web site: http://www.wisbar. org/AM/CustomSource/ASPCode/caseindex.asp?l ap=1&MoreOpener=&ci=1&OrdMode=DESC&O ffsethi=20&Lio=1&Area=6&Numlines=20.

Milwaukee Public Schools. (n.d.). Retrieved June 5, 2006, from Web site: http:// mpsportal.milwaukee. k12.wi.us/portal/server.pt.

National Education Association. (n.d.). Retrieved June 10, 2006, from Web site: http://www. nea.org/index.html.

National Labor Relations Board. (n.d.). Retrieved June 5, 2006, from: Web site: http://www.nlrb. gov/nlrb/home/default.asp.

National School Boards Association. (1996). *The school personnel management system* (rev. ed.). Retrieved June 5, 2006, from Web site: http://www. nsba.org/site/index.asp.

State Employment Relations Law. (n.d.). Retrieved June 10, 2006, from Web site: http://www.law. cornell.edu/topics/Table_Labor.htm.

Toledo Public Schools. (n.d.). Retrieved June 5, 2006, from, Web site: http://www.tps.org/.

GLOSSARY

Ability to pay One of several criteria used to determine a school district's efforts relative to the compensation of employees.

Accuracy A criterion used to assess the efficiency of a selection process.

Active delivery method A format used within the orientation process and the staff development process whereby employees exhibit simulated or actual job behaviors.

Adverse impact A management practice that has a disproportionate effect on a protected class group.

Affective needs Psychological needs of employees within the recruitment, selection, orientation, and development processes.

Affirmative action Employment practices designed to afford certain protected class persons preferential treatment within the employment process.

Age Discrimination Employment Act (ADEA) A federal act that prohibits employment discrimination against persons over 40 years of age regarding selection, compensation, termination, and related personnel practices.

Agency shop A type of union security requiring employees to pay their fair share obligations for contract bargaining and contract administration.

Alternate ranking A norm-based assessment technique used to evaluate jobs and/or individuals by focusing on either the most important job and the least important job or the highest-performing employee and the lowest-performing employee.

Americans with Disabilities Act of 1990 (ADA) A federal act that states that employers may not discriminate against an individual with a disability in hiring or promotion if the person is otherwise qualified for position.

Applicant ratio The number of applicants applying for each position (10:1, 20:1, etc.).

Application form An instrument designed to collect preemployment information from applicants.

Appropriate bargaining unit The members of a bargaining unit as agreed to by labor and management or as designated by a third party with vested authority.

Appropriate labor market A group of public school districts selected for assessing compensation data.

Arbitration A process that involves an impartial third party who collects pertinent facts from the disputants and proceeds to make recommendations based on the findings.

Assimilation The acclamation of employees either to the school district or to a new work assignment.

Audit A formal review and evaluation of an administrative process.

Award system The process of rewarding the job performance of employees.

Base pay The amount of pay generally reflected on a salary schedule for a position, excluding any forms of supplemental pay.

Base rate The percentage of employees who would perform successfully if a predictor were not used to select employees.

Base year A term used by enrollment techniques and staffing plans to denote the current year of operation.

Bayesian estimation process (BES) A nonlinear enrollment projection technique that incorporates objective and subjective information.

Bayesian normalization process Part of the Bayesian estimation procedure that combines subjective and objective information.

Behaviorally anchored rating scales (BARS) A criterion-referenced system for performance appraisal that utilizes job behaviors as anchor points for assessing job performance.

Benchmark positions Positions that are consistent across school districts and that share common responsibilities and reporting relationships.

Benefits A form of compensation in addition to base pay that can be either direct or indirect such as vacation and insurance.

Bona fide occupational qualification (BFOQ) A skill or a trait that is absolutely necessary for effective job performance of a specific position and can be used to exclude applicants from employment consideration.

Bonus pay A source of pay that is a one-time occurrence and fails to be incorporated into the base salary of an employee.

Bonus systems A method of pay that is a one-time occurrence and fails to be incorporated into the base salary of an employee.

Burden of proof Denotes the responsibility of a party (school board or individual) for providing supporting evidence within a dispute process.

Business leave A type of leave where each party stands to gain or lose within a transaction.

Cafeteria benefit plan A benefit plan in which position holders elect benefits they will receive within a specified dollar amount.

Career stages Stages through which a position holder passes from career outset to retirement. These stages have been described as establishment, advancement, maintenance, and withdrawal.

Certification bar A criterion used to evaluate a petition for changing the status quo of a public school district relative to recognition, decertification, and/or changing union membership.

Checklist A criterion-based job performance assessment technique design to assess either the presence or absence of specific personal characteristics or job behaviors.

Civil Rights Act of 1964 (CRA) Federal legislation that prohibits all forms of discrimination on the basis of race, color, religion, sex, or national origin.

Closed shop A type of union security requiring employees to join a union after employment and to stay in good standing with the union.

Coaching A managerial technique used to shape the job behaviors of an employee.

Communication mediums Those outlet sources involving printed, verbal, and electronic methods for communication.

Community concerns One of the sources of concerns for newly appointed or newly assigned personnel that relates to the broadest aspect of their job assignment.

Compensation planning tools Procedures and process used by a public school district to establish equitable levels of compensation for employees.

Compensation policy A formal statement that reflects the goals and intentions of the board of education related to compensation practices.

Compensation structure Interrelated provisions governing salaries, wages, benefits, incentives, and noneconomic rewards for school personnel.

Compensatory evaluation model A formal model that can be used by a public school district to determine internal consistency and external competitiveness.

Compensatory model of decision making An empirical procedure for combining all information about an employee's performance on each dimension with a single summary statistic.

Compression An auditing criterion that reflects the functional growth potential associated with a particular salary range.

Concentration statistic An index that reflects the distribution of protected class persons across different job categories within an organization.

Confederate A person taking part in an experiment and representing the interest of the investigator within the study.

Congruent role-playing An orientation/development technique where an employee role-plays the responsibilities of an assigned position.

Consent agreement A memorandum drafted by a third party reflecting the mutual agreement of labor and management within the dispute resolution process.

Construct validity A type of validity appropriate for assessing abstract concepts such as leadership, satisfaction, or motivation.

Contested election A union election process involving more than a labor organization vying to represent a group of employees.

Contextual knowledge A level of learning that is specific to a particular situation.

Convergent validity A psychometric measure assessing the degree to which measures purported to share common variance with an abstract construct.

Cost benefits A criterion used to define an appropriate labor market that is sensitive to expenditures (cost) and gains (benefits).

Cost-of-living adjustment (COLA) A change in compensation received by employees that reflect increases in goods and services for a defined labor market.

Criterion A standard, benchmark, or expectation by which to evaluate personnel performance, policies, processes, procedures, and organizational outcomes.

Criterion contamination The degree to which job tasks and behaviors are unique to the actual criterion and the predictor but not the ultimate criterion.

Criterion deficiency The degree to which job tasks and behaviors are unique to the actual criterion.

Criterion measures Part of a selection paradigm that reflects actual job performance exhibited by employees.

Criterion-referenced systems A performance appraisal process that compares an employee's job performance to an external standard.

Criterion-related validity A psychometric property that reflects the degree of shared variance between a measure and a standard (criterion).

Criterion relevance The degree to which job tasks and behaviors are reflected by the ultimate criterion, actual criterion, and predictors.

Critical incidents checklists A performance appraisal system that incorporates the most important aspects of job performance either for effective or ineffective job performance.

Decertification The dissolution of a union that has been representing a bargaining unit.

Declaratory ruling A ruling to determine if a proposed item is a mandatory subject for collective bargaining.

Defined benefit A type of retirement system that entitles an employee to a fixed income based on dollar contribution, chronological age, and appropriate job experience.

Defined contribution A type of retirement system that requires a specific amount of contribution for investing and uses investment returns to determine retirement income.

Demotion A job change by an employee from a position of higher value to a position of lower value.

Development A human resource function that is designed to enhance the skills, knowledge, abilities, and/or affective reactions of an employee.

Development needs The skills, knowledge, abilities, or affective deficiencies to be addressed through a remedial process.

Development process A process designed to assist position holders to raise their level of performance in present or future assignments to performance expectations.

Discriminant validity A pschometric index that assesses the relationship among purportedly dissimilar items.

Discrimination Employment practices that have a disproportionate impact on certain individuals.

Dismissal A personnel action initiated by the system to sever an employment relationship.

Disparate impact A legal doctrine used to establish prima facie evidence for discrimination based on the intentions of the employer.

Disparate treatment A legal doctrine used to establish prima facie evidence for discrimination based on the actions of the employer.

Disproportionate impact An employment action that has a greater implication for protected class groups than nonprotected class groups.

Diversity analysis A breakdown of a school district workforce by the protected class statuses of employees.

Due process A process that protects system members or union protection against infringement on employment rights. Requires showing of "just cause" and the use of "rules of reasonableness."

Earning potentials The economic dollar value that describes the range between the minimum and the maximum dollar values associated with a particular salary/wage level.

Eclectic evaluation model An empirical procedure for combining information about an employee's performance on dimensions of job performance, utilizing certain aspects of the multiple-cutoff and compensatory models.

Economy of scale A criterion used to define a relevant labor market that is based on the size of a public school district.

Effectiveness The degree to which organizational, group, or individual aims or intended effects are accomplished.

Efficiency Outcomes or results evaluated in terms of organizational resources expended.

Elasticity A percentage that reflects changes over time in the theoretical growth potential of a salary range.

Election bar A statutory criterion for evaluating the timeliness for an election petition.

Emergency leave A privilege granted by school districts or labor contracts that affords an employee time off the job for incidents requiring the immediate attention of an employee.

Employee preference A method for defining the use of privileges granted employees whereby usage requires only notice to exercise the privilege.

Employer preference A method for defining the use of privileges granted employees whereby usage requires the discretion of administrators.

Employment decisions Part of the selection process that involves the concurrence of applicants and employers.

End run A collective bargaining term that describes how a union bargaining team bypasses the management team at the bargaining table and negotiates directly with the board of education.

Enrollment projection A technique used to provide an estimation of future students attending a public school district.

Enrollment trend A graphic representation of students attending a school district across a specific period of time.

Equal employment opportunity Employment practices designed to be facially neutral with regard to the protected class status of an individual.

Equal Employment Opportunity Commission (EEOC) Established as the administrative agency for Title VII (Civil Rights Act of 1964).

Ethics Personal principles and beliefs used to guide decision making or to direct overt actions.

Exclusive representation A collective bargaining term denoting that all employees within a bargaining unit must be represented by a single bargaining agent (union).

Exempted employees Individuals not covered by the Fair Labor and Standards Act.

External environment Forces external to the organization over which it has no control, such as federal, state, and local regulations; court decisions; public opinion; economic fluctuations; and political movements or activities influencing system courses of action.

External labor market Target organizations that are viewed as similar to an object organization for the purposes of assessing compensation data.

Facially neutral Employment practices that fail to consider any protected characteristics of individuals within a decision-making process.

Fact finding A dispute mechanism procedure to resolve an impasse within the collective bargaining process.

Fair share The amount that nonunion members pay for the cost of negotiating and administering a labor contract.

False negative Employee that exhibits substandard performance on job predictors but performs satisfactory on the job.

False positive Employee that exhibits satisfactory performance on job predictors but performs unsatisfactory on the job.

Family and Medical Leave Act of 1993 Federal legislation that requires a covered employer provide up to 12 weeks of unpaid leave if the employee provides appropriate documentation substantiating the need for leave.

Final offer arbitration A dispute mechanism for resolving a contract impasse, and where either union or managements offers are selected in totality.

Fixed-rate salary schedules A compensation structure that affords automatic movement based on certain factors such as education and experience.

Flagship school districts A criterion used to define a relevant labor market that is based on those school districts perceived as similar from a political perspective.

Flow statistics An index that describes the number of applicants applying and the number of applicants employed according to protected class characteristics.

Forced distribution technique One type of ranking technique used to evaluate either persons or positions.

Form A standardized method of recording data.

Formal compulsory systems Nomenclature used within the development process to describe the structure of the program and the type of participation.

Formal voluntary systems Nomenclature used within the development process to describe the structure of the program and the type of participation.

Full-time equivalent (FTE) A term used to describe students or staff in projection techniques that prorates individuals by time of involvement.

Gain-sharing A type of incentive compensation where awards are based on group performance rather than on individual effort.

Goal-setting techniques Mechanisms used for establishing objectives to move from a current state of operation to a desired state of operation.

Goal-sharing systems One of many systems used to enhance the earning of employees.

Goal structure A hierarchy of assumptions ranging from broad to narrow organizational intent (mission, purpose, goals, objectives, and targets). Developed to identify desirable future outcomes.

Good faith bargaining An abstract measure to reflect the willingness of labor or management to reach an agreement on items being negotiated.

Graphic rating A performance appraisal technique for evaluating job performance along a single continuum by denoting the level of performance with an adverb, number, or behavior incident.

Green circle employees Individuals found to be compensated at less than the minimum value of a pay level as revealed through an auditing process.

Grievance procedure A prescribed series of steps or a line of appeals designed to resolve a disagreement, dissatisfaction, dispute, or conflict concerning conditions of employment.

Ground rules The guidelines negotiated at the beginning of the collective bargaining process that determine the basic protocol for negotiations.

Head count A term used to describe students or staff in projection techniques that fail to prorate individuals by time of involvement but uses each individual as a unit of analysis.

Health maintenance organization (HMO) The Federal Act of 1973 requires employers to offer an HMO (medical organization) to their employees as an alternative to conventional group health plans.

History A type of threat pertaining to internal validity that relates to the passage of time and suggests external factors other than the desired treatment that influences outcomes in assessment.

Human resource function Personnel is one of the major functions of school administration, including these processes: planning, bargaining, recruitment, selection, induction, development, appraisal, compensation, justice, continuity, and information.

Impasse A breakdown in the negotiation process due either to failing to agree to negotiate an item or failing to reach an agreement on an item being negotiated.

Impasse procedures Dispute mechanisms typically involving mediation, fact finding, and arbitration.

In-basket exercise A selection technique used frequently in assessment centers that involves an analysis of memorandums directing the activities of a potential employee.

In-part principle A collective bargaining principle that forbids any retaliatory action on the part of an employer if the cause is related on tangentially to rights afforded union membership.

In-service education Planned programs of learning opportunities afforded staff members for the purpose of improving the performance of individuals in assigned positions.

Incentives Forms of compensation in addition to base salary that link rewards to outstanding performance.

Individual concerns An interest of employees within the orientation process that focuses on the immediate job setting.

Individual portfolios A performance appraisal technique relying on examples of work compiled by an employee.

Informal compulsory systems Nomenclature used within the development process to describe the structure of the program and the type of participation.

Informal voluntary systems Nomenclature used within the development process to describe the structure of the program and the type of participation.

Information policy A procedural document pertaining to the collection, maintenance, and usage of formal records maintained by an organization.

Information process A series of phases used to describe the acquisition, uses, and evaluation of data by an organization.

Information system A systematic plan designed to acquire, refine, organize, store, maintain, protect, retrieve, and communicate data in a valid and an accurate form.

Initial service period That part of the development process that pertains to the earliest stages of employment.

Instrumentation A type of threat pertaining to internal validity that suggests outcomes are due to changes in calibration of the measuring instrument rather than intended treatment conditions.

Integrated information system An electronic collection of data that addresses all the human resource functions.

Interest arbitration A dispute resolution process for resolving impasse with the negotiation process.

Interim appointment period That part of the development process that pertains to the time period encapsulating the initial period of employment.

Internal consistency A criterion for evaluation of compensation systems that focuses on the interrelationship among positions.

Internal environment Forces within the school system, such as mission, goals, processes, performance culture, and leadership styles, that influence organizational courses of action.

Internal labor market Those current employees desiring to move from their current job assignment to another job assignment.

Item-by-item arbitration A dispute mechanism where the arbitrator has the choice of recommending the proposals of labor and of management either in part or in whole.

Job A group of positions identical with respect to their major tasks.

Job analysis A formal set of procedures used to identify and define job tasks and behaviors.

Job categories Includes professionals, office and clerical personnel, skilled and semiskilled operatives, unskilled laborers, and support personnel.

Job descriptions A formal document that describes a position and the position requirements.

Job evaluation The process by which jobs are compared in order to determine compensation value and ensure pay equity.

Job fairs A recruitment technique that involves multiple school districts at the same location and provides potential applicants with multiple opportunities.

Job predictors Assessment measures used to forecast tasks and behaviors required for job performance.

Job satisfaction Individual inclination, expression, feeling, or disposition relative to a work assignment and the environment in which it is performed.

Job simulations A set of job tasks designed to approximate actual job behaviors and duties.

Labor contract A master agreement resulting from the collective bargaining process that specifies the terms and conditions of employment.

Learning curve A graph depicting proficiency rates over periods of time.

Least-qualified job incumbent Any employee within a job classification that has the lowest qualifications.

Local education association (LEA) A collective bargaining term used to describe the union organization at the public school district level.

Management by objectives (MBO) A narrative system of performance appraisal that focuses on establishing and assessing goals mutually determined by the employee and employer.

Market assessment A compensation term that pertains to the process of collecting data considering salary and fringe benefit information.

Maturation A type of threat pertaining to internal validity that suggests changes in outcomes are due to biological changes in participants rather than treatment conditions.

Mean survival ratio The average succession rate calculated as part of a particular enrollment projection technique.

Mediation A dispute resolution technique based on persuasion as a means for resolving an impasse.

Mediator One who performs mediations to resolve an impasse.

Meet-and-confer model A weak form of bilateral decision making where the inputs to the board of education is only advisory.

Mentor programs Programs established by a school system to enable outstanding experienced teachers to serve as coaches, guides, and/or role models, especially for beginning teachers, teachers changing from one grade position to another or to another school, and to enhance the performance of other experienced teachers.

Merit systems A method of compensation where salary increases are based solely on the job performance of employees.

Minimum job requirements The least level of skills, knowledge, and abilities that is necessary for job consideration.

Minority Part of a population differing from others in some characteristics (cultural, economic, political, religious, sexual, or racial) and often subjected to differential treatment.

Misconduct Deliberate violation of system employment standards relating to felony, insubordination, embezzlement, exceeding authority, misappropriation of funds, drug and alcohol abuse, off-duty conduct, and employment creating a conflict of interest to detrimental effect on the system.

Mission statement The policy pertaining the overarching purpose of a school system.

Mixed-rate salary schedules A pay system that involves granting increases according both to job performance and to fixed factors.

Mortality A type of threat pertaining to internal validity that occurs when participants withdraw their participation because of training conditions.

Motivation theories Assumptions regarding determinants that influence personnel to cooperate in putting their abilities to use to further organizational aims. Among those cited in the literature are two-factor, social comparison, consistency, reinforcement, and expectancy theories. Beliefs school officials hold about how motivation influences personnel decisions.

Multiple-hurdle model of decision making An empirical procedure for combining information about an employee's performance on each dimension when a minimum level of performance is required on each dimension.

Narrative system A family of self-referenced systems that compare different dimensions of job performance as exhibited by employees.

National education affiliation (NEA) A collective bargaining term used to describe the parent union organization at the national level.

National Labor Relations Board (NLRB) A federal agency responsible for all collective bargaining activities within the private sector.

Need A discrepancy between an actual and a desired state.

Negotiations The process used by unions and management to establish a master agreement for determining compensation, fringe benefits, and conditions of employment.

Nonexempted employees Individuals covered by the Fair Labor and Standards Act.

Norm-referenced system An assessment appraisal process that compares the job performance of an employee to the job performance of other employees.

Norms Unwritten group rules or values shared by members regarding work behavior. Statistical norms are averages sometimes construed as standards (goals).

Numerically anchored rating system A performance appraisal process that requires the immediate supervisor to rate employees on a scale anchored by numbers.

Objective theory of job choice A theory for recruitment that focuses on the economic incentives associated with jobs/organizations.

Objectives What is to be accomplished, for what purpose, to what extent, by whom, with what resources, and within what time frame, and should be measurable as well as linked to broad system aims and strategies.

One-shot case study A weak assessment design that involves evaluating the reactions of employees after receiving the treatment.

Open shop A union security measure that describes a bargaining unit comprised both of union and of nonunion members.

Organization culture Values, standards, and attitudes of appropriate conduct and fair treatment established and reinforced by the organization and system members.

Organization manual A document (handbook) describing the formal organization structure and related policies, processes, programs, rules, and regulations.

Organizational structure A formal or informal layout of a school district that contains line and staff relationships.

Orientation goals A systematic organizational plan to assist personnel to adjust readily and effectively to new assignments so that they can contribute maximally to the work of the system while realizing personal and position satisfaction.

Orientation periods Crucial times within the assimilation process where employees acquire knowledge about their jobs, the system, and the community.

Orientation policy A formal action on the part of a school board that recognizes the importance of orientation and authorizes the expenditure of district funds for the orientation process.

Orientation process The procedures and methods used to assimilate a newly assigned employee within the work environment.

Paired comparison ranking technique A norm-based job performance assessment technique that involves dyadic pairings among all employees comprising a work group.

Parent organization A union term used to describe the affiliation of a local education association with a state and national education association.

Part-time employees Individuals that work all year on less than a full-time basis.

Partial pick-up A method used by school districts to pay part of the employees' required contribution to a state retirement system.

Passive delivery methods A means of delivering orientation and development programs that require an individual to only listen and are in contrast to active delivery methods.

Performance appraisal system Techniques and procedures used by an organization to assess the job performance of employees.

Performance criteria Outcome measures used to assess or to evaluate the position holder's performance.

Personal leave A privilege granted employees either by board policy or by labor contract that permits time away from the job.

Personal recommendations Job nominations made by persons generally unknowledgeable about an employee's professional competencies.

Pick-up A method used by school districts to pay the employees' required contribution to a state retirement system.

Pick-up of the pick-up A method used by school districts to pay all of the employees' required contribution to a state retirement system and to pay the portion of the pick-up as part of the contribution.

Placement The assignment of an individual to a specific position within an organization.

Portfolios An assessment technique for evaluating performance that relies on the compilation of work materials and outcomes.

Position concerns Part of the orientation process that emphasizes the interest of an employee on the actual job assignment.

Postcontrol group design A program assessment format that compares a treatment condition to a control condition.

Practice significance The functional utility of a process, procedure, or practice to achieve a purpose.

Pre-posttest design A program evaluation format that involves comparing pretreatment performance to posttreatment performance.

Preappointment period Part of the orientation process that pertains to the time involving recruitment and selection.

Predictive validity An empirical paradigm for assessing the appropriateness of a measure or process based on prejob performance and postjob performance.

Predictor deficiency The portion of variance in a predictor of job performance that fails to relate to the actual or ultimate criterion measure.

Predictor relevance The portion of variance in a predictor of job performance that relates to the actual or ultimate criterion measure.

Predictor variables Actual measures used to delimit an applicant pool and to select employees.

Pregnancy Disability Act of 1978 (PDA) Prohibits discrimination in employment practices on the basis of pregnancy, childbirth, or related medical conditions.

Prenegotiations planning Initial phase of the collective bargaining process, which includes such activities as developing the bargaining structure, analyzing the current contract, anticipating issues, preparing the financial outlook, and formulating strategy and tactics.

Pretesting The first phase of assessment associated with the pre-posttest design.

Prima fasci evidence A legal term implying that on the surface it appears to be.

Privacy Act of 1974 Federal legislation that places limits on the collection and dissemination of personal information of members of affected organizations.

Privacy laws Legislative acts addressing scope of access to personal records of students and employees.

Procedural denial A ruling issued within the impasse or grievance process when a party fails to follow the appropriate protocol.

Procedural justice Refers to organizational procedures employed to arrive at impartial adjustment of conflicting claims, rights, or adherence to employment standards. Focuses on conformity to truth, fact, or reason.

Procedural knowledge A type of learning concerned with an understanding of fundamental processes usually associated with fulfilling job requirements.

Professional recommendations A job reference addressing the employment competencies of an applicant.

Promotion A job change by an employee from a lower-level position to a higher-level position.

Protected class status Protection of specific groups of individuals from discrimination in employment on the basis of group characteristics (age, sex, race, etc.).

Quadrant analysis A graphic display used to analyze the configuration of an organization's selection and staffing processes.

Quickie strike A labor stoppage technique used by unions that affords no warning to the employer.

Ranking systems A family of norm-referenced systems that compare the job performance of one employee to the job performance of other employees.

Ratification process The approval mechanism used by labor and management to adopt the contents of a proposed labor contract.

Rating system A family of criterion-referenced systems that compare the job performance of an employee to external standards.

Rationality An auditing criterion pertaining to an expected salary differential between a supervisor and a subordinate.

Recognition procedures Formal process followed by employees to acknowledge a union.

Recruitment A human resource function involving the generation of applicant pools.

Recruitment message The communication between an organization and an applicant independent of mode.

Red circle employees Results from an auditing process that indicates those individuals that are paid more than the suggested market value for a position.

Redress sought The type of relief requested by employees filing a grievance.

Reference Information obtained from external sources about applicants, which can be either professional or personal.

Regression Either a type of threat pertaining to internal validity or a statistical technique used for assessing covariation.

Relevant labor market A composition of school districts deemed via a policy decision to be comparable for the assessment of compensation data.

Reliability Refers to those measures that give consistent results either over periods of time or among different raters.

Restricted range A small amount of variability associated usually with an assessment outcome from performance appraisals or selection predictors.

Rights arbitration A type of dispute mechanism for resolving an impasse within the grievance process.

Role-playing A experimental techniques requiring an individual to act out specific behaviors.

Salary Amount of money received for services rendered by employees exempted from the Fair Labor Standards Act of 1938.

Scope of bargaining The substance of economic and noneconomic issues to be negotiated at the bargaining table.

Screening decision One phase of the selection process that involves delimiting the initial applicant pool usually on the basis of paper credentials submitted by job candidates.

Selection A type of threat pertaining to interval validity that suggests that outcomes obtained are an artifact of the particular participants rather than the treatment condition or an administrative task performed by an organization to choose among applicants for employment purposes.

Self-representation A means whereby an individual rather than a labor union represents the interest of an employee to the board of education.

Self-referenced systems One dimension of job performance exhibited by a single employee is compared to another dimension of job performance exhibited by the same employee.

Shaping A mechanism for altering the job performance of an employee through incremental proactive steps.

Sheltered contributions Monies pay pretax for fringe benefit options.

Sick leave bank An income protection mechanism requiring individuals to contribute sick days to a bank and affording individuals with an opportunity to borrow sick days from the bank.

Simple ranking technique A norm-based job performance assessment technique for aligning employees or jobs along a single continuum relative to specified criteria.

Simulations A family of techniques used to refine managerial skills through role-playing of job behaviors in a protective setting.

Site-based decision-making council A local body afforded authority for managerial decision making.

Skill deficiency Lacking the technique knowledge to perform in a satisfactory manner.

Skill obsolescence Possessing job skills or job knowledge that are dated and no longer sufficient for satisfactory performance.

Socialization Formal and informal experiences through which members become adjusted to the values, roles, relationships, and culture of the organization.

Span of control The scope of positions supervised by a mangerial employee.

Spreadsheet A computer program used to analyze numbers in a row and column accounting format. Useful in budgeting, collective bargaining planning, forecasting school enrollment, and staff projections.

Staff development Systematic means for continuous development of performance capabilities of system personnel.

Staff positions Positions depicted on a staffing chart that are related indirectly to line positions and usually perform support services.

Staffing chart A management vehicle that displays the allocation of staff for particular work units.

Staffing ratio The relationship between student enrollments and staffing allocations as expressed by a statistic.

Standard of comparison The criterion to which an employee's level of job performance is compared.

Standard of living index Changes in the costs associated with goods and services for a particular group of employees.

State education association (SEA) A parent organization for a bargaining unit at the state level.

State employment relations board (SERB) A governmental state unit responsible for administering the collective bargaining process within a particular state.

Statistical significance The empirical utilization of a process, procedure, or practice to achieve a purpose within the bounds of certain probabilities.

Stock statistics An index that reflects the degree of utilization of protected class persons relative to their distribution in the labor market.

Strike To quit or cease working in order to compel employer compliance with a demand.

Subjective theory of job choice A theory for recruitment that focuses on the psychological rewards associated with jobs/organizations.

Substantive denial A response to a grievance request based on the content of the grievance.

Succession process The movement of students into and through the school system and is the building block for the survival ratio projection technique.

Sunshine laws A group of laws pertaining to the openness of meetings and the availability of information to the public.

Supply and demand A criterion used to define a relevant labor market that is concerned with a specific geographical area competing for the same resources.

Survival ratio technique An enrollment projection technique relying on student movement into and through a school system.

Sympathy strike A work stoppage technique where bargaining units uninvolved in a dispute support the actions of a bargaining unit involved in a dispute.

System concerns Needs newly appointed employees have that exceed their concerns about the job itself.

Technology Systematic advancements for improving standard operating procedures within an organization.

Temporary employee An individual that works full time for less than a contract year without any future employment obligation on the part of a school board.

Tenure An official status granted after a trial period to a teacher or a member of another covered professional class to protect the individual from summary dismissal.

Termination Severance of an employment relationship.

Testing A type of threat pertaining to internal validity that suggests outcomes of an assessment are due to the pretest rather than to the treatment condition.

Transfer An administrative action where an employee is assigned to another position within the organization.

Turnover Changes in the composition of the workforce due to resignation, transfer, retirement, or behavioral reasons.

Uncontested election A union election process involving only a labor organization vying to represent a group of employees.

Uniform benefit plan All employees receive the same fringe benefit package regardless of their individual needs.

Union shop A collective bargaining term requiring all employees to join and stay in good standing with the union. Always illegal in the public sector but is common in the private sector.

Vacation Time away from the work environment granted employees in continuing employment and working a full work year.

Values Ideals, customs, and beliefs of system members for which a group has an affectionate regard.

Variable benefit plan Employees choose among benefits based on need rather than receiving a fixed benefit package. Sometimes referred to as a cafeteria plan.

Variable-rate salary schedules A compensation structure that advances employees solely on the basis of their job performance. Sometimes referred to as merit systems.

Verbally anchored rating systems A type of graphic rating scale used to assess job performance of employees while relying on adverbs (i.e., always, sometimes, etc.).

Wage Amount of money received for services rendered by employees covered by the Fair Labor Standards Act of 1938.

Wall-to-wall bargaining A collective bargaining term that reflects only a single bargaining agent representing all employees of a school district albeit under different contracts.

Wild cat strike A work stoppage by a labor union that is unannounced and not sanctioned by the parent organizations.

Work diaries An assessment technique for evaluating jobs or individuals on the basis of a written narrative compiled by employees.

Work itself theory of job choice A recruitment theory that focuses on duties and job tasks associated with jobs/organizations.

Work sample A predictor used within the selection process that involves an actual job task.

Zipper clause A collective bargaining term that is part of a labor contract and indicates that all items of interest are addressed for the duration of the contract.

AUTHOR INDEX

SUBJECT INDEX